# Unsettling the World

# MODERNITY AND POLITICAL THOUGHT

Series Editors:
**Morton Schoolman**, State University of New York at Albany

**Kennan Ferguson**, University of Wisconsin–Milwaukee

This unique collection of original studies of the great figures in the history of political and social thought critically examines their contributions to our understanding of modernity, its constitution, and the promise and problems latent within it. These works are written by some of the finest theorists of our time for scholars and students of the social sciences and humanities.

## Titles in the Series

# Unsettling the World

## Edward Said and Political Theory

Jeanne Morefield

ROWMAN & LITTLEFIELD
*Lanham • Boulder • New York • London*

Published by Rowman & Littlefield
An imprint of The Rowman & Littlefield Publishing Group, Inc.
4501 Forbes Boulevard, Suite 200, Lanham, Maryland 20706
www.rowman.com

86-90 Paul Street, London EC2A 4NE

British Library Cataloguing in Publication Information Available

**Library of Congress Cataloging-in-Publication Data**

Names: Morefield, Jeanne, 1967- author.
Title: Unsettling the world : Edward Said and political theory / Jeanne
  Morefield.
Description: Lanham, Maryland : Rowman & Littlefield, 2022. | Series:
  Modernity and political thought | Includes bibliographical references
  and index. | Summary: "Jeanne Morefield synthesizes Palestinian American
  theorist and cultural critic Edward Said's critical humanism as a
  conceptual approach for addressing crises in contemporary global
  politics that demands reflection about historical context and the nature
  of the collective public before considering solutions to perceived
  problems. Said's approach to humanistic inquiry speaks directly to the
  way scholars of international ethics who speak from a liberal
  internationalist perspective react to global crises by fixating on the
  international status quo, often advocating global order for global
  order's sake. In the process, Said's humanism transforms the very idea
  of what it means to theorize global ethics in a postcolonial age and
  offers a clarifying way to navigate through foreign policy discussions
  with conflicting interest groups and ideologies"-- Provided by
  publisher.
Identifiers: LCCN 2022002853 (print) | LCCN 2022002854 (ebook) | ISBN
  9781442260283 (cloth) | ISBN 9781538168622 (paperback) | ISBN
  9781442260306 (epub)
Subjects: LCSH: Said, Edward W. | International relations--Moral and
  ethical aspects. | Humanistic ethics.
Classification: LCC JZ1306 .M69 2022  (print) | LCC JZ1306  (ebook) | DDC
  327.101--dc23/eng/20220304
LC record available at https://lccn.loc.gov/2022002853
LC ebook record available at https://lccn.loc.gov/2022002854

*For two dreams.*

# Acknowledgments

Thanking everyone who contributed in some fashion to the writing of a book this challenging to write is impossible. But I will try my best. For starters, I am enormously grateful to the two people who have spent the most time with the entire manuscript: James Tully and Michael Goodhart. Without their encouragement and thoughtful suggestions, the book would not exist as it does. The series editors for Modernity and Political Thought, Morton Schoolman and Kennan Ferguson, were also extraordinarily helpful and careful readers, and I thank them heartily for encouraging me to write for the series in the first place. I am also deeply grateful to all the people who commented on portions of this text in progress as well as reflecting on bits and pieces of my thinking about Said as it evolved, in particular: Arash Davari, Patchen Markell, Bashir Abu–Manneh, Asav Siniver, Duncan Bell, Craig Borowiak, Elizabeth Wingrove, Paul Apostolidis, and Hagar Kotef.

Over the years, I have benefited enormously from spirited conversations with friends and colleagues about this book, about Said and his work, and about the relationship between that work, political theory, and imperialism. These include: Patrick Porter, Eskandar Sadeghi, Lawrie Balfour, Murad Idris, Joshua Foa Dienstag, Samuel Moyn, Davide Panagia, Melvin Rogers, Sarah El–Kazaz, Onur Ulas Ince, Jacqueline Rose, Akeel Bilgrami, Ella Myers, Nicholas Kompridis, Allison Weir, Jack (Chip) Turner, Inés Valdez, Elyse Semerdjian, Gaurav Majumdar, Paul Bové, Joseph Carens, Jennifer Nedelsky, Yves Winter, Catherine Liu, Jennifer Pitts, Dipesh Chakrabarty, Daniel Lee, Joshua Cohen, Alisa Kessel, Romand Coles, Adom Getachew, Robert Vitalis, Jason Frank, Mary Katzenstein, Peter Katzenstein, Jonathan Kirschner, Turkul Isiksel, Susan Buck–Morss, James Muldoon, Yasamin Altaïra, and Anna Apostolidis.

Thank you to the librarians at the Columbia University Library Archives for allowing me access to Said's papers. Thank you to Whitman College for a long–ago sabbatical that proved so productive and the University of Birmingham for their initial support and a place to thrive. I am also hugely grateful to Oxford University and New College for giving me a new intellectual home during some dark academic times and for providing me with the funds to pay for bits and pieces of this project. I am particularly grateful to my political theory colleagues for opening Oxford's doors to work like this. In particular, huge thanks to Lois McNay, Teresa Bejan, Sophie Smith, Amia Srinivasan, and Elizabeth Frazer for their constant support as I navigate the intricacies of this internal/external world.

This book would not look like it does without the help of some very talented people. Judy Dunlop was initially described to me as a "celebrated" indexer and this has proved to be the case. Very few people could have navigated the unresolved intricacies of Said's work with such precision and sympathetic finesse. Jon Sisk, Sarah Sichina, and Caje Brennan Knight at Rowman and Littlefield were also extraordinarily helpful, patient, and attentive throughout the editing process. Additionally, locating the credits for the stunning art that graces the cover of this book was a journey in and of itself. Credit goes to Zied Hadhri (Jebiniana, Tunisia 2012) for the outstanding picture of a mural created by the Tunis–based art collective, Ahl Alkahf, whose goal is to "de-centralize art and open it for the public." But locating the rights to an image produced by an anonymous collective required the help of a whole host of people (Zied Hadrhi, Jacob Geuder, Shuk Ying Chan, Liona Neubert) who helped relay messages from Berlin, to Shanghai, to Tunis, to Berne, to Oxford—a contrapuntal ensemble that I like to believe would have made Said proud.

My family has been ebbless in their support for me and this project. Huge thanks go to my mother, Kathy Morefield, who put her razor-sharp editing skills to work on the proofs and to both she and my father, John Morefield, for modelling for me—my entire life—what committed social activism looks like. Thanks to Paul Apostolidis who has patiently listened to my perorations about this project for longer than anyone else; to Anna Apostolidis who has grown into herself as an intellectual in the midst of the book's becoming; and to Niko Apostolidis, whose growing capacity to self-reflect and thrive is both amazing and humbling.

This book is also indebted to three, great thinkers, whose voices are no longer with us. First, Charles Mills, who died in 2021, was a brilliant, funny, lion in the field, whose world–transforming challenge to the epistemological assumptions of political philosophy—as the epistemological assumptions of White ignorance—has had a profound impact on my thinking. Next, the wonderful Isaac Kramnick, my co–advisor at Cornell, died in 2019. Isaac modelled for me what it is to study the political thought of (as Said would put it) "unsystematic" thinkers working across genres and political spaces. Because Isaac never once said, "you can't do that, that's not political theory," I am the political theorist I am today.

And finally, this book is dedicated to Edward Said, a man I never had the good fortune to meet but who I feel I know, both through those who did, through his many interviews, and through his writings. Said's words ring in my ear every time I set out to theorize and rage at the fragmented, co–constituting, imbricated, fraught, unjust world enabled and furthered by imperialism, in the past and in the now. I wish I had met that fierceness in person, but I am eternally grateful to have been influenced by the fiery core of his mind.

# Contents

# Series Editor's Introduction

Jeanne Morefield's *Unsettling the World: Edward Said and Political Theory* is the twentieth volume in Modernity and Political Thought (MPT), the Rowman and Littlefield series on contemporary political theory. It follows the recent publication of volumes on Lincoln by Steven Johnston, Rawls by J. Donald Moon, Publius by Jason Frank, and Hume by Davide Panagia.[1] MPT has long been a series of works by today's distinguished political thinkers who reintroduce and refigure canonical political theorists and philosophers in relation to the politics of our modern world. Our long list of earlier volumes includes studies on the thought of Augustine (William E. Connolly), Hobbes (Richard E. Flathman), Burke (Stephen K. White), Emerson (George Kateb), Rousseau (Tracy B. Strong), Thoreau (Jane Bennett), Adam Smith (Michael J. Shapiro), Foucault (Thomas L. Dumm), Hegel (Fred Dallmayr), Arendt (Seyla Benhabib), William James (Kennan Ferguson), Merleau-Ponty (Diana Coole), Aquinas (Shadia Drury), Deleuze (Nicholas Tampio), and Schmitt (Kam Shapiro).[2]

Each of these works proposes interpretations and arguments about key figures in the history of political theory and recognizes their singular importance in modernity. In particular, contributors to MPT critically examine how major political theorists shape our understanding of modernity—not only its origins and constitution but also its overt and latent problems, promises, and dangers. In addition to the individual works themselves, the series illustrates how the history of political thought can be brought to bear on modernity's political present to acquire deeper insight into its possible political futures. As a whole, MPT offers a unique presentation of the discussions and debates that define much of political theory today.

Empire has long been the central subject of Jeanne Morefield's scholarship. Both her previous monographs, *Covenants without Swords: Idealist Liberalism and the Spirit of Empire* and *Empires without Imperialism: Anglo-American Decline and the Politics of Deflection*, are concerned not only with practices of European, American, and especially English imperialism but also with their justifications and rationalizations.[3] Each of these works takes seriously the intellectual structures and underpinnings of the Anglo-imperial projects by delving into the complexities of the academic, policy, and conceptual debates of the past hundred years regarding empire. Recalling these works and the intellectual milieu they illuminate shows what led Morefield to her work on theorist Edward Said, one of the twentieth century's most incisive and well-known critics of imperial thinking.

The word *empire* itself descends from the Roman term *imperium*, which signifies absolute and unconstrained power. In its current incarnation, it implies a distant occupation, domination from a distance, a place where the mechanisms of politics arise not from the constituent people or the autochthonous land but rather from the barrel of a gun. Empire would therefore initially seem to be at radical odds with liberalism, the political theory of individualism, choice, and self-determination. And yet, as theorists from Frantz Fanon to Uday Mehta have pointed out, modern forms of liberalism and empire not only seem to be historically coincident, but they also seem to emerge in concert, supporting one another in their development and justification.[4] Morefield's research has described and analyzed this twinning, tracing how ideas of imperial power and concepts of liberalism develop around one another.

Morefield's first book, *Covenants without Swords*, examines the milieu from which the current Anglo-American conceptualization of international relations arose. It focuses particularly on two of the interwar era's most influential and renowned theorists, Gilbert Murray and Alfred Zimmern. Murray and Zimmern helped craft both the institutions designed to shape the international world, such as the League of Nations, and the then emergent field of international relations. Both trained as classicists—Murray in Greek poetry and drama, Zimmern in ancient Greek politics—were hired at Oxford University and began to engage with liberal political organizations.

In England, the political presumptions of liberalism had for a generation been based on a particular and peculiar form of Hegelianism. Relying heavily on Hegel's notion of universal spirit—the necessity for the individual to fuse with a collective identity—liberals nonetheless wished to reject his assumption that the highest form of association was the total correlation between each citizen and the state. This forced British liberalism into a particularly unstable configuration, one that sought to promote both individualism and social connection. As a result, prewar liberalism tended to rely on metaphors of organic association, particularly of the patriarchal family.

As German militarism and antidemocratic practices intensified in the early twentieth century, Hegel's influence on liberalism receded. Yet politics required a historical grounding. Both Zimmern and Murray introduced the polis of Athens to fill this void—in their telling, a regionally specific, overtly democratic, and participatory governance that called on a shared literary and oration culture to thrive. This classical Hellenism provided the progressive Left with a new template for liberalism but one with its own fissures and contradictions. And it was in its applications to the international arena, especially in conceptualization of Britain's worldwide empire, that the implications of this organicist classicism would illuminate liberalism's incompatibility with racial egalitarianism.

This model of politics, based on the presumptions that associations should always be natural and that people had the rights to form their own associational life, was soon forced to come to terms with increasingly strong anti-imperialism in Britain's colonies. While some settled lands dominated by Europeans were allowed limited self-determination (e.g., Canada, New Zealand), those where anticolonial pressure came from the indigenous peoples were further repressed. For Zimmern and Murray, liberals who rejected embracing state power as nothing more than force, the only solution was to enlarge their conception of order. Developing the "Liberal spirit" (Murray) or making the world "interdependent in spiritual relations" (Zimmern) seemed to solve the problem: As "uncivilized nations" were guided by the universalism of liberalism, they could evolve their own associational maturities.

A League of Nations, then, solved many of the intellectual desires of liberals. It could allow for the organicism of peoples, stop the madness of war, and teach developing nationalities the moral goods of liberal order. It could accept and reinforce racial and civilizational hierarchies while denouncing the multiple forms of violence used to keep those hierarchies in place. Neither a government nor an empire, such a league could allow for the flourishing of justice and peace through negotiation and technical superiority. As such, Europe, particularly England, could lead the way toward a world of natural order and cooperation.

Morefield's concern with these two thinkers, both widely forgotten today, has less to do with the creation of the institutions they helped build. To be sure, most people think of the League of Nations as merely a failed precursor to the United Nations, and the British Empire has faded into history. Instead, she sees this particular liberal internationalism as a template, one upon which both contemporary scholarship and international policy relies. By naturalizing states, hierarchizing cultures, and universalizing a particular kind of political existence, the liberal internationalists of a century ago predetermined the sorts of questions asked within the fields of international relations and its institutions. Such now-familiar questions as, Which aspects of transnational politics count as organic and are by nature immutable, and which are seen as open to forceful remaking and monetary inducement? continue to underpin international diplomacy, military operations, nongovernmental organizations, and transnational trade.

This intellectual tendency (some might think of it as mendacity) to celebrate empire's "civilizing processes" while denying the oppression and brutality they entail, underpins the thesis of Morefield's second book, *Empires without Imperialism*. The seeming contradiction inscribed by the title aptly illustrates the British dream world of a painless, frictionless, and innocent imposition of power over the world's peoples. Nor is this strictly an English delusion. Morefield traces resonances between early-twentieth-century justifications for liberal international empire and those promoting the military power of the United States eighty years later.

In both cases, her subjects are intellectuals with a high political profile—academics at ease in the halls of power, framing international force in ways that make its deployment more comfortable. In the British group, she returns to Zimmern, as well as Jan Smuts, Lionel Curtis, and other participants in Cecil Rhodes's Round Table (what we would now consider a think tank). In more recent years, Donald Kagan, Michael Ignatieff, and Niall Ferguson have all served up apologetics and justifications for American empire. All these thinkers, Morefield explains, "deflect attention away from imperial violence" and toward an idealized and sanitized collective identity.[5]

While their methods vary, their goals were similar. To show the lines of connection, Morefield pairs them up. Each chapter analyzing an Edwardian theorist is followed by one addressing a contemporary neoconservative, showing continuities between their political programs and their conceptual rationalizations. The Round Table's embrace of the cross-cultural validity of British forms of governmentality sits neatly alongside Ferguson's assumption that a globally integrated capitalism supports world order. What is most important, she shows, is not the particular figure making the arguments that support empire, though she delves deeply into each, but the specific logics that justified imperial power.

Three conceptual parallels thus make up the core of this analysis. The first, expanded from her previous work, is the role that classicism plays in the project. Athens specifically becomes a stand-in for the early twentieth and twenty-first centuries. By idealizing this "cradle of democracy," apologists for empire can point to a utopian correlation between civic participation, egalitarian legal responsibility, and patriotic celebration. The expansion of this model to the rest of the world, then, can be displaced from the barrel of the gun to the imagined brilliance of the Athenian populace. The parallel also encourages elisions: Ignoring such other aspects of ancient Greece as slavery, the disenfranchisement of foreigners, and the oppression of women encourages silence about contemporary racial hierarchies, technological superiority, and military occupation. Supporting Pericles's "imperial ideal of freedom" allows for an allegedly reluctant military and economic domination of the world.[6]

The second parallel emerges from the explicit assumption that the rest of world ultimately aspires to the way of life of those who control empire. The benefits of British ideals or of US capitalism become built into the rationales of conquest and occupation. Those Indians who reject the British way of life or Iraqis who fail to appreciate being forced into a representative democracy show their ignorance of the great gifts being bestowed upon them. By embedding this hierarchy, those who embrace empire can reimagine it as a civilizational munificence rather than an extractive exploitation of land, people, and resources. In each case, the authors under analysis are "providing readers with metanarratives intended to restore their faith in the superiority of their own civilization and ameliorate any doubts that the imperial state to which they belong has ever engaged in anything worthy of critique"[7]

The third parallel between the Edwardian and the contemporary defenses of empire is built on the conflation of international organization with holism and domination. For these theorists, the contradictions between mechanisms of world order building and their desire to reject domination for its own sake back their work into a conceptual corner. For some, a turn to naturalizing metaphors solves this problem. If the British Empire or the League of Nations can be likened to the natural world, then the hierarchies—and violence—internal to the way each operates can be dismissed: different parts of an organism, where certain ones necessarily follow others. Differences can be celebrated at the same time as their dependences can be enforced. For other thinkers, the conflict between order and violence demands the resolutions that only the strong can meet. But because mere military strength cannot justify domination, this strength emerges from the morality of an embrace of tragedy: Terrible things happen in the world, and only some have the ethical fortitude to make the hard decisions.

All these approaches, for their differences, hold that the world must be ordered, lest it fall into chaos; that the tools and abilities to so order the world properly belong to the organizations and institutions that have previously done so; and that the overlap of military power with those organizations and institutions is merely coincidental. Such a vision is able to stuff the whole architecture of empire into a putatively anti-imperial form. Dissecting and displaying the strategies used in this project, Morefield redirects our attention to the continuities of empire across the past hundred years.

Her subjects in both books are those striving for political and conceptual power over empire. The cut of Morefield's critique comes from the dramatic gaps between what her subjects imagine they are doing (creating a world of peace and order) and what they are actually doing (justifying a world of White supremacy, extractive capitalism, and colonial and postcolonial domination). In the case of those theorists of the early twentieth century, the past years have clarified the truth of her exposé. For the theorists of the early twenty-first, the purposes and logics of their political projects are laid bare.

This book proves different. Morefield turns to a theorist engaged in precisely the opposite project. Said opposes empire. He insists on the full humanity of the oppressed; the value of imagination; the fragilities of life; and the complexity of the connections between knowledge, action, place, and power. Rather than undercutting these insights, Morefield shares them. And in moving from critique to critical exegesis, she invites her readers to share in that transformation, which points not to a new world order but to a new world.

We are grateful to Jon Sisk, vice president and senior executive editor for American government, American history, public policy, and political theory at Rowman and Littlefield, for the thoughtfulness and professionalism that make it possible for authors and editors alike to produce their best work. His support of a series dedicated to examining authors through the lens of modern thought has led to a compilation of volumes that as a whole refigure the relationship between critical thinkers and the contemporary world. Authors, editors, and publisher together strive to provide an indispensable set of volumes that, taken in their totality, provide a guide to the complexities and nuances of history's most important political philosophers. Under his stewardship, Rowman and Littlefield's Modernity and Political Thought continues to define the importance of the study of political theory today.

Kennan Ferguson, University of Wisconsin at Milwaukee
Morton Schoolman, State University of New York at Albany

# Prelude

"If you're an exile . . . you always bear within yourself a recollection of what you've let behind and what you can remember, and you play it against the current experience. So, there's necessarily that sense of counterpoint. And by counterpoint, I mean things that can't be reduced to homophony . . . . And so, multiple identity, the polyphony of many voices playing off against each other, without, as I say, the need to reconcile them, just to hold them together, is what my work is all about. More than one culture, more than one awareness, both in its negative and its positive modes."

—Edward Said[1]

It is difficult for me to fully describe the experience of writing this book. As a scholar whose interdisciplinary impulses have always compelled me toward the centripetal point where history, theory, international politics, and culture intersect, I have long been drawn to Said's work. But I must confess, before writing this book, I tended to assume Said rather know Said. Like most people who have studied political theory anytime over the last nearly forty years, I had read *Orientalism* and, like most people, tended to know the main arguments of this astonishingly influential and field-transforming book. Over the years, however, as my scholarly interest in imperialism grew, so, too, did my interest in Said's work. *Culture and Imperialism* proved essential reading during the writing of my last book, as I struggled for a theoretical language to help situate thinkers and texts within the riotously complex world of Anglo-American imperial rhetoric. Likewise, the central ideological phenomenon I explore in that book—what I term a liberal imperial "politics of deflection"—found its antidote in the take-no-prisoner's demand for critical reflection that Said developed in *Humanism and Democratic Criticism.* More than anything, Said's insistence in that text and elsewhere that intellectuals themselves play a role in keeping public conscience from falling asleep or looking away in times of historical forgetting resonated with all the ways I most wanted to inhabit the world, as a scholar and a political being.

So when I first started writing this book, I thought, rather smugly, "How hard can this be? I've written books about imperialism before. I love what I know of Said's work, and I know what moves me about it politically and theoretically." And then I began the actual writing and almost immediately slammed hard into the brittle wall of that hubris. My scholarship up to that point had largely been oriented toward critiquing the work of thinkers I believed were important but, frankly, disliked. Hated, even. And as I soon discovered, it is considerably easier to write about a thinker you hate—be it Jan Smuts or Niall Ferguson—than it is to write about a thinker you love. Love evokes all kinds of complicated critical disquiets and emotional minefields. How do you do justice to someone whose work continuously astounds you with its scythe-like ability to cut through liberal imperialism's thick wall of deflection? How do you honor the work of all the other people who have tried to shine a light on this work without parasitically replicating their insights? How do you cope with the hurt you feel in the pit of your stomach when this same person writes something that disappoints you?

And the internal tensions of Said's own work made writing from love even more of a quagmire. How was I supposed to grapple with all the ways Said's reckoning with experience seemed to resonate with my comparatively privileged experience without trivializing his? How was I supposed to grapple with Said's *own* privilege in comparison to that of other exiles and refugees without trivializing their experiences? How was I supposed to unpick the tangled knot of unresolved tensions that are the heart and soul of Said's work—because they are also the heart and soul of what it means to analyze the presence of the imperial past today—and simultaneously translate its frequent opacity without getting lost in its studious lack of closure?

Writing about Said is like standing in the middle of a raging cyclone, with all the moving pieces of imperialism—cultural, historical, rhetorical, artistic, political, and material—swirling about you at the same time, and it is your job, as a critic, to engage them all. At the same time. Despite the wind. Despite the mess. Not to reconcile them, just to hold them together. Said's intellectual intuitions flow from the subjective instability of exile, and his intellectual heroes are people who were "unsystematic" and "involved in culture, in political struggle."[2] Coming to terms with the instability at the core of his thought, his lack of systematicity, and his radical openness to polyphony and tension is essential for understanding the fluidity of his thinking. And yet as glorious as it can be to stand with Said in the midst of the unsettling storm, letting the vibrancy and chaos of the world he describes wash over you, it can also be infuriatingly confusing and mind-numbingly complex. And there are times—particularly if you are a political theorist with some ancient, lingering desire for philosophical resolution baked in your DNA—when Said's own refusal to resolve *anything* can compel you (hypothetically speaking, of course) to throw *The World, the Text, and the Critic* across a crowded coffee shop in frustration, much to the consternation of the other patrons.

Beyond the complexities of Said's thought, there is the sheer vastness of Said's own work that extends well beyond *Orientalism* and *Culture and Imperialism*. A scholar of astonishing breadth, Said wrote about literature, culture, ideology, music, theory, criticism, history, philosophy, philology, imperialism, rhetoric, and politics, and all at the same time. Moreover, Said's intellectual generosity and his willingness to travel with his own theory meant that he was continuously giving interviews (many of which were then collected in edited volumes) and speaking for academic and nonacademic audiences alike, expanding his scholarly and political contributions to the world well beyond his writing. Yet the baffling amount of work by Said pales in comparison to the baffling, mountainous weight of the secondary literature about Said, what Gauri Viswanathan called a "growth industry" in 2002 that shows little sign of abating since his untimely death in 2003 and, if anything, has recently taken on renewed life.[3]

And then there is the disconnect between the vastness of the secondary literature on Said and the fact that so little of it has been written by political theorists. In other words, scholars of comparative literature, history, sociology, anthropology, philosophy, Middle Eastern studies, race and ethnic studies, postcolonial theory, and subaltern studies have written about Said's work for at least the last forty years, and over this same period, virtually every field in the humanities has been transformed by that work. By comparison, political theorists have largely ignored Said, and he has remained a marginal figure in the field, assumed but not engaged. Thus, the learning curve involved with writing this book was steep, and I spent a not insignificant amount of time while researching feeling overwhelmed by the need to familiarize myself with what sometimes felt like an exponentially expanding realm of inquiry.

In the introduction and at points throughout the book, I think more critically about the structural and substantive hurdles that might account for political theorists' lack of interest in Said. For now, suffice it to say, my limited exposure as a political theorist to his work meant that not only did I spend a lot of time playing scholarly catch up, but I also frequently felt like a bumbling outsider who had stumbled into an intricate world constructed completely from theoretical scaffolding for which I had no conceptual reference. In some ways, writing a book about Edward Said and political theory can feel like standing against the wall at a crowded cocktail party full of super-cool people, having multiple fascinating and inspired conversations in a language with which you are only half familiar. I struggled with this foreign idiom of signs and genre and narration and fiction and theories I hadn't engaged since

I took literary theory as an undergraduate. At other times, this sense of intellectual alienation felt almost paralyzingly like unworthiness. How dare I, a facile interloper into a world so gorgeously well trod by the likes of Homi Bhabha, Bruce Robbins, Timothy Brennan, Paul Bové, Gayatri Spivak, Akeel Bilgrami, Jaqueline Rose, Hamid Dabashi, and Rashid Khalidi—people who not only wrote beautifully about Said but also actually *knew* him personally—suggest there was anything new to learn from a fresh engagement with his work?

And still, at other times, I was simply taken aback by the querulous disbelief with which a sizable number of political theorists responded to my project. While most theorists were genuinely curious to learn more about Said, numerous people asked me questions that suggested they had no idea why I would write about someone whose oeuvre was so clearly inappropriate to the reasoned study of politics and philosophy. In the course of presenting bits and pieces of this book at various political theory seminars or conference panels over the years, I have fielded comments that range from the bemused to the outright hostile. "I liked much of what Said stood for," one workshop participant noted plaintively, "but did he always have to be so *angry*?"

And then, in the middle of all this intellectual uncertainty, I went into exile.

# Introduction

## *Two Dreams: Edward Said and Political Theory*

Shortly after Edward Said's death in 2003, the prolific and revered Palestinian poet Mahmoud Darwish wrote a lengthy poem in honor of his good friend entitled "Edward Said: A Contrapuntal Reading." The poem is a tribute to Said's life and mode of being in the world. It is the kind of beautifully fleshed out portrayal of a brilliant and complicated personality that could only be written by someone who knew him well, in all his complex iterations. That closeness is apparent throughout, from the very form of the poem (which moves in and out of an imagined conversation between Darwish and Said) to Darwish's gentle teasing of Said's expensive tastes, Upper West Side lifestyle, and Protestant work ethic:

> New York. Edward wakes up to
> a lazy dawn. He plays
> Mozart.
> Runs round the university's tennis
> court.
> Thinks of the journey of ideas across
> borders,
> and over barriers. He reads the *New York Times.*
> Writes out his furious comments. Curses an Orientalist guiding the
> General to the weak point
> inside the heart of an Oriental woman. He showers. Chooses his
> elegant suit. Drinks
> his white coffee. Shouts at the dawn:
> Do not loiter.[1]

But the poem also engages seriously and with pathos Said's intellectual and emotional struggles with identity, with politics, and with the tensions that cling like limpets to the very fact of living and being in exile. At one point in the conversation, the fictional Darwish asks the fictional Said about the time he returned to visit his childhood home in Jerusalem. Said himself had already detailed the sense of alienation he felt in that moment in a 1992 piece, "Palestine, Then and Now." There, Said describes how the house ("now occupied not by an Israeli Jewish family but by a right-wing fundamentalist Christian and militantly pro-Zionist group") was shut to him. "I did not, could not, enter," he wrote. The house staring down at him "from behind its shaded windows" symbolized in shuttered finitude the fact that "Palestine as I had known it was over."[2]

The Said of the poem, however, stands not outside the house but at the doorway, looking into the faces not of fundamentalist Christians but of Israeli Jews. The poem's Said expresses reservations about the experience, and Darwish presses him: Were you afraid? What frightened you? And the Said of the poem—Darwish's Said—answers thus:

> I could not meet loss face
> to face. I stood by the door like a beggar.
> How could I ask permission from strangers sleeping
> in my own bed . . . . Ask them if I could visit myself
> or five minutes? Should I bow in respect
> to the residents of my childish dream? Would they ask:
> Who is that prying foreign visitor? And how
> could I talk about war and peace
> among the victims and the victims' victims,
> without additions, without an interjection?
> And would they tell me: There is no place for two dreams
> in one bedroom?[3]

I begin this introduction with Darwish's poem rather than with a straightforward exposition of why I think Said's methodological orientation is important to political theory because my goal is not to privilege that method *as* method. In other words, my reading of Said's approach resists the possibility that it can and should serve as a broad theoretical framework for analysis (what Said once called a "theoretical machine"), into which we can fit bits of culture, politics, and imperialism like puzzle pieces, that then makes sense of the whole ensemble.[4] Said's "method," by my reading, is too fractured for that kind of introduction. Because it begins from a loss that can never be fully embraced—a loss one can never look fully in the face—it must be approached differently: from the side, backing in, waking up to what it means from inside or, rather, from the doorway.

Beginning a book on Said and political theory in the midst of an imagined conversation with his friend allows us to experience Said's approach to the world for what it is: not a method but an unsettling disposition—toward criticism, toward politics, toward discourse, toward culture—that originates in exile and loss. Darwish's poem places us right in the midst of that loss, back at the site of disruption, and there we wake up to all of its complexities and contradiction. We experience, with Said and Darwish, the fractured discomfort of losing one's home without ever losing one's love of home. We experience, with Said and Darwish, what it feels like to be both engaged and disengaged with place and people, to stand at the doorway, neither here nor there. In the eyes of the querying occupants of the house, we perceive both the alienation of being out of place—a prying foreign visitor—and the inherent trickiness of memory that draws the heart back to one's childhood bedroom. In Said's fretful hovering, in the midst of his open insecurity about discussing peace between the victims and the victims' victims, we experience fully the instability of belonging, the open sympathy with the loss of others, and the "plurality of vision" to which instability and sympathy give rise.[5] Said's is a disposition grounded in this insecure moment and in a capacity to hold, without reconciling, "two dreams." It is, in essence, a disposition in which the critic is "constantly being unsettled and unsettling others."[6]

The primary goal of this book is to argue that Said's unsettled and unsettling disposition toward culture, power, and politics has much to offer political theorists today. In particular, scholars interested in the entanglements of theory with imperialism, race, and settler colonialism can find in Said's work an orientation toward inquiry that illuminates the discursive complexities of imperial history while highlighting the affiliations between that history, contemporary politics, and resistance. Said's work does this by unsettling the surety of the ground on which we theorize and by insisting that criticism begin from a place of connection rather than reconciliation or foreclosure. For those of us theorizing from within or under sheltering wing of America's global power, this also means remembering, as Said puts it, "[w]hen we consider the connections between the United States and the rest of the world, we are so to speak *of* the connections, not outside and beyond them."[7] Theorizing from within these connections comes with a particular set of responsibilities that entail confronting, rather than looking away from, the impact of American imperialism on the world.

Making this point is hardly a straightforward proposition, however, and not simply because Said's critical disposition resists a straightforward telling. Rather, my argument is overdetermined, from the beginning, by Said's looming absence from political theory scholarship, an absence rendered deeply uncanny by the fact that he literally remade the intellectual landscape all around us. Indeed, my suggestion that Said might prove useful to political theorists interested in empire and imperialism will no doubt strike anyone who isn't a political theorist as ludicrously obvious, maybe even slightly dim, like recommending to a person with an interest in oceans that they consider thinking more deeply about water.

Not only was Said one of the most influential intellectuals of the late twentieth century, but he also fundamentally transformed the way imperialism is studied. *Orientalism* in 1978 kindled a scholarly movement, inaugurated the field of postcolonial studies, and shifted the intellectual horizon of the humanities in ways that are truly incalculable. Indeed, today *Orientalism* has so thoroughly saturated the intellectual airwaves of the modern academy that, for many scholars of comparative literature, anthropology, Middle Eastern studies, and history, it is effectively, as Eqbal Ahmad puts it, "learnt by osmosis."[8]

And yet, Said's influence goes far beyond *Orientalism*. A hugely productive scholar and innovative thinker, his writings, speeches, and interviews on literature, theory, music, and politics have been the subject of sustained attention for decades by some of the most well-known scholars of our age.[9] Said is widely credited as the person who introduced the study of Foucault to the American academy, and his global intellectual influence can still be seen in the abundance of critical articles and books dedicated to his work that appear every year.[10] Moreover, as a public intellectual, Said did more, in Rashid Khalidi's words, "than any other individual to establish the idea of the basic humanity of the Palestinian people in the minds of the American public."[11] All in all, as David Harmon put it shortly after Said died, his career didn't just track the great shifts in academic, political, and media culture that began in the 1970s. Rather, "Said was in the vanguard of all of them."[12]

Regardless of that influence, there have been shockingly few political theoretical engagements with Said's work and not a single book-length treatment of his political thought by a political theorist. This disinterest has persisted over the years, despite Said's career-long exploration of themes that have remained perennially fascinating for theorists: exile, cosmopolitanism, belonging, identity, worldliness, humanism, nationhood, sovereignty. Even more curious, it has persisted in the face of major changes in the field. For roughly the last twenty years, increasing numbers of theorists have expressed interest in questions of empire and imperialism, a phenomenon that accelerated substantially over the last decade. From Cambridge School investigations of ideas in context, to critical theoretical reappraisals of modernity, to normative global justice reconsiderations of reparations, to democratic confrontations with settler colonialism, political theorists from across methodological perspectives have collectively helped to establish the sustained investigation of the relationship between political theory and imperialism as an accepted realm of inquiry in our subdiscipline.[13] Alongside this interest in imperialism, political theory—as a subdiscipline and academic endeavor—has also begun opening its doors to thinkers who have been traditionally excluded from the formal canon. This important development has led to a flowering of new work on transnational Black political thought, indigenous political thought, and increasing interest in the work of scholars from Asia, Africa, and Latin America, both historical and contemporary.[14] It has also contributed to the rising prominence of "comparative political theory" as a field and the expansion of lively and productive debates about what scholars think that field should be.[15]

And yet, despite these developments, a majority of political theorists have remained roundly and robustly immune to Said's charms in a manner that goes beyond mere unseeing or misrecognition. For more than forty years, political theorists haven't merely ignored Said's work; they have assumed, misrecognized, and in some cases dismissed it in ways that have left lingering, almost palpable traces on the field. If postcolonial theory in general is, as Leela Gandhi describes, a "theoretical resistance to the mystifying amnesia of the colonial aftermath," then the niggling presence of Said's absence in political theory has much to tell us about the mystifying hold of colonial amnesia on a community of scholars theorizing in that aftermath, *even as* that community struggles to rectify years of silence about imperialism.[16]

This book is thus decidedly different from most books in the Modernity and Political Thought series, each of which engages a well-known, canonical thinker (or thinkers) in nuanced and novel ways. By contrast, writing a book about Edward Said's political thought means beginning from an absence, a Said-shaped hole that requires both explanation and explication. The double goal of that follows: to introduce Said's work to a field that has largely ignored him and then begin to make a case for why he should not be ignored.

## SITUATING EDWARD SAID

Edward Said was born in Jerusalem in 1935 and spent a considerable portion of his childhood moving between that city and Cairo. His family were Palestinians but also Anglicans, making them, as he explained in a 1987 interview, a "minority within the Christian minority in an Islamic majority setting."[17] In 1947, the Said family was forced to abandon Jerusalem before the Palestinian-Israeli war and returned to Cairo, where Said attended the elite Victoria College—the "Eton of the Middle East." In 1951, he moved again, this time to the United States, to complete high school at another elite boarding school, Mount Hermon. Thinking back on this period of his life—on his complex class, religious, and family identity and the movement of his childhood—Said observed that all these years later, he still "retained this unsettled sense of many identities" along with an acute memory "of the despairing feeling that I wish we could have been all-Arab, or all-European and American, or all-Orthodox Christian, or all-Muslim, or all-Egyptian."[18] Said's feeling of being "out of place"—the title of his 1999 memoir—would influence his scholarship and politics for the rest of his life.

From Mount Hermon, Said went on to study at Princeton and Harvard and then, in 1963, took up a position as instructor in English at Columbia University, where he would spend the rest of his career until his death of leukemia in 2003. As Said later recalled, his career at Columbia in the 1960s was largely unconventional until the Six-Day War of 1967 and subsequent events in the Middle East changed his thinking on the relationship between scholarship and politics for good.[19] "Until 1967," he notes in his memoir, "I succeeded in mentally dividing U.S. support for Israel from the fact of my being an American pursuing a career there."[20] Thereafter, Said began to practice the form of public intellectualizing that would so characterize the rest of his career as a Palestinian academic in America. In 1969, he published "The Arab Portrayed," an essay that foreshadows many of the themes he would develop in *Orientalism*.[21] But the idea of Orientalism as a "style of thought based upon an ontological and epistemological distinction made between 'the Orient' and (most of the time) 'the Occident'" only truly crystalized for Said as he observed the depictions of Arabs flowing through the Western media in the wake of the 1973 Yom Kippur War.[22]

Today, most political theorists are aware of Said's work because of this innovative reading of "the other," although this awareness rarely translates into close familiarity with *Orientalism* as a text. In other words, many of us—with significant exceptions—read *Orientalism* as undergraduates and then proceed through the rest of our academic careers assuming that we understand what it is about: the idea of "the other" in the context of European imperialism in Asia and the Middle East. And yet, the richness and novelty of *Orientalism* far exceeds this single problematic. As a whole, Said's approach in this book transforms the academic study of imperialism from engagement with a fixed, historical set of facts and practices whose policies, theories, cultures, and impact run solely in one direction—from Western metropoles to Asian, African, and Latin American sites of occupation—into engagement with the "constantly expanding," "inexorably integrative" ideological formation that buttressed domination in the past, rationalizes imperial politics in the present, and renders the impact of the former invisible on the latter.[23]

In *Orientalism* and elsewhere, Said approaches imperialism as a dynamic process that orders the world spatially and temporally through forms of knowledge and cartographic common sense that he famously called "imaginative geography."[24] Deeply influenced by Foucauldian readings of power, *Orientalism* explores the workings of this "knowing vocabulary"—this "comparative framework"—that reduces the complex dynamism and heterogeneity of Asia and the Middle and Near East "to a kind of human flatness," easily analyzed through ready-made categories of difference and essence.[25] Over the course of the eighteenth and nineteenth centuries, Said argues, Orientalists refined the key features they associated with the East—"its sensuality, its tendency to despotism, its aberrant mentality, its habits of inaccuracy, its backwardness"—and productively contrasted them with opposing Western characteristics—rational, democratic, active, and history making.[26] His antidote to this fixing and flattening is a wholesale interrogation of Orientalism in action coupled with an investigation of those tension-filled, human-created moments he termed history's "disruptive detail."[27] The subjects of Said's inquiry in *Orientalism* range from well-known European figures from the eighteenth and nineteenth centuries (e.g., Renan, Flaubert, Balfour, and Macauley) to obscure travel writers and polemicists, while the texts he examines similarly run the gamut from works of high literary and philosophical achievement to letters, pamphlets, journals, and travel and guide books.

The most striking feature of *Orientalism*, however, is Said's departure from mainstream literary theories of the time, which, in his words, "isolated textuality from circumstances."[28] By contrast, with Raymond Williams, Said argues that texts are "produced and live on in the historical realm."[29] For Said, analyzing the emergence and circulation of Orientalist texts requires first bringing them into conversation with power and context (an approach he refers to as "worldly") and then situating them within the military, political, cultural, and material apparatus that supported Europe's rapidly expanding imperial influence in the East. Thus, Said argues, "my contention is that Orientalism is fundamentally a political doctrine willed over the Orient because the Orient was weaker than the West, which elided the Orient's difference with its weakness."[30] Ultimately, as Leela Gandhi argues, *Orientalism*'s most powerful and controversial innovation was its assertion that understanding how the West came to dominate the East politically requires a deeper understanding of how the West studied, imagined, quantified, described, and *knew* the Orient—and *knew* itself to be fundamentally different from the Orient.[31]

In sum, the methodology Said develops in *Orientalism* engages the discursive mechanisms through which imperialism and imperial knowledge order the world by flattening complexity, naturalizing differences, telling developmental stories about far-off peoples and places, and narrowing the narrative aperture of history such that alternative accounts of colonization, precolonial time, and resistance simply disappear and "history" becomes the history of colonization alone.[32] Said's work more broadly continues to draw on these themes, exploring how active traces of the imperial past on the present (including the grotesque inequality of resources between the global North and South) still appear sui generis, untethered from a history of imperialism, slavery, settler colonialism, dispossession, and resource extraction—the natural order of things.

Not only do *Orientalism*'s conceptual and methodological innovations exceed what most political theorists know about that text, but also Said's conceptual and methodological innovations far exceeded *Orientalism*. Again, Said was a scholar of astonishing breadth. He was an early champion (and early critic) of Foucault, he cotranslated Erich Auerbach's "Philology and 'Weltliteratur,'" and he was one of the first scholars in North America to combine Foucault's insights with a Gramscian critique of hegemony.[33] From the early 1970s, Said entered into the debates between structuralist and post-structuralist scholars, often by insistently connecting language to politics and domination, specifically to the political and material project of imperialism.[34] This early work lays the foundations for the anticolonial mode of humanism and worldly criticism Said developed later, an approach that combined Fanon with Gramsci, Auerbach with C. L. R. James, Césaire with Vico.[35]

Thus, Said's theoretical sensibilities were, from the very beginning, radically open and radically political. From as early as 1969, he was writing about Palestine-Israel and linking his work on discourse, history, and imperialism to critiques of Israeli state violence and Palestinian dispossession.[36] Indeed, Said considered *Orientalism* to be part 1 of a trilogy that helped illuminate the current situation in Palestine. In that first part, he examines the relationship between knowledge, power, and the rhetorical and ideological justification for European imperialism in the Orient. In part 2, *The Question of Palestine* (1979), he extends his analysis of this justificatory discourse to critique the imperial origins of the Israeli state and the rhetorical framing of Arabs as supine, violent Orientals. Part 3, *Covering Islam* (1981), brings this analysis up to date through an investigation of the Western media's generalizations about Islam, generalizations, Said argues, that "have become the last acceptable form of denigration of foreign culture in the West."[37]

Over the course of his career, Said wrote dozens of books, many more articles, and numerous collections of essays; gave countless speeches; and sat for long, intensive interviews. He was also an extraordinarily self-reflective scholar, "traveling"—as he might put it—with his own theoretical and conceptual insights.[38] *Culture and Imperialism* (1992), for instance, demonstrates Said's post-*Orientalism* growth as a scholar, showcasing in particular the increasing urgency with which he believed it necessary to pair poststructuralist-inspired accounts of the constitutive, disciplinary power of imperial culture with genealogical investigations of anticolonial resistance. In this book, he also develops a more sophisticated reading of how ideas travel from the periphery to the center and back again. Here and in other texts, Said stresses the need to cultivate what he calls a "contrapuntal" orientation toward history, culture, and politics that "sees Western and non-Western experiences as belonging together because they are connected by imperialism."[39]

Said also had a complicated relationship with postcolonialism, the field that, as Rosi Braidotti puts it, "nonetheless celebrated him as a foundational figure."[40] As chapter 4 explores in greater detail, Said objected vigorously to the affiliation between some postcolonial scholarship and an essentializing identity politics, a trend of which he was deeply skeptical throughout the 1980s and '90s. In a 1991 article for *Raritan* entitled "The Politics of Knowledge," Said describes his experience of being excoriated by a professor of history after he presented a paper at a seminar on colonialism and the nineteenth-century English novel. This professor, according to Said, felt it was unacceptable that Said failed to mention a single living non-White male thinker. Said recalls that he left the seminar with the distinct impression that any politics sympathetic to "the other" (a category that, again, his work had helped raise to the level of scholarly consideration) was expected to "mention some approved names . . . as if the very act of uttering them was enough," as if this uttering "took the place of evidence, argument, discussion."[41] For Said, such an approach pushed against the grain of the contrapuntal, worldly, humanist critique he develops in his work, a critical disposition that, by its nature, resists essentialism at every turn.

Throughout his scholarship, Said repeatedly tied this resistance to both his own experience of living in exile and to the more generally productive qualities of an "exilic" perspective that resists domination and upends univocal accounts of identity and history. As he put it in 1984s "Reflections on Exile," "Most people are principally aware of one culture, one setting, one home; exiles are aware of at least two, and this plurality of vision gives rise to an awareness of simultaneous dimensions, an awareness that—to borrow a phrase from music—is contrapuntal."[42] Said's pairing of exile and counterpoint here illustrates how so many of the key concepts that circulate through his work emerges from this dialectical and often deeply personal mode of reflection on experience, history, culture, politics, and loss. Scholars across fields have found this exilic wrestling with polyphony and tension productively unsettling, often in ways that transformed their own thinking. Reflecting on his first encounter with *Orientalism* in 1980, for instance, Partha Chatterjee remembers reading the text in the midst of having his house repainted. "I read right through the day and, after the workmen had left in the evening, well into the night," he recalls. "Now whenever I think of *Orientalism*, the image comes back to me of an empty room with a red floor and bare white walls, a familiar room suddenly made unfamiliar."[43] Chatterjee's words here capture the most arresting aspect of Said's work in a nutshell: his capacity to *defamiliarize* a political, cultural, and intellectual landscape that had, until that moment, been simply and commonsensically known. In the process, Said changed the way scholars thought about imperialism in the past and present.

Throughout all these productive years, as Said taught and wrote and transformed and unsettled multiple academic fields, he also came to prominence as one of the most prolific and committed public intellectuals in America, intervening again and again in important debates about contemporary US foreign policy, particularly when it came to Palestine-Israel. Said's career as a public voice for Palestine was long and diverse, but it can be usefully understood, as Ardi Imseis argues, in terms of three distinct roles that he played in advancing discourse on the subject. First, Said "had an enormous impact as a *narrator* of contemporary Palestinian experience," constantly drawing attention, through various media and public intellectual outlets, to the ways Palestinians had been denied "permission to narrate" that experience.[44] Said did this by exploring, for instance, the imperialist assumptions at work in the Balfour Declaration and the historical persistence of Orientalist language in Western portrayals of Arabs and Palestinians today. In the introduction to *The Politics of Dispossession* (a collection of essays he wrote between 1969 and 1993), Said notes that his most specific task throughout all the essays was "to make the case for Palestinian presence" and "to try and change the public consciousness in which Palestine had no presence at all."[45]

Second, Said was a consistent *critic* of power, not just Israeli and Western, "but also of Arab and Palestinian power."[46] Throughout the 1970s and 1980s, along with Darwish and other cultural and intellectual figures, Said supported the Palestinian Liberation Organization's (PLO) political struggle for sovereign statehood.[47] From 1967 until 1991, Salah Hassan argues, the vision of sovereignty that Said championed "modelled a cosmopolitan, exilic, and secular Palestinian national subjectivity that was Third-Worldist, revolutionary, and avant-gardist."[48] From early on, however, Said critiqued the oil money flowing in to support the PLO from some of the most reactionary regimes in the Middle East, regimes whose goal was to preserve the status quo with Israel rather than support the emergence of an anticolonial, Palestinian state. All this came to a head in 1993, when he broke from Arafat and the PLO over the Oslo Accords which he presciently believed were doomed to failure.[49] And yet, instead of withdrawing from politics when Arafat and the PLO accepted the internally divided form of self-government that exists today, Said transformed his own aspirations, rejecting what Joseph Masad calls the PLO's "game of pragmatism" for a "renewed vision" of a secular, democratic state.[50]

Thus, the third role Said played in advancing discourse about Palestine, according to Imseis, was that of *visionary*, someone who consistently saw the problems associated with various plans for peace, articulated those problems, and put forward his own interpretations. After Oslo, Said became increasingly critical of the now widely accepted "two-state solution," which he believed was compromised from the beginning by both "Israel's massive geographic and demographic transformation" of the Occupied Territories *and* the reality of the fact that Israeli Jews and Arab Palestinians had been living together in the same region for so long.[51] For the rest of his life, he championed a binational, secular, "one-state solution." This solution, he explains in 1999's "Truth and Reconciliation," "does not mean a diminishing of Jewish life as Jewish life or surrendering Palestinian Arab aspirations and political exis- tence" but rather "self-determination for both peoples." At the same time, he argues, it "does mean being willing to soften, lessen, and finally give up special status for one people at the expense of the other."[52] For this position, Said was often the object of liberal criticisms (for rejecting the Oslo agree- ment); of conservative ire (for continuing to point out Palestinian oppres- sion); and, as he later recalled, of "extreme left-wing nationalist hostility" because of his belief in "the idea of co-existence between Israeli Jews and Palestinian Arabs."[53]

As a Palestinian in exile, constantly negotiating and interrogating the space between imperial history, the Palestinian present, and the global impact of America's militarism, Said's work as a narrator, critic, and visionary made him, in Masad's words, a "veritable passport for the Palestinian cause, allow- ing it to cross borders into territories where it was previously denied entry."[54] But this extraordinary effort did not come without cost. As Alexander Coburn wrote in a 2006 article for the *Nation*, "The FBI was probably tap- ping Edward Said's phone right up to the day he died in September 2003."[55] Indeed, the FBI began its file on Said in 1971, according to David Price, and continued their surveillance of him for the rest of his life, enlisting the help of employees "at Princeton and Columbia Universities" and at the Harvard University Alumni Office, all of whom gave FBI agents detailed education and bibliographical information on Said.[56] Over the course of his career, Said was dubbed "Professor of Terror" and received "innumerable death threats," and his university office was set afire.[57] During an interview in 1986, Salman Rushdie asked Said what it was like to write and speak about Palestine in America today. Said responded by noting that he had effectively "become tokenized, so that whenever there is a hijacking or some other such incident, I get phone-calls from the media asking me to come along and comment." It is, he continued, a "very strange feeling to be seen as a kind of representative of terrorism."[58] This mischaracterization of Said's politics and intentions was often purposely reinforced by public figures. For instance, then Israeli ambas- sador to the United Nations Benjamin Netanyahu once engaged in a fatuous piece of 1980s performance art by insisting that he would not appear in the same building as Said for a television debate because "he wants to kill me."[59] Through such antics was Said's fate as Terrorist Professor Number 1 sealed.

It is important to note, however, that it wasn't just Said's work about and for Palestine that made him appear particularly dangerous to large swathes of the conservative and liberal chattering classes in America. Rather, Said was dangerous precisely because his scholarship suggested that American foreign policy today might usefully be analyzed through the same critical lenses through which we study imperialism. Nowhere is this more obvious than in the central role played by Said's scholarship in the rhetorical justification for the passage of H.R. 3077, the International Studies in Higher Education Act, passed by the US House of Representatives in 2003. The act sought to shift allocation of funds for international studies, areas studies, and language studies at American universities away from the oversight of scholars toward the authority of an "international advisory board partly composed of non-academics invested in national security."[60] In the hearings leading up to this bill, leading neoconservative academics soberly linked the need for H.R. 3007 to the disturbing domination of anti-American bias in the American academy. In his testimony before the House Subcommittee on Select Education for Hearings on International Education and Questions of Bias, Stanley Kurtz (then a fellow at the Hoover Institute) warned Congress that "postcolonial theory" was now the "ruling intellectual paradigm in academic area studies (especially Middle Eastern studies)." Kurtz went on to tie this theory explicitly to Said, who, he argued, "equated professors who support American foreign policy with the nineteenth-century European intellectuals who propped up racist colonial empires." In the screed that followed, Kurtz argued that not only did Said think the "very idea of American democracy a farce" but also that his dangerous approach now threatened to transform Middle Eastern studies into a coven of extremists whose perspectives might infect the "teachers responsible for educating America's young children about the meaning of September 11."[61]

For Kurtz, Said wasn't dangerous just because he wrote for and about Palestine. Said was dangerous because he viewed American interventionism and foreign policy through the same critical, postcolonial lenses that he viewed European imperialism. Kurtz is thus palpably uncomfortable with Said's conflation of American and European imperialism and palpably fearful that this conflation was becoming normalized within the academy in ways that might negatively affect US foreign policy and the minds of America's youth. A generation of students, Kurtz warned, was now on the verge of succumbing to the nigh hegemonic influence of a postcolonial, Saidian critique of imperialism whose goal was to deexceptionalize American power in the world.

And yet, for all that Kurtz feared the tentacular power of Said's theory in June 2003 (just two months before Said's death), he needn't have been overly worried. Large sections of the academy (particularly those subfields dedicated to the study of politics) remained staunchly resistant to postcolonialism as well as to the critical study of imperialism. As Jennifer Pitts notes in her adroit 2010 review article "Political Theory of Empire and Imperialism," as a field, political theory had come "slowly and late to the study of empire relative to other disciplines." Moreover, she notes the discipline's remarkable imperviousness throughout the 1980s and 1990s to the "powerful theoretical and thematic developments" of postcolonial theory more generally, despite the fact that the two fields clearly have convergent theoretical and historical interests.[62] In the course of making this argument, Pitts briefly mentions Said but only twice: at the beginning of the essay, when she refers to *Orientalism*'s status as the text that launched postcolonial studies, and then again toward the end, when she notes the "vast influence of Said's *Orientalism* on literature and history."[63] Between these bookended references, Said's "vast influence"—an influence that clearly kept Kurtz and legions of neoconservatives up at night—quietly disappears.

Pitts's article suggests that the Said-inspired plague of postcolonial scholarship Kurtz believed was devastating the academy had clearly failed to infect the subdiscipline of political theory. But for our purposes, her article is even more illustrative. On the one hand, Pitts's observation about a field that both is impervious to postcolonial theory and came "slowly and late" to the study of imperialism begins to circle in on some of the structural reasons that help explain political theory's overall lack of interest in Said. In other words, as I argue later, political theorists probably aren't reading Said for the same two professional reasons it took us so long to start analyzing imperialism in the first place: the internal divisions that striate political science as a discipline and the double layer of unseeing that flows from these divisions. On the other hand, Pitts's acknowledgment of Said's influence on the humanities in this article, coupled with her decision not to closely engage the substance of his thought, also suggests that a different kind of disconnect is often at work for political theorists when it comes to Said. In what follows, I explore some structural and substantive explanations for this disconnect in turn.

## WHITHER SAID? STRUCTURAL UNSEEING

In the vast majority of universities in North America and Europe today, political theory remains a subdiscipline of political science, a discipline that, for a variety of reasons, has had a difficult time identifying and theorizing imperialism. The origins of this difficulty can, in part, be traced to the formalization of the discipline and its subdisciplines in the immediate postwar period, a time of professional hiving-off in which nearly all thinking about global politics was corralled into the field of international relations (IR).[64] The segregation of inquiry within the discipline thus broke down along lines determined by the idea of the state; that is, between "domestic," "comparative," and "international" realms of analysis. Such divisions were far less common prior to the war, when academics in Europe and America who considered themselves scholars of politics often theorized broadly about international and domestic politics, moving between the realms of philosophy, law, history, classics, and global affairs with an ease that seems astonishing from our contemporary perspective.[65] Over the years, however, professional divisions within political science have ossified to such an extent that the fields of political theory and IR, for instance, now occupy what Duncan Bell describes as "parallel universes" with markedly different literatures and understandings of the very same terms (e.g., *liberalism*, *idealism*, and *realism*).[66]

By 1960, the distinction between political theory and IR was so obvious to Martin Wight that he breezily insists it "requires no explanation."[67] IR scholars, Wight argues, in his influential essay "Why Is There No International Theory?" were interested in the "untidy fringe" of political activity taking place *between* states, while political theorists were oriented toward the normative, stationary, and domesticated project of theorizing the good life *within* states. It was not until the late 1970s that Rawlsian-inspired theorists like Charles Beitz and Henry Shue began challenging at least part of this distinction by suggesting that philosophical theories of justice might usefully be applied to the international sphere.[68] Overall, however, it remains the case that political theorists are largely uncomfortable theorizing about global politics, and indeed historically, the structural scission of the field has actively discouraged them from doing so except in normative and analytical terms that steer well clear of the power politics associated with the "untidy fringe."

Additionally, Wight's observation about the *methodological* border between political theory and IR reflects the increasing salience of *sovereign* borders within IR scholarship. Following the period of "sustained reflection about the organization of international knowledge" that occurred after the war, the emerging discipline of IR concretized around approaches aimed at legitimizing the subfield's relationship to political science, thus establishing, in Hans Morgenthau's words, the "proper place of international relations and area studies as academic disciplines."[69] These approaches associated the work of IR primarily with the relationships *between* sovereign states, an assumption that is still foundational for much of the subdiscipline to this day. Whether they are imagined by liberals as inclined toward cooperation, by realists as inevitably drawn to power politics, or by constructivists as responsive to international norms regimes, sovereign states remain, by and large, the primary units of analysis for the majority of mainstream IR scholars today. As a field, IR continues to naturalize this orientation by *prospectively* narrowing the discipline's interpretive frame to three dominant, state-oriented approaches: idealism/liberalism, realism, and constructivism. IR scholars also do this by *retroactively* reading the contested landscape of world history through these same lenses.[70]

Because the discipline of IR associates both its own disciplinary history and the history of international politics more broadly with the relationships between states, imperialism—as a transnational, global mode of power—tends to fall out of its conceptual frame. As such, the long-term impact of imperialism on the formation of contemporary international politics and the discipline is also rendered invisible. But, as David Armitage points out, the European and American intellectuals who were most involved in the debates that established the postwar international order (and eventually the discipline of IR) were never merely concerned with a world of states. They were also profoundly anxious about the "drawn-out transition from a world of empires to a world of states."[71] Indeed, in Armitage's words, most of the world's population, "for most of history lived not in nation states but in empires," and imperial politics remained centrally important to American and European foreign policy discussion through the mid-twentieth century.[72] Within the developing field of American IR, this manifested itself, according to Robert Vitalis, as a preoccupation on the part of some of the discipline's founding thinkers with colonial administration and non-White migration.[73]

And yet, despite the importance and presence of imperialism in the founding of the contemporary world order, the dominant IR Weltanschauung to emerge after World War II naturalized an international terrain imagined largely through sovereign states. From the beginning, this conceptual apparatus necessarily occluded not only the lingering impact of imperialism (and the ongoing impact of racism) on world politics and foreign policy but also contemporary forms of "informal imperialism," ranging from structural adjustment programs to CIA-sponsored coups to drone strikes. In the North American academy, this blinkered self-understanding has resulted in a discipline grounded in what Vitalis argues are the two entwined myths of IR: a conviction that the United States is not and has never been an imperial power and a belief that the discipline itself has never showed much interest in the study of race and imperialism.[74]

On its face, this blithe unseeing of imperialism's living impact on the world resembles what Jodi Byrd calls "colonial agnosia." Read in the context of US settler colonialism, "colonial agnosia" for Byrd is the inability "to connect the present tense presence" of living Indigenous people and Indigenous bodies "to the larger systems of domination that continue to inform Otherness within U.S. settler imperialism."[75] As a mode of misperception, it enables mainstream accounts of American IR to proceed *as if* imperialism was a purely historical and European phenomenon and *as if* the discipline's interest in race and imperialism had no long-term impact on both the shape of American foreign policy and the intellectual object that is political science today. Because of this, argues Vitalis, most mainstream IR scholarship just assumes that until Michael Doyle wrote *Empires* in 1986, political science was simply uninterested in imperialism.[76] The "norm against noticing," as Vitalis calls it, deflects attention away from imperialism in history; away from the work of midcentury Black scholars like Merze Tate, who *did* actually write about imperialism; and away from the racist and imperialist concerns of the early discipline and American foreign policy. In this reading, for instance, the original name of *Foreign Affairs*—the *Journal of Race Development*—can simply fade into history, known but militantly unseen.

All this contributes to a situation in which political scientists are not just reluctant to utter the word *empire* aloud, but also it simply wouldn't occur to many of them to do so. In IR, realists, idealists, and constructivists alike prefer terms like *great power* or *hegemon* to describe the military, political, and economic "primacy" of the United States. Combined, the "norm against noticing" and the laser-like focus on sovereignty mean that, aside from the subdiscipline's vibrant postcolonial contingent, the few IR scholars who theorize imperialism do so by treating it as a (largely historical) species of *state* power.[77] In *Empires*, for instance, Doyle defines an empire as a "relationship, formal or informal, in which one *state* controls the effective political sovereignty of another" and imperialism as "simply the process or policy of establishing or maintaining an empire."[78]

Finally, the emphasis in IR and political science on the state as the primary unit of analysis has the unfortunate side effect of sometimes reducing questions about imperialism to questions about status or essence. This focus on what Paul Kramer calls "thingness" tends to come into play with particular ferocity when discussing American foreign policy. Throughout the postwar period, for instance, mainstream American political scientists have occasionally stopped to utter the word *imperialism* aloud, but it almost always focused on a single vexing question: *Is* the United States an empire? If so, as Kramer puts it, "[W]hat type [is it?]" and Does it measure up "to the rubrics built to account for other empires"?[79] The resounding response to such questions is almost always no. The United States is not an empire because it does not look like European empires, because it nominally supports the sovereignty of other states, and because it does not self-identify as such. Unfortunately, this assumption about American "thingness" (not an empire) tends to mute inquiries into how America came to have the kind of hegemonic global power that it does in the first place. For contemporary realists like Stephen Walt and John Mearsheimer, the United States is simply the "luckiest great power in history."[80] For liberal internationalists like G. John Ikenberry (the subject of chapter 6), other states voluntarily relinquished military leadership to the United States after World War II, "just as Hobbes' individuals in the state of nature construct and hand over power to the Leviathan."[81] Hans Morgenthau's approach to imperialism in *Politics among Nations*, however, might be the most stark in its studied blindness. In the midst of a discussion about America's acquisition of the Virgin Islands and barely a decade after the end of America's nearly twenty-year occupation of Haiti, Morgenthau looks around at the world and decides to call the United States a "status quo" rather than an imperial power.[82]

Thus have IR scholars traditionally called American global power—with its long history of annexation, occupation, continental colonialism, electoral interference, assassination, and counterinsurgency—anything other than imperial: because America is not an empire. The basic problem with this fixation on *essence* is that it precludes richer analyses of *action*. In other words, perseverating on the "*Is* the United States an empire?" question forecloses the "When is the United States *acting* imperially?" question. Said, by contrast, focuses on imperial*ism* as a dimension of power rather than *empire* as a moniker. When one makes this conceptual shift, it becomes easier to compare the discursive hallmarks associated with America's foreign policy actions in the present to those of imperialisms in the past. This is, of course, precisely the line of questioning that most troubled Kurtz about Said's scholarship, and it is also a line of questioning that is structurally very difficult for political scientists to access. As a result, even sympathetic critics of American hegemony are frequently hamstrung by the limitations of their disciplinary language when it comes to explaining that hegemony.[83] Worse, scholarly champions of the "American-led liberal world order" (the subjects of chapter 6) often fall back on a justificatory logic that looks, for all intents and purposes, like imperialism while insisting the United States is not an empire.

The overall impact of these disciplinary divisions and conceptual blind spots on the field of political theory is a double layer of unseeing. First, given the professional divisions in the field, political theorists largely avoid thinking about international politics and foreign policy. When they do think about it, as I argue further in chapter 2, is it usually through the register of analytic philosophy and normative theory. With very few exceptions, scholars of global justice, such as Shue, Beitz, Michael Blake, Martha Nussbaum, Mathias Risse, Simon Caney, Joseph Carens, and David Held, adhere to largely Rawlsian-inspired modes of ideal moral theorizing that have only a thin conceptual connection to the actual political history of imperialism and its long-term impact on global power politics today.

At the same time, most critical scholars in political theory who are committed to analyzing the relationship between history, race, and politics; to thinking in complex ways about the circulation of power in our neoliberal era; and to engaging questions of political subjectivity from the perspective of race, class, gender, and sexuality have largely ceded the realm of "international politics" (as a field of contemporary inquiry) to IR scholars and ideal moral theorists.[84] This discomfort with challenging the domestic-international divide (which often maps onto the critical-analytical divide in political theory) affects the work of even the most critical thinkers in the field of political theory today. In her challenge to liberal theory, for instance, Nancy Fraser situates liberalism's assumptions within an account of the modern welfare state and what she calls a "history of capitalism" that takes place in four stages: mercantile, liberal, state-managed, and financial "neoliberal globalization."[85] What her state-centered narrative fails to address, however, is the absolutely essential (some would say constitutive) role played by extrastate forces of production (colonialism, slavery, resource extraction, land dispossession) in the development of capitalism at *every single one* of those stages.[86]

Second, because political science has traditionally passed off thinking about extrastate politics to IR and, as a field, IR is often allergic to thinking about imperialism, political theorists largely avoided the topic throughout much of the 1980s and 1990s, when disciplines in the humanities were being actively transformed by Said's scholarship and by postcolonial theory. Even political theory's eventual "turn to empire" in the early 2000s—a "turn" in which I am proud to have played some small part—reflected this disciplinary isolationism. The main problematic that structured much of our work at the time was the connection between historical liberalism and imperialism. In essence, we were largely interested in the professional and intellectual entanglements of liberal thinkers like John Stuart Mill with the material and political benefits of an imperial system grounded in extraction, dispossession, hierarchy, and exclusion. Very few of us doing this research in the early 2000s, however, looked for conceptual guidance in the work of scholars from those disciplines outside political theory that had been deeply influenced by postcolonialism and for whom imperialism had been an object of inquiry for decades. This double unseeing—first unseeing imperialism, then unseeing postcolonial theory and the study of imperialism outside political theory— reflects the field's baseline insularity and a general reluctance to access the political-theoretical intellectual insights of scholars in other fields. By way of example, in 2005's *Edgework*—a book ironically about interdisciplinary thinking—Wendy Brown observes that the "work of thinking about political matters theoretically *has lately* been undertaken in disciplines as far removed from each other and from political science as art history, anthropology, rhetoric, geography, and literature."[87] Whether Brown is unaware of the fact that scholars in these disciplines have been thinking "about political matters theoretically" for decades or whether she just doesn't consider those political insights sufficiently theoretical is unclear. What is clear is that the disciplining power of our discipline first made it difficult for political theorists to see imperialism as an object of analysis and then, once scholars had begun to think critically about imperialism, to find inspiration in the postcolonial scholarship of thinkers outside of political theory.

This same insulating tendency to constrain political theory's conceptual gaze vis-à-vis political science also contributes to a theoretical common sense that, I argue, obscures Said's work. In essence, Said's analysis is located in neither the "national" nor the "international" but rather in that complex discursive and material universe that maintains imperial domination and expresses itself through myriad transnational forms of power-knowledge and countless overlapping connections. His emphasis on "worldlines"—his cross-, trans-, sub-, and antinational way of reading culture and history—can make his work almost indecipherable for scholars used to containing their analyses of politics within textual and geographical sites encircled by what G. D. H. Cole once called the "ringed fence" of state sovereignty.[88]

Said's theory of imperialism challenges that ringed-fence orientation at every turn. Rather than assume, with Doyle, that imperialism is "simply the process" by which one state establishes and maintains "effective political sovereignty" over another, a Said-inspired approach understands imperialism as a complex dimension of power that unfolds on a variety of levels that far exceed one state's physical occupation of another state's sovereign territory. As he explains in "Zionism from the Standpoint of Its Victims," it would be a "serious underestimation" of imperialism if one were to "consider territory in too literal a way." Instead, he continues, "Gaining and holding an imperium means gaining and holding a domain, which includes a variety of operations, among them constituting an area, accumulating its inhabitants, having power over its ideas, people, and of course, its land, converting people, land, and ideas to the purposes and uses of a hegemonic imperial design."[89] In other words, for Said, "laying claim to an *idea* and laying claim to a *territory*" are two sides of the same multivalent, multivocal, "constitutive activity."

For Said and for scholars inspired by his approach, the "constitutive activity" of imperialism manifests itself through a discursive process that makes distinctions among and between those peoples being dominated; expands and solidifies disparities in power and status between the colonizers and the colonized; and tells affirmative, identity narratives about "*our* culture"—the culture of the metropole.[90] Imperialism from this perspective, as Kramer explains, isn't merely the instrumental application of power by one state onto another. It is rather a system of power in which "asymmetries in the scale of political action, regimes of spatial ordering, and modes of exceptionalizing difference enable and produce relations of hierarchy, discipline, dispossession, extraction, and exploitation."[91] In order to sustain and expand this scalar world, imperialism—as an ideology and a political practice—has to function on a number of different political, philosophical, cultural, artistic, military, architectural, geographic, and economic registers simultaneously.

Said insists that those who want to grapple with imperial power—and the complex legacy of cultural, political, and material relations it engenders—necessarily must work on an interdisciplinary level and must be willing to engage the transnational linkages between imperialism and its vivifying culture(s). Moreover, a definition of *empire* and *imperialism* that does not take into account the dense ideological and cultural assemblage necessary to rationalize and naturalize domination cannot adequately grapple with the way imperialism functions in a putatively postimperial age. In essence, any definition of *imperialism* that stops at the level of "state control"—be it formal or informal—will necessarily fail to fully account for the way the very terms and institutions of contemporary international political and economic organization have been determined by former empires and great powers in such a way as to render their historic connections to imperialism invisible over time.[92] Imperialism, in Said's sense, necessarily overflows its definitional floodgates, filling up postcolonial space in a manner that won't be contained by the pedantic question that routinely shuts down inquiry in our discipline: "*Is* America an empire?"

At the very outset, then—before one even begins to scratch the surface of his work more generally—Said's scholarship breaks most of political science's methodological presumptions. It violates the distinction between domestic and international politics, between IR and political theory, between political and cultural theory, and between American foreign policy and European imperial history. Said's approach thus unsettles the containers in which political theorists, IR scholars, and political scientists are meant to confine their thinking. This may explain why Said's work has been so hard to see and, at the same time, why seeing it is more important than ever.

## WHITHER SAID? SEEING WITHOUT SEEING

Several years ago, I presented an early draft chapter from this book at a workshop held by a large political science department at a large American university. That admittedly now-underformed chapter focused on Said's critical reading of humanism and the conceptual and political possibilities of that reading for political theory and for IR. During the discussion that followed, one older, well-known political theorist raised his hand to offer a comment on Said that I would hear, in multiple forms, over the course of writing the book: "I always found Edward Said fascinating as a thinker. But did he have to be so angry?"

About a year later, at the annual meeting of the American Political Science Association (APSA), I gave a brief introduction to a panel about the relationship between postcolonialism and political theory, in which I talked extensively about Said's influence. In the spirit of the panel, I suggested that political theorists had much to learn from the work of a man whose scholarship fundamentally transformed many of our cognate disciplines. When the last speaker on the panel concluded their remarks, a man in the front row immediately raised his hand. In the midst of explaining why he believed the insights of postcolonial theory were irrelevant to the study of imperialism in the history of political thought, he paused and, with an exasperated sigh, blurted out, "Why do we need Edward Said? All he did was read five novels and tell the rest of us how to think about empire!"

That same year, at another annual conference, I found myself listening to a plenary given by a scholar whose work I greatly admire. In the course of the talk, this scholar offered a razor-sharp critique of political theory as a field, focusing on what Charles Mills has termed "White ignorance" and the conceptual implications of that ignorance for research.[93] The speaker called boldly for a conceptual paradigm shift that sought inspiration from the way scholars in other fields have addressed issues of historical racism and settler colonial violence. As a theoretical orientation toward this interdisciplinarity, the speaker turned to Brown's suggestion in *Edgework* that political theorists employ what she terms a "contrapuntal strategy" that "agitates" along disciplinary parameters.[94] And yet, as appropriate as this contrapuntal approach might be for challenging political theory's disciplinary isolation, Brown did not invent or develop the idea; Edward Said did. Brown's unseeing of Said is indicative of a weighty double silence, a silence that mutes Said's rich and generative voice from political theory discourse more broadly and even from a plenary (and a book) dedicated to interdisciplinarity.

I begin this section with these reflections not to cast blame on any of the political theorists involved for either mis-seeing or not seeing Said. Indeed, throughout the process of working on this book, the vast majority of political theorists with whom I've spoken about the project have read something by Said at some point in time and been genuinely curious and enthusiastic to learn more about his work. Moreover, as someone who has been known to bang her head against a desk in frustration while struggling to understand Said's sometimes maddeningly open-ended arguments, I am fully sympathetic to the frustrations voiced by political theorists who struggle to translate Said into a familiar idiom. Rather, I begin with these observations to help paint a general picture of the kinds of seeing, unseeing, or misrecognition that cloud our collective imaginations and make it more difficult for political theorists to fully engage Said's work.

Brown's failure to mention Said's innovative reading of counterpoint, for instance, reflects one important feature of contemporary political theory as a subdiscipline that presents a challenge for thinkers who want to engage Said's scholarship: the unfortunate isolationism of our field. In the case of *Edgework*, this isolationism is so acute that it prevents Brown from acknowledging the copacetic theorizing of a scholar in another discipline while she is in the midst of arguing for an approach that "agitates" along disciplinary borders. More commonly, the bunkered quality of political theory research manifests itself in a hesitancy to explore the theoretical work of political thinkers who never made it onto the list of approved names established during the early postwar period, when political theorists, like their IR brethren, endeavored to legitimize the subdiscipline vis-à-vis political science.[95] While the field today is in the midst of an important "decolonizing" move to open its doors to alternative approaches and noncanonical thinkers, contemporary political theory is still veined by informal and formal "hedges" that, as Hobbes put it in regard to laws in the commonwealth, exist not to stop students and scholars in their tracks but to "keep them in the way," encouraging them to engage particular thinkers and themes while discouraging them from peeking over the hedges to see what people might be up to in neighboring fields.[96]

This does not mean that, over the years, political theorists haven't written about Said or been drawn to his conceptual universe. Brown herself is among that small group of theorists who occasionally refer to his work, and she does so in a way that is fairly typical in the field: by evoking a particular Saidian concept from *Orientalism* (or, more rarely, from another text) as a way of setting the stage for an argument to come. In *Walled States, Waning Sovereignty*, for instance, she briefly refers to Said's concept of "imaginative geography" in order to introduce the book's idea of a "mental organization of space."[97] Pitts's article similarly uses *Orientalism* as a framing device to stress the importance of imperialism studies on other fields. But in both these texts, Said's conceptual innovations for Brown and Pitts are largely emblematic or catalytic; they demonstrate a direction and open up inquiry but don't require engagement on their own terms *as* theory.

Amy Allen's and Frederick Dallmayr's theoretical evocations of Said's life and work are similarly gestural rather than substantive. Allen thus begins her important book *The End of Progress* with a quotation from *Culture and Imperialism*, in which Said criticizes the thinkers of the Frankfurt School for their "blithe universalism" and refusal to connect their sustained critiques of modernity and domination with the histories of imperialism, racism, and anticolonial resistance.[98] With exquisite clarity, Allen's book systematically explores this blindness in the work of Jurgen Habermas, Axel Honeth, and Rainer Forst, linking critical theory's failure to address racism and imperialism to its attachment to an essentially Eurocentric idea of progress in history. And yet, for a book that takes not just its inspiration but its organizing problematic from Said's scholarship, Allen goes on to mention Said only a few times in a 258-page book, and each time, she does so in the service of identifying the problem at hand: Eurocentrism in critical theory and poststructuralism.[99]

Dallmayr's *Beyond Orientalism: Essays on Cross Cultural Encounter* similarly begins with a grateful dedication to Said for showing the way. "In the attempt to transgress 'Orientalism,'" he notes, "I am strongly and lastingly indebted to Edward Said whose book of the same title opened the eyes of the reader to the complicity of much traditional scholarship with European colonial expansion."[100] Dallmayr proceeds to reference *Orientalism* several times in the introduction but, as with Allen, he does so largely in the service of indicating a direction of travel rather than a deep engagement with that text or with Said's work more generally. Thus, Said opens the door for Allen and Dallmayr; he inspires their endeavors. The expansive corpus of his work, however, invites no further inquiry.

For Brown, Pitts, Allen, and Dallmayr, Said exists as a pivotal figure who sets the terms of a broader debate but whose work ultimately does not inspire the same close reading and scrupulosity as do thinkers more obviously associated with the political theory canon (Allen) or thinkers from other traditions writing in an idiom that more closely resembles something that looks like canonical political theory (Dallmayr). To be fair, all these scholars are genuinely moved by Said's work and take him seriously as an intellectual figure. By contrast—and I count myself among this group for much of my career—it is more often the case that political theorists simply *think* they know what Said wrote about and stood for. Sometimes this takes the form of a baseline awareness of *Orientalism*'s main themes and a sense that the book is largely an engagement with literary texts. Occasionally that surface awareness can morph into the slightly exasperated tone of the man in the front row of the APSA panel. For this man, Said was a professor of comparative literature, someone whose main intellectual domain was the novel, and didn't that make his scholarship about imperialism more than a little presumptuous?

Unfortunately, many of the most virulent reactionary responses to Said's work over the years echo this critique of his interdisciplinary hubris. So powerful are these claims about Said's presumptiveness that they are still being trotted out regularly to this day, years after his death. In his 2013 article "Enough Said: The False Scholarship of Edward Said," for instance, Joshua Muravchik refers to the "deviousness and posturing and ineffable vanity" of a man who could have stuck to analyzing literature and whose influence could have remained an "academic matter" but who had the temerity to make policy observations and engage in political activism.[101] In the summer of 2020, Caroline Glick lambasted Said posthumously for the "postcolonialist crusade he waged against the United States," a crusade that has now become the "reality on the streets of America's great cities." With Muravchik, Glick (whose own academic credentials consist of a BA in political science from, ironically, Columbia) expresses a deep irritation with *Orientalism* as a text and with the long-dead-but-still-threatening Said for having a degree in one thing and daring to weigh in on another. "Although his field of expertise was comparative literature," Glick laments, "Said became a celebrity intellectual for a work that had nothing to do with comparative literature."[102]

Setting aside the obvious distortions of Muravchik and Glick, it is not entirely without reason that some political theorists would react to Said's theory with irritation, not because he was a comparative literature professor who dared to talk about politics or because he "only read five novels" and told the rest of us what to think about imperialism, but because his overall style is strikingly different from that of most political theorists and/or anyone who has devoted their careers to developing expertise in a single field. Said was a professor of comparative literature who insisted on interdisciplinarity, describing the mono-focus of academic specialization as a form of "guild solidarity" that produces increasingly narrow interpretive communities and intellectual constituencies who collectively worked to reify and privatize the "untidy realm" of history.[103] In an intellectual environment where academic fields tend to "subdivide and proliferate," scholars often proceed like the blind men in the story who misidentify the elephant as they work their way around the discrete parts of the animal, failing to see the astonishingly complex overlap of discourses, politics, ideology, and culture that sustains imperialism over time.[104]

As Conor McCarthy puts it bluntly, "Said practiced interdisciplinarity on a grand scale."[105] His is a disruptive mode of intellectualizing that roams expansively beyond fields of expertise, moving in and out of genres and theoretical approaches with, at times, head-spinning alacrity. Reading imperialism through Said-inspired eyes requires not only a willingness to situate texts within the whole "economy" of discourses that give imperialism life but also a willingness to expand the definition of what counts as "texts" worthy of critique to include, for instance, the rhetorical utterances of public intellectuals, travel narratives, maps, and educational manuals. Criticism must be capacious enough to travel across areas of expertise and between high and popular culture, while scholars themselves must embrace forms of intellectual amateurism that thinks expansively beyond disciplinary specializations.[106]

But beyond his refusal to stay within disciplinary boundaries, Said both *uses* theory and *theorizes* differently from the way most political theorists use theory and theorize. Perhaps because of our affiliations with political science and our somewhat more complex relationship with political philosophy, political theorists frequently err on the side of systematic clarity, parsimony, and conceptual closure. By contrast, Said argues that he had been most influenced by the scholarship of "people who are unsystematic." As he explained in a 1997 interview, you "cannot derive a systematic theory" from Gramsci, Fanon, or C. L. R. James because they "were involved in culture, in political struggle," in eclectic forms of aesthetic expression, and in the "adaptation" of conventional disciplines like philosophy, psychology, and political science.[107] Their writings were also highly unconventional, produced under unusual circumstances (Gramsci's fragmented prison notebook), written for political struggle (Fanon's political pamphlets), or committed to mixing genres (James's historical plays).

From Said's perspective, this kind of openness to approach, context, and genre is necessary for engaging a global phenomenon/discursive universe as culturally and politically complex as imperialism. The "worldly" disposition he champions is thus inherently field transcending, radically secular, and engaged with politics and history in ways that provide neither normative solutions to political/ethical problems nor the kind of conceptual scaffolding that would enable the critic to explain political and cultural phenomena in systematic terms. From the perspective of political theorists interested in conceptual clarity, Said's intellectual nomadism can feel hopelessly unkempt or, in Iskander and Rustom's words, "theoretically unhoused, methodologically untidy and spatially fluid."[108] In addition, because political theorists are often trained to *think through* a particular thinker's perspective into the world—to bring, for instance, a Foucauldian analysis to bear on immigration, to provide a Rawlsian perspective on human rights—following the diverse theoretical influences that exit and enter through the revolving door of Said's prose (from Vico to Foucault, Adorno to Fanon, Auerbach to Raymond Williams, Gramsci to C. L. R. James) can feel like an exhausting form of intellectual whiplash.

As I explore further in chapter 2, this might help explain why, on those rare occasions when political theorists have seriously engaged with Said's scholarship over the years, they often combine a sincere appreciation for his political vision and intellectual bravery with a deep frustration at what they see as his lack of systematic rigor. Said frequently responded to these kinds of criticisms by both acknowledging and embracing them. Yes, he notes in his important afterword to the 1995 edition of *Orientalism*, the book has certainly been the subject of heavy criticism from some British and American academics for its "residual humanism"; its "theoretical inconsistencies"; and its "insufficient, perhaps even sentimental, treatment of agency." "I am glad that it has!" he responds enthusiastically. "*Orientalism* is a partisan book, not a theoretical machine."[109]

Said's reaction here beautifully captures why political theorists might have a difficult time appreciating his thinking: because much of the work we do as political theorists consists of building theoretical machines. In other words, while our styles, approaches, methodologies, and traditions might differ, the field is united, as John Dryzek, Bonnie Honig, and Anne Phillips put it, "by a commitment to theorize, critique, and diagnose the norms, practices, and organization of political action in the past and present, in our own places and elsewhere."[110] In essence, we construct theoretical machines to help us understand politics in conditions both foreign and familiar, historical and contemporary. We create frameworks on which we hang arguments that illuminate the world. Said does something similar. He similarly draws on a variety of theoretical inspirations to craft arguments that make sense out of imperialism, culture, and politics. But his commitment to the unfinished, unsettled, and unsettling qualities of reading the world through exile and imperialism means that his interpretive impulses constantly leak through the gears and levers of theory's machine.

Perhaps the best way to illustrate this idea is through a comparison with a political theorist whose thinking is, in some notable ways, similar to Said's: Hannah Arendt. Like Said, Arendt was an exilic intellectual and a critic of Zionism whose work is also similarly difficult to pin down from the perspective of either academic political theory or political science.[111] Indeed, Seyla Benhabib's prosaic description of Arendt's enigmatic style could very well be a description of Said's; it is also frequently "too systematically ambitious and overinterpreted to be strictly a historical account" and "too anecdotal, narrative, and ideographic to be considered social science."[112] Like Said, Arendt's work is often described as too much like journalism for serious scholarship and yet too theoretically sophisticated for journalism. Also like Said—and in marked distinction from nearly all American and European political theorist of the early-postwar period—Arendt wrote about the relationship between imperialism and political ideas, what she terms the "boomerang effect."

In *The Origins of Totalitarianism,* Arendt insists that the nineteenth-century scramble for Africa contributed to the expansion of Nazism in Europe by provided a template on which the most brutal tendencies of nationalism could effloresce, unrestricted by the legal strictures of the nation-state.[113] Because imperialism allows for the "expansion of political power without the foundation of a body politic," capitalists and colonial administrators within the colonies could bend all the "state's instruments of violence, the police, the army" toward the goal of unchecked capital accumulation now explicitly understood in racist terms.[114] Different in kind from "exaggerated nationalism," this system of "race thinking," Arendt argues, became the "main ideological weapon of imperialistic politics."[115] Africa thus set the "preparatory stage for coming catastrophes" in Europe by providing a training ground for unbounded practices of economic extraction and racist violence that, when coupled with the power of the state, would return, like a boomerang, in the form of Nazi genocide.[116]

Of course, Arendt was not the first European political theorist to consider the negative impact of imperialism on domestic politics. In 1788, for instance, Edmund Burke inveigled against Warren Hastings and the East India Company "Nabobs" for bringing the attributes of "tyrants, robbers, and oppressors" back with them from their time exercising unchecked power in India.[117] In 1933, Harold Laski insisted that no group of individuals who "exercise the powers of a despot can ever retain the habit of democratic responsibility" and went on to describe at length the impact of these learned "habits of imperialism" on British political life.[118] But Arendt's analysis of imperialism, like Said's, was more genealogical in its orientation than either of these accounts, weaving together the rise of nationalism, capitalism, imperialism, and scientific racism as historically situated phenomena, exploring how the symbiotic relationship of these phenomena contributed to an environment in which total state power could circulate unchecked. Also with Said, Arendt understands the *movement* between Europe and the colonies as crucial to understanding European politics itself, and she makes this argument through careful analysis of the historical relationship between power and knowledge; that is, between developing accounts of racial difference and forms of domination abroad and at home.

The boomerang thesis is, in effect, a highly convincing theoretical machine that explains the rise of authoritarianism in Europe in the early twentieth century, through an exploration of European actions in the colonies. But the movement of that theory—the swoop and return of the boomerang—is ultimately temporally and spatially fixed. In spatial terms, it flies forth from its specified beginning (Europe), toward the outer limits of its arc (Africa writ large and timeless), and back to its origins transformed (as the totalitarian impulse). In this narrative, the relationship between imperial power and the colonized/occupied space is both directionally *known* (from Europe to Africa and back) and univocal (Europeans act, Africans suffer, Europeans turn that action onto themselves). In this metaphor, the preoccupation of the political theorist is centered on the need to critique the effect of a discrete (if prolonged) practice of imperial aggression on the political culture of the metropole, ignoring or occluding the actual lived experiences of human beings in the colonized world prior to imperial occupation and after, human beings who also responded to, challenged, or entirely transformed European ideas and practices.[119] From Arendt's perspectives, precolonial political culture and/or the problems and promises of the political/philosophical ideas that circulate in a colonial context have nothing to teach us. These innovations and transformations lie outside the explanatory intention of Arendt's theoretical machine, which is to explain the rise of totalitarianism in Europe. No more, no less. As Arendt put it three years after *Origins* in an entry in *Denktagebuch*, the "real tragedy" of imperialism was not imperialism itself but rather that imperialism was the only way for Europe to solve "national problems that had become insoluble."[120]

Arendt's obvious racism (which I explore in chapter 4) aside, it would be unfair to declare here that she simply didn't care about the long-term impact of European resource extraction, land dispossession, and racial violence on the colonies *themselves*. More likely, these concerns simply didn't register *as* concerns because they are not part of the original framing of the boomerang theory. Again, in spatial terms, the boomerang leaves Europe, enters Africa, and returns transformed, but not by Africans. In temporal terms, that period is compressed between the late-nineteenth-century European "competition" for dominance over the African continent and World War II.[121] The explanatory machine thus grinds to a halt when confronted with the confounding specter of racism and imperialism elsewhere and in other times.

Arendt's heavily critiqued account of the American civil rights movement in 1959's "Reflections on Little Rock," for instance, is startling not only for its anti-Black racism but also for its literal understanding of the American state as democratic, republican, and anti-imperialist. American racism—which for many White Americans and clearly for Arendt only became apparent in the context of the civil rights movement—could be tied neither to the internal occupation of the North American continent nor to a centuries-long history of chattel slavery, much less to the rapidly increasing interventionism of the United States in the global South during the postwar period. The fact that the "color question" had become an issue in the mid-twentieth century, Arendt argues, "is sheer coincidence as far as American history and politics are concerned." The "color problem in world politics," she continues, "grew out of the colonialism and imperialism of European nations—that is, the one great crime in which America was never involved."[122] Arendt's theoretical machine thus blinded her to American imperialism that resembled European imperialism (e.g., the occupation of the Philippines and Puerto Rico), to its settler colonial history, to the relationship between colonial capitalism and slavery, and to the particular type of imperialism that most defined her historical moment: what Kwame Nkrumah calls "neo-colonialism" or "imperialism in its final and perhaps its most dangerous stage."[123]

In making these observations about the temporal and spatial limitations of Arendt's boomerang thesis, I am in no way implying that the thesis itself cannot serve as a powerful form of anticolonial critique. Aimé Césaire and W. E. B. Du Bois both developed complex economic and cultural theories of the colonial boomerang (also in relation to Africa) that predate Arendt's analysis and that open up political horizons that extend far beyond Europe's tragedy.[124] Likewise, the scholarship of contemporary historians like Rashid Khalidi and Keith Wattenpaugh demonstrates that explorations of imperial blowback in a limited and specific context (e.g., the long-term impact of the League of Nations' mandates on Middle Eastern politics) can be extraordinarily revealing of the current moment.[125] Rather, I suggest that the limitations of Arendt's boomerang thesis's limitations make it less well equipped to capture the broad, living complexity of imperialism as an unfolding phenomenon and to fully grasp the extent to which the dense, multivocal connections between the metropole/great power and the colonized/occupied/invaded regions of the world are both historical and *ongoing*.

The flight of Said's critical disposition, I argue, better captures this complexity. It is curtailed by neither the temporal nor spatial limits of a boomerang nor the anticipated outputs of a theoretical machine. Its internal propulsion is multidirectional and unsettling. As chapter 3 discusses in greater detail, Said imagined the relationship between the metropole and the colonies not in univocal but rather in *contrapuntal* terms, always aware of both "metropolitan history" and "those other histories against which (and together with which) the dominating discourse acts."[126] Said's theoretical orientation toward imperialism tacks back and forth between metropolitan centers and colonies, between sites of colonial domination and resistance, and between the present and the past. Imperialism, for Said, isn't over once the boomerang has completed its arc through the sky. Rather, it is continuous, a "contested and joint experience" without clear end.[127] Theory cannot be a machine because imperialism is always exceeding the intentions of the theorist and the limitations of the machine.

At the same time, Said's other assertion in his afterword to *Orientalism*— that it is a "partisan" book—also helps explain his relative absence from political theory. Said never disguised his political commitments under a veneer of scholarly objectivity, and this refusal to tone down his politics could sometimes create professional challenges. He had a difficult time, for instance, finding an academic publisher for *Orientalism*. Basic Books, which had published *Beginnings* in 1975, refused to publish it. Said then approached the University of California Press with his proposal, but an editor there responded by expressing doubts that a book meant to be both an "unorthodox scholarly polemic" and "political polemic" would be of interest to any press.[128] When *Orientalism* was published by Vintage Books, it attracted attention for both, precisely as Said had intended. But his blurring of the lines (in *Orientalism* and elsewhere) between theory, history, imperialism, culture, and partisan politics also transgresses certain norms of academic comportment, which are particularly complicated for people who study politics as an academic subject.

As I argue in greater detail in chapter 5, there is still a widespread discomfort among political theorists with scholarship that seems *too* political, that might accidentally veer off track into what Jurgen Habermas calls "distorted communication" or communication that, as Michael Freeden puts it, "lags in the status stakes behind the high prestige of political philosophy, whether analytical or critical."[129] Said, the committed public intellectual and theorist *of* public intellectualizing, continually crossed the invisible style line between political theory and political expression that exists in our field. That Said's work refuses to color within this line, that many of his writings are partisan, that he brought his political sensibilities to bear on his scholarship and his scholarship to bear on his politics continues to make him the target of academic critics.

Moreover, not only is Said's work partisan, but his support for Palestine also made it easier for his critics to stereotype him as an "angry" Arab. Michael Walzer, for instance, famously reacted to Said's review of *Exodus and Revolution* with hyperbolic, finger-wagging incredulity.[130] "For Jewish supporters of Israel," Walzer opines in a 1986 exchange, "there is only one politics, and we cannot design it for ourselves; Said designs it for us in the image of his rage."[131] That Said makes no such claim about Jewish supporters of Israel—that to do so would have violated every one of his humanist impulses—seems not to have mattered to Walzer. Said, he implies, was by definition an enraged Arab: out of control, boiling in his support for terrorist destruction.

By the summer of 2019, it was clear to many observers of political science as a discipline and political theory as a subfield that things both had changed regarding the politics of Palestine and, in some ways, had stayed exactly the same. This dynamic was played out with excruciating clarity at the annual convention of the APSA, when a small group of political theorists introduced a motion to the "Foundations of Political Theory" section in support of the boycott, divest, sanctions (BDS) movement. In anticipation of this motion's consideration, the usually sparsely attended business meeting was packed to the rafters with not just political theorists but also some of the most influential lions of the discipline. The exchange that took place was largely civil, and one came away with the sense that there were people of goodwill on both sides of the issue. But the event was also notable for several reasons. First, with a few important exceptions, the generational gap between those in the room sympathetic to the Palestinian cause—whether they supported the BDS motion or *not*—was stark. Second, as if in affirmation of Said's long-standing observation that Palestinians have historically been denied "permission to narrate" their own experiences, not a single Palestinian academic spoke. Indeed, not a single Muslim political scientist spoke, even though there were several in the room. And this unwillingness to speak was no doubt related to the third notable aspect of this exchange: Michael Walzer was, after all these years, still very much a presence in the room and still insisting loudly and for everyone to hear that those political theorists sitting at the front of the room in support of the motion were obviously being manipulated by terrorists.[132]

Is it any wonder, given the continuingly fraught status of Palestinian politics in our discipline, the continuing absence of Palestinian voices at our debates, and the fact that people in our professional circles are still allowed to publicly call those with whom they disagree "terrorists" and/or "dupes of terrorists" that the work of Edward Said would simply fail to rise to the level of visibility in our collective academic consciousness as political theorists? Worse, that he would continue to be seen without seeing, a spectral nonpresence in a field currently striving to confront imperialism?

I argue in this book that theorists should consider embracing Said's polemical style not *despite* but *because of* its polemicism. Because unlike Walzer's condescending dismissiveness, Said's polemic is characterized by more than a desire to castigate and silence his opponents and call their characters and intentions into question. Rather, Said's partisan style models what he calls "adversarial critique," interrogating those institutions, discourses, and sometimes individuals who make imperialism "both so possible and so sustainable."[133] Said aims his "adversarial critique" not just at politics and knowledge but at *self*-knowledge, at the epistemological presumptions and disciplinary blinders that suppress different interpretations of the world, alternative visions of politics, and the voices of people who aren't allowed to narrate their own experiences. This mode of partisan critique does not ignore more subtle, less polemical-seeming forms of polemics, the soothing civilizational nostrums and smoothly insistent narratives about "who we are" and "our values," for instance, that populate liberal internationalist rhetoric and moral philosophical treatises alike. Said's polemic calls out unseeing in others but also unseeing in ourselves as critics, focusing in on the silencing assumptions that nestle in "our" intentions as scholars or "our" moral intuitions about what "we" owe to the global poor. The aim of this adversarial critique is not merely to win arguments but to stop conscience before it can, in Said's words, "look away or fall asleep."[134] Critics do this not merely by building better theoretical machines but by unsettling the very ground on which theorizing takes place.

One political theorist today whose lifetime of work closely resembles this deeply reflective mode of critique is James Tully, who, not surprisingly, is also one of the few political theorists to have drawn sustained inspiration from Said's scholarship over the years. Tully has been fascinated throughout his career by the dialogical possibilities that emerge from political contestation, from difference, and from the history of colonial occupation and resistance. Within the struggles for recognition by indigenous activists, for example, Tully finds multiple, lively forms of "doing democracy" that can be repressed by neither preemptive acts of misrecognition nor exclusionary institutional claims about citizenship.[135] With Said, Tully is attentive to the "journey back" of formerly colonized people into the colonizing metropoles and the "new forms of multiculturalism and multi-civilizationalism" such a journey creates on the ground. In his recent work, Tully turns to Said's "contrapuntal ensemble" to help him describe the discursive landscape on which it is possible, as he calls it, to "deparochialize" or "decolonize" dialogue. Tully argues that Said, like Charles Mills, provides political theorists with a way of reflecting on their own epistemological surety and, in the process, open doors to alternative "epistemologies of the global south."[136]

Said's writings differ from Tully's in their more explicit partisanship and in their polemicism. In other words, Said was committed to the proposition that it was possible both to engage in processes of self-critique and self-reflection that opens the world up to a multiplicity of perspectives *while also* writing from within the middle of a political struggle in which one takes very public sides. Unlike many political theorists whose political sympathies appear in gestures and along the edges and interstices of their scholarly work, Said's politics—informed as they were by the instabilities and "privileges" of exile—are at the front and center of almost everything he wrote, informing his arguments and widening the ambit for criticism at the same time. Said not only fought for Palestine in his public scholarship and journalism—first as an advocate of sovereign statehood, then as the champion of a single, multiethnic state—but he also fought tooth and nail to destabilize Orientalist and imperialist knowledge and reveal the complicated, fraught, joyous, violent, unjust, multivocal, unreconciled, cohabiting, hybrid, polyphonous reality of political life. For Said the partisan—Said the smasher of theoretical machines—one does this by constantly unsettling others and, most importantly, by constantly being unsettled.

## PARAMETERS AND ORGANIZATION OF THE BOOK

An enormous challenge of writing a book about Edward Said and political theory (if you are a political theorist) is confronting the absolutely mind-boggling body of work he produced throughout his career. Again, Said himself was a hugely productive scholar whose work consists of multiple published books, dozens of essays and chapters in edited volumes, hundreds of articles on a variety of topics in numerous news outlets, and countless interviews in which he further explicated, defended, and reflected on his work, sometimes traveling with it to places that significantly enhanced his original intention. Perhaps even more daunting, however, is the even more enormous literature *about* Said. Said didn't just inaugurate postcolonialism as a scholarly realm of inquiry; he also inspired a virtual cottage industry of books and edited volumes dedicated to his work, a massive universe of texts so vast that it is virtually impossible to identify them all. And every year, like clockwork, they keep coming, adding to the ever-towering wall of secondary literature by scholars in various fields—anthropology, comparative literature, Middle Eastern studies, history—writing about Said's work in the context of already-established bodies of literature about Said in their own disciplines.

By contrast, when political theorists evoke Said's work, it is usually in reference to something else or as deep background for critical inquiry. This does not mean, as Tully scholarship demonstrates, that political theorists universally ignore Said, and the chapters that follow explore the work of those thinkers in greater detail. Given the relative absence of that work, however, my argument consists primarily of reflections on Said's ideas that I believe resonate with debates in political theory that interest me most: about subjectivity and identity, about coexistence and global justice, and about the historical and contemporary entanglements of liberalism and imperialism. My goal is also to think, with Said, about expanding the field in more worldly directions that challenge distinctions both between IR and political theory and between political theory and the rest of the humanities.

Ironically, however, in the process of trying to contain an argument that, in large part, consists of a plea for interdisciplinarity, I have made the strategic choice *not* to go down the many, many rabbit holes that lead to the vast world of postcolonial debates about Said. In other words, this book can only touch on some of the most long-standing and intense discussions regarding Said's work that have raged in other disciplines. For instance, I linger only briefly on debates regarding Said's approach to narrative and representation, and I do not devote much time to similarly important discussions of his controversial attitude toward secularism.[137] Likewise, I do not explore the impact of Said's work on the relationship between postcolonial theory and subaltern studies or the internecine details of *Orientalism*'s tumultuous reception.[138] Finally, I have only been able to touch with the lightest brush the work of postcolonial IR scholars who have written about Said and some very recent work (published after this manuscript was submitted) by some political theorists approaching aspects of Said in novel ways.[139]

Rather, this book seeks to make good on an observation of Akeel Bilgrami in his loving introduction to Said's last collection of essays, *Humanism and Democratic Criticism*. Because of his political courage, his fight for Palestinian freedom, and his commitment both to understand domination and to further resistance in his most important writings, Bilgrami argues, "Edward Said's intellectual legacy will be primarily political—not just in the popular imagination, but also perhaps in the eyes of academic research."[140] I argue that the time has come to integrate Said's insights into the academic study of political theory.

The themes I explore thus spring from my own sense—as a political theorist and a scholar of imperialism—of what I believe to be most urgent about Said's work for the field broadly construed: his exilic destabilizing of critical subjectivity, his contrapuntal commitment to locating imperialism at the center of critique, his practice of public intellectualizing, his search for humanist connection while also querying those connections, and his radical insistence on analyzing the United States in light of its imperial past and present. At every stage of this book, as I've engaged these themes and explored criticisms of Said's work, I have been keenly and personally aware—on an intellectual level—of just how maddeningly counterintuitive Said's critical intuitions can be for political theorists, how much they require letting go of our expectations for resolution and closure, even as they demand public and scholarly intervention. Said's work ultimately asks us to reorient ourselves away from settled intellectual homes toward the "precarious exilic realm" wherein we both wrestle with the complexity "of what cannot be grasped" and "go forth to try anyway."[141]

Five chapters in this book explore these themes in Said's work, and the sixth provides an example of what I hope resembles a Said-inspired political theory practice. Chapter 1, "Writing at a Distance: Exile, Critique, and Loss," dives into the sometimes-unnerving contradictions of Said's exilic disposition, from his reflections on his own life in exile to his discordant prose style, focusing on the productive criticism that he believed flows from this unsettling disclosure. The chapter looks closely at Said's 1982 essay "Secular Criticism" and explores his approach to analyzing filiative and affiliative modes of ideological connection. Chapter 1 concludes by turning from Said's theoretical writing about exile to his exilic writing in 1984's *After the Last Sky.* This book, I argue, offers the reader a powerful glimpse into the attached and detached mode of seeing at work in Said's exilic orientation and provides a fuller sense of how this orientation twins a critique of power, nationhood, and exclusion with a deep sympathy for the ties that bind love to home, love to loss, and love to loss of home.

Chapter 2, "A Cluster of Flowing Currents: Theory Unresolved and Groundless," begins to think more about the implications of this exilic approach for political theory research, focusing in particular on the way that approach unsettles questions of identity, history, coexistence, and justice. It begins with an exploration of two political theorists who have devoted time to Said's scholarship, Fred Dallmayr and Joan Cocks, focusing on both their appreciation for his political passion and their ultimate disappointment with his rejection of philosophical closure. The chapter also compares Said's unclosed, ungrounded theory to mainstream cosmopolitanism and global justice literature to the work of Iris Marion Young on Palestine-Israel. The chapter focuses in particular on what Said calls a "method for thinking about a just peace" in Palestine-Israel. I conclude with an examination of Said's ethical impulse toward ungrounded subjectivity, which, I argue, enables a mode of theorizing that opens our eyes to political possibilities foreclosed by philosophical resolution.

Chapter 3, "Into the Language of Music: The Colonizer and the Colonized Together," investigates Said's powerful conception of counterpoint through a close analysis of 1993's *Culture and Imperialism*. It focuses on the affiliation between Said's approach to contrapuntal criticism and anticolonial resistance, exploring some of the political tensions generated by his Foucauldian orientation and some contemporary Marxist criticisms of that orientation. The chapter investigates Said's understanding of counternarrative resistance and his reading of Fanon's "integrative view of human community and human liberation," which, he argues, transforms "social consciousness beyond national consciousness."[142] I conclude with some thoughts on the relationship between Said's "critical practice as a form of resistance" and his sense of the world as a "contrapuntal ensemble," both rent asunder—and connected by—imperialism.[143]

Chapter 4, "Reading You in Your Presence: Political Interpretation and Worldly Humanism," explores Said's influential theory of worldliness and his controversial notion of humanism. The chapter first contrasts Said's concept of worldliness with the Cambridge School's "ideas in context" approach and then traces the evolution of his humanism from his early career through some of his last essays. I also explore the "slowness" of Said's worldly humanism, contrasting this interpretive pace with the kinds of humanism associated with the "turn to ethics" in political theory. I compare Said's belief in worldly humanism's capacity to resists the "disappearance of the past" with both Michael Ignatieff's self-proclaimed "humble humanism" and Walzer's "thin universalism." I conclude by turning again to Arendt's theory, focusing on her approach to the "loss of the world," and critically reimagine it alongside the interpretive and political promise of Said's humanist vision.

Chapter 5, "The Honeypots of Our Mind: Public Intellectuals in an Imperial World," is the last thematic chapter of the book, and it focuses on Said's commitment to theorizing the relationship between public intellectuals and political power, as well as his critique of public intellectuals who transmute imperial power into quasi-scholarly narratives about "our culture." The chapter thinks again about the status of public expression in political theory and Said's complex and controversial insistence on speaking and writing as a public intellectual. It examines his equally complex and controversial understanding of exile as a "metaphysical" condition, his rigorous critique of a certain type of pronoun politics (e.g., narratives about "who we are" as a nation), and his recentering of public intellectuals *within* the connections between the United States and the rest of the world. I also take an extended look at some of the many criticisms that have been leveled against Said's public intellectualizing over the years.

The final chapter of the book, "The Treason of the Intellectuals: Reading Said against Liberal Narcissism," conducts a Said-inspired investigation of the cultural and political entanglements between liberalism and imperialism, or, as Duncan Bell frames it, "between the dominant ideology of the contemporary Western world and some of the darkest, most consequential entanglements of its past."[144] So proliferous has been recent scholarship about these entanglements that they can no longer be ignored, even by liberal scholars committed to American global hegemony like G. John Ikenberry, whose work has long depended on a studious unseeing of the historical connections between liberalism and nineteenth-and twentieth-century imperialism.[145] And yet, given the intensity of this recent engagement, it seems all the more strange that political theorists and scholars of politics would largely continue to ignore Said's work, despite the fact that he was, as Cindi Katz and Neil Smith explain, "one of the first—certainly the most trenchant—among intellectuals to expose the connections between liberalism, the Enlightenment, and imperialism."[146] This chapter seeks to address that lack of interest in Said by thinking about the prolix relationship between liberalism and imperialism through his interpretive intuitions.

Chapter 6 thus makes the case that Said's critical orientation provides political theorists with a profoundly generative approach for transforming our increasingly robust historical critiques of liberal imperialism into equally robust critiques of liberal imperialism in American foreign policy discourse today. The chapter digs into contemporary political theoretical approaches to the study of liberalism, interrogating the difference between studies of liberalism as a political philosophy and studies of liberalism as a historical ideology. It analyzes current liberal internationalist discourse and its relationship to American foreign policy, focusing in particular on ardent defenders of the "American-led, liberal world order." I then lay out a Said-inspired critique of liberal internationalism that bridges the divide between IR and political theory while challenging the omnipresent "we" narratives that too often plague both subfields. I end with some thoughts on the "treason" of the intellectuals in a world transformed by Trumpism and consider Said's humanist alternative to a politics of rage and reaction: an alternative that imagines "the other"—the immigrant, the resident of the "shithole country," the person on the other end of the drone strike—"reading you in your presence."[147]

Ultimately, the reading of Said that I develop throughout this book is grounded in my belief that his interpretive practice lends itself extraordinarily well to the difficult task of integrating critical accounts of the past with the political imperatives of the present. Said's critical disposition is so relevant to this task and I have absorbed it so thoroughly that I often found, in the midst of writing, that I would lose track of where his voice ended and mine had begun. And while I strove throughout for consistency of voice to capture the life of the Said who is no longer with us and the words of Said that live on— the voice of Said that reads history and the intensity of Said who demands justice in Palestine *now*—I realized at some point that my prose had become horribly tangled in the past and the present and the presence of the past. At the end of the day, I can only apologize to those readers who are irritated by my swinging between verb tenses and suggest that it is part and parcel of what it means to write about Edward Said. "He was," as Hamid Dabashi puts it, "never the past participle of anything—he is always the present tense of somewhere else."[148]

Toward the end of his poem for Said, Darwish returns to ruminate on the relentless insecurity of exile and on the futility, violence, and impossibility of capturing either hope for the future or the enormity of the struggle for justice in Palestine in a poem. Darwish, clearly knowing Said's resistance to resolution and to readings of place and identity that foreclose complexity, frames his friend's imagined last words as both a directive and a puzzle:

> He also said: If I die before you,
> my will is the impossible.
> I asked: Is the impossible far off?
> He said: A generation away.
> I asked: And if I die before you?
> He said: I shall pay my condolences to Mount Galilee,
> and write, "The aesthetic is to reach
> poise." And now, don't forget:
> If I die before you, my will is the impossible.

Said's impossible will—his exilic refusal to resolve opposing experiences and visions but instead to just hold them together—makes his disposition toward politics, power, critique, and culture both astonishingly powerful and, as Darwish well knew, enormously unsettling. Indeed, it is precisely Said's insistence on keeping theory open by holding contradictions and complexities without resolving them that has most frustrated some of the few political theorists who have devoted time to his work over the years. And yet, this book argues, it is precisely Said's refusal to resolve the antinomies of imperialism that makes his approach so necessary for political theory today. These worlds in tension *are* the two dreams in one bedroom, and as much as they may fight to push each other out, Said refused to let them go. And neither, I argue, should we.

# 1

# Writing at a Distance

## *Exile, Critique, and Loss*

Edward Said begins his most influential essay about exile with this sentence: "Exile is strangely compelling to think about but terrible to experience."[1] Read on its own, this declaration/provocation feels flippant, even dismissive, a hyper-intellectualized response to what can be a terrifyingly violent state of homelessness, deprivation, and loss. But Said's attitude toward exile and the critical disposition he develops from it were anything but flippant. Indeed, in Said's work, the jarring, uncomfortable, unhealable wounds of exile—in all their unfused, irritating resistance to coherence—make possible a unique way of seeing that is both critically incisive of culture and politics and deeply, empathically connected to culture and politics. What is true of all exile, Said thus argues, is "not that home and love of home are lost, but that loss is inherent in the very existence of both."[2] In other words, exile truly just is always both/and for Said: both compelling to think about and terrible to experience.

Nowhere is the both/and quality of Said's approach to exile more apparent than in 1986's *After the Last Sky*. Written in conversation with Jean Mohr's haunting photographs of ordinary Palestinians going about their everyday lives, the book explores the "subjectivity and historical consciousness of being Palestinian."[3] And it does so—at least for Said—from a distance. *After the Last Sky*, as Said notes in the introduction to the 1998 edition, is thoroughly an "exile's book," written during that period when his then affiliation with the PLO made it impossible for him to return to Jerusalem, the place of his birth, a city he had not seen since 1947. For Said, however, this distance is both a blessing and a curse. "I write at a distance," he notes, explaining that if he were not in exile,

> possibly there would be no problem in finding a direct and simple narrative to tell the tale of our history. When I let myself go and feel as if everything in the Palestinian situation flows directly from one original trauma, I can then see

a pattern emerging inexorably, as intertwined and as recountable as any other sequential tale of misfortune. What I have found is that if you seize on all the evidence that appears intermittently—another massacre, one more betrayal, a damaging defeat—you can easily construct the plot of a logically unfolding conspiracy against us.[4]

Here Said is simultaneously reflective about his own limitations as a Palestinian living in America acutely aware of his own loss, and sympathetic to nationalism's pull—even as he ultimately resists the intertwined conclusions of that pull. And yet, as *After the Last Sky* repeatedly demonstrates, the pain of exile also provides Said with a searingly uncomfortable glimpse into affiliative connections between plotlines and tragedy, people and nation—a way of seeing in which he ultimately finds critical inspiration and political meaning,

In what follows, I look more closely at Said's thoughts on exile by first interrogating the many discordant tensions that persist throughout his writings on the topic. In particular, this first section examines the sometimes-unnerving contradictions of Said's own prose style, a broken cadence that can never fully express the political and cultural phenomena that it seeks to capture. Section 2 then turns to a closer investigation of the kinds of productive critique Said believed could be generated through exilic disclosure. Focusing in particular on Said's important 1982 essay, "Secular Criticism," I explore his understanding of the relationship between exilic criticism and the necessary unearthing of filiative and affiliative modes of ideological connection. The final section then turns from Said's writings about exile to Said's exilic writing in *After the Last Sky.* I argue that through an exploration of Said's intimate comingling in this text of his own exilic distance and the Palestinian experiences he observes—in exile, in Gaza, in the West Bank—we get a powerful glimpse into the way attachment and detachment work through exile to paint a picture of political life that is both critical of the powers that obscure and dominate while deeply sympathetic with the ties that bind love to loss and loss to home.

## STRANGELY COMPELLING BUT TERRIBLE TO EXPERIENCE

That exile would come to play such a vital role in Said's scholarship is not entirely surprising, given his personal and family history, but it certainly wasn't inevitable. As Bill Ashcroft and Pal Ahluwalia note in their biographical introduction to Said's work, during the 1960s, Said was "well on the way to establishing a distinguished but unexciting career as a Professor of Comparative Literature." Then the 1967 war broke out, and "he found himself in an environment hostile to Arabs, Arab ideas and Arab nations."[5] Suddenly, Ashcroft and Ahluwalia continue, Said was "surrounded by an almost universal support for the Israelis, where the Arabs seemed to be 'getting what they deserved' and where he, a respected academic, had become an outsider and a target."[6] As Said explains in his 1999 memoir, *Out of Place*, after 1967, "I was no longer the same person." "The shock of the war," he continues, "drove me back to where it had all started; the struggle over Palestine."[7] And that internal return had a politicizing effect on both Said and his scholarship. The year 1967, he recalls, was the "dislocation that subsumed all the other losses," including both the "disappeared worlds of my youth and upbringing" and the "unpolitical years of my education, the assumption of disengaged teaching and scholarship at Columbia, and so on." Even this shift toward political engagement, however, was itself not inevitable. Said recalls, for instance, being discouraged from politics by his parents, who worried "about what the Zionists will do" and begged him to stick to the apolitical life of a literature professor.[8]

Said did not do this, however, and the paradox of his dual identity as both Arab and American began to be reflected in his work. In 1968, he launched himself into the role of an explicitly political, public intellectual with the publication of "The Arab Portrayed," an essay that, among other things, calls the American Left to account for its hypocrisy. The dominant stereotypes of Arabs in circulation after 1967, Said argues, "draw on exactly the values disclaimed by 'liberals' (whether Jewish or not)" when discussing Israel. In other words, American liberals might abhor racism, but they were happy to employ racist values ("however they might be whitewashed") when discussing Arabs. In fact, such stereotypes were considered "eminently suitable" for describing the Palestinian people as a whole.[9] In many ways, then, "The Arab Portrayed"—with its nod to what he would one day call the "knowing vocabulary" associated with mainstream liberal and academics narratives about Arabs and Muslims—provides a preview into Said's later work, particularly *Orientalism* and *Covering Islam*. The re-ignition in 1967 of the "continual loss of Palestine," for Said, also compelled him to think more reflectively and constructively about both his internal experience of exile in general and the implications of that experience for his developing style of criticism. In "Secular Criticism," "Reflections on Exile," and elsewhere, Said transforms this insolidity into a productive wedge for prising open vexing questions about the relationship between identity, narrative, text, and colonial context.

Of course, both the experience of exile and the practice of ruminating on the relationship between this experience and critical/artistic production is hardly unique to Said nor to his historical moment. As he argues in "The Mind of Winter," the "canon of modern Western culture is in large part the work of exiles."[10] Scholars have long been intrigued by the experience of exile and by the fact that some of the greatest works in the history of philosophy, art, and literature—from Ovid to the surly Samuel Johnson stewing angrily in his juices in Ireland—have flowed from the minds of individuals steeped in the unfamiliarity and insecurity of being cut off from their homelands. Throughout his career, Said was similarly moved by the critical and aesthetic work of intellectuals writing from a distance, struggling under the weight of alienation. In particular, along with so many others, Said was fascinated by the *textual* productions of exile, an affinity perfectly captured in the cover art for 2002's *Reflections on Exile and Other Essays*: a close-up of Domenico Peterin's 1865 painting *Dante in Exile* focused squarely on the book clasped in Dante's lap.[11]

If this affinity for exilic texts was not unique to Said, neither was his decision to theorize *out of* his own experience as an exile. Indeed, many of the intellectual heroes to whom he pays homage in his work did precisely this. In 1953's *Minima Moralia*, for instance, Theodore Adorno channels (albeit in an indirect way) his own experience in America during World War II into a more expansive rumination on the ethical benefits of homelessness for the critic, arguing that, in a postwar context, it is morally necessary "not to be at home in one's home."[12] Drawn toward the insight that comes from exclusion and marginalization, Said's thoughts on exile are explicitly indebted to the work of scholars like Adorno (writing far from his homeland), Antonio Gramsci (writing from within a homeland that denied him a home), and Frantz Fanon (writing prophetically far from home about the seductive dangers and necessities of homeland). Moreover, even the controversial idea of exile as metaphor (which Said developed most extensively in *Representations of the Intellectual* and which I explore further in chapter 5) has a storied history that long predates the advent of modernity. The Jewish tradition, for instance, has attached symbolic meaning to exile for millennia, perennially ending the Passover seder with the words "Next year in Jerusalem," a hope that, as Ian Buruma points out, has remained an abstraction for most utterers throughout the history of Judaism.[13]

The uniqueness of Said's approach to exile, I argue, can be found neither in his fascination with exilic intellectuals as such nor in his concern with text, perspective, and/or metaphor. Rather, what makes Said's notion of exile so unique and profoundly powerful is his paradoxical refusal to square the circle between his conviction that exile was both a necessary "habit of life" for the critic *and* a completely horrible, frequently intolerable way of living.[14] Much of his work on the topic is wracked by precisely this discomfort between loss and insight, between the incredibly uncomfortable, unstable, psychologically exhausting, sometimes-violent qualities of the exile's lived life and the productive quality of the exilic disposition. Indeed, irreconcilability is precisely what makes Said's understanding of exile so generative for critique. Exilic loss provokes juxtapositions in subjective consciousness: the ongoing temporal clash of the present with the past, for instance, the grating disconnect between feelings of attachment to a natal community and detachment from that community. Under the right circumstance, this rasping discomfort can, Said argues, gives rise to a profound form of insight. Thus, his pronouncement that exile is "strangely compelling to think about but terrible to experience" is both a declaration of the obvious and a provocation to criticism.[15]

Said begins "Reflections on Exile" by defiantly interrogating its terribleness. Whereas the romantic ideal of exile in Western literature and philosophy often focuses on isolated intellectuals forced from home—think Cicero languishing in Thessalonica—exile today, Said argues, is primarily a mass phenomenon.[16] For this reason, thinking expansively about exile requires the contemporary critic to "map territories" of experience that push beyond those in the Western canon. Mapping such territories means one "must first set aside Joyce and Nabokov" and purposefully turn one's mind instead to the "uncountable masses for whom UN agencies have been created."[17] The average experience of exile is thus markedly less contained and significantly less safe than Joyce's long, voluntary sojourn in Trieste; Nabokov's comfortable travels through the American academic landscape; or Said's own Ivy League existence. Since World War II, Said continues, imperial expansion, ethnic cleansing, and spasms of state violence all over the globe—but particularly in the formerly colonized world—have resulted in waves of mass migration, floods of refugees, and a constantly expanding global population of displaced and stateless persons.[18] Contemporary exiles may sometimes look like Said himself—drinking his white coffee in his elegant suit in his Upper West Side apartment. More likely, they will resemble the exhausted, traumatized children trudging hundreds of miles with their parents through Mexico, expelled from Central America by the violent political legacy of US imperialism, searching for a safe place to make a life, if not a home. Syrians caught perennially in the no-man's-land of Greek refugee camps, entire Rohingya communities languishing in temporary settlements in Bangladesh, and the third-generation Palestinians making a life in the Shantila refugee camp in Beirut: these are the contemporary faces of exile.

Given the scale of this dislocation and the poverty, violence, and sheer human suffering that accompany it, Said wonders aloud in the essay about whether this accumulation of experiences can have any meaningful critical or political purchase on the world or whether exiles themselves are not "manifestly and almost by design irrecoverable." The fact that, throughout his work, Said looks straight into the desperate and disparate faces of exile, sees the experience for what it is—often horrifying in its alienation and loss, lambasted by trauma and violence—and still insists it is not merely compelling to think about but absolutely necessary for critical inquiry and politics is a testament to how strongly he believed in its illuminative power.

Throughout his work on exile, Said repeatedly draws the reader's attention to the tensions of the exilic experience and the extent to which those living in exile bear within themselves a recollection of what has been left behind, which they then play constantly against the current experience in all its unsettling and untenable iterations. This ebbless loss, this constant friction between past and the present—between home and displacement, the memory of safety and the trauma of lived life—resists reconciliation at every level. His decision to move with abrupt alacrity in "Reflections on Exile" between the shivering specter of mass migration and the solitary turmoil of the exile's internal life reinforces this sense that the abrading tension between mass political phenomena and subjective experience is simply irresolvable.

Said's refusal to reconcile the experience of exile as a "horrendous" phenomenon with his equally emphatic insistence on its critical vitality is reflected in the very structure of his prose and in the paradoxical rhythm of his observations. "Reflections on Exile" is littered with conflicting images that Said simply allows to coexist, layering one on another without apology, from the refugee with the ration card in one sentence to the Urdu poet in a café in Beirut in the next. These images sit cheek by jowl within the flow of the essay, often without clarification or transition, and the juxtaposition is both uncomfortable and jarring. Likewise, Said makes contrasting, nearly simultaneous conceptual claims about exile here, sometimes heaping one argument on another. Thus, in one paragraph he dismisses literary and religious traditions that have wrongly cast the exilic experience as somehow "good for us" in the face of humanitarian catastrophe and then, in the next, pivots to a discussion of the dignity exilic poets lend to situations "legislated to deny dignity."[19] Said also resists defining exile, even as he makes distinctions between individual and mass exilic experiences. He argues in one moment that anyone who wants to theorize exile "must set aside Joyce and Nabokov" and concentrate instead on ration-card-clutching masses of refugees. Then, six pages later, he notes that "some distinctions can be made" between exiles and refugees.[20]

In the end, reading Said on exile can feel like an exercise not just in prosaic whiplash but also in frustrated anticipation of a conceptual closure that never comes. In the course of "Reflections on Exile," readers are tossed between competing and unresolved assertions about the political, rhetorical, material, and cultural experiences of exile that, on both an aesthetic and a philosophical level, can often leave one craving some kind—*any* kind—of resolution.

Numerous authors over the years have been critical of these many inconsistencies, particularly Said's pattern of letting discordant conceptual claims simply stand next to each other without any attempt to work out their contradictions. David Kettler rightly notes that Said begins "Reflections on Exile" with a rejection of the idea that "exile somehow serves humanism, as some sort of school for virtue" but then ends the piece with the claim, according to Kettler, that exile is a "symbolic embodiment of subjectivity." It turns out, he argues, that Said thinks exile is "good for us after all."[21] For Kettler, Said's concern for refugees and the victims of genocidal violence and mass migration is largely an empty gesture, a rhetorical nod toward mass political suffering that he feels compelled to acknowledge before rushing to get to the real object of his concern: the exilic intellectual. Said's manner of evoking the "tortured conditions of exile" and then immediately retreating into considerations of individual subjectivity, Kettler insists, ultimately *depoliticizes* the experience of exiles themselves while simultaneously "devaluing the sufferings of the defeated and excluded whose pitiful state is initially mobilized against humanistic glorifications of exile."[22]

Frederick Aldama takes this depolitization argument ever further, accusing Said not just of being disingenuous in his concern for refugees but also of actively disparaging the material bases of exilic suffering in the service of developing an idealized version of the isolated intellectual, exiled and alone, hovering above the fray.[23] "Whether isolated colonizer or quixotic adventurer," Aldama claims, "Said's conception of the individual remains unmoored from history—isolated from the people and their transformation *en masse* of the material conditions of the world."[24] Both Kettler and Aldama wonder how it is that exile can be so many things at once for Said: both a mass phenomenon and deeply personal, both a material experience and an intellectual position, both antihumanist and humanistic, both intolerable and necessary. How can these observations exist side by side without canceling each other out?

Said's response to such criticisms was, as Masad once beautifully put it, to "unsettle rather than accommodate his audience," to keep digging into the paradoxical and the contradictory.[25] Inconsistencies are, Said maintained, at the core of his work because they are the hallmark of the exilic experience, captured in the irritating rub between state violence and individual suffering, between mass migration and the longings of the lonely poetic soul, between political violence and political art. This is the essence of exile, and Said's absolute refusal to resolve these inconsistencies in his own writing—even from one sentence to the next—reflects the tenacity with which he believed the exilic experience resists closure. Rather, for Said, the gap between the past and the present—home and resettled life, the inner and outer world—are perennially unsutured, like an irritating open wound whose healing is relentlessly stymied both by "terminal loss." As he puts it in "Intellectual Exile: Expatriates and Marginals," being an exile in today's world means living away from home while also "living with the many reminders that you are in exile, that your home is not in fact so far away, and that the normal traffic of every day contemporary life keeps you in constant but tantalizing and unfulfilled touch with the old place."[26]

And yet, it is precisely the nagging pain of this wound—the "agonizing distance" between subject and homeland—that gives rise to what Said believed is a particularly powerful way of seeing and interpreting the world.[27] To be clear, there is nothing Pollyannaish about Said's observation that exile sometimes enables the "crippling sorrow of estrangement" to be transformed "into a potent, even enriching motif of modern culture."[28] Indeed, "Reflections on Exile" itself is replete with examples of the disquieting political and cultural effects that can follow from the loss of the exile's "native place."[29] Because "homecoming is out of the question," Said notes, life in exile is perennially insecure, and while the intensity of loss may ebb and flow, that insecurity never abates. Exiles are thus prone to particular kinds of emotional and political dysfunctions and neuroses. "Exile is a jealous state," Said argues, and exiles often "look at non exiles with resentment. *They* belong in their surroundings, you feel, whereas an exile is always out of place."[30] The desire to combat this rootlessness and insecurity can drive exiles to draw lines around their community in an attempt to re-create—to reconcretize—a connection that can never be entirely repaired.

Thus, at its worst, exile can lead to an "exaggerated sense of group solidarity, and a passionate, stubborn hostility to outsiders, even those who may in fact be in the same predicament as you."[31] This passionate hostility can then turn inward on the community itself. What, Said queries,

> could be more intransigent than the conflict between Zionist Jews and Arab Palestinians? Palestinians feel that they have been turned into exiles by the proverbial people of exile, the Jews. But the Palestinians also know that their own sense of national identity has been nourished in the exile milieu, where everyone not a blood-brother or sister is an enemy, where every sympathizer is an agent of some unfriendly power, and where the slightest deviation from the accepted group line is an act of the rankest treachery and disloyalty.[32]

Given this intransigence, these layers of resentment that themselves become a kind of identity all its own, is there a difference between the extremes of exile and the "bloody minded affirmations of nationalism?" Said asks. Do "nationalism and exile have intrinsic attributes," or are they "simply two conflicting theories of paranoia?"[33] Both emerge from a desire for habitus, from a compulsion to differentiation between inside and outside, from an often exclusive desire for belonging, and both have particularly modern manifestations that can render them dysfunctional in particular ways.

Said's response to his own provocation is not merely to emphasize the material differences between these experiences—such as nationalism's sometimes attachment to state and military power versus the exiles' relative disempowerment—even though these differences can be significant. Rather, he responds by once again drawing the reader's attention to the through lines of disruption and loss. Unlike nationalism, Said argues, exile is "fundamentally a *discontinuous* state of being."[34] People living in exile are constantly being drawn up hard against the jagged edge of today's indeterminate reality contrasted with yesterday's experience of belonging. The past is endlessly mediated by not just distance but also time and the trickiness of memory. The present is undermined and defamiliarized by both the uncertainties of daily existence and the intrusion of the mediated past. As Said put it in a 1991 interview, if you are an exile, "you always bear within yourself a recollection of what you've left behind and what you can remember," and you constantly "play it against the current experience."[35]

Thus, the "double perspective" produced by the exile's internal knowledge of "what has been left behind and what is actually here and now" means that exiles never see things in isolation. Rather, every "scene or situation in the new country necessarily draws on its counterpart in the old country."[36] This internal sense of playing against can—under the right conditions—lend itself to a critical temperament that resists resolution, certainty, and homophony, a temperament that understands that, despite the assurances of nationalism and the universalist exhortations of triumphant empires, "no one today is purely *one* thing."[37] Rather, Said argues, an exilic disposition that begins from a place of multiple identities—from the midst of the "polyphony of many voices playing off against each other"—has no need to reconcile these identities. Its goal, rather, is "just to hold them together."[38] Loss is thus the pebble in the exile's shoe that pains with every step and, in that unsettling pain, fosters a critical consciousness particularly adept at denaturalizing and historicizing dominant modes of political and cultural discourse that seek to compartmentalize and homogenize. In essence, for Said, the braided experiences of loss of home, detachment from home, and love of home enable a uniquely piercing form of insight into the inner workings of cultural/political discourses, an insight particularly adept at revealing the affiliative connections that transform discourse into coherence.[39]

## FILIATION, AFFILIATION, AND THE WORK OF EXILE

Developed most fully in 1982's "Secular Criticism"—his seminal introductory essay to *The World, the Text, and the Critic*—Said's approach to affiliation begins by differentiating between filiative and affiliative relations, linking one to perceptions of family and nature and the other to cultural construction. Drawing on the insights of both Antonio Gramsci and Raymond Williams, Said argues that, just as one cannot choose one's family, one cannot choose one's filial connections to one's natal place. At the same time, he argues, the constellation of cultural and social objects—traditions, truisms, forms of knowledge, dominant discourses, historical narratives—associated with that place relies on a more complicated set of constructed connections, or *affiliations.* Said understood the relationship between filiation and affiliation as the "passage from nature to culture"; the "filiative scheme," in this sense, "belongs to the realm of nature and of 'life,' whereas affiliation belongs exclusively to culture and society." The affiliative world thus entails more concerted forging of connections in multiple forms, including "guild consciousness, consensus, collegiality . . . the hegemony of dominant culture."[40]

Making this conceptual distinction is crucial for Said, not merely because of what it describes, but also because it helps make visible the frequent conflation of the filiative with the affiliative; that is, the way filiation can stand in for and/or obscure what are actually affiliative connections. Indeed, he argues, exploring the cooperation between the two modes of relation—the way affiliation sometimes reproduces filiation and "sometimes makes its own form"—is essential to developing a mode of critical consciousness able to think beyond "organic complicity."[41] Said suggests that because filiative connections are meant to connote the "mere natural continuity between one generation and the next," they can become a kind of common sense.[42] Defenders of the putative coherence of "Western civilization" over time, for instance, often imagine it in filiative terms as a cultural inheritance linked directly to a particular population through genealogical descent. Such an approach narrows the circle of what is considered acceptable for criticism, excluding, for instance, the "nonliterary, the non-European" and the universe of political and discursive phenomena that go into maintaining that distinction.[43] Reading Western culture filiatively also obscures precisely the kinds of productive contrasts—between the active, enlightened West and the supine, barbaric East—that Said explores in *Orientalism*, contrasts without which, in Stuart Hall's words, the "West may not have been able to recognize itself as the summit of human history."[44]

Ultimately, Said argues that understanding culture in affiliative terms means directing critical awareness at the active and creative fusing of particular ideas with particular peoples through discourse. Making the affiliative connections between "the West" and its civilization the explicit subject of criticism denaturalizes those connections. This perspectival shift highlights the intellectual work of human beings—situated within a complex web of cultural/political/material power—as they spin artful links between themselves and their natal culture, links that are then contrasted negatively with accounts of the colonized "other."

For Said, the instability of exile—the way it wrenches the critic out of their situated perspective and compels an often-unbidden reflection on the relationship between place and people, self and home—makes possible a way of seeing and critiquing that reveals how "affiliation sometimes reproduces filiation, sometimes makes its own forms."[45] To demonstrate this point, he turns, in "Secular Criticism," to the example of German philologist and literary critic Eric Auerbach, who wrote his groundbreaking work *Mimesis* while living in exile in Istanbul during World War II. Not only does Said consider *Mimesis* a work of individual genius, but he is also completely fascinated by the fact that a text many believe to be a "massive reaffirmation of the Western cultural tradition" was "built upon a critically important alienation" from that tradition.[46] In other words, for Said, *Mimesis* reflects more than just Auerbach's extraordinarily thorough education and his unparalleled "familiarity with European culture." It is also an "exile's book" written by a man cut off from the culture that he knew so well.[47]

In his critical introduction to the fiftieth-anniversary edition to the book, Said notes that *Mimesis* would have looked very different if the author had written it from home. Indeed, Said continues, Auerbach himself observed that had he been in Germany, with access to his library, the material "would have swamped him."[48] Instead, *Mimesis* is a prescient and audacious text, Said argues, precisely *because* it had to be constructed from memory. In *Mimesis*, Auerbach does more than admire a "Europe he lost through exile," Said maintains. Writing in exile allowed him to see Europe in a new light as a "composite social and historical enterprise, made and remade unceasingly by men and women in society."[49]

*Mimesis* is thus a particularly powerful example, for Said, of affiliative making at work. Deprived of his books, his library, his interlocutors, and all intellectual ties to the cultural constellation about which he writes, Auerbach's efforts to rearticulate that culture from memory expose the ideological and political effort that goes into forging culture more generally.[50] *Mimesis* suggests that the heritage of the West is—like all cultural and political systems—what Said calls a "compensatory order" comprised of institutions, sets of beliefs, and world visions that provide "men and women with a new form of relationship" beyond filiative immediacy. As a text, *Mimesis* draws attention to the way texts themselves are rarely the seamless products of an interface between author and culture but rather are "produced and live on in the historical realm."[51]

Throughout much of his work—whether explicitly devoted to the theme of exile or not—Said models how an exilic "double perspective" can uproot and unknot various unseen affiliative connections, not just between cultural forms, but also between culture and power. Always unstable, always balanced in the doorway between loss and place, Said aims this mode of critique squarely at the system of "associations between forms, statements and other aesthetic elaborations" that link Western culture to the "institutions, agencies, classes, and amorphous social forces" of imperial rule.[52] Thus, Said argues, in the imperial and Orientalist imaginary, Western culture circulates independently from the multiplicity of political, material, and military linkages that tie European (and the European-settler-colony-now-global-hegemon that is America) to the colonized and formerly colonized world. Culture in this imperial context, Said argues in another 1982 essay, works to "make invisible and even 'impossible' the actual *affiliations* that exist between the world of ideas and scholarship, on the one hand, and the world of brute politics, corporate and state power, and military force on the other."[53] By contrast, the detachment of the exilic critic from her natal culture creates an opening for a mode of seeing—a disposition born of disruption—able to identify and render visible those ongoing affiliations between ideas and power.

Thus, for Said, the experience of being torn from the seamless connection between self and homeland makes it more possible for the detached exilic critic to identify and theorize affiliative connections between culture, power, and homeland more generally. Importantly, for Said, the experience of *being* detached from their culture of origin never completely vitiates the exilic critic's *feelings* of attachment. In other words, because exile is a "median state, neither completely at one with the new setting nor fully disencumbered of the old," Said argues, the experience of being an exile is "predicated on the existence of, love for, and a real bond with one's native place."[54] Moreover, as Said argues in the conclusion to *Culture and Imperialism*, the loss that inheres within the experience of exile never dulls the "real bond" a person feels for their homeland, but it does have the perverse effect of making all experiences seem temporary, "*as if* they were about to disappear."[55] Looking at lived life through the lens of loss—through the detached experience of someone who still feels the "sweetness" of home but who knows that the recapture of that sweetness is impossible—can give rise to a form of persistent reflection on subjectivity, a nagging mode of questioning the relationship between the current moment and the past that prompts exiles to treat the now as provisional, to look on it and wonder what might be worth saving and what, if necessary, could be given up.[56] It is almost as if, for Said, once one has experienced the pain of seeing filiative relationships transformed into all their complex affiliative pieces, one can never go back to a state of unseeing. It becomes less likely, he muses, for the exile to accept pat explanations of belonging that flow, seemingly without effort, from the nationalist's "pride in one's heritage" or a "certainty about who 'we' are."[57]

At its best, then, love of a home that is lost can produce a form of detached attachment in the exilic subject. This detached attachment is both removed enough from the immediacy of national belonging to denaturalize it and attached enough to the visceral memory of place to sympathize with the pull of national home. Hence, the orientation that flows from this experience of loss does not have to be fatalism, according to Said, nor disdain for the ties that bind people to their sense of place. Rather, the experience of being caught between worlds can enliven a form of unclosed consciousness that is both open to an understanding of what it feels like to be connected while also possessed of a nettling need to question fundamental certainties about connection—about the affiliative relationship between identity, culture, and place.[58]

Of course, Said is aware that the unsettling exilic experience of seeing the world in provisional terms doesn't inevitably resolve itself into a critical perspective capable of profound insight, and indeed, the sheer awfulness of living in exile just as often promotes seclusion, retrenchment and a resentful interiority. Still, he maintains, despite these possibilities and problems—despite the fact that exile is a "jealous state"—if one can break out of the desire to turn inward while refusing "to sit on the sidelines nursing a wound," then "there are things to be learned" from exile.[59] Thus, despite the fact that exile is terrible to experience, Said believed that the "productive anguish" it inspires can serve as "an alternative to the mass institutions that dominate modern life," that it can foster a critical, compassionate, and necessary counterweight to political and cultural narratives that never pause to query the "certainty about who 'we' are."[60] In sum, the disruptive but still profoundly sympathetic account of loss and identity implicit in Said's detached attachment promotes a political, critical, and ethical disposition grounded in subjective instability. This instability elucidates both commonsense forms of filiation and identity on the one hand and an appreciation for love of home on the other. And it does this by refusing to reconcile the two.

## *AFTER THE LAST SKY*: THE PERILS OF ATTACHED DETACHMENT

As provocative and conceptually arresting as Said's writings about exile can be, however, they often lack the immediacy and urgency of Said's exilic writing. In other words, to fully understand the revealing power of exile as a mode of critical seeing, it is useful to pair Said's meta-exilic commentary with work where he writes as an exile, embedding his own roaming, exilic consciousness within his reading of politics, text, and context. In particular, Said's reflections on Palestine (including those captured in interviews) are often inflected with insights he draws from his own precarious status as a

Palestinian intellectual in exile. These works tend to have an internal rhythm different from many of his other writing because they engage with the specificities of Palestinian life and politics through Said's own (knowingly) filtered perspective. As Denise deCaires Narain puts it, "Said's writings on Palestine focus heavily on the specific realities of Palestinians, but his writing about *writing* seldom incorporated this material."[61]

While I don't entirely agree with DeCaires Narain's overall character-ization of Said's "writing about writing," I agree that Said's approach to exile is often expressed most powerfully in those texts committed to mak-ing the Palestinian cause visible and Palestinian narratives audible. In such vital works as 1979's "Zionism from the Standpoint of Its Victims," 1984's "Permission to Narrate," 1988's *Blaming the Victims*, and the dozens of articles and texts he wrote desperately (and presciently) to highlight the struc-tural flaws of the Oslo Accords, Said engages in an explicit mode of exilic analysis that requires him to explore his own biographical connections to the material. As he explains in the introduction to *The Question of Palestine* (a book whose content made it almost unpublishable in 1979),

> I have been conscious of trying to present more than a summary of recent his-tory, or a prediction of tomorrow's developments. My hope is to have made clear the Palestinian interpretation of Palestinian experience, and to have shown the relevance of both to the contemporary political scene. To explain one's sense of oneself as a Palestinian in this way is to feel embattled. To the West, which is where I live, to be a Palestinian is in political terms to be an outlaw of sorts, or at any rate very much an outsider. But that is a reality, and I mention it only as a way of indicating the peculiar loneliness of my undertaking in this book.[62]

In this introduction and elsewhere, Said makes himself explicitly vulner-able, revealing the pain that attaches itself to the experience of living as a Palestinian exile in a country whose mainstream discourse is committed to either erasing or demonizing Palestinians. In his writings, Said often makes his experience of exile an essential vector through which to explain the poli-tics and history of Palestine. Again, in Masad's words, Said transforms him-self into a "veritable passport for the Palestinian cause, allowing it to cross borders into territories where it was previously denied entry."[63]

As I explore later, Said's exilic mode of critique allows him to engage in a contrapuntal mode of global analysis that interrogates imperialism—in the past, in the present, and in the presence of the past—by pushing back against the wall of unseeing and deflection that has surrounded receptions of the Palestinian experience in Europe and America since the 1917 Balfour agree-ment. In terms of sheer immediacy, however, none of his political writings is as deeply revealing of Said's exilic method-in-the-raw as *After the Last Sky:*

*Palestinian Lives*, a book that takes its title from another poem by Mahmoud Darwish, "The Earth Is Closing in on Us":

> Out of the windows of this last space. Our star will hang up mirrors.
> Where should we go after the last frontiers?
> Where should the birds fly after the last sky?[64]

Written in dialogue with Jean Mohr's haunting black-and-white photographs, the book unfolds as a series of themed, personal and political, reflections on the lives of ordinary Palestinians, exploring the meaning of the Palestinian experience through a stylistic cadence that traces the discordances of that last space. As Salman Rushdie put it in his beautiful introduction of the book's themes, for Said the "broken or discontinuous nature of Palestinian experience entails that classic rules about form or structure cannot be true to that experience." Rather, Rushdie continues, "it is necessary to work through a kind of chaos or unstable form that will accurately express its essential instability."[65]

The book was published in 1986, nearly a decade before Said's return to Jerusalem for the first time since his departure in 1947. *After the Last Sky*, Said notes in the introduction to the 1999 edition, is thoroughly an "exile's book," crafted from a self-aware distance, in spectral communication with Mohr's images of ordinary Palestinian people living ordinary lives in the disordered world of the late 1970s and early 1980s (with a smattering of pictures from 1967 and the 1950s). These photographs concentrate, for the most part, on capturing the day-to-day world of Palestinians in the Occupied Territories, in Israel, and in the diaspora of the Arab world—children, refugees, poets, professors, laborers, activists, musicians, students, mothers, fathers, bus drivers, grocers, doctors, and dressmakers. Throughout the book, the exilic Said moves back and forth between the proximity of his own experience and the geographic, political, and sometimes-temporal distance of the photographs, reading each image through loss. The book ruminates extensively on the relationship between people and places; on the transformation between present and past landscapes; and on the lingering, troubling role memory plays in Palestinian identity.

Mohr's images are jarringly and unabashedly situated alongside Said's reflections on home, violence, loss, nationhood, states, refugee camps, the *Nakba*, marriages, daily struggles, and triumphs. Through them, Said explores broader questions of power, politics, and identity that are both enabled and unsettled by this disrupted mode of being. The photographic image—which Said describes as the "culmination of a sequence of capturings"—lends itself particularly well to this mode of reflection, allowing him to layer accounts of lives interrupted through time on top of and next to one another, challenging, with every layer, the incorporeal quality of exilic memory.[66] As with his other work, Said is largely concerned with generating questions rather than answers, although in contrast to such essays as "Reflections on Exile" and "Intellectual Exile: Expatriates and Marginals," the questions he poses in this text are both more personal and less obviously instructive. Thus, throughout the book, Said explores most of the major themes of exile about which he theorizes in his academic writing, but because of the intimate, fugal quality of that exploration, the themes themselves feel strikingly close and particularly revealing.

Chapter 1 begins, for instance, with Said's reflections on a black-and-white photograph of a 1983 wedding party standing proudly and awkwardly at a border of sorts: "outside of a drab Arab city" and "outside of a refugee camp" that would soon thereafter be ravaged by intra-Palestinian fighting.[67] Crushed between sites of home, temporary home, and unsettling violence, the image sets the stage for a chapter devoted to considering states, statelessness, and the internal subjectivities that statelessness provokes. As Said puts it, whereas "our interlocutors" in Israel, Europe, America, and the Arab states all have the "luxury of a state" from which to articulate their various opinions about the status of the Palestinians, Palestinians themselves do not. Rather, he argues, we "lead our lives under a sword of Damocles."[68]

In the process of this exploration, Said engages themes from his scholarly writing on exile, such as the exilic temptation to self-isolate and retrench. The collective response to prolonged and exhausting statelessness, he writes, is "more precarious now than it was, but I detect a general turning inward among Palestinians, as if many of us feel the need to consolidate and collect the shards of Palestinian life still available to us."[69] Situated among the shards of life that Mohr gathers and preserves in his photographs, Said's words—uttered from across the world—crystalize this particular exilic desire to circle the wagons around an inner core in the midst of radical uncertainty. And yet, in contrast to the didactic tone he adopts in "Reflections on Exile," when Said describes the often-insular, "jealous state" of exile in *After the Last Sky*, one is struck by the closeness of his voice and his spontaneous sympathy for the act of "turning inward," both here and now and in the midst of grappling with distance. Unsettled from across the world, Said finds home in the solemn stares of a Palestinian wedding party. In this moment, "turning inward" not only makes intuitive sense, but it is also clearly the only option.

Said's situated sympathy with retrenchment—sandwiched between a photograph of children walking arm in arm down the street in Jerusalem and one of distant figures gathered on a rise outside a village near Ramallah—makes his recovery of this indwelling in the next sentence seem like a natural progression. Turning inward, he explains, is not quietism at all, nor is it resignation. Rather it springs from the natural impulse to stand back when the headlong rush of events gets to be too much, perhaps, for us to savor life as life, to reflect at some distance from politics on where we came from and where we are, to regrasp, revise, recomprehend the tumultuous experiences at whose center, quite without our consent, we have been made to stand.[70]

In this moment, Said links the desire to turn inward both with the move to regroup and recover *and* with the distance necessary for reflection, revision, and recomprehension. In this moment, Said captures precisely the mode of detached attachment—a vision caught in the to-and-fro of the journey in and the journey out—that makes exilic inquiry such a productive and painful form of criticism.

Said's detached view sits alongside his careful exposition of specific qualities associated with exilic life, particularly the brutal juxtaposition between past and present that, once again, he follows through Mohr's images. In the "small but clear formed human figures" standing outside the town near Ramallah, "surrounded by a dense and layered reality," Said sees shards of his own past life, a long-ago fragment of a childhood memory from a long-ago trip to Ramallah. This memory is fractal, plagued with all the instabilities of exilic memory more generally; what exactly was the reason he was locked out of a playhouse as a child? How do those memories of standing outside that theater in Ramallah—cut off from the security of his family and the insecurity of a grown-up world—map onto Mohr's "telescoped vision of small figures assembled in a detached space?"[71] How does detachment itself—the detachment of the figures, the detachment of memory, the detachment of time—contribute to his own seeing and unseeing?

Over and over, Said uses his reflections on these photographs to explore some of the "things to be learned" from exile. In the exuberant visage of the elderly Palestinian villager smiling through the starburst crack of a pair of broken eyeglasses, for instance, he locates the indeterminacy endemic to the exilic vision: "one lens that is clear, another that is hopelessly impaired. . . . What is good and whole is never so good and whole as to overrule the bad and vice versa."[72] Said allows the complexity of this cracked vision to steer him through the book, through his own sense of distance, disrupting both his memories and even his lack of memories—of that "other," earlier Nazareth, for instance, where his mother was born, that he never saw for himself. In the end, this inability to see straight—to resolve the unfused and unorganized strings of culture and identity that remain in a state of flux for so many exiles—leads Said to a series of profoundly attached-detached observations about exilic life more generally and the contemporary situation in Palestine in particular.

Beyond illustrating the detached attachment of exile, *After the Last Sky* also paints rich, complicated portraits of individual Palestinians defiantly living (sometimes thriving) in the midst of repression, dispossession, and apartheid. Perhaps more importantly, it also reveals and interrogates the complex realities of Palestinians as a people. This, in itself, is an important corrective to the relentless media campaign within Israel and the West either to treat Palestinians as a "pretext for a call to arms" or to deny their coherence as a nation altogether.[73] Elsewhere, Said describes this as the "inadmissible existence of the Palestinian people," a willful call to *unsee* most famously encapsulated in Golda Meir's 1969 quip: "Who are the Palestinians? There are no Palestinians."[74]

At the same time, *After the Last Sky* is also a book about the insecurity and uncertainty of *peoplehood* as a concept. Through his own experience and his engagement with the experiences of others, Said explores the ways national identity (both subjective and collective) are necessarily framed in relation to a traumatic past and to an unsettled, insecure present:

> Dispossession and dispersion have meant a fundamental discrepancy between "us" and wherever each of us now happen to be. Each of us bears the loss of place and of history acutely, the given we share at the root of our various lives. There is no way for us to feel the accumulations of our past except as a gap, an apparently unchanging abyss separating us from the national fulfilment we have not been able to attain. As internal exiles in Israel, as detainees on the West Bank or Gaza without sovereignty over land, as refugees and itinerant exiles, we are not likely to recuperate our loss of a settled national existence. The tie between us and our past was not only severed in 1948; it is periodically and ritually resevered in the sustained war upon our national peoplehood by Israel.[75]

This fundamental rift between "us" and "wherever each of us happens to be" is both material and political, grounded in forms of human suffering that can't be relegated to the distant past because the ties that bind the Palestinians to each other and to a homeland are perennially being "resevered" by the Israeli state. This ongoing trauma alters the way exiles understand their connections to each other and to their own pasts. For Said, "no clear and simple narrative is adequate to the complexity of our experience" as a people and as a "community set apart from others," whose identity has been forged and reforged through the experiences of expulsion and violence and the everyday work entailed in survival. Indeed, he continues, the "further we get from the Palestine of our past, the more precarious our status, the more disrupted our being, the more intermittent our presence."[76]

Thus, out of this attached and detached mode of engagement flows Said's broader observations about filiation and affiliation, nationalism and identity that are, at the same time, deeply sympathetic to the ties that bind a people to each other and homeland and deeply critical of national belonging as a culturally constructed project. Often, Said uses Mohr's photographs—these sequences of "capturings"—to highlight the subjective, fractured, constructed quality of peoplehood. Reflecting, for instance, on nearly identical pictures of "peasant women" (one from 1950 in Irbid and one from 1979 near Mount Carmel), Said explores how these kinds of images can and have been interpreted: as reflections on the "timeless East," as examples of the "miserable lot of women in Islam," and/or as proof positive of Palestinian existence over time. The truth is, he argues, the reader knows these are photographs of Palestinians "because I have identified them as such; I know they are Palestinian peasants, and not Lebanese or Syrian, because Jean has been my witness." But, he continues, in themselves the pictures are mute and thus invite the "embroidery of explanatory words."[77] This doesn't mean there is no *there* to be captured. Indeed, as Said points out in notably Marxist terms, if anything, these exotic, romanticized images probably depict the ongoing reality of a people "who have little control of either the product of their labor or their own laboring capacity."[78] Said's transition in the next paragraph to a discussion of Philip Baldensperger's famously Orientalist text about Palestine, 1913's *The Immovable East*, again highlights—through the jolt of juxtaposition—the multiplicity of interpretations that scholars and observers have affixed to Palestinian peasants, all of which freeze them in time, none of which identifies the one relatively consistent through line of peasant life: their alienated labor.

What Said finds most striking about Baldensperger's and other Orientalist descriptions of Palestinian peasants, is the recurrent historical contrast between their urge to record and systematize "our passive scattered incoherence" and the absence of "Palestinian writings on the same subject."[79] Over the years, he argues, nationalist narratives have emerged to speak back to this gap. "Our history," he notes in the chapter on statelessness, "is forbidden, narratives are rare: the story of origins, of home, of nation is underground." When an origin story appears, he continues, "it is broken, often wayward and meandering in the extreme, always coded, usually outrageous—mock-epics, satires, sardonic parables, absurd rituals—that make little sense to an outsider."[80] Here and elsewhere in *After the Last Sky*, Said reveals—in the most intimate and painful of ways—the deeply *affiliative* connections at work in the construction of national identities, affiliations that might be overlooked by an observer speaking/theorizing from the perspective of settled and thus unreflective belonging.

In the process of grappling with the Palestinian experience from a distance, through an engagement with images of the present and his own contested and complex past, Said marvels at the "imbalance in consciousness" that springs from the coexistence of a deeply unorganized and disrupted twentieth-century Palestinian history and "our declared and apparently coherent" political, social, and cultural status as a people.[81] "There is no great episode in our history," he continues, that could be seen to establish a roadmap for the future, because "our past is still ragged, discredited, and unassimilated, partly because we endure the difficulties of dispersion without being forced (or able) to struggle to change our circumstances." For Said, there is no "dominant theory of Palestinian culture, history, society" and "we cannot rely on one central image." There is, he insists, "no completely coherent discourse adequate to us."[82]

Moreover, this absence he describes of a coherent discourse and a central image sits uncomfortably alongside a political imperative *to be* something in the context of other Arab states that are both Arab and otherwise: Arab and Lebanese, Arab and Jordanian, Arab and Kuwaiti. And yet, at the same time, the discomfort around Palestinian identity also lays bare the way these other nation-state identities are also "partly invented and partly real."[83] Looked at in the context of the same history that produced the absence of a "coherent" Palestinian discourse, these Arab states themselves seem just as "ragged," equally the products of imperial (and mandated) power, equally tainted by hybridity and disruption, resistance and accommodation, power and time.

Throughout the book and through his reflections on Mohr's photos, Said's observations also demonstrate the ways Palestinian national identity is consistently rendered geographically impossible by the ongoing imperial context of domination and dispossession in which Israeli planning policies seek to create "interconnections" between Jewish communities while restricting "uncontrolled Arab settlement" (a policy that Said rightly understood would ultimately undermine the Oslo agreements).[84] At the same time, the book does not shy away from a rigorous critique of sectionalism and violence within the movement for Palestinian liberation, even as it links this violence to a long historical chain of violence: "the violence of our uprooting and the destruction of our society in 1948, the violence visited upon us by our enemies, the violence we have visited on others, or, most horribly, the violence we have wreaked on each other."[85] *After the Last Sky* is thus a detached-attached account of both Palestinian identity and national identity more broadly, about the constructed and contested nature of that identity, its potential for violence, and its simultaneous necessity as a mode of anticolonial politics. As a text, it reveals the intimate and contradictory reasons, as Said argues slightly later about Fanon's thought, that "nationalism, for all its obvious necessity, is also the enemy."[86]

At the same time, *After the Last Sky* demonstrates exilic criticism's compassionate sympathy for what moves people to embrace nationalism and sometimes violence, *even as* it exposes nationalism itself as a contested, invented, potentially exclusive and violent phenomenon. Said makes this clear by, again, reflecting on the fact that he writes "at a distance," acknowledging, with humility, that he hasn't "experienced the ravages" of those Palestinians whose lives are materially affected, day after day, by the violence of dispossession and dispersal.[87] This distance, he acknowledges, makes it easier for him to critique and then walk away. And yet, at the same time, Said insists, distance is what reveals the affiliative narratives that flow from trauma, from massacre, from a rootless desire for foundation. Multiple times in this text, Said demonstrates—through reflection on his own experience—both the limitations of detachment (how *not* experiencing the ravages makes it harder for him to feel the pull of nationhood) and the revelatory quality of detachment (how distance enables perspective into the nationalist "plot of a logically unfolding conspiracy against us"), all while experiencing—in a distanced but attached way—what it is to lose home without losing love of home.

One thus comes away from reading *After the Last Sky* with a deep appreciation for the struggles and everyday triumphs of Palestinian people *as a people* and with a keener awareness of why nationhood and identity claims are essential to resisting the relentless onslaughts of a state and a world that refuses to acknowledge its existence. Simultaneously, Said's reflections sketch out why nationhood and identity are themselves constructed categories with complex modern histories that can turn inward, exclusive, bitter, and violent. Ultimately, the book leaves readers holding these two closely felt experiences—of attachment and detachment, filiation and affiliation—together with compassion and without resolution. Indeed, *After the Last Sky* leaves one with the distinct impression that resolution would not only misrepresent reality but also simultaneously betray the diverse experiences of real people whose inhabited lives reflect this paradox.

*After the Last Sky* models a form of cracked-lens insight into the affiliations between culture and power that holds contradictions without resolving them while also refusing to dismiss the desire for belonging, even as it exposes the multiple conflicts that belonging (and the desire for belonging) can evoke. Said demonstrates, again and again, the kinds of insights that a detached-attached exilic perspective elicits while troubling and undermining his own memories, his own sense of place, and his right to "write at a distance." Loss, Said concludes, is "absorbed into our notion of the present." Therefore, the best that you can do, under the circumstances, is to "tell your story in pieces, *as it is*."[88] Such fractured narrative is always preferable, in Said's account, to forced coherence. Or, as he puts it with characteristic provocation in his moving review of Mona Hatoum's "Art of Displacement," "[b]etter disparity and dislocation than reconciliation under duress of subject and object; better a lucid exile than sloppy, sentimental homecomings; better the logic of dissociation than an assembly of compliant dunces."[89]

# DISTANCE, LOSS, AND CRITIQUE

At the end of the day, *After the Last Sky* and Said's other exilic writings demonstrate a disposition toward politics and culture that is always both/and: both critical and empathetic, both detached and attached. The exilic subject begins their analysis of the world from the perspective of loss; that is, from the position that the ground on which they stand is not the home with which they identify, a home to which they can never return nor fully reoccupy but for which they, like Said, continue to feel deeply, even at a distance, even as the shiftiness of memory, qualifies and deepens that sympathy. Beginning from loss—and from a sense of insecurity about one's own relationship to home and to memory—prods into being modes of reflective humility that lead the exilic critic to the door where they can look in and look out, with clarity and compassion, on the complex relationship of the past to the present, the filiative to the affiliative. This sympathetic perspective doubles back on itself, generating a constant mode of questioning nestled in the fundamental question Said asks in *After the Last Sky*: "Do we exist? What proof do we have?"[90]

Said's approach thus assumes that "homes are always provisional" and that the borders and barriers within which we find ourselves "can always become prisons."[91] This unresolved, "precarious exilic realm" is tinged throughout by the perennial suffering that accompanies loss, a lingering pain that can and does elicit "rancor and regret, as well as a sharpened vision."[92] For Said, the choice is clear: One can either sit on the sidelines and permanently mourn "what has been left behind," or one can embrace the sharpened vision, the "different set of lenses" this unsettlement makes possible.[93] This means holding, without resolving, exile's tensions: strangely compelling to think about and terrible to experience.

Perhaps not surprisingly, it is also Said's insistence on just holding without resolving contradictions that has most frustrated some of the political theorists who have devoted time to thinking about his work over the years. And yet, as I argue in the next chapter, it is also precisely his refusal to resolve the antinomies of exile that makes Said's approach to identity, politics, and place so necessary for political theorists today, particularly those theorists most interested in the injustices that result from the living legacy of imperialism: the global maldistribution of resources, the racist violence and exclusions of nationalism, the blindness of American exceptionalism, and persisting forms of domination that continue to deny victims of settler colonial dispossession the right to narrate their own experience. Most importantly, Said's unsettled, exilic disposition models for theorists a language through which we can disrupt the deep-rooted silences and modes of unseeing that flow from an insouciant attachment to "our mode of theorizing" and "our way of life." As Said notes at the end of *Culture and Imperialism*, embracing the "independence and detachment" of someone who both loves and has lost their homeland makes it far more difficult to write the world from a place of unreflective certainty. At the same time, disentangling the theorizing subject from a position of supreme confidence about "who 'we' are" opens up new possibilities for criticism, even as it provides no clear answers or obvious solutions to the pressing political problems of our age.[94] And yet, as Said puts it in the last sentence of the last essay in *Humanism and Democratic Criticism*, only in the "precarious exilic realm can [one] first truly grasp the difficulty of what cannot be grasped and then go forth to try anyway."[95]

## 2

# A Cluster of Flowing Currents

## *Theory Unresolved and Groundless*

In the last paragraph of his 1999 memoir *Out of Place*, Said returns to a broader question that begins the book: the significance of his rich, complicated, multiethnic, multilocational early life for his intellectual self in the present. Writing this memoir—reconstructing memories, flirting with nostalgia, grasping at loss—had been, Said argues, an act of much-needed escape from the anxiety and pain he experienced during another twelve-month round of therapy for the leukemia that would eventually kill him. "My other writings and my teaching," he notes in the preface, "seemed to take me far away from the various worlds and experiences of this book."[1] But, he continues, surely his political writings and his critical studies must somehow be related to this memoir, must somehow have worked their way into the substance of his past as he reconstructed it in the present. The final paragraph of *Out of Place* circles back to the impact of that dissonance on Said's own sense of self:

> I occasionally experience myself as a cluster of flowing currents. I prefer this to the idea of a solid self, the identity to which so many attach so much significance. These currents, like the themes of one's life, flow along during the waking hours, and at their best, they require no reconciling, no harmonizing. They are "off" and may be out of place, but at least they are always in motion, in time, in place, in the form of all kinds of strange combinations moving about, not necessarily forward, sometimes against each other, contrapuntally yet without one central theme. A form of freedom, I'd like to think, even if I am far from being totally convinced that it is.[2]

The "cluster of flowing currents" Said describes here is neither comfortable nor integrated, but it is instead open to the multiplicity of experiences that have informed not just his own identity but also the intellectual stance he felt best lends itself to critiquing, diagnosing, and describing a global

political/cultural environment shaped by the "strange combinations" of imperial history. For Said, this unsolid self also provides the best location from
which to theorize, imagine, and fight for a better world.

Said's unresolved, ungrounded approach to identity and to critical subjectivity could not be more different from that of many scholars collectively
engaged in the broad yet oddly insular field called political theory, a field in
which the "we" who philosophize remain largely identified with place and
tradition, even as that place and tradition goes without utterance. This chapter
begins to think through what an exilic, Said-inspired, unresolved subjectivity might mean for political theory and, in particular, for political theorizing
around questions of identity, history, coexistence, and justice. It does this by
first engaging the work of political theorists who have taken Said's approach
seriously and then been ultimately disappointed by his rejection of closure.
It then compares Said's unclosed theory to mainstream cosmopolitanism and
global justice literature. The chapter concludes with a closer look at Said's
"method for thinking about a just peace" in Palestine-Israel. Throughout the
chapter, I return to the kinds of questions, modes of political life, visions
of history, and possibilities for the future that are occluded by a theoretical
insistence on reconciliation and an understanding of identity as a "solid self."
The ethical impulse toward ungrounded subjectivity in Said's exilic disposition, I argue, ultimately makes possible a mode of political theorizing that not
only more fully describes a world still seeped in the affiliative connections of
imperialism but also opens our eyes to political visions foreclosed by a political theory that seeks to resolve, rather than unsettle, the world.

## RESOLVING SAID

Over the years, political theorists who have written sympathetically about
Said at any length have tended to engage his work in the service of thinking
through some of the thornier political and conceptual problems associated
with multiculturalism, cosmopolitanism, nationhood, and identity. While
neither of the theorists analyzed in this section focus on Said exclusively nor
for any length of time, both Fred Dallmayr and Joan Cocks do engage ear-
nestly with his work in the context of thinking through shortcomings in other
literatures. Both have been inspired by Said's work, and both are extraordinarily appreciative of his passion and insight.[3] Both, however, are critical
of Said for what they see as his failure to develop a robust epistemology or
an adequate moral philosophy. Said's work may be brilliantly insightful and
even inspirational, they agree, but his approach is ultimately so committed to
loose ends that it fails to provide satisfactory answers to the important questions of political life. In other words, in his exilic unwillingness to resolve

antinomies, Said fails to provide for them acceptable *theoretical* solutions to *political* problems.

Dallmayr, for instance, believes that Said's political commitment to the cause of the Palestinian people is admirable but ultimately undermined by the deconstructive impulse of his exilic method, a method hamstrung, he insists, by the same apolitical—even antipolitical—tendencies that plague poststructuralist theory. Dallmayr thus begins his 1997 article "The Politics of Nonidentity: Adorno, Postmodernism, and Edward Said" by tying anti-foundationalism and postmodernism to the philosophical revolt against Enlightenment certainties. As someone who is himself explicitly indebted to Said's groundbreaking, Foucault-inspired approach in *Orientalism*, Dallmayr acknowledges that this revolt springs, in part, from a legitimate desire to diversify the Eurocentric canon and resituate philosophy within a "properly global and multicultural environment."[4] He worries, however, about what this anti-foundationalist destabilization of Enlightenment cogito means for political theory. "Does it mean the simple demise or 'end of the subject' in favor of some kind of objectivism or reifying heteronomy?" he asks, or does such destabilization lead inevitably to the "erasure of boundaries between self and other," culminating in a generalized "nondistinction or indifference" between the two?[5]

Of course, Dallmayr continues, destabilizing questions like this are obviously not new to philosophy and, in fact, played a substantive role in the development of Hegel's dialectic. The problem, he maintains, is that anti-foundationalists and poststructuralists have thrown out the Hegelian baby with the Enlightenment bathwater and, in so doing, have perversely reinforced an incoherent form of nonidentity. In other words, in the absence of a dialectical commitment to reconciliation—especially to the kind of reconciliation embodied in the ethical world of Hegelian *Sittlichkeit*—postmodernist jettisoning of cogito simply reifies heteronormativity and annihilates the distinction between self and other, reducing the world to universal sameness, or in Dallmayr's words, to a bleak "no-man's land bereft of all distinction."[6]

The rest of the article seeks alternatives to this no-man's land, first in a favorable account of Adorno's negative dialectic that transitions to a disappointed discussion of Said's unhoused, exilic approach. By retaining a Hegelian commitment to "'ethical life' and the possibility *Sittlichkeit* holds for a 'reconciliation' of opposites," Dallmayr argues, Adorno's critique of Enlightenment subjectivity manages to escape the political and philosophical nihilism of nonidentity.[7] The ethical impulse of *Negative Dialectics, he continues, lies in precisely the "distant hope" that it is possible, in Adorno's words, to "break through the fallacy of constitutive subjectivity" and chart a course beyond alienation. This "reconciled condition," according to Adorno, avoids the "philosophical imperialism" of appropriating difference. Instead, he continues, the "alien, in the proximity it is granted, remains what is distant and different, beyond the heterogeneous and beyond that which is one's own."*[8] Adorno's embrace of heterogeneity is acceptable, in Dallmayr's mind, precisely *because* his challenge to universalism is hitched to a "reconciled condition," however distant.

Dallmayr next identifies Said as another contemporary theorist who resituates philosophy within a "properly global and multicultural environment" by challenging the adamantine coherence of Enlightenment subjectivity through a turn to disruption that, he argues, Said combines with a laudable commitment to political transformation. Unfortunately, Dallmayr concludes, Said's concern for politics is ultimately undermined by his simultaneous commitment to remaining conceptually open and to always holding and never letting go of the myriad tensions between filiative and affiliative modes of belonging that adhere to the exilic experience. For Dallmayr, Said's unwillingness to abandon this disruptive tension for even the distant hope of ethical reconciliation denotes a failure of political imagination and an inability to successfully navigate the "border between vagrancy and a differently committed politics."[9]

In contrast to Adorno, he concludes, Said's recipe for undermining the brittle fixedness of Enlightenment subjectivity in the absence of resolution concludes in the same kind of ethical and political no man's land as that of the poststructuralists. From Dallmayr's perspective, in defiantly linking critique to dislocation, disruption, and heterogeneity without a commitment to *Sittlichkeit*, Said's exilic consciousness remains "*disengaged* from concrete contexts and loyalties." Ultimately, given the interminable distance between the exilic subject and the object of critique, he wonders, how can Said, or thinkers of a Saidian persuasion, ever really "engage themselves" with "real-life problems or events?" In other words, having sundered all concrete attachments, can exilic intellectuals ever be committed to anything but the "principle of nomadism?"[10]

Dallmayr illustrates this point through a reading of *Orientalism* that he then traces through *Culture and Imperialism*. Echoing the observations of a number of Said's critics over the years, Dallmayr questions Said's hesitancy when it comes to claiming authenticity for any cultural or political expression. In other words, Said maintains throughout *Orientalism* that reading "the Orient" as a "constituted entity" also requires the critic to call into question claims that frame actual, existing cultures in Asia and the Middle East as historically authentic, the product of "some religion, culture, or racial essence proper to that geographical space."[11] Dallmayr acknowledges that Said refined and clarified this position over the years in response to his critics by focusing more intentionally on the emergence and sustained presence of anticolonial resistance in Asia and the Middle East. In *Culture and Imperialism* and elsewhere, Said argues that making counteridentity claims is often an important, strategic necessity for resistance movements, and this, according to Dallmayr, goes a long way toward counterbalancing his dismissal of "authentic" culture in *Orientalism*. He insists, however, that it is ultimately not enough. For Dallmayr, Said's absolute commitment to the idea that human experience is "historical and secular"—always open to interpretation and analysis and never limited by national, ethnic, or doctrinal borders or "exhausted by totalizing theories"—simply sets his theory adrift.[12] For Said, he concludes, "all identities or distinct differences are basically arbitrary."[13] Thus, for Dallmayr, Said's mode of analysis, like that of the poststructuralists, ultimately cycles into an abyss of disengaged nonidentity, where all attachments melt into air, and we are left finally with nothing but an "intellectual nomadism and an indifferent cosmopolitanism."[14]

From Dallmayr's perspective, Said quite simply fails to provide philosophical grounding for his political investments, including his long-term investment in Palestinian politics. While Said may genuinely desire to engage the cause of the Palestinians, and while he clearly has a connection to the issue through his own status, Dallmayr concludes that Said "does not seem particularly concerned with the distinctiveness of Palestinian traditions nor inclined to share or participate in their life-forms or religious beliefs."[15] Why he comes to this conclusion is unclear. Aside from Said's well-known commitment to secularism and secular criticism, the idea that Said was "not inclined" to "participate" in Palestinian life forms is simply untrue. As *After the Last Sky* and many of Said's other writings on exile and politics demonstrate vividly, he felt a profound connection to Palestine, Palestinian culture, and the lives of Palestinian people, people who must now, he insists in his famous essay on the subject, be given "permission to narrate" those lives.[16]

At the end of the day, it seems that for Dallmayr, Said's philosophical and political resistance to reconciliation *must* translate, somehow, into an insouciant politics, despite evidence to the contrary. In other words, Said's irresolution and his rejection of philosophical and political closure coupled with his belief in the constructedness of identity, Dallmayr's analysis implies, can only result in a nomadic lack of concern for the actual cultural/religious lives of Palestinians. Thus, Said's lifetime of activism and his involvement in the cultural world of Palestine—from his friendship with poets and artists to his long-term support for the National Conservatory of Music in the West Bank, now the Edward Said National Conservatory of Music—are not legible for Dallmayr because they cannot be linked to *Sittlichkeit*. They remain, in other words, ungrounded. This leads Dallmayr to the ironic conclusion that Adorno was a more genuinely *political* thinker than Said, despite Adorno's notorious rejection of political praxis (manifest most famously in his decision to call the police to break up a group of striking students at Frankfurt University in 1968).[17] Dallmayr's straight line—between the "distant hope" for *Sittlichkeit* and politics—not only does a disservice to Adorno's much more complex reading of the relationship between negative dialectics and praxis, but it also flatly refuses to see the thing right in front of his eyes: Said's enduring personal and political investment in the "life world" of Palestine and the Palestinian people.

Joan Cocks paints a similarly admiring but dissatisfied, portrait of Said's commitment to irresolution. With Dallmayr, she is inclined to see in Said's writings a potentially fruitful response to the thorny questions of identity, multiplicity, and difference that were gradually beginning to penetrate the reluctant world of political theory toward the end of the 1990s. In her 2000 article for *Constellations* "A New Cosmopolitanism? V. S. Naipaul and Edward Said," Cocks notes that the end of the Cold War, the expansion of globalization, the rise of ethnic nationalism, and the emergence of multicultural politics all set the stage for what remains an ongoing debate in political theory and political philosophy between cosmopolitan thinkers and their communitarian, conservative, and liberal-nationalist critics. Cocks rightly intuits that Said's exilic approach is doing something distinct from mainstream philosophical cosmopolitanism, and she sets out in the article to determine whether this approach has the potential to successfully navigate the "tensions between particularism and universalism" that dominated those debates.[18]

The debates that Cocks identified twenty years ago still exist in some form today within the mainstream of political theory, and despite the increasing importance of postcolonial and anticolonial approaches to globalization, resistance, and self-determination in the field, they still tend to focus primarily on the relationship between universal theories of justice and democracy on the one hand and the importance of particularity and community on the other.[19] Over the last twenty-five years—appearing in multiple iterations, through various academic outlets—major figures in political theory and political philosophy, such as David Held, Thomas Pogge, David Miller, Martha Nussbaum, and Will Kymlicka, have engaged in a variety of exchanges that circle around one basic question: What matters more for politics? A universal conception of justice arrived at through reason (as articulated by most cosmopolitans) *or* the recognition of particular conceptions of the good life (as articulated by communitarians and pluralists)? While a new generation of scholars like Mathias Risse and Laura Valentini may attempt to merge or meld these positions, the basic dichotomy—the positions themselves—remain the same.[20]

Nancy Fraser characterizes this ongoing set of arguments as a clash between two opposing philosophical perspectives, one oriented toward "the right" (which she associates with "Kantian *Moralität*") and the other toward "the good" or "the ethical" (which she, like Dallmayr, associates with Hegelian *Sittlichkeit*). In part, Fraser argues, this contrast boils down to scope. "Norms of justice are thought to be universally binding," she maintains. "[T]hey hold independently of actors' commitments to specific values." By contrast, she continues, claims of recognition and of difference are "more restricted," and they involve "qualitative assessments of the relative worth of various cultural practices, traits, and identities," and "they depend on historically specific horizons of value, which cannot be universalized."[21]

Cocks considers the possibility of finding in Said's work a potential bridge— a "third way" of sorts—between "the right" and "the good." Ultimately, however, while sympathetic to his mode of theorizing, she concludes that Said's "exilic consciousness is not generalizable" for two reasons. First, echoing Dallmayr's critique, she concludes that the "detachment" implicit in Said's notion of exile leads to an overvaluation of the "outsiders' and [skeptics'] autonomy," an emphasis that renders the exilic critic aloof from the very people he claims to care most about.[22] Second, Cocks thinks that Said's exilic perspective is ultimately hamstrung by its failure to adequately "map out and fight for clear political alternatives to the nation-state."[23] In other words, because Said's mode of criticism does not systematically address the philosophical tension between particularism (nationalism) and universalism (cosmopolitanism), by theorizing a third option (whatever that may be), it is not "generalizable" as an alternative mode of political thinking. This is effectively the same critique made by Dallmayr in another form: Because Said refuses to resolve tensions between the particular and the universal by not addressing "alternatives to the nation-state," his approach lacks ethical purchase as a theory of politics. It may be disruptive, it may be critical, it may even be artful, but it isn't political theory.

From my perspective, the problem with Cocks's reading is apparent in the very title of the article: "A New Cosmopolitanism?" From the very beginning, Cocks approaches Said's exilic project through the lens of political theory's cosmopolitanism debate even as she explores (and then dismisses) the pos- sibility that he might provide us with a "new" perspective on this debate. She concludes that Said's inability (or unwillingness) to articulate a distinct realm outside of the nation-state in which political ethics might circulate and differ- ences might be negotiated means that his approach fails the litmus test that would make it "generalizable" for politics. Nearly twenty years later, in a piece on Said and Freud, Cocks makes almost the exact same argument, although she now frames it not in terms of a nationalism/cosmopolitanism dichotomy but in light of a "citizen/stranger" divide. While Said "can be congratulated," she argues, for standing on the side of "strangers"—exiles, refugees, immigrants, stateless people—this stance is finally "doomed to political impotence unless the sensibility that informs it percolates through the world's popular majorities so that it can be democratically institutionalized in the admission and membership rules and practices of what we still conceive of as nation-states."[24] In other words, once again, unless Said's stance on the margins can be translated into an alternative to the nation-state, it fails to deliver on its political potential.[25] With Dallmayr, Cocks also seems to believe that a critical disposition that begins from a position of unfixedness—from the perspective, in her words, of the "border crossing stranger"—simply cannot foster a new political imaginary because it cannot fully appreciate connection, community, the space of politics, and the pull of tradition. It is incapable, in other words, of speaking to that urgent core of political life that requires situatedness, history, rootedness, and democratic traditions—all practices, she maintains, we still associate with national communities.

At the end of the day, if the litmus test of a politically satisfying theory is its capacity to provide either well-theorized alternatives to dislocation and nonidentity (in the present or as a "distant hope") *or* to produce conceptually rigorous "alternatives" to the universal-particular dichotomy, then Said's work will always fall short. Without detracting from those political theory traditions that aim to achieve such goals, I do think that proclaiming Said's approach "doomed to political impotence" because it does not share those goals somewhat misses the point. The strength of Said's critical disposition—what makes it so potentially potent as an approach for political theorists—is precisely its capacity both to disrupt *and* to understand the need/desire for connection, place, and justice. There is nothing flippant about this approach, nothing that privileges "vagrancy" over commitment. Instead, Said's detached attachment requires the exilic critic to embrace instability for both its critical and ethical capacities.

In other words, because the starting point of exile for Said is not "vagrancy" for its own sake but simply the reality of irretrievable loss, his political commitments circulate differently—and to different effect—than do those of Dallmayr or Cocks. As he explained in a 1986 interview,

> For me, the figure of the exile is terribly important, because you reach a point where you realize that exile is irreversible. If you think of it in this way, then it becomes a really powerful image; but if you think that the exile can be repatriated—find a home—well, that is not what I'm talking about. If you think of exile as a permanent state, however, both in the literal and in the intellectual sense, then it's a much more promising, if difficult thing.[26]

This is not a "view from nowhere" (in Nagel's sense) but rather a disposition toward the world that emerges from a disrupted core bearing within itself the tactile memory of rootedness, of home.[27] Exile as a "permanent state" is both a critical and a substantive position for Said, neither a rootless cosmopolitanism nor a vague liberal multiculturalism, but an unresolved tension out of which flow the ethical and political commitments that Cocks and Dallmayr tend to characterize as ephemeral.

Over and over again in his work, Said demonstrates how loss of home— loss of comfort, loss of surety, loss of family, loss of connection to tradition— can open the exilic mind to a uniquely reflective critical practice with ethical implications. The exilic disposition both reveals and scrutinizes the affiliative relationship between culture, identity, and power *while also* politicizing these relationships in ways that expose, connect, and transform. Because loss of home is not the same as loss of love of home, the questioning impulse that flows from exile neither denies "distinct features" nor unquestioningly validates them.

Neither does the exilic perspective Said cultivates concede to fatalism. Indeed, Said argues, while constantly treating experience as if it were about to disappear "may seem like a prescription for an unrelieved grimness of outlook and, with it, a permanently sullen disapproval of all enthusiasm or buoyancy of spirit," this is not necessarily the case. Rather, standing on unstable ground, aware of "both the old and new environment," torn by connection and alienation, the experience of exilic loss "gives rise to an awareness of simultaneous dimensions," a unique form of insight into the construction of affiliative connections and a deep sense of what those connections can mean.[28] This insight neither diminishes awareness of human connection nor the pain of its loss and, in contrast to Dallmayr's assertion that dwelling in the irresolution of loss distances the exile from "real life problems and events," it ultimately opens up the world to new experiences of these problems and events. In the process, exile in this critical sense works to "diminish orthodox judgment" while cultivating an "appreciative sympathy" for the experiences of others and alternative modes of life.[29]

It is Said's dedication to this unstable subjectivity that is not only unsettled but also profoundly unsettling to others, that most differentiates his exilic mode of seeing/reading culture and politics from what Dallmayr describes as "indifferent cosmopolitanism." Indeed, reading the debates about cosmopolitanism within political theory that have taken place over the last thirty years *through* a Said-inspired exilic subjectivity highlights the marked distinction between these perspectives. At the same time, such a reading also exposes the profoundly *settled* sensibilities that have so often shaped (and continue to shape) the theorizing of both cosmopolitans and their critics. These largely unacknowledged assumptions of attachment and identification are representative of those epistemological biases that continue to shape much political theorizing precisely at a moment when, according to Dallmayr, it is meant to be engaging a "properly global and multicultural environment."[30]

## COSMOPOLITANISM AND THE GROUNDED "WE"

Superficially, the distinction between Said's exilic approach and mainstream cosmopolitan theory seems perfectly obvious. As Said's work since *Orientalism* and the multiple strains of postcolonial criticism that it inspired more than ably demonstrate, the putatively universal theories on which cosmopolitanism largely depend reflect a Eurocentric vision of the world that was developed in the global/historical context of imperial domination. Both *Orientalism* and *Culture and Imperialism* are concerned largely with exploring the complicated convergence "between the great geographical scope" of European empires and the "universalizing cultural discourses" that sustained them, discourses that "assume the silence, willing or otherwise, of the non-European world." Within such discourses, Said continues, there is "incorporation; there is inclusion; there is direct rule; there is coercion," but only infrequently is there an "acknowledgement that the colonized people should be heard from, their ideas known."[31] Since 1978, much of the postcolonial scholarship inspired by Said has focused on interrogating more extensively these twin occluding impulses: the tendency of universalist discourses to colonize all theory and, simultaneously, to silence the voices of the colonized. For Said and for such scholars as Dipesh Chakrabarty, engaging in postcolonial critique entails "provincializing" Western philosophy itself by, as Chakrabarty puts it, investigating how the "reason" of the Enlightenment, "which was not always self-evident to everyone has been made to look obvious far beyond the ground where it originated."[32]

That a majority of mainstream cosmopolitan theorists in political philosophy and political theory today still rely on the universal presumptions of Enlightenment thought—most notably, the conviction that, in Nussbaum's words, "reason rather than patriotism or group sentiment" ought to guide moral action—is beyond dispute.[33] Indeed, their commitment to the cosmopolitan idea of a universal reason that transcends state boundaries is precisely what differentiates Rawlsian-inspired global justice scholars like Henry Shue and Charles Beitz from Rawls himself, who believed that principles of justice must be channeled through social groupings or "peoples."[34] Regardless of the particularities of their approaches—the "strong" or "weak" forms of thinking they propose—most cosmopolitan political theorists today (e.g., Shue, Beitz, Nussbaum, Mathias Risse, Simon Caney, Joseph Carens, Seyla Benhabib, Thomas Pogge, and David Held) generally agree that human beings within nation-states have obligations to human beings in other parts of the world and that a right understanding of these obligations can be determined through (some form) of Kantian, Stoic, or Rawlsian reason.

This is true even of a cosmopolitan philosopher like Anthony Appiah, who is both specifically concerned with the relationship between non-Western modes of life and cosmopolitan theory and committed to making "difference" a fundamental feature of his theory. Appiah's notion of "universality plus difference," for instance, remains largely wedded to the same logic of "incorporation" and "inclusion," which Said read through the universalizing impulses of imperialism. Indeed, Appiah's "universality plus difference" tends to first assume a universality that we all desire and/or have already experienced and then conflate anticolonial or postcolonial criticisms of that universal vision with attempts by activists to "preserve culture" in the face of economic globalization.[35] Such attempts, he continues, fail to adequately appreciate the extent to which these cultures have *already been* globalized, despite the activism of truculent culture warriors.

Cosmopolitan theory has, since the "turn to empire" and the growing interest in anticolonial, postcolonialism, indigenous, comparative, and Black political thought in the field, come in for some long-overdue criticism and supplementation. As scholars like Gurminder Bhambra have so ably demonstrated, mainstream cosmopolitanisms have historically failed to adequately theorize the Eurocentrism of their putatively universal vision.[36] Additionally, scholars of the history of political thought, such as Adom Getachew and Ines Valdez, have also begun to seriously theorize alternative, non-European forms of cosmopolitanism articulated by anticolonial Black thinkers like W. E. B. Du Bois and Marcus Garvey, thinkers routinely ignored by the mainstream cosmopolitan literature.[37] This postcolonial and anticolonial work is incredibly necessary and, in many ways, a late recognition by political theorists of Said's influence since *Orientalism*. It has inspired discussions between political theorists and political philosophers, such as James Tully and Charles Mills, about the need to engage comparative, historical traditions from a place of "epistemic humility." The goal, in Tully's words, is to reintegrate these traditions into the "dialogues of encounter, interchange, and interaction that shaped the modern world, with its unequal interdependent relationships and corresponding forms of relational subjectivity."[38]

The comparison I want to make, however, between Said's exilic orientation and mainstream cosmopolitan literature is slightly different. Rather than focusing on cosmopolitanism's universal orientation, the Eurocentric and Orientalist sensibilities that orientation enables, and the global dialogues it occludes, I argue that reading cosmopolitanism through Said's unstable exilic vision also shines a bright light on the *fixedness* of the cosmopolitan subject and the blinkering effects of this epistemological fixedness.

This reading is sympathetically aligned with Charles Mills' critique of the "White ignorance" that has dominated mainstream, Anglo-American liberal and analytic thought—particularly in North America—for so long. Taking the epistemological orientations of Rawls and Rawlsians as his primary example, Mills argues that they assume a pristinely reasoning subject that remains resolutely blind—deeply and emphatically impervious—to the constitutive power of racism and imperialism as sociological and historical facts. Mills argues in *Black Rights, White Wrongs* that White ignorance has been able to flourish for so long precisely because a "[W]hite epistemology of ignorance" has safeguarded it against its own assumptions and against acknowledging the "dangers of an illuminating blackness or redness." "Only by starting to break these rules and meta-rules," he argues, "can we begin the long process that will lead to the eventual overcoming of this [W]hite darkness and the achievement of an enlightenment that is genuinely multiracial."[39] Reading mainstream cosmopolitanism through exile, I suggest, provides one sympathetic mechanism for disrupting, exposing, and ultimately breaking these rules and meta-rules.

Again, many mainstream cosmopolitan theorists working in North America and Europe today assume that human beings have moral obligations, grounded in reason, that transcend the boundaries of the contemporary nation-state, obligations that require them to reflect on questions of justice dealing with peoples and events in parts of the world that may not immediately appear to concern them. Cosmopolitans thus ask such questions as: What obligations do citizens in the First World/global North owe to citizens in the Third World/global South? To what extent are First World citizens responsible for rectifying poverty in these countries? Under what conditions should liberal democracies intervene in the sovereign politics of states committing human rights abuses against their own people? What role should universal concerns for human rights play in the construction of transnational economic policies? What responsibilities do countries in the First World/global North have to mitigate the effects of climate change? Cosmopolitan theorists who are explicitly concerned with questions of global justice, such as Charles Beitz, Martha Nussbaum, Thomas Pogge, and Onora Nell, address these questions by drawing on different (although uniformly Eurocentric) philosophical traditions, but all of them argue strenuously that considerations of justice ought to extend to the human community beyond national borders. As David Miller argues, these formulations share the "idea that we owe all human beings moral consideration of some kind."[40] With Mathias Risse, they tend to frame both their questions and affirmative claims about the rest of the world as some version of: "What We Owe to the Global Poor."[41]

Over the years, debates between cosmopolitans and their critics (like Miller) have tended to focus on the role of local or national communities in the formation of moral obligations, and they almost always revolve around questions of *identification*. In other words, these debates are centrally concerned with the extent to which individuals within nation-states can actually sustain a robust sense of moral and political connection to others with whom they do not identify as fellow nationals. For cosmopolitans, cultural and political identification with "the other" isn't necessary because people are capable of understanding moral obligation through reason. But for a communitarian critic like Alasdair MacIntyre, this hubristic faith in reason ignores entirely the role that identification with one's national or local community plays in the development of moral consciousness. "The self," MacIntyre maintains, "has to find its moral identity in and through its membership in communities."[42] Conservative scholars also focus their critiques on this question of identification. Legal theorist Jack Goldsmith, for instance, argues against the idea that the United States has any "cosmopolitan duty" to "take affirmative steps that would help other nations and their peoples" on the grounds that individuals first learn their duties to others within local and national communities. In Goldsmith's words, "cosmopolitan duty" makes little sense in a world where individuals "tend to focus their attention, energies, and altruism on members of their community (friends, family, and compatriots) with whom they identify and share a common bond."[43]

Pluralist and liberal multiculturalist critics like Will Kymlicka similarly couch their critiques in terms of identification. In his rebuttal of David Held's approach to globalization, Kymlicka suggests that Held's analysis of nation-states as "communities of fate" underplays the very real role that national and local communities play in fashioning people's responses to globalization. It is absolutely true, he argues, that many of the material and political forces that shape people's lives cut across national borders, a reality increased in an era of globalization. But, he insists, what "determines the boundaries of the 'communities of fate' is not the forces people are subjected to, but rather how they respond to those forces, and in particular, what sorts of collectivities they identify with when responding to those forces."[44] Finally, even some postcolonial critics of mainstream cosmopolitanism still sometimes privilege identification *even as* they rethink and trouble it. Robert Young, for instance, argues that cosmopolitanism "raises the question of how new forms of belonging in a world marked by migration, diaspora, and transnational labor" might be interpreted "in relation to those older forms of singular identification," such as nation-states.[45]

What most cosmopolitan theorists and their critics share, however, is a relatively untroubled surety about the fixedness of the position from which they validate or minimize identity. In other words, cosmopolitans consistently ask questions about "our" ethical obligations toward "others": non-nationals, refugees, potential victims of genocide. Critics then raise concerns about the extent to which citizens within national communities can identify with a broader conception of humanity through reason. But whether they take identification as key to morality or not, neither Nussbaum and Beitz on the one hand nor MacIntyre, Goldsmith, and Kymlicka on the other, question *their own* untroubled identification with a community of origin. Few of them wonder whether the ground on which *they* stand—as theorists writing about the promises or problems of cosmopolitanism—is solid. Nor do they consider what questioning the solidity of that ground might do to or for their theorizing. Assuming themselves to be safely situated within their natal communities or within their communities of choice, able to return home when and if they like, these thinkers theorize broadly about the extent to which people who may or may not be like them can identify or need to identify with a global moral community. Whether they do this by drawing on an Enlightenment tradition in which reason remains resolutely unencumbered by bonds of home *or* a Burkean tradition that ties virtue to the "little platoons" of home, their own subjective position remains untroubled.[46]

By contrast, Said's exilic subject begins their analysis of the world from the perspective of loss; that is, from the position that the ground on which they stand, critique, and theorize is not the home with which they identify, a home to which they can never return or fully occupy but for which they continue to feel deeply. This sympathetic, attached and detached, perspective, as Said demonstrates in *After the Last Sky*, necessarily generates a disruptive mode of questioning nestled in the fundamental question, "Do we exist? What proof do we have?"[47] The perspective of the exile in the world, Said argues, is thus structured by a tendency to evaluate current experiences "*as if* they were about to disappear" and thus to query experiences by asking, "What would you save of them, what would you give up, what would you recover?"[48] In other words, beginning from loss, from a sense of insecurity about one's own relationship to place and to memory, prods into being modes of reflection that open up identity, politics, culture, and theory itself to contestation.

Because exilic critics begin from a place of instability rather than closure, Said maintains, they are less likely "to derive satisfaction" from compensatory affiliative connections—from "substitutes furnished by illusion or dogma, whether deriving from pride in one's heritage or from certainty about who 'we' are."[49] They are thus more likely to ask questions about the world that differ significantly from those of settled cosmopolitans and their critics, questions that boil down to "What do *we* owe to others, and what enables or prohibits *us* from identifying with those others?" Rather, the exilic intellectual who begins from the unstable ground of wondering, "Do we exist? What proof do we have?" begins by questioning the very category of the "we" itself. Such a perspective queries the affiliative connections that naturalize the categories of "us" and "them" in a global context perennially constructed and disrupted by the lingering and ongoing effects of imperialism. It interrogates the history whereby "we" came to be "us" in relation to "them" in the first place.

Thus, when oriented toward those same problems of global injustice that preoccupy cosmopolitans, an exilic perspective is more likely to invert the question "What do 'we' owe others?" and to ask instead, "How, in a world framed by histories of violence and colonial dispossession, extraction, domination, encounter, and connection did 'we' become 'us'?" As such, it pushes the question of identification—and all the subsequent questions of distribution, justice, reparations, obligation, and intervention that flow from it—inward, backward, and outward, toward a deeper investigation of the current moment. It explores those affiliative connections between culture, politics, domination, forgetting, and collusion that, when woven together, set the stage for the current international institutions, norms, and legal regimes that cosmopolitans like Thomas Pogge believe "enhance the fulfilment of human rights."[50] An exilic inclination reorients the object of theoretical concern away from the shivering, starving, bomb-throwing masses of the world ("them") toward a frank investigation of how they came to be "them" in the context of "us." Looking at the world through the lens of exile entails seeing the current configuration of global politics—the "us" and the "them"—in Said's words, "not simply as they are, but as they have come to be that way."[51]

The disruption of identification—and thus of affiliation—that is so essential to Said's exilic approach has implications, I argue, for political theorizing beyond the "cosmopolitan/global justice and its discontents" debates and, thus, beyond "the right versus the good" framing. It can, in particular, provide a much-needed counterweight to the philosophical move whereby political theorists respond to instances of clear injustice by theorizing from a settled place of identification, whether that place (and the affiliations that sustain it) is explicitly acknowledged or not. Beginning from "out of place" responds to the object of inquiry—the site of injustice and domination—by reframing the world as, in William Spanos's sympathetic rendering of Said's method, a "domain of questions rather than answers."[52]

My argument here is sympathetic to, but different from, that articulated by critics of the ideal theorizing that so predominates global justice scholarship in Europe and America today. Michael Goodhart, for instance, notes that most global justice theorists rely primarily on what he calls an "ideal moral theory" (IMT) orientation, with Rawlsian origins. Indeed, Goodhart argues, global justice theorists may argue among themselves about whether Rawlsian principles can be applied in a direct fashion to global politics (e.g., Beitz) or whether, as Rawls believed, they ought to be channeled through social groupings (e.g., Michael Blake), but they never question the universal applicability of this ideal theory, and they assume it can address global justice "without any particular difficulty."[53] The problem with this IMT approach, Goodhart continues, lies in its commitment to positively theorize something called "justice," against which "injustice" can then be determined. Most scholars of global justice today, Goodhart argues, believe that "injustice can only be conceived as the absence or opposite of justice" and, they then insist with Rawls, there is "no other way" to adequately respond to injustice than by positively theorizing justice.[54]

For thinkers committed to this IMT methodology as defined by Goodhart, an approach that fails to fully clarify justice in philosophical terms can only ever be terrifyingly relativist. As A. John Simmons puts it, "to dive into nonideal theory without an ideal theory in hand is simply to dive blind, to allow irrational free rein to the mere conviction of injustice and to eagerness for change of any sort."[55] Goodhart, by contrast, argues that this attachment to a positive theory of justice elevates philosophy and morality *over* politics, over lived political experiments with solutions, with practices of solidarity, with multiple forms of resistance emerging from actual sites of global and local contestation, *rather than* from the realm of ideal theory.

I am in full agreement with Goodhart's argument and to the principled gauntlet he throws at the feet of this powerful mode of approaching global justice that has dominated political theorizing about international politics since the 1970s. At the same time, as a Said-inspired exilic critique of the cosmopolitanism and its critics reveals, both ideal and nonideal theorists (i.e., both liberal and communitarian, Enlightenment and conservative, normative and "grounded") share an assumption: that, underneath it all, lies identification with place. In other words, much political theorizing today either assumes the foundation from which the theorists' unhampered reason takes flight *or* assumes the theorist takes identification with place as the source of morality itself. Whether explicit or tacit, this identification sense sets parameters for the kinds of questions that scholars ask about political life by effectively freezing people and place in the moment in which the subject theorizes: What do "we" (First World subjects) owe "them" (the global poor)?

The limitations of this approach—the narrowing of its epistemological and conceptual parameters—persists even for political philosophers like Pogge, who approach global inequality from a position he calls "ethical cosmopolitanism" that takes seriously the "common and very violent history through which the present radical inequality accumulated."[56] In other words, for Pogge, because the wealthy nations of the world still benefit from the unequal distribution of resources generated over centuries through imperialism, richer states have an ethical duty to help poorer states financially. And yet, Pogge's attachment to the subject in place—to the cosmopolitan subject attached to the First World, speaking to other subjects in the First World, about solutions intended for the Third World—precludes any prolonged investigation into imperial history itself. The history of imperialism may set the stage for Pogge's analysis, but it plays an oddly small role in his actual theory. His philosophical solution to the global maldistribution of resources remains resolutely presentist and untouched by the actual *details* of imperial history or the way specific policies of extraction, slavery, land dispossession, and resistance evolved and circulated in various colonial contexts and continue to evolve and circulate through the discursive, political, and economic connections between the formerly imperial and postimperial world today.[57] The question is always "How do we make this right?" not "How did we get here?" Or "How might knowing how we got here change our reaction to the present"? Or "How is it that the 'we' for whom I theorize is in a position to determine how to make this right?" Or "How has the identity of the 'we' for whom I theorize been shaped by its relationship with 'the other'?" Or "How might previous experiments with remedying global poverty generated by activists from both the global North and the global South serve as inspiration for my theory now?" Or "How might the experiences, perceptions, theoretical orientations, history of resistance, and political desires of people throughout the global South impact the texture of 'our' response to the legacies of colonial injustice today?"

This presentism attached to the subject in place affects even those forms of political theorizing that profess to think in more capacious terms about identity itself and about the relationship between identity, pluralism, multiculturalism, sovereignty, and justice. In this next section, I explore an example of such an approach, Iris Marion Young's application of "self-determination as non-domination" to Palestine-Israel. I compare it to Said's exilic orientation toward the same subject. Ultimately, I argue, the disruptive and destabilizing quality of Said's critical disposition exposes the co-constituting narratives of imperialism and shared history that lurk in the background of Young's approach to identity in the region. It also reveals avenues for justice and coexistence that a more settled reading of identity fails to see.

## A METHOD FOR THINKING

Despite the normatively ascriptive title, Iris Marion Young's 2005 article "Self-determination as Non-domination: Ideals Applied to Palestine-Israel" attempts to marry a framework for guiding "thought and action" (what she calls, "self-determination as non-domination) with a robust, multicultural concern for the relationship between national/ethnic/religious identity and place.[58] Young's goal in this piece is to challenge the idea that the "self-determination" of peoples should be based on "non-interference." With Said, Young believes that the "unequal relations of interdependence" between

Israelis and Palestinians today result from a history "of unjust domination that should be recognized" but that, she argues, cannot be "completely undone."[59] Therefore, attempts at separate statehood ("self-determination as non-interference") simply replicate the already-existing forms of exclusion and apartheid. Young thus argues that rather than ground a recipe for self-determination on the assumption "that peoples are separate or separable," anyone interested in justice and peace today should consider reconceptualizing self-determination more generally in a way that acknowledges the overlapping interconnection between groups that "dwell together in territories." For Young, it is essential to forefront the fact that the "activities of those in one group often affect the possibilities of action for others."[60]

Young's hope is that an alternative approach that privileges "non-domination" rather than "non-interference" can pry open political thinking to alternative modes of coexistence that acknowledge the "dense interrelation" of Israeli Jews and Palestinians by creating a "number of smaller and dispersed Palestinian and Jewish-identified units" with equal rights, brought together in a loose federal system.[61] Her argument is thus extraordinarily interesting not only for the way it reimagines the political landscape of Palestine-Israel but also for the way it highlights the moral and political complexity and limitations of sovereignty as non-interference. It does this by allowing for a more flexible conception of the relationship between identity, self-determination, and place.

What Young never does, however, is question the fixity of identity itself. In other words, her argument starts from the presumption that Palestinians, like other "traditional," indigenous people, understand their own identities in relation to "particular locales."[62] The goal of self-determination as non-domination, Young continues, is to both account for this feeling of identity in place and combine it with a normative vision of federated sovereignty. Palestinian and Jewish communities, she imagines, would occupy the same large, federated state, but these communities would be considered autonomous units, and the political relationships between these units would be construed in such a way as to give expression "to the self-determining desires of those peoples."[63]

But this is where her approach becomes somewhat static. Young has acknowledged that Israeli Jews and Palestinians have been a part of each other's histories for a very long time, but she doesn't seem to believe that this historically "dense interrelation" could have any impact on the development of either group's sense of identity over time *or* impact the way they think about each other now. Jewish and Palestinian peoples simply *are* for Young and the goal of political theory is to provide a way for them to coexist "together in difference."[64]

"Self-determination as Non-domination" thus inadvertently flattens the identities of both Palestinians and Israelis and obscures their conjoined historical development. Missing, for instance, from Young's account is sustained engagement with dominant Zionist discourses about Palestinian Arabs that circulated during the mandate period and provided substantial ideological justification for the dispossession of Palestinian land, both before and after 1948. These discourses explicitly constructed the Palestinian people as nomadic and/or lazy natives who were either not terribly attached to the land or (as with predominant nineteenth-century framings of indigenous people in North America) were passing out of history anyway, ultimately and tragically doomed to disappear.[65] Young's oddly ahistorical account of Palestinian and Israeli identity in this article fails to acknowledge the rhetorical environment in which the modern state of Israel was created, an environment in which Zionists and colonial administrators worked to generate narratives about Palestinians as a people without place, a people unable to explain their own cultural stories because they have been, in Said's words, denied "permission to narrate" those stories.[66] In this way, Young's article inadvertently replicates the Orientalist rhetorical move by which Palestinians are simply *known* in their entirety—"recorded and systematized" by imperialists, journalists, political leaders, peacemakers, and political theorists alike.[67]

Young's analysis may acknowledge the "dense interrelation" between Palestinians and Israelis, but in the end, the density of that interrelation has little impact on her understanding of either groups' evolving identities over time, nor does it take into account the ideological environment around identity construction in Palestine-Israel today. As with both most mainstream cosmopolitan theory and that of its critics, identification with community and with place seems to linger in the background of Young's theory *even as* she strives to think in more complicated ways about self-determination and coexistence. This same tendency, Cristina Beltrán argues, is apparent in Young's work more broadly. Thus, even as Young commits herself in *Justice and the Politics of Difference* to the "laudable effort of replacing an exclusionary meaning of difference with an emancipatory one," Beltrán maintains, she remains wedded to an understanding of community that is hesitant to trouble the internal coherence of group identity, particularly those comprised of marginalized subjects.[68] For Beltrán, Young appears reluctant "to grapple with these subjects' more ambiguous agency," in particular, "their capacity for disciplinary exclusions."[69] The theoretical model that Young "applies" to the future coexistence of both Israelis and Palestinians ("self-determination as non-domination") rests on a similar assumption of internal coherence that masks power relations within and across the two communities, despite their fraught histories, internal and shared.

Said, by contrast, approaches the situation in Palestine-Israel from the unresolved and unsettled perspective of exile—a perspective that, in this case, is personally invested in the politics and identity narratives of the very region he analyzes. He thus assumes that the relationship between power politics and identity formation is fraught and dynamic, that the politically imbricated and internally complicated nature of the "dense interrelation" between Arabs and Jews in the land of Palestine-Israel has had lingering, transformative, trauma-tizing effects on the nature of both groups' senses of self and senses of "the other." This dispositional tendency to disrupt the very identities at the heart of his own experience and at the core of the politics with which he engages, has a number of effects on both Said's analysis of the relationship between identity and power politics in the region and his approach to identifying a "just peace."

First, Said argues more generally that dominant political and cultural nar-ratives can have a profound impact not only on the way marginalized and oppressed groups are seen by others but also on the way these groups experi-ence the world and themselves. For instance, he argues in 1988's "Identity, Negation, and Violence," political narratives about powerful identities in history—for example, "America is a force for good in the world"—tend to resist both historical and factual contestation. Attached to hegemonic states and populations, these deflective narratives routinely come up against the resistance of obdurate peoples like the Viet Cong, the Sandinistas, and the Black Panthers, whose political claims (indeed, whose very existence) call attention to the historical facts and contemporary political formations that belie the seamlessness of that narrative.[70] The dominant discursive response to such disruptions is often to pathologize resistant groups, to frame them as dispositionally irrational and illegitimate, caught in the grips of an extremist indecency that places them at odds with democracy, pluralist coexistence, and peace itself.

The identity-in-history narrative of Israel as a democratic bastion in an irra-tional and arid Arab landscape is similarly dominant, Said argues, and simi-larly deflective, relentlessly configuring and reconfiguring Palestinians as antidemocratic extremists, prone to violence and irrational religiosity, while simultaneously denying them permission to narrate their own experiences. These narratives—coupled with the unwillingness of much of the world to simply hear them—has had lasting effects on Palestinians themselves. In a context where there are "no acceptable narratives to rely on," Said argues, and "no sustained permission for you to narrate, you feel yourself crowded out and silenced." These silencing "processes of identity enforcement," Said continues, are likely "to produce rejecting, violent, and despairing responses by groups, nations and individuals whose place in the scheme is perforce inconsequential."[71]

In Palestine-Israel, Said continues, such "processes of identity enforce-ment" have influenced the evolving relationships between Arab Palestinians and Israeli Jews and simultaneously helped shape their understanding of themselves and each other. For Said, this imbricated history means that any approach to self-determination that treats identity groups as if they are linear reflections of people in place (e.g., Young's assumption that "traditional" and indigenous peoples have direct and uncomplicated relationships with the land) will fail to fully confront the ideological complexity of identity formation, the historically constitutive relationships between identity groups, and the fraught political terrain on which such self-determination is meant to unfold. And while it would be a mistake, Said continues, "to ascribe all the problems" in Palestine-Israel "to this maelstrom of escalating identity demands," it would also be a mistake to ignore that maelstrom altogether.[72]

Second, for Said—whose support first for a two-state and then a one-state solution in Palestine-Israel combined activism on the part of the Palestinians with a sympathetic compassion for the historical suffering of the Jewish people and their legitimate presence in Israel—"processes of identity enforcement" in the region have always been overlapping and mutually reinforcing, and it is necessary to treat them as such. In particular, he insists, these two communities are connected by suffering. In 1997's "Bases for Coexistence," for instance, Said argues that the "sheer enormity" of what happened to Jews in Europe between 1935 and 1945 "beggars our powers of description and understanding."[73] Reading the history of Nazi genocide, he continues, "with comprehension and compassion" also means understanding that the "distortions of the Holocaust created distortions in its victims which are replicated today in the victims of Zionism itself, that is, the Palestinians."[74] Said goes on to clarify that his goal in tracing these distortions is never to argue for a moral equivalence between "mass extermination and mass dispossession." It would be "foolish," he maintains, to even try such a thing. "But," he continues, these experiences—these two histories, these two evolving identities— "*are* connected" in the struggle over Palestine.[75] "The injustice done to the Palestinians," Said thus argues, is not ancillary to but *constituted by* "these two histories," as well as being the "crucial effect of Western anti-Semitism and the Holocaust."[76]

Reading identity and the dense interrelation of the victims and the victims' victims on the land of Palestine-Israel as connected by suffering was, for Said, part of interpreting the circumstances of the present, "not simply as they are, but as they have come to be that way."[77] His insistence on approaching politics, culture, and activism from this unsettled and interrogative position means that his understanding of the current injustice—the ongoing dispossession of Palestinian land, the violence and apartheid of Israeli annexation policies, the corrupt self-absorption of the Palestinian Authority—and its "solution" looks distinctly different not only from those of theorists like Young, who have tried their hand at addressing the situation. It also differs from the way political theorists often approach concepts like justice, democracy, or "the political" more generally through reconciliation and closure: Dallmayr's desire for resolution, for instance, Cocks's search for an alternative to the nation-state, the cosmopolitan/global justice fixation with providing fully articulated theories of justice. In essence, trying to understand Said's approach from the position of an academic field whose response to political problems is often to theorize resolution or provide philosophically coherent alternatives to political, cultural, economic injustice on a global and local scale can be a challenge, particularly because most of the time, Said's writings about Palestine resist precisely the kinds of meta-interpretive explanations that are so central to the field as a whole. Said's work on Palestine dwells not at the level of methodology but rather *in the fray*: in the actual politics of injustice; in the lived political narratives of identity making; in the visceral discursive landscape where activism, rhetoric, and "solutions" all circulate through the realm of a power politics that understands claims about injustice and justice to be, in Goodhart's terms, "ideological claims."[78]

Occasionally, however, Said steps back and elaborates his methodological orientation toward justice in Palestine, as he does in a piece he wrote toward the end of his life for the edited volume *What Is a Just Peace?* The overall goal of this diverse collection of essays, as explained by the editors, is to provide a counterbalance of sorts to the long, continuously re-energized philosophical debate about "just war." Despite the prolix nature of that political/philosophical endeavor, they argue, "surprisingly little conceptual thinking has gone into what constitutes a peace that is a just one."[79] The various contributors to the volume all seek to address this problematic from a variety of intellectual perspectives. Said's response to the question is different from all of them and is captured in the very title of the chapter: "A Method for Thinking about Just Peace." This "method," Said notes, requires approaching the subject itself as a "series of reflections rather than a string of assertions or affirmations." It therefore begins at precisely the point where "most peace-making efforts normally stop."[80] In other words, most approaches to peace-making, he argues, reach their conclusion when they've established which geographic and/or political arrangements are presumed most fair and best able to achieve peaceful coexistence.[81] Peace-making in this key, imagines that the goal is first to identify the communities to be divided and then to establish the relationship of these communities to the land and to each other, to create fair processes for negotiation, to identify a system of fully articulated political and human rights that will connect them, and, potentially, to devise a scheme for dealing with acknowledgment, truth, and reconciliation.[82]

Said, however, begins his analysis from a place of disrupted identity; that is, from the exilic assumption that the ground on which he stands is unstable, that history and time can change one's perception of place and self, and from a conviction that the "reality of simultaneous voices" is a constant feature of life in a contemporary landscape that bears all the traces—present and remote—of imperialism, racism, and dispossession.[83] None of this means that Said was not, again in Dallmayr's words, "particularly concerned" with the distinctiveness of Palestinian life. Throughout his career, he wrote about Palestinian art, Palestinian cinema, Palestinian culture, and the existence of a distinctly Palestinian Arab community on the land before Zionism. Indeed, for Said, engaging with Palestinian distinctiveness was necessary to Palestinian survival and necessary to counteract the Orientalist logic behind traditional historiographies that portrayed pre-1948 Palestinian culture as barbaric, nomadic, and on the natural verge of civilizational extinction. As he puts it in "Invention, Memory, and Place," perhaps the greatest challenge faced by the Palestinians as a people "has been over the right to a remembered presence and, with that presence, the right to possess and reclaim a collective historical reality."[84] And yet, at the same time, Said resolutely refuses to essentialize Palestinian identity. He also insists that the Jewish experience on the land is not only meaningful on its own terms but also *part of* that identity. The simple fact, he insists in "A Method," is "that Jewish and Palestinian experiences are historically, indeed organically, connected: to break them asunder is to falsify what is authentic about each."[85]

Said thus grounds his method in the conviction that Palestinian and Israeli histories—and the historical development of their identities throughout the twentieth century—must be approached "together, contrapuntally," because neither of these identities and histories is a "thing in itself, without the other."[86] In other words, most people committed to finding some form of just solution to the conflict in Palestine-Israel approach it as if the current tensions, dispossessions, and separations capture the essence of the situation. We are, Said notes, "perpetually at the starting point, looking for a solution now, even as that 'now' itself bears all the marks of our historical diminishment and human suffering."[87] Such presentist approaches both replicate the historical "amnesia" of imperial history and foreclose the contrapuntal connections between the two communities. Rather, for Said, Palestinian and Israeli identities have co-evolved through the unfolding colonialist logic of the mandate period, the mass immigration of displaced Holocaust survivors from Europe, the Palestinian exodus of 1948, the 1967 war, the first Intifada, the rise of Hamas, the establishment of the Palestinian Authority, the ongoing land dispossession, and the brutal geographic incising and settler colonial dispossession that continues to this day. The historical trauma of dispossessed Palestinians is hopelessly entangled with the historical trauma of Jewish Holocaust survivors, which means that for Said, there is a basic irreconcilability between Zionist claims to the land and Palestinian dispossession. Thus, the way forward, for Said, must remain attentive to the living past, to Palestinian silence, and to how peacemaking in the "now" often deflects attention from a deeper interrogation of the very affiliative connections that naturalize the circumstances of the present.

But beginning from a compassionate, exilic place of disruption that assumes a maelstrom of escalating identity demands and co-constituting, contrapuntal histories also means assuming the "dynamic and developing nature" of a just peace itself. For Said—speaking as both a Palestinian exile and a scholar of imperialism—a just peace must, by necessity, reject solutions that artificially freeze in place the imbricated, riotously polyphonous identity communities that emerge from the prolix process of imperialism. Turning to the history of Ireland, Said notes that for hundreds of years, Britain "had accustomed itself to seeing Irish people as savages deserving death or permanent servitude." In 1921, after decades of resistance and insurrection, peace negotiations that included partition eventually did take place between the British and Sinn Féin. "The position of each side varied accordingly," Said argues, and the different strategic styles of each that emerged in the process of these negotiations reflected not merely the Irish people's "traditional" connections to the land or the British people's presumptions about civilizational superiority, but also, the actual lived history of connection, coexistence, and exploitation— "suffering, poverty, dispossession, forced settlement, famine, and the like"— between them.[88] Whatever we call a "just peace" in Palestine-Israel, Said thus argues, it must reflect the changing complexities of the two communities' shared history; it must be a "fluid, rather than a stable, concept."[89]

Assuming that a just peace is fluid rather than stable, Said maintains, also means privileging the long-term possibility of an "emergent composite identity based on that shared or common history, irreconcilabilities, antinomies and all."[90] Such a composite identity, he argues, resists attempts to shoehorn Palestinians and Israelis—these "two communities of suffering"—into fixed categories. Rather, it begins from a position that accepts the "overlapping and necessarily unresolved consciousness of Palestine-Israel through its history."[91] Beginning with an acceptance of both overlap and irresolution— rather than from an attachment to *Sittlichkeit* or an identity in place—means assuming that emerging, composite identities will refuse both assimilation and what Dallmayr refers to as the "erasure of boundaries between self and other."[92] Said argues instead that composite identity is not the end goal itself but only part of the "extremely long-term project" that is a just peace, a project that requires work, openness, ongoing effort, and a subjective commitment to something that looks very much like what James Tully refers to as "epistemic humility."[93] In other words, as Said describes it, the long-term project of a just peace assumes that it is possible for Israelis and Palestinians to construct a "composite identity" in which "the other" is understood to be both "valid but incomplete as usually presented" and to acknowledge that, despite their conflicts and antinomies, their histories "can only continue to flow together, not apart."[94] Importantly, Said acknowledges, this fluid project must accept the "crucial role of education" in challenging the "constitutively bellicose" and Orientalist "clash of civilization" narrative.[95]

A just peace, Said thus insists, "does not bring quiet and the end of history at all, but rather a new dynamic," a living engagement/entanglement with identity and place that fully engages both the injustices committed against Palestinians and the historic injustices of the Holocaust.[96] And if one begins from this place—from a place that privileges an unresolved method for thinking about the overlapping histories of Arabs and Jews on the land of Palestine-Israel rather than running to resolve conflict, to clarify identity, to articulate a solution right now—it is also necessary, as Said argues in 1999's "The One-State Solution," for members of each community to treat the existence of the other as a "secular fact" that "has to be dealt with as such."[97] Beginning from any position that regards either groups' relationship to the land as effectively transcendental or essential creates the fundamental problem of choosing between origin stories. Does one go back, Said wonders, to the Old Testament or to the Golden Age of Islam or to the pre-1948 period? Any of these choices, he continues, has the potential to lead to "exterminism or separatism." Rather, for Said, beginning from an unfixed position that accepts the contrapuntal histories of Jews and Palestinians as a secular fact ultimately requires a secular solution: the creation of a unitary state grounded in the Right of Return for both Jews and Palestinians and in the "rights and institutions of common secular citizenship, not of ethnic or religious exclusivity."[98]

As I discuss in the introduction, Said's position on the preferability of the one-state over the two-state solution changed over the course of his life, becoming particularly obvious, in his mind, after the unraveling of Oslo. But, ultimately, through his years of writing, activism, and bitter experience, Said came to the conclusion that if you begin with a method for thinking about a just peace that takes the historically complex and interconnected relationship between Jews and Palestinians seriously, then the possibilities of a unified state emerges as the most feasible among a number of political solutions. Likewise, any plan that begins from a place of separation reproduces "abridged memory, conflict, apartheid."[99]

The fact that Young so completely and emphatically rejects the possibility of the "one-state solution" has much to tell us about her approach to identity. Even though she is attentive to the "shared problems" of Palestinians and Israelis, even though she acknowledges the "dense interrelation" between the two communities, her argument proceeds *as if* Israeli Jews and Palestinian Arabs inhabit communities that are effectively *sui generis*. Young thus argues that the creation of a single, secular state in Palestine-Israel is undesirable because it necessarily fails to adequately address the internally coherent identity needs of Jews and Palestinians. Her belief that this is true appears to be based on an unstated assumption that communal identity is fixed and that this fixity necessarily translates into the desire for a self-determination that will enable the expression of that identity. "Peoples, such as the Jewish people and the Palestinian people," she therefore concludes, "have a legitimate claim for a social and political means to govern themselves in their own ways and to enact public expressions of their history and culture as a people." The "humanist vision" of a secular state, she continues, "conflicts with these goals."[100]

But Young's argument here assumes that the identity goals of the Palestinians and Israelis are known to them entirely, accepted by everyone, fixed in the present, and unchanging. Their identity needs now will be their identity needs in the future. Such an understanding—which Beltrán sees as one of the "problems with unity" that haunt Young's work—does not comport with the actual history of the region and the "dense interrelation" of Jews and Palestinians on the same land. By contrast, Said argues that if our method for thinking about a just peace is committed to understanding Palestinian and Israeli identities not just as they are "but as they have come to be" in the context of "shared or common history, irreconcilabilities, antinomies and all," then secular coexistence presents itself as the best option. Moreover, Young frames her reasons for applying "self-determination as non-domination" to the situation in Palestine-Israel as a means to "guide thought and action" by wresting "political imagination away from unexamined assumptions," thus enabling a "critical distance from existing facts, so they can be better evaluated."[101] But ironically, it is precisely her move toward closure—toward providing an alternative model for living together in difference that is critically distant from context—that occludes options for coexistence, options that potentially bubble up from the complicated multicultural, multiethnic, multireligious historical facts of Palestine itself.

Said, by contrast, begins his method for thinking by resisting the need to theorize from the precarious cusp of the "now," resisting resolution, and resisting the foregrounding of alternatives with which to guide action and thought. With Young, Said believes in the necessity of "critical distance," but that distance springs from the detached attachment of exilic loss rather than the imposition of normative models to "guide thought." Thus, while Said's exilic disposition observes from a distance, it is also connected—through memory, through community, through activism, through critical engagement, through love of a home lost—to a world of multiplicity and to the "reality of simultaneous voices." The exilic momentum of Said's method pushes us away from our unacknowledged/untheorized assumptions of identification toward an unhoused perspective where we can observe politics and culture not just as problems to be solved but as a "series of reflections" to be engaged.

On the one hand, Said's unsettled exilic disposition illustrates how imperial processes in the history of Palestine disassociated evolving Zionist narratives from historical context, from the "institutions, agencies, classes, and amorphous social forces" of the mandate period that continue to contribute to an environment where Palestinians are still denied permission to narrate their own experiences. On the other hand, this dispositional openness toward connection and history also gestures toward historical examples of meaningful coexistence on the land that is now Palestine-Israel, examples that suggest different modes of being in the present. As Said puts it in 1999's "The One-State Solution,"

> Palestine is and has always been a land of many histories; it is a radical simplification to think of it as principally or exclusively Jewish or Arab. While the Jewish presence is longstanding, it is by no means the main one. Other tenants have included Canaanites, Moabites, Jebusites and Philistines in ancient times, and Romans, Ottomans, Byzantines and Crusaders in the modern ages. Palestine is multicultural, multiethnic, multireligious. There is as little historical justification for homogeneity as there is for notions of national or ethnic and religious purity today.[102]

Such a vision should not be confused with a vague multiculturalism that celebrates difference, that depoliticizes identity by subsuming subaltern citizens into liberal, neocolonial norms. Rather, Said's reading of Palestinian pasts and futures—his insistence on emphasizing the "co-creation" of modern Palestinian and Israeli identities—neither rejects the power of identity nor trivializes its liberatory impact on anticolonial politics.

Instead, Said argues that anticolonial politics, by virtue of the discourses, histories, and power constellations that shape the imperial life world, must think critically about identity *even as* anticolonial movements mobilize identity for liberatory purposes. Fanon and Césaire, he argues in his earlier "Representing the Colonized," understood the need "to abandon fixed ideas of settled identity and culturally authorized definition," even in the midst of nationalist struggles. For both men, he continues, the point of wrestling with identity is to "become different . . . in order that your fate as colonized peoples can *be* different."[103] Likewise, thinking about a just peace through Said's contrapuntal lenses ultimately invites partisans—both Israelis and Palestinians—to imagine the future not from a fixed "certainty about who 'we' are" but from the possibility that "we" and "the other" have been—and can be—otherwise.

# LOSS, DISCLOSURE, AND FUTURE

In a 1984 article, "The Future of Criticism," written to commemorate the passing of literary theorist Eugenio Donato, Said argues that there is an "urgent and irreducible bond between what critics do and who they are, and this bond cannot otherwise be reproduced, codified, or transmitted as 'criticism' *tout court*."[104] For some political theorists, however, it is precisely the lack of codification, reproducibility, and, most importantly, reconciliation and resolution in Said's approach that make his work so frustrating. And yet this frustration, I believe, somewhat misses the point of the exilic disposition that Said works up through the "cluster of flowing currents" that birth his exilic perspective. The uncomfortable paradox of loss reveals a world of critical vistas and conceptual landscapes on which to investigate and interrogate hitherto obscured affiliative connections. Such an orientation toward global justice, for instance, might recast the question "What do we owe others?" in the same way that Said recasts the question of Palestine-Israel: not as a "string of assertions and affirmations" but as a "series of reflections."[105] These reflections, as Said describes them in "The Future of Criticism," reveal "non-dominative and non-coercive modes of life and knowledge" that seek not to "apply" normative frameworks but rather to think through connections, in the past, present, and future. Indeed, these modes of knowledge are, Said insists, "essential components of the desired future."[106] They open up our political horizons to richer notions of justice, self-determination, and coexistence while upending the "we" that theorizes and the "they" on the receiving end of that theorizing.[107] They suggest paths for criticism that begin from unsettled ground and gesture toward different ways of living and coexisting. They suggest modes of thinking, not about how, in Hagar Kotef's words, "one side can triumph, but how the space can be shared in just and nonviolent ways."[108]

So important did Said believe this disruptive, unsettled, self-reflective mode of life and knowledge to be that he urged scholars who had not experienced the ravages of exile to adopt it. Chapter 5 examines in greater detail the problems and promises of Said's controversial commitment to exile as a "*metaphorical* condition," an orientation that he locates squarely within his equally emphatic commitment to the political praxis of public intellectualizing. First, however, the next two chapters explore the broader critical and political horizons that exilic instability reveals. "Most people," he argues toward end of "Reflections on Exile," "are principally aware of one culture, one setting, one home." Exiles, however, are "aware of at least two, and this plurality of vision gives rise to an awareness of simultaneous dimensions, an awareness that—to borrow a phrase from music—is contrapuntal."[109] Chapters 3 and 4 delve more deeply into the complexity of Said's contrapuntal vision and the related concepts of worldliness and humanism. I argue that his "awareness of simultaneous dimensions" provides a model for political theorists interested in ungluing theory from its indwelling foundation, its tendency to enclose and delimit politics and "the political." Instead, a critical perspective influenced by Said asks us to think more capaciously about an orientation toward critique that pulls the "intertwined and overlapping histories" of the colonizer and the colonized from the margins to the center, jettisoning the "solid self" and embracing the "cluster of flowing currents" that make exile what it is: always becoming and never become.

# 3

# Into the Language of Music

## *The Colonizer and the Colonized Together*

Three years before his death in 2003, Edward Said sat down for an interview with two professors of geography from CUNY Graduate Center, Cindi Katz and Neil Smith. Not surprisingly, many of the questions they asked during this fascinating conversation concerned Said's field-transforming approach to the spatial politics of culture and imperialism. At one point, however, Katz poses what might seem to be the slightly incongruous question of an academic geographer: "How does music," she asks Said, "work for you spatially?" Said responds immediately. One of the reasons he had long been drawn to the work of pianist Glenn Gould, he notes, is Gould's "geographical realization of music," his ability to perform a "contrapuntal scheme" like a Bach fugue "so that you can actually see it on different levels."[1] This spatial-visceral quality of performance, Said argues, transforms something that looks clear-cut and temporally progressive on the page (a Bach fugue) into an embodied space one occupies and experiences on multiple levels.

Music, he continues, thus resists the "ordinary solicitations of argument," the way it "goes from a to b to c to d and then you're home." Rather,

> Sometimes it's a rhythmical question that might settle the issue, at other times it's a tonal question, a question of timbre, different kinds of organizations all of them leading me constantly into the language of music. And searching for an answer I know can't ever come, but there's a kind of tension between music and sound, you might say, that's permanent, which is deeply interesting to me.[2]

The tension Said describes here—between music and sound, between multiple voices, between tone and timbre—resists progressive narratives and transforms flat annunciation into inhabited space. And it is precisely through this language of music that Said also expresses his critical strategy of reading culture, power, and imperialism contrapuntally: as the interplay of "various themes" with "only a provisional privilege being given to any particular one." In the "resulting polyphony," he continues, "there is concert in order, an organized interplay that derives from the themes, not from a rigorous melodic or formal principle outside the work."[3]

The impulse toward counterpoint in Said's thought is related—on multiple, braided levels—to the "habits of life" inimical to exile, although in some ways, they would seem to exist in contradiction. For the exile, he argues, the expressions and activities of everyday life "occur against the memory" of things experienced "in another environment," the one lost and left behind. Thus, for the exile, "both the new and the old environments are vivid, actual," expressing themselves in a manner that is both perennially disruptive and, Said insists, sometimes uniquely pleasurable, even necessary.[4] In other words, exile is an unsettling mode of life experienced "outside the habitual order," whereas counterpoint, in the musical terms Said uses to describe it, implies organization, concert, and—as captured in the score of a Bach fugue—order.

But this is where Said's description of Gould's performance is so helpful. As anyone who has ever listened to a recording of Gould's *Goldberg Variations* knows, while the variations themselves may be known, Gould's experimentation, his barely audible vocalization underneath the melody, the tension between music and sound opens up vistas for the listener to occupy, see, and feel, even though the expressions of those feelings and visions—the way Gould picks up and puts down various modes of invention each time he performs—can't be anticipated. And yet there is an order there. It may not exist in "formal principles" rigorously imposed on the work from the outside, but the variations themselves—the changes in tone, timbre, or rhythm that settle and unsettle—these *are* the work. In essence, you can't always know how and when contrapuntal voices will connect, but you do know that eventually they will.

Similarly, when thinking critically about text, culture, and politics, Said assumes that the world itself is the work. And this work, as nearly the entirety of his scholarship suggests, is affiliatively connected through imperialism. In Said's words, the "great imperial experience of the past two hundred years is global and universal; it has implicated every corner of the globe, the colonizer and the colonized together."[5] But, as in contrapuntal music, this global, "imperialist ensemble," he argues in *Culture and Imperialism*, lacks an "overarching theoretical principle" of governance.[6] It is, rather, "fissured" throughout with domination and resistance, with multiple "interdependent histories and overlapping domains," and with the "continuous history of struggle."[7] Imperialism, Said insists, is a "contested and *joint* experience" and must be treated as such.[8]

Thus, in Said's mind, a "global, contrapuntal analysis" should be modeled "not on a symphony but rather on an atonal ensemble." We must reject univocal accounts of history, culture, and politics and, instead, "take into account all sorts of spatial or geographical and rhetorical practices—inflections, limits, constraints, intrusions, inclusions, prohibitions—all of them tending to elucidate a complex and uneven topography."[9] The "plurality of vision," he continues, that can sometimes flow from the ungrounded, exilic experience, is particularly suited for identifying and analyzing the myriad contrapuntal affiliations that sustain and enliven this complex world. As he notes in his introduction to *Culture and Imperialism, if you are an exile, you often belong to "both sides of the imperial divide,"* which enables you *"to understand them more easily" and to see beyond the "defensive little patch" of one's own culture to "some sort of whole"—albeit a qualified, fissured, atonal whole, forged through the contested experience of imperialism.*[10] Not surprisingly then, Said focused a sizable portion of his inquiry in *Culture and Imperialism* on scholars and intellectuals from the global South who were often, but not always, "exiles, expatriates, or refugees and immigrants in the West," thinkers who crafted counternarratives of resistance that treated "non-Western and Western experiences as belonging together" because, at the end of the day, like an atonal ensemble, "they are connected by imperialism."[11]

This chapter begins with a detailed exposition of Said's contrapuntal mode of criticism through an analysis of the text in which he develops the concept most fully, 1993's *Culture and Imperialism*. It then examines how Said's thoughts on the relationship between contrapuntal criticism and the historical continuity of anticolonial resistance influenced his account of both Foucauldian poststructuralism and academic Marxism by engaging some Marxist critiques of Said's own approach. The third section explores Said's understanding of counternarrative resistance, focusing on his reading of Fanon's more "integrative view of human community and human liberation," which, he argues, involves a "transformation of social consciousness beyond national consciousness."[12] I conclude with some thoughts on Said's approach to "critical practice as a form of resistance" in a world fundamentally and inescapably shaped by imperialism.[13]

## CULTURE AND IMPERIALISM

Said elaborates the concept of counterpoint most fully in 1993's *Culture and Imperialism*, a book that, with *Orientalism, assumes imperialism and colonialism were/are never simply collective acts of acquisition, accumulation, and domination. Rather, imperialism and colonialism are enhanced and supported—sometimes even impelled—by complex ideological formations that assume "certain territories and people require and beseech domination, as well as forms of knowledge affiliated with domination."*[14] These ideological formations rely on a complex chain of signifiers to both identify and instantiate differences between the colonizer and the colonized: *subject races, dependency, developed, expansion, authority.* Like *Orientalism,* the book also interrogates the continuity of such ideas over time and the way these ideas continue to influence the politics of the contemporary world. Before we patronizingly dismiss Joseph Conrad's attitude toward native autonomy in *Nostromo* as a product of his times, Said thus cautions, it would behoove us to note that similar attitudes continue to haunt the logic of the foreign policy establishment in Washington. Imperialism "did not suddenly become 'past'" once decolonization ended, Said insists, and the power makers in today's global hegemon are just as likely to represent foreign "others" as strange, violent, and beseeching of domination as were their explicitly imperial progenitors in Britain and France.[15]

*Culture and Imperialism,* however, differs significantly from *Orientalism* in its emphasis on the "dynamic global environment" created by imperialism.[16] It is, in essence, a book that goes beyond an analysis of domination's relationship to Orientalism and imperialism. Instead, it engages in a multileveled reading of the complex relationship between domination and resistance. Said's augmentation of his original thesis follows his intellectual and political development after 1978. Indeed, as Gauri Viswanathan points out, one of the most striking things about Said as a scholar, thinker, and activist was his willingness to revisit "arguments made in his books and essays not merely to defend and elaborate on them but, more important, both to mark their limits and probe their extended possibilities, especially in contexts other than those which first gave rise to them."[17] Throughout the 1980s, Said listened to and engaged with critics of *Orientalism,* like Aijaz Ahmad and Robert Young, who argue that the book elides accounts of anticolonial resistance, that in focusing so entirely on domination at the expense of anticolonial struggle, Said was ultimately unable to wrest himself, in Young's words, from the "coercive structures of knowledge that he is describing."[18] Said's decision to engage deeply with anticolonial resistance in *Culture and Imperialism* is a testament to the way he was willing to challenge and "travel" with his own theory.

This is particularly apparent in Said's changing and conflicted attitude to Foucault and poststructuralism. Again, Said played a critical role in introducing Foucault's theory to American academics in the early 1970s, but this initial appreciation for Foucault's approach, as Karlis Racevskis puts it, "was not to last." Most scholars like Racevskis argue that Said's "growing disenchantment with Foucault's thinking" became apparent in the "many essays he wrote and the interviews he gave over the years following the publication of *Orientalism*."[19] And yet, one can see quite clearly Said's irritation with certain aspects of Foucault's work from at least the early 1970s. In 1971, for example, he was already arguing that the biggest problem with Foucault's approach is its failure to "account seriously" for the forces of change that propel the development of one epoch to the next. "It is as if," he continues, "like nuclear elements with an assigned half-life, periods simply live and pass off, leaving their place to be covered up in the same slot by other periods."[20] Said expanded this critique in the early 1980s, taking Foucault to task for his mono-focus on the *effects* of disciplinary power rather than on resistance to that power. By Said's lights, Foucault' unwillingness to fully analyze resistance and resistance movements rendered him, at best, a mere "scribe of domination" and, at worst, a co-conspirator with the status quo.[21]

And yet, Said's own relationship to Foucauldian criticism was far more complicated than his disapproval would suggest. In *Orientalism* and elsewhere, Said interrogates the profuse forms of disciplinary knowledge (circulating through text, art, philosophy, theory, narrative, and culture broadly construed) that sustained civilizational and developmental readings of the East. To develop this analysis, he drank deeply and with gusto from the well of Foucauldian criticism, arguing in *Orientalism* that without Foucault's approach, "one cannot possibly understand the enormously systematic discipline by which European culture was able to manage—and even produce—the Orient."[22]

How do we square Said's reliance on a Foucauldian analysis of power with his simultaneous critique of Foucault for his failure to address resistance and change? Some scholars insist that you simply cannot. Ahmad, for instance, argues that Said's commitment to both dispositions means that his work is "self-divided," plagued throughout by a basic, unsettling irreconcilability between modes and schools of thought.[23] Other detractors insist that Said was never truly committed to a Foucauldian approach and that his turn to it in *Orientalism* is purely situational, "utterly, even boringly, symptomatic and indicative" of the Left's turn toward poststructural analyses in the wake of 1968.[24] But as Leela Gandhi argues, Said's embrace of Foucault can itself hardly be reduced to a derivative symptom of a disappointed era. Rather, she contends, both his fascination with, and criticism of, the conceptual tools of poststructuralism was prompted, in part, by a desire to expand the critique of Western metaphysics generated from *within* the West *beyond* the West and, in the process, to demonstrate the complicity of Western metaphysics itself with the violence of the "civilizing mission."[25] In Gandhi's sense, Said's use of Foucault should also be read as an immanent critique of poststructuralism's unacknowledged attachment to a potentially imperializing universalism.

Throughout the 1980s, in "Traveling Theory" and other works, Said expanded his critique of Foucault by refocusing his own analysis on both the historical durability of anticolonial resistance over time and the challenge such resistance poses to "master narratives" of power that can never fully contain the "essential untidiness" of history.[26] As a text, *Culture and Imperialism* is devoted to exploring what it means to read culture and power, not in the context of one, overarching theory of domination, but rather, through the "dynamic global environment" created by imperialism.[27]

Counterpoint provides Said with the perfect critical metaphor to capture the dynamism of that global environment. A classically trained musician who wrote extensively about music, Said references counterpoint in his earliest writings, from his ruminations on the performance of Glen Gould to his later explorations of the exilic experience in "The Mind of Winter" and "Reflections on Exile," both of which were published in 1984.[28] It is in *Culture and Imperialism*, however, that Said truly develops the concept, describing a contrapuntal world shaped by imperialism as the polyphonous interplay of "various themes" with "only a provisional privilege being given to any particular one," a "concert in order" derived "from the themes" themselves, "not from a rigorous melodic or formal principle outside the work."[29] Said thus cautions against approaching the "cultural archive" associated with the West—its literature, philosophy, histories—as the univocal efflux of one, unsullied source flowing, unaltered, into the world, touching and reshaping the inert cultures of the non-West along the way. Rather, he urges his readers to approach these archives contrapuntally, "with a simultaneous awareness both of the metropolitan history" narrated by Western authors and "those other histories against which (and together with which) the dominating discourse acts."[30]

Reading culture contrapuntally thus means starting from the assumption that, for at least the past several hundred years, the cultural productions we associate with "the West"—its literature, philosophy, art—has evolved dynamically and organically alongside and in relation to an expanding imperial geography. Again, for Said, while no single overarching theoretical principle governed this imperialist ensemble, the "great experience" of imperialism ultimately implicated nearly every culture and society on the globe, "the colonizer and the colonized together."[31] Said's goal in *Culture and Imperialism* is to reconnect power, culture, and imperial experience while reading texts from "the West" and from "the peripheries" together in a manner that upends the all-knowing, universalistic gaze associated with those European and Orientalist assumptions that help sustain empire. Approaching culture contrapuntally implies jettisoning the privilege of associating "'objectivity' to 'our side'" and "'subjectivity' to 'theirs.'"[32] In a nutshell, reading culture contrapuntally, for Said, means treating the histories of the West and the non-West (or the global North and the global South) as integral parts of each other's becoming.

*Culture and Imperialism* does this by working at three different but interrelated levels of analysis. First, through an analysis of imperialism's impact on the culture/politics *of* the West itself. Second, through an investigation of the culture/politics produced by intellectuals and activists who moved back and forth between the metropole and the periphery—a phenomenon Said terms the "voyage in." And third, through an analysis of the historical longevity of anti-colonial resistance and its relationship to migrant and hybrid cultures.[33] At every level, Said examines the intersection of power, domination, culture, writing, and resistance, exploring their overlap with one another, following the deeply unpredictable, layered quality of the atonal ensemble that is imperialism. At every level, these connections suggest that colonial domination, colonial resistance, and the shared experience of both are deeper, richer, and infinitely more complicated than hegemonic narratives of "Western civilization," civilizational improvement, or economic development would suggest. Furthermore, for Said, at every level, reading domination and resistance together has explicitly political implications for scholarship and criticism.

Said is thus very intentional in the way he takes the relationship between Europe and the colonial world as a "point of entry" for studying Western cultural practices. The cultural archive of the West is neither, Said insists, *sui generis*, forged either from the raw material of pure expression transformed by inspired savants into "inviolable masterpieces," nor sewn from a cultural fabric woven over generations from the filiative attachments of a perfectly coherent (and superior) tradition. Rather, expressions of art, philosophy, and culture and the associated political and legal regimes presumed to constitute "Western culture" writ large should be read, Said insists, as always imbricated with the historical fact of imperialism—that is, in light of Europe's extended contact with, and domination of, the colonial "other."[34] Thinking in this way about European culture means abandoning a "simple causality" between Europe and the non-European world, wherein the relationship between culture and empire is understood to be instrumental and sequential.[35] For instance, as Said argues, just because Jane Austen and Charles Dickens wrote works related to empire *before* Britain's imposition of the Raj in 1858 does not mean that these works *caused* the transition to indirect rule. Rather, both texts reflect and legitimize certain aspects of imperial politics and culture and do so in complicated and subtle ways that, at the time, helped broaden the ideological horizon on which Britain's expanding nineteenth-century empire could unfold.

Said's contrapuntal reading of Austen's *Mansfield Park*, for instance, illustrates not only how the events in the novel rely materially on Britain's plantation economy in Antigua but also on the interpellation of plantation authority into the Bertram estate through Sir Thomas's treatment of the novel's young protagonists. Here, Said argues, Austen "synchronizes domestic with international authority" in a manner that makes apparent "that the values associated with higher things such as ordination, law, and propriety must be grounded firmly in actual rule over and possession of territory."[36] Thus, *Mansfield Park* not only connects the "actualities of British power overseas to the domestic imbroglio" at the core of the novel, but it also demonstrates how ideas about dependent territories and subject races were broadly normalized during this era, diffusing beyond the realm of colonial administrators to touch on the world of "novel-readers educating themselves in the fine points of moral evaluation, literary balance, and stylistic finish."[37] Thus *Mansfield Park*, with other texts of this genre, "unobtrusively" opens up what Said calls a "broad expanse of domestic imperialist culture" that makes intuitive sense out of Britain's ensuing territorial, political, and economic expansion.[38]

Additionally, a contrapuntal perspective like the one Said describes looks not only for material connections (e.g., the presence of the sugar economy within the novel's narrative structure) and internal resonances (e.g., between domination in the Caribbean and domination on the Bertram estate) but also discrepancies and elisions. For instance, making contrapuntal connections "between coronation rituals in England and the Indian durbars of the late nineteenth century," Said argues, entailed a willingness to think through and "interpret together" discrepant experiences, "each with its particular agenda and pace of development, its own internal formations, its internal coherence and system of external relationships, all of them co-existing and interacting with others."[39] Kipling's novel *Kim*, Said notes by way of illustration, played a very particular role in the development of the Victorian novel in England, but the picture it paints of India in 1900 "exists in a deeply antithetical relationship" with the actuality of life in India and the development of the independence movement there. That discrepancy—between the rhetorical power of Kipling's *idea* of India in the metropole and the actual political and cultural texture of the independence movement—is important for understanding the cultural ensemble of empire. Representing and interpreting the novel and the movement in abstraction from each other, Said argues, "misses the crucial discrepancy between the two given to them by the actual experience of empire" and thus misses something crucial about the experience of imperialism during this period.[40]

Because *Kim* is an imperial novel written to represent India to men and women in Britain, it is also important to note its many "suppressions and elisions."[41] Conspicuously absent, for instance, are any signs of Indian social and political creativity or autonomy, any whiff of rebellion, or anything that would trouble the Orientalized vision of India as sublimely placid and immutable. Similarly, interpreting Camus's essays and novels as "interventions in the history of French efforts" to make and keep Algeria French, tells us substantially more about his writing and Camus's "state of mind" than if we read them—as does, for instance, Michael Walzer—as the agonized, internal musings of one man's inability to come to terms with love, justice, and the "brutality of colonialism."[42]

Said's move here, to place texts like *The Stranger* and *Kim* in their colonial contexts and read them for both discrepancies and elisions, is not unlike the move by scholars of the history of political thought today to reconsider many of the great canonical texts of European political philosophy in light of these theorists' involvement with imperialism, settler colonialism, and slavery. Consider, for instance, David Armitage's and Herman Lebovics's different but equally important revisiting of John Locke's *Two Treatises of Government* in light of Locke's relationship to both the idea of America and to the actual Carolina Colonies. Both readings not only significantly enhances our understanding of Locke's theory of ownership and labor, but they also offer enormous insight into both patterns of late-seventeenth-century colonial capitalism as well as broader liberal assumptions about property accumulation.[43] Hence, like Said, both Armitage and Lebovics treat the "relationship between the 'West' and its dominated cultural 'others'" as a "point of entry into studying the formation and meaning of Western cultural practices themselves."[44]

Crucially, Said's contrapuntal analysis both resembles and predates much of the political theory work that emerged in the 1990s and early 2000s that reintegrated the history of empire with the history of European political thought, work authored by the likes of Uday Mehta, James Tully, Jennifer Pitts, Sankar Muthu, Duncan Bell, Karuna Mantena, myself, and many others. In some ways, Said's approach in *Culture and Imperialism* both anticipates this shift in the historical study of political thought and pushes beyond it by insisting that texts associated with "the West" be read contrapuntally alongside anticolonial texts about the same region and the same history. He argues, for instance, that we ought to read Camus's assumptions about and incorporations of Algerian history in conversation with anticolonial texts about the same region written at the same time or after independence. Reading Camus and Abdallah Laroui contrapuntally, for instance, fills in the material and psychological reality of an apartheid-like occupation that structured the everyday lives of so many Algerians, a reality that remains largely in Camus's peripheral vision. Through Said, we get a clearer sense of the rhetorical *work* these absences do for Camus's narrative: the questions they elicit, the questions they repress, the subjectivities they create and occlude.[45] This Algerian perspective, Said argues, "may unblock and release aspects hidden, taken for granted, or denied by Camus."[46]

This means that, for Said, interpreting the presence of colonialism and imperialism in the cultural archive of the West also entails reading "the colonizer and the colonized together." If, he argues, "French and Algerian or Vietnamese history, Caribbean or African or Indian and British history are studied separately rather than together, then the experiences of domination and being dominated remain artificially, and falsely, separated."[47] Bringing these experiences together requires the reader not merely to approach "histories written by Algerians" as supplements to enhance and complexify the work of scholars like Camus (or Locke). It also requires a more conceptually disruptive commitment to reversing the directionality of the imperial gaze by analyzing the movement, integration, reception, and impact of thinkers from the colonial world who "write back to the center," in Salman Rushdie's words, rather than stand at the windowsill of the West petitioning to be heard.[48] In essence, like listening to one of Gould's *Goldberg Variations*, it requires engagement with the whole atonal, imperial ensemble *rather than* just simply following the melodic intention of the metropole where it takes us on the historical page.

Given his affinity for the reflective, wandering attributes of exilic subjectivity, it is hardly surprising that many of the thinkers on whom Said focuses in *Culture and Imperialism* were exiles, refugees, or immigrants: scholars, thinkers, students, and activists like C. L. R. James, Frantz Fanon, and Aimé Césaire, who moved between the periphery and the metropole and back again. From their complex, embedded, and distanced—attached and detached—positions, these intellectual activists, Said argues, made a "conscious effort to enter into the discourse of Europe and the West, to mix with it, transform it," and "to make it acknowledge marginalized or suppressed or forgotten histories."[49] The writings of these authors, Said thus insists, cannot be described as merely the "reactive assertion of a separate colonial or native identity" forcefully expressed against a coherent metropolitan identity.[50] Rather, both the content and directionality of their thought—and their own subject positions—were much more complicated from the very beginning.

Approaching the scholarship and artistic production of these thinkers contrapuntally rather than univocally, Said maintains, requires a re-orientation toward both the idea that the metropoles into which they ventured were somehow unaltered by non-European cultures *and* the idea that the texts they wrote represent authentic, native responses untouched or unstructured by the connective tissue of imperialism. Rather, for Said, when James, Fanon, and Césaire sojourned into the heart of the empire—into Paris, into London—they found these spaces were *already* abuzz with the political, artistic, and intellectual activity of communities from the periphery, communities who were busy shaping the cultures of the metropole but whose impact on those cultures has been largely ignored by mainstream historians. For example, Said, notes, most histories of European modernism simply omit discussion of the "massive infusions of non-European cultures into the metropolitan heartland" during the early years of the twentieth century, despite the obvious influence they had on artists like Picasso.[51] These mass infusions of "large-scale mass movements" spilled over from the colonial periphery into the center, establishing beating hearts of anticolonial activity within the belly of the imperial beast itself and helping sew connections between the artistic and political movements that played a vital role in what Said terms the "global history of modernism." As testament to the living political and cultural power of these transnational communities, Said points to the way FLN fighters often referred to France as the "Seventh Wilaya"—the other six understood to constitute "Algeria proper." In this manner, he argues, was the "contest over decolonization" relocated "from the peripheries to the center."[52]

Said's contrapuntal approach transforms how scholars interpret the "imaginative geography" of imperialism. It does this by highlighting the *movement* of anticolonial thinkers between colonial contexts permeated by immigration and political mobilization. In this reading, no longer do the European and "the other"—the "here" and the "there," "our" culture and "theirs"—exist in suspended animation, separated by a developmental and temporal logic of civilization that works its way into common sense and imagined divisions. Rather, Said insists, it is important to understand that by the time Fanon, Césaire, and James journeyed into their respective metropolitan societies for an education—societies that largely believed themselves to be "homogenously [W]hite and Western"—these metropoles were already being altered by migrant communities from the colonies.[53] From the waves of non-White immigration within the British Empire that so terrified Edwardian liberals, to interwar Paris's emergence as the "center of African diasporic intellectual production," to those countless Indian students at the London School of Economics whose connections to each other and to radical thinkers like Harold Laski would have an enduring impact on postcolonial politics in India and Africa, to France's status as the Seventh Wilaya, the actual cultural and political flows of imperialism consistently belied the purity and primacy of Western civilizational narratives.[54] Thus, the writings produced through the "incursions" of Fanon, Césaire, and James into the metropole—their "voyage in"—are concerned with the "*same* areas of experience, culture, history, and tradition" that had, Said argues, been hitherto understood as the pristine, unaltered province of the metropole.[55]

Provincializing European imperialism in this fashion, for Said, reveals that history never runs "unilaterally" from north to south, west to east, becoming "more sophisticated and developed, less primitive and backward as it goes."[56] Rather, as Said's gorgeous exposition of James's *The Black Jacobins* demonstrates, imperial history takes place within a great, contrapuntal ensemble of connections and divisions reflected in James's own complicated relationship to the culture he critiqued, expanded, assailed, and reimagined. Thus does

*The Black Jacobins* move, with chilling, terrifying alacrity, between visceral images of the middle passage, to the complicated class politic of the San Domingo settlers; to the beginnings of revolt, to Toussaint's intimate borrowing from the language of French liberty found in Rousseau, Raynal, and Diderot. The text is its own contrapuntal ensemble, written from within a culture of protest and resistance and, perhaps not surprisingly—given Said's fascination with counterpoint in musical performance—written as a play originally intended for Paul Robeson, who ultimately appeared in a London production, alternating the Toussaint and Dessalines characters with James himself.[57]

For Said, scholar-activists like James and the Lebanese historian George Antonius addressed the colonizing world "from within it," and on cultural grounds, "they disputed and challenged its authority by presenting alternative versions of it, dramatically, argumentatively, and intimately."[58] In other words, James wasn't just writing a better, truer history of France, Haiti, and the West Indies. He wasn't just filling in blank spaces that had been hidden or suppressed by Western historians—although he was doing that, too. Rather, through his writing and activism, James *bridged* "Caribbean, specifically Black, history on the one hand, and European history on the other," creating new, argumentative, discursive links between the two histories that he then interpreted through the ongoing struggle for African and West Indian liberation.[59]

Thus, for Said, treating "non-Western and Western experiences as a belonging together because they are connected by imperialism" meant more than reading parallel sets of texts—Western and non-Western—alongside each other. It also specifically meant situating these texts and connections within the history and unfolding context of anticolonial resistance that, Said emphatically highlights, was an enduring and continuous feature of imperialism. As he makes clear in a 1993 interview about *Culture and Imperialism, all the great resistance movements of Africa, Asia, and Latin America*

> traced their history back to the first people who resisted the [W]hite man coming. There's a continuity of resistance. For example, the Algerian FLN which defeated the French and achieved independence in 1962, saw themselves as continuing the resistance begun in 1830 by Emir Abd el-Kadar in Algeria. They saw themselves as part of the same history. That's what I was trying to show. There's a continuous history of struggle. Imperialism is never the imposing of one view on another. It's a *contested and joint* experience. It's important to remember that.[60]

Said stresses the continuity of anticolonial resistance—from Abd El-Kadar to the FLN—in order to emphasize the "contested" nature of the colonial experience. Highlighting contestation, he argues, challenges both the "linear and subsuming" narratives associated with Orientalist and civilizational narratives of progress as well as contemporary academic and social science accounts of "development" that similarly locate progress and movement in the West alone, transforming the rest of the world into passive recipients of Enlightenment discourse. It is still the case that dominant political and social science interpretations of anticolonial movements too often view these movements as sporadic, local responses to the long unfolding of European rule *or* as derivative mass phenomena that mimic European ideas of liberation.[61] This is not, however, how the relationship between the colonizer and the colonized played out in reality, Said argues. It was never the case, he maintains, that the imperial encounter "pitted an active Western intruder against a supine or inert non-Western native; there was *always* some form of active resistance, and in the overwhelming majority of cases, the resistance finally won out."[62]

Said's analysis in *Culture and Imperialism* and elsewhere thus highlights how imperialism, as a cultural and political assemblage, was always deeply fissured by the "overlapping" experiences of and relationships between protest movements in Africa, India, and "elsewhere in the peripheries" and within metropolitan cities themselves, spaces and connections wherein the "incorporative, universalizing" logic of imperialism was challenged and disassembled.[63] Often participants in these movements developed transnational connections to participants in other parts of the world, sewing networks of resistance, shared literatures, political and narrative strategies, and modes of reading and writing against domination.[64] Activists involved with "Home Rule" movements in India, Ireland, and Egypt, for instance, were in lively conversation with each other throughout the nineteenth and into the early twentieth centuries in ways that shaped and transformed these movements and their goals.[65] Likewise, the Pan-African Congresses of the early twentieth century and the 1955 Bandung Conference in Indonesia (attended by twenty-nine newly independent states from Africa and Asia) were explicit testaments to the networks of transnational organization and solidarity between anticolonial resistance movements in the mid-twentieth century.[66]

In sum, the process of decolonization Said describes was staggeringly diverse, complex, and interwoven, involving "different histories and geographies," different groups of individuals and activists, different modes of political resistance ranging from revolutions to strikes, marches to retaliation, "retribution" to "counter-retribution."[67] Reading imperial history through these generative networks of resistance and these multiple histories challenges unidirectional accounts of culture and power that naturalize domination on a global scale.

Moreover, Said's contrapuntal reading of decolonization and imperialism situates domination and resistance on the same discursive and political landscape by again integrating rather than sequestering these histories. In other words, the process of decolonization was shot through with both the interventions of colonial officials—writing "about the nature of the Indian mentality" or the "land rent schemes of Bengal"—and the extant responses of anticolonial intellectuals and public figures who appealed to publics within their own communities to expand their influence and mobilize for independence.[68] Moreover, Said argues, while the timetable of resistance varied historically from region to region, ultimately, the great decolonization movements of the twentieth century fundamentally transformed the domestic politics of newly liberated states, their relationships to other nations in the postcolonial block, *and* the "internal situations" of states in Europe and the global North.[69] His contrapuntal approach to imperialism and resistance is, ultimately, a gauntlet thrown at the feet of universalist, Western narratives of human development, which tend to sideline both the history of anticolonial resistance and the impact of the colonies on metropolitan culture and politics.

The tendency to simply elide that contrapuntal history is still so prevalent in political theory as a field that it can even present itself in the work of political theorists who are explicitly interested in the imperial history of European political thought and European imperialism. Anthony Pagden, for instance, has spent his career writing close, genealogical excavations of the universalist responses developed by early-modern and modern European and American thinkers like Vitoria, Gentili, Pufendorf, and Grotius to the theological, legal, and political puzzles produced by imperial governance and occupation. His work often exposes the theoretical and political questions left unanswered in the work of these thinkers and then, through close investigation of context, traces these questions and ideas from one thinker to the next through history.[70]

At the same time, Pagden is also committed to reading a fairly unaltered version of Kantian thought (particularly with regard to human rights) into contemporary international politics, from the League of Nations to the European Union.[71]1 Thus, even as Pagden notes that the European Union is "confined to Europe," he argues that "it is a 'Europe' whose understanding of itself . . . is constantly expanding" and may in fact someday include its ancient enemy, Turkey.72 In one sentence, seemingly without noticing, Pagden makes the argument that the European Union—the apotheosis of Kantian thought in his mind—is evolving in a less Western, more open and inclusive direction, *as if* most international law from the nineteenth century onward had not developed within the context of a Europe that was *already* "expanding" its influence around the world through imperialism.

Additionally, Pagden's analysis of the contemporary European Union is stunningly silent about the "non-European" citizens and residents of Europe, many of whom are not recent arrivals but, as Said reminds us, longtime residents of the Continent, particularly of metropolitan cities.[73] He is also silent on the impact of anticolonial movements on the formulation of European international law itself and silent about the long-term impact of laws and institutions (such as the League of Nations' mandate system) that were intended to extend a version of imperial rule into the post-imperial age.[74] Pagden's unwillingness to challenge the coherence and contemporary relevance of a certain brand of Kantian-inspired, human-rights-oriented cosmopolitanism stands in stark contrast to much of his work on imperialism, which is sensitive to the contrapuntal complexities of historical context. At the same time, by both consistently privileging the Kantian ideal today and maintaining that it is "inescapably" the child of a "specifically Western belief in the existence of a single human nature," Pagden's work constricts political possibilities in the present, insisting with Habermas (whom Pagden quotes approvingly in the final lines of 2015's *The Burdens of Empire*), that "normatively speaking," there is no "coherent alternative" to Kantian cosmopolitanism today.[75] Said's contrapuntal sensibilities challenge this univocal orientation toward Kantian narratives by reading the history of the "West" and the "non-West" together because they are united by imperialism and resistance.

At the same time, Said argues that his contrapuntal approach poses a significant challenge to seemingly more sympathetic forms of analysis, namely Foucaultian poststructuralism and academic Marxism. At moments during his career, Said accused thinkers from both schools of ignoring racism and failing to be "reliable allies in the resistance to imperialism."[76] His criticisms, however, have not been without pushback, and as this next section explores, such responses open up particularly interesting sets of questions about both Said's method and his politics of resistance.

## CRITICISM AND THE IMPERIAL ENSEMBLE

Said develops his critique of Foucault most fully in 1982's "Traveling Theory," focusing on what he sees as the internalizing tendency toward self-reproduction at work in Foucault's theory of power. For instance, Said argues, Foucault's insistence that "power is everywhere" (in *Discipline and Punish*, *History of Sexuality*, etc.) has the somewhat-perverse effect of rendering power inescapable. In his "eagerness not to fall into Marxist economism," Said continues, Foucault dismisses and "obliterates" the role of class, economics, insurgency, and rebellion from his analysis.[77] The "disturbing circularity" of this theory of power—with its totalizing, weblike mechanisms and disciplinary effects—ultimately and ironically begins to mimic precisely the universalizing metaphysics *against which* it emerged in protest.[78] In the end, Said argues, Foucault's critique of power—draws a "circle around itself, constituting a unique territory in which Foucault has imprisoned himself and others with him."[79]

In "Traveling Theory" and elsewhere, Said takes Foucault to task for arguing from this conceptual prison. Foucault's satisfaction with delineating the effects of disciplinary power rather than theorizing the structural relationship between power and resistance, Said argues, makes him vulnerable to charges that he is either complicit with the status quo or an actual "scribe of domination."[80] For Said, the basic problem with Foucault's theory—what keeps it from transgressing the circle in which it is penned—is his failure to recognize that in history "there is always something beyond the reach of dominating systems, no matter how deeply they saturate society," no matter how entangling the disciplinary micro-networks.[81] Said is deeply frustrated with the way a theory that provides such a vivid explication of cultural hegemony, regulation, and power seems completely unable to account, in a colonial context, for the long-term historical existence of anticolonial movements and resistance cultures, both inside and outside Europe. The long-standing reality of resistance highlights, he maintains, the limitations of Foucault's thought.

Said's critique of academic Marxism similarly predates *Culture and Imperialism*. In *Orientalism*, for instance, he explores the ease with which Marx deployed such tropes as "Oriental despotism" and an "Oriental mode of production."[82] He is also extraordinarily critical of contemporary literary Marxists for declaring the "serious study of imperialism and culture off limits."[83] In 1982's "Opponents, Audiences, Constituencies, and Community," Said makes an argument similar to the one that he would eventually make most forcefully in *Culture and Imperialism*: that such Marxist theorists as Terry Eagleton and Frederick Jameson still all too frequently articulate their political analyses through a closed intellectual language so grounded in an internal logic that it becomes immune to the "extra-academic world outside."[84] In *Culture and Imperialism, Said extends this critique to the Frankfurt School, accusing them, too, of remaining "blinded to the matter of imperialism." "Frankfurt School critical theory," he argues, "despite its seminal insights into the relationships between domination, modern society, and the opportunities for redemption through art as critique, is stunningly silent on racist theory, anti-imperialist resistance, and oppositional practice in the empire."[85]

Amy Allen makes these exact words a point of departure for her own criticism of the Frankfurt School in *The End of Progress*, although as I explore in the introduction, the book then proceeds to largely ignore the substance of Said's own theory. It is strange, then, given the slightness of Said's presence in the book, that some political theorists have criticized Allen for what they see as her *overreliance* on, what Robert Nichols calls, a "basically 'Saidian' framework," which, for Nichols, has the unfortunate effect of mirroring the philosophical approach Said refutes.[86] According to Nichols, the core problem with Said's approach to imperialism—what he also refers to as a "Saidian formulation"—is that it understands imperialism itself primarily in terms of a "set of explicitly or implicitly held propositions about the world, especially about the universality or superiority of one's own way of life."[87] This formulation, he argues, relies too exclusively on the cultural "idea of empire" and not enough on the material and social processes that created and sustained this idea. As such, according to Nichols, both Said and Allen tend to privilege an *epistemological*—that is, cultural or ideal—explanation for empire over a material explanation. While Said, he continues, is "surely right" to argue that the "idea of empire" was necessary to European imperialism's political project, "it was surely not *sufficient*."[88]

While clearly sympathetic to both Said's and Allen's projects, Nichols still maintains that their excessive dependence on this ideas-based approach ultimately replicates (in reverse) critical theory's own "blithe universalism" and, as such, transforms the question of imperialism into a moral crusade aimed at "rooting out false claims that have normatively problematic consequences." In this reading, Said's version of an imperialism structured by discourse and culture is ultimately transformed into another dominant explanatory narrative—like Foucauldian poststructuralism, critical theory, and/or Western philosophy writ large. By contrast, Nichols argues, what we need to better grasp the scope and impact of imperialism is a "social theory" that has "better explanatory power" over the myriad material and social processes—with all their "tendencies and contradictions"—that vitalize imperialism.[89] Quoting directly from *Culture and Imperialism*, Nichols argues that, while he may be able to elucidate the contours of a world "united into a single interacting whole as never before," Said's theory lacks the critical capacity to *explain* the material and social processes that went into the creation of this whole.[90] For Nichols, by not grappling with social theory, Said's approach has the unfortunate effect of transposing the political question of imperialism into a moral question. In other words, from the perspective of this "Saidian formulation," some narratives about the world are judged to be truer than and normatively superior to false narratives, when in reality, imperialism involves such a "complex set of social processes" that it cannot be reduced to "for or against" propositions.[91]

Nichols, of course, is not the first person to argue that Said's approach transforms the relationship between "the West" and "the Rest" into an inverse of Enlightenment universalism, a parallel cosmos driven by a normative imperative to tell different, better, and truer stories about the world. Aijaz Ahmad spends a not inconsiderable amount of time in 1992's *In Theory*, making a similar critique of Said's method. Ahmad argues that Said's approach in *Orientalism* takes the relationship between the West and its "other" and creates a new interpretive axis to rival European high humanism. Said's formulation, he argues, not only replicates the universalism of the Western approaches that Said criticizes, but it also devalues the transnational character of class, privileges discursive interrogation over political economic analysis, and restricts anti-imperial critique to the realm of the textual.[92] From this perspective, Said simply shifts the register of criticism from one key to another—from class to discourse—thus reinforcing rather than deconstructing precisely the "doctrinal walls" he set out to challenge while simultaneously occluding the material "facts" of imperialism. These "facts," Ahmad insists, can best be accounted for by the "particular constellation of concepts" that Marxism provides.[93] Ultimately, with Nichols, his criticism suggests that Said's analysis is vulnerable to totalism and that his rejection of class for culture mimics the worldview he claims to challenge. Said, they both imply, never fully confronts his own universalism and the extent to which his method transforms culture into another aggregating vessel that contains the world.

Ironically, both authors end up articulating a criticism of Said that is, in some ways, exactly opposite the ones made by Dallmayr and Cocks and yet has many of the same features. In other words, both Dallmayr and Cocks suggest that Said's understanding of politics is finally hamstrung by his refusal to provide an ethical alternative to imperialism and domination other than unhoused movement and unsettling hybridity. Said's theory has, in this sense, no closure and, therefore, no politics. For Nichols and Ahmad, by contrast, Said's cultural theory of imperialism (posed in opposition to Western Enlightenment theory) constricts possibilities for material and social theories of imperialism. It is too closed, too epistemological, and therefore has no politics.

This leads Ahmad to reach conclusions about Said's intentions that are similar to those of Dallmayr. Both believe, for instance, that Said is only vaguely interested in non-Western culture and, specifically, in the communal life of Palestinian people. For Dallmayr, Said "does not seem particularly concerned with the distinctiveness of Palestinian traditions nor inclined to share or participate in their life-forms or religious beliefs."[94] Ahmad echoes these concerns, arguing that Said can only express his relationship to the political struggle for liberation in Palestine through the "lonely splendor of a representative" rather than an embedded participant.[95] And while it was written before the publication of *Culture and Imperialism*, Ahmad's *In Theory* uses a number of articles Said wrote after *Orientalism* to extend this same critique to Said's fascination with the anti-colonial "voyage in." Ahmad is troubled by what he sees as Said's preference for authors who wrote their anti-colonial texts in the context of privileged access to European cultural politics *in* Europe over authors who wrote their anticolonial texts while living and struggling in the colonies. For Said, Ahmad maintains, the "struggle against imperialism now simply does not take place in the countries that are actually imperialized" but is transformed into a "moveable feast and it goes where the experts go!"[96] Does Said actually want to engage anti-colonialism resistance from the peripheries, Ahmad's work suggests, or does he really just want an excuse to theorize high-humanist culture *in* the West *through* anticolonialism?

Said himself never makes any of this easy. In Ahmad's words, Said is notable for many things, including his "irrepressible penchant for saying entirely contrary things in the same text."[97] For Ahmad, this is most shockingly apparent in Said's near-simultaneous concern in *Orientalism* with the idea that the Orient has been misrepresented by the West and his Foucaultian-inspired conviction that there is no "Oriental essence" *to be* misrepresented.[98] Said acknowledges that his work is not consistent but never apologizes for it precisely because he believed theoretical "machines" failed to adequately capture ideological structures like Orientalism that rely on persistent *inconsistencies:* for example, the Arab who is both inscrutably wise and ignorant, violent and indolent, feminized and hypersexualized. Ahmad, however, tends to read Said's penchant for saying contrary things as a reflection of his elitism, an unwillingness to just articulate his own discomfort with resistance politics, and a smuggled-in desire for universal theory.

While one can, with Viswanathan, read Said's propensity to change his mind more charitably than does Ahmad, I think a better way to interpret the frustration of theorists who accuse Said of both not paying sufficient attention to social and economic theory and also remaining attached to a totalizing cultural worldview is to think of this critique in terms of a basic disconnect between *their* goals for theory and *Said's* goals for theory. In essence, for Ahmad and Nichols, Said does not pay sufficient attention to the social and political-economic causes of imperialism. Because his causal theory is incomplete, his vision of a world "united into a single interacting whole as never before" must be understood as totalizing in a manner that mirrors the imperatives and elisions of high European philosophy and the Frankfurt School's unfortunate orthodoxies.

I want to suggest, however, that arguing thus overlooks or underplays several key aspects of Said's approach, beginning with his desire to fill in some of the conceptual and historical gaps left by *other* social theories. For Said, "one of the main flaws in the enormous literature in economics and political science and history about imperialism" was precisely the fact that "very little attention has been paid to the role of culture in keeping an empire maintained."[99] In this light—and in relation to the extant body of scholarship on imperialism—Said's putative lack of concern with social and material theory makes considerable sense. Moreover, as I take up further in chapter 5, transforming Said into someone for whom culture is the prime mover of imperialism requires his critics to excise multiple moments of sympathy and rupture in his writings where he demonstrates a clear affinity for Marxist and dialectical approaches. His observations about peasant life in Palestine, for instance, are couched in the explicitly Marxist language of alienation.[100] He is also quite clear that his critique of Marxism emerges *not* from some metaphysical dismissal of class and capitalism but rather from the unhoused, exilic qualities of his own subjective orientation and his discomfort with "-isms" of any kind.

Never once does Said dismiss the voraciously destructive and constructive quality of colonial capitalism, but rather, he routinely highlights the extent to which it was consolidated through the plantation system, through slavery, and through the relentless, grinding vortex of dispossession, expansion, and monopoly. His work is preoccupied with the way these original connections to colonial capitalism linger on in today's global economic and political environment. And while Nichols's critique seems to imply that a more appropriate title for *Culture and Imperialism* would be *Imperialism as Culture*, the *and* is actually important for Said. The relationship between culture and imperialism is contrapuntal and multivocal; one phenomenon cannot describe the totality of the other, and a concern for cultural analysis neither vitiates nor privileges material analysis. As Hamid Dabashi argues, Said's work can be used to flesh out the linkages between Orientalist configurations of culture and global capitalism, thus demonstrating the variety of ways by which his legacy today "can be extended into a decidedly Marxist direction, even though he himself was not a Marxist."[101]

Finally, and perhaps most importantly, by mapping Said's contrapuntal project onto a realm that resembles the metaphysical inverse of the Enlightenment project, his critics sideline the political imperative Said attached to an understanding of the world as one, contrapuntal ensemble, whose atonal resonances emerge from the history and contemporary reality of imperialism. In other words, there is indeed a "oneness" in Said's work—a reiterated claim that imperialism frames the world as "some sort of whole." This does not, I submit, translate into a metaphysical accounting of the world grounded in a set of normative propositions. Rather, while Said's understanding of counterpoint assumes that some hegemonic, narrative accounts of imperialism make it more difficult to identify the way imperialism actually operated in the world, he also thought that these same narratives suppress liberatory forms of politics and culture grounded in the substantive connections—material, cultural, and political—between human beings in the global North and the global South. These connections are often generated not only through imperialism's own history of violence and dispossession but also through the borrowing, innovation, shared experiences, shared practices, and shared resistances that imperialism engenders.

Thus, writing contrapuntal history—thinking and reading contrapuntally—is never merely about articulating a set of propositions that one is "simply for or against." Rather, the internally dynamic, atonal, hybrid, riotous circulation of culture and resistance within the contrapuntal ensemble means that the interpretive impulses of counterpoint have to be similarly multivocal and similarly atonal. In political terms, this means that because men and women in the global North and the global South "belong to the same history," if we chose to listen to just one theme from that complex ensemble—one history, one explanatory factor, one social theory—then we lost sight of the transformative potential that weaves its way through the shared whole.[102]

Reading imperialism as a contested and joint experience thus not only gives us insight into imperial domination and resistance in the past, but it also provides forms of narrative resistance in the present and for the future. Thus, while Jonathan Arac argues that contrapuntal criticism is "not itself narrative" but rather a "technique of theme and variations," there is also a way in which writing contrapuntal criticism becomes an act of *narrative* resistance in an age when the history of imperialism has been increasingly erased from narratives about global history.[103] Said calls these resisting themes "counternarratives," modes of retelling that envision the world otherwise. By examining, collating, and comparing texts and contexts as they emerge out of the unfolding imperial ensemble, critics identify patterns, expose alternative histories, reveal paths unseen, and moot possibilities for the future that would otherwise remain submerged and unarticulated. Generating counternarratives provides one way for the contrapuntal readers to puncture the "semi-official narratives that authorize and provoke certain sequences of cause and effect while at the same time preventing counter-narratives from emerging."[104] For example, one particularly common imperial sequence, Said argues, is the "old one," in which the United States—a "force for good in the world"—is forced to confront "obstacles posed by foreign conspiracies, ontologically mischievous and 'against' America."[105] The cause-and-effect sequence at work within this narrative transforms American military aid (in Vietnam, for instance) into a benevolent gift that is then refused by insurgents and terrorists. Writing narratives that trouble these "semi-official" imperialist sequences, Said argues in 1984's "The Future of Criticism," translates into what he calls "critical practice as a form of resistance."[106]

This counternarrative practice presents itself in multiple iterations throughout Said's work. In chapter 4, for instance, I explore how counternarrative plays an important role in Said's humanist commitment to "protect against and forestall the disappearance of the past." For the rest of this chapter,

however, I explore the role of counternarrative in Said's reading of anticolonial nationalist programs generated through the writings and expressions
of sojourning, migrant scholars like James, Césaire, and, most importantly,
Fanon. Their narrative visions of the world, Said maintains, simultaneously
disrupts the smooth skein of Western philosophy, highlights the need for
autonomy and liberation, and insists on the fact that the experience of imperialism is "really an experience of interdependent histories."[107] Produced by
thinkers invested both in anticolonial struggle and in the cultural archive
of the metropole, these counternarratives were not written to posit a set of
simple propositions that one is for or against. Rather, Said argues, James,
Césaire, and Fanon articulate forms of liberation and resistance—as well as
alternative-connective narratives of radical politics and human comity—that
reintegrate the contested and joint experience of imperialism into the atonal
ensemble of the world. Said is attracted to these narratives precisely because
they dovetail with his own political orientations. "I'm not a separatist," he
once explained in an interview. "My whole effort is to integrate areas of experience that have been separated both analytically and politically."[108] For this
reason, the historical counternarratives Said finds most attractive are oriented
toward disrupting analytical and political binaries generated *through* imperialism in order to transform a world connected *by* imperialism.

## RESISTANCE, COUNTERNARRATIVE, LIBERATION

In numerous publications and interviews from the 1980s onward—including 1986's "Intellectuals in a Post-colonial World" through the collection
of essays published in 2003 as *Humanism and Democratic Criticism*—Said
expresses an acute interest in the kinds of resistances that emerge from the
"holding and crossing over" between imperialism and anticolonialism.[109]
These modes of "liberationist anti-imperialism" advocated by thinkers like
Fanon, Césaire, and James, Said argues, use nationalist counternarratives to
explode the "shackling unity" of imperialist "master narratives" while at the
same time (or ultimately) rejecting nationalism. This "earlier generation of
resistance writing," he argues, was carried out "by dozens of scholars, critics,
and intellectuals in the peripheral world."[110] They channeled the "nomadic,
migratory, and anti-narrative energy" of exile, Said argues, into an "integrative
or contrapuntal orientation" toward history, culture, and politics, an orientation that expressed itself in historical counternarratives and critical accounts
of imperialism that challenged fixed doctrines and "encoded orthodoxies."[111]
Because they were so embedded in international and transnational dialogues
with others in anticolonial resistance movements, the works of Fanon, James,
and Césaire consistently point to the multiplicity of connections that exist

both between the colonizer and the colonized and among the resisters themselves. The very fact that imperialism is a contested and joint experience, ironically, then suggests possibilities for expansive, nondominative forms of political life and belonging in the future. In Fanon's political vision, for instance, Said found an "alternative way of conceiving human history" and a vision for the future based on a "more integrative view of human community and human liberation."[112]

Said uses a comparison of Foucault and Fanon—born a year apart, both educated in France—to illustrate this point. Both men, Said argues, were interested in thinking critically about the "problematic of immobilization and confinement at the center of the Western system of knowledge and discipline."[113] Fanon's work and his political program were, however, geared toward resisting colonial domination, and as such, his challenge to the "immobilization and confinement" of Western philosophy is embedded in a conceptually sophisticated description of the relationship *between* the colony and the metropole. These connections work at a variety of levels for Fanon: through the individual psyches of the colonized and the colonizer, through the economic system of racial capitalism and domination, and through the transference of wealth from the colony to Europe.[114] By contrast, according to Said, Foucault's intellectual interests lay in developing a "microphysics of power" rather than a "serious consideration of social wholes."[115] Instead of seeking out connections, Foucault's theoretical impulses circle inward, Said argues, away from critical resistance and solidarity.

Again, for Said, Foucault's analysis is vital. "More than anyone before him," he argues in a 1984 memorial article for *Raritan,* Foucault's work exposes those unconscious, unwritten "rules," whereby doctors and/or historians and/or administrators become "epistemological enforcers of what (as well as how) people thought, lived, and spoke." "If he was less interested in how the rules could be changed," Said continues, "it was perhaps because as a first discoverer of their enormously detailed power he wanted everyone to be aware of what disciplines, discourses, epistemes, and statements were *really* all about, without illusion."[116] Said is also aware of and sympathetic to Foucault's fascinating—if brief and rather late—interest in certain kinds of resistance, particularly the kinds of embodied "responses, reactions, results, and possible inventions" that "may open up" when we see power in relational terms.[117] But the point of such critical investigations, Foucault argues in 1982's "The Subject and Power," is not to understand resistance for resistance's sake but to use its "antagonisms" as a "chemical catalyst" through which to deepen our understanding of power relations, and this was never enough for Said.[118] By contrast Fanon, Said insists, understood resistance as both a critical catalyst and a political end. Thus, he concludes, while both Fanon and Foucault had "Hegel, Marx, Freud, Nietzsche, Canguilhem, and

Sartre in their heritage," only Fanon presses "that formidable arsenal into anti-authoritarian service."[119]

Said argues that Fanon's pushing of "Hegel, Marx, Freud, Nietzsche, Canguilhem, and Sartre" through the lens of colonialism and colonial resistance amounts to more than mere adaptation, more than the simple application of European thinkers in a colonial context. In an essay written shortly after the publication of *Culture and Imperialism*, 1994's "Traveling Theory Reconsidered," he pushes this idea further. He rejects arguments that suggest, for instance, that Fanon's theoretical apparatus in *The Wretched of the Earth* is "little more than a replication of Lukács, with the subject-object relationship replaced exactly by the colonizer-colonized relationship."[120] Rather, Said argues, Fanon uses the field of Algerian resistance and its suppression to fundamentally transform Lukács's "subject-object dialectic." In Algeria, Said argues, Fanon saw that the antinomies Lukács insisted were integral to the subject-object relationship under capitalism in Europe failed to adequately explain the subject-object distinction in the colonies. "In the colonies," Fanon explains in stark, concise terms, "the economic infrastructure is also a superstructure. The cause is effect: You are rich because you are [w]hite. You are [w]hite because you are rich."[121] Upon closer examination, Lukács's antinomies reveal less about transplanted forms of capitalist domination in Algeria than they do about the kind of history European thinkers *tell* themselves *about* themselves.[122] Fanon then broadens this insight, expanding his analysis of the fraught nature of colonial capitalism by paying particular attention to the role nationalism would play in both decolonization and anticapitalist struggles in the future.

The fact that Fanon's reading of Lukács evolves and transforms within a colonial context poses a challenge to "other worldly" theories (like Foucault's) that can ostensibly travel anywhere in the world but remain unchanged, that see the world and claim, in Said's words, to "account for everything."[123] In contrast, Said read in Fanon's transmutation of Lukács a direct attack on the "permanence of vision" so central not only to Orientalist modes of approaching "the other" and the developmentalist logic of social science but also to Enlightenment and postmodern approaches to power. Said's interpretation of traveling theory thus opposes "facile universalism or over general totalizing" while simultaneously exploring how theory's transformation through imperialism can generate new ways of imagining the world that go beyond "borrowing and adaptation." Fanon's rearticulation of nationalism's complicated dialectic via Marx and Lukács, for instance, challenges, reshapes, and refracts Lukács's theory in ways that reignite and reinvigorate what Said calls the "fiery core" of the original approach.[124]

Said is also profoundly moved by Fanon's "noticeable pull away from separatist nationalism toward a more integrative view of human community and human liberation."[125] However, he continues,

> I want to be very clear about this. No one needs to be reminded that throughout the imperial world during the decolonizing period, protest, resistance, and independence movements were fueled by one or another nationalism. Debates today about Third World nationalism have been increasing in volume and interest, not least because to many scholars and observers in the West, this reappearance of nationalism revived several anachronistic attitudes. In all these views, I believe, there is a marked (and, in my opinion, ahistorical) discomfort with non-Western societies acquiring national independence, which is believed to be "foreign" to their ethos.[126]

Thus, Said does not want his feelings about nationalism to be confused with what he sees as an essentially imperialist and/or Orientalist argument that understands "Western" nationalisms as circulating in a separate universe from "Third World" nationalisms and that identifies the problems of nationalism in the formerly colonized world with a misfit between Western and non-Western values. All cultures borrow from each other, Said maintains. Indeed, the history of most cultures *is* the history of borrowing.

Said's approach is in sympathy with Partha Chatterjee's argument about nationhood as a "derivative discourse."[127] For Chatterjee, the project of anticolonial nationalism is overdetermined from the outset by the fact that the nation-state itself—as a historical object and bounded form of political organization—was predetermined by European empires, a problem Gandhi identifies in 1910's *Hind Swaraj*, when he accuses his young nationalist interlocutor of wanting "English rule without the Englishman" or "the tiger's nature, but not the tiger."[128] There is thus, Chatterjee argues, an "inherent contradictoriness" in anticolonial and postcolonial nationalism "because it reasons within a framework of knowledge whose representational structure corresponds to the very structure of power nationalist thought seeks to repudiate."[129] Said agrees with Chatterjee about both the contradictoriness and the tendency for postcolonial nationalism to becomes a "panacea for *not* dealing with economic disparities, social injustice, and the capture of the newly independent state by a nationalist elite."[130] Too often, he argues, have anticolonial nationalist movements resolved themselves in this way.

With Fanon, however, Said refuses to reject nationalism completely. "I do not want to be misunderstood as advocating a simple anti-nationalist position," Said clarifies. It is a historical fact, Said continues, that assertions of national identity—the creation and emergence of new cultural and political practices—were hugely mobilizing and helped birth political struggles that ultimately led to decolonization. "It is no more useful to oppose that," he quips, "than to oppose Newton's discovery of gravity."[131] At the same time, he insists, we can identify within these movements historically strands of thinking that saw nationhood as both essential to and not sufficient for liberation in the long term. The form of resistance Said theorizes begins with nationalism but, once independence is achieved, insists that "new and imaginative re-conceptions of society and culture" are required "in order to avoid the old orthodoxies and injustices."[132] His appreciation for Fanon springs precisely from Fanon's impassioned articulation of these "pitfalls of national consciousness." "If I have so often cited Fanon," Said notes, "it is because more dramatically and decisively than anyone, I believe, he expresses the immense cultural shift from the terrain of nationalist independence to the theoretical domain of liberation."[133] In essence, Said is drawn to Fanon's writing for the way it captures the tensions of anticolonialism.

Said brings to his reading of Fanon the same exilic disposition he brings to so much of his work: a heightened appreciation of both what it means to be attached to a national community and what it is to experience ongoing, unquiet detachment from that community, to see the national ties that bind as a complex overlay of affiliative connections that structure and exclude. The exilic critic both knows and appreciates the necessity of belonging—particularly for marginalized, oppressed, and stateless peoples—and knows firsthand what it is to experience the retaliative violence and expulsive force of nationalism as it circles in and pushes out—as it binds, defines, and curtails. Said believes that, as a partisan and a traveler, attached and detached in his political inquiry and his passionate advocacy, Fanon was able to write back to the colonial, national, and anticolonial project in ways that simultaneously gestured toward the necessity of national identity, the ultimate limitations of nationalism as a political project, and the possibilities for a more inclusive liberation.

The "voyage in" that Fanon experienced, Said argues, allows for the development of political visions that "break down the tyranny of the dominant discourse" and reanimate and reconnect imperialism and colonial connection "in its positive dimension" as a differently configured form of "human history."[134] For Fanon, this is a two-part task: one aimed at the colonized; the other, at the colonizer. First, Fanon insists, having been so deeply affected by the radical alienation and "depersonalization" of colonial control, the colonized had to reassert themselves as valid subjects and explode the striated landscape of occupation and the "compartmentalized world" in which they had been penned.[135] "The famous dictum," Fanon maintains in the first chapter of the *Wretched of the Earth*, "Concerning Violence," "which states that all men are equal will find its illustration in the colonies only when the colonized subject states he is equal to the colonist."[136] Such a process entails both organization and self-transformation, a "collective self-criticism with a touch of humor because everyone is relaxed, because in the end we all want the same thing."[137] At the same time, by Fanon's lights, this kind of resubjecti-fication by subjects who have been so deeply dehumanized by the marginaliz-ing violence of the colonizer necessarily required violence. As Said describes it, violence for Fanon, is the "synthesis that overcomes the reification of [w] hite man as subject, Black man as object."[138]

For Fanon, however, overcoming this reification through the mobilization of anticolonial nationalism also leads to a series of disconnects within nation-alism that mirror disconnects within imperialism. In his analysis of chapter 2 of *The Wretched of the Earth*, "Spontaneity: Its Strength and Weakness," the musically attuned Said focuses on Fanon's analysis of the "time lag and rhythm difference" between what Fanon identifies as "the leaders of a nationalist party and the mass of the people."[139] In the process of copying their methods from Western nationalist parties, Said continues, "all sorts of tensions develop within the nationalist camp—between country and city, between leader and rank file, between bourgeoisie and peasants, between feudal and political leaders—all of them exploited by the imperialists." In this contrapuntal tension between the idea of nationalism and its experience—the tension between music and sound, as it were—Fanon identifies one of the core problems of anticolonial nationalism: a disconnect between advocates of official nationalist ideology and advocates of an unofficial nationalism who are often hounded, imprisoned, and silenced. Fanon's response, according to Said, is to highlight the impact of this underground party by dramatizing "its existence as a counter-narrative." The way Fanon draws attention to these counternarratives, Said continues, makes it more obvious for the nationalist that, in "breaking down colonial oppression he is automatically building up yet another system of exploitation" with a "[B]lack face or an Arab one."[140] Counternarratives thus shine a spotlight on a double-edged reality: that "racialism and revenge" cannot, in Fanon's words, "sustain a war of libera-tion." Or, as he puts it, the "battle against colonialism does not run straight away along the lines of nationalism."[141]

Said argues that, for Fanon, precisely because the colonizer and the colo-nized are connected through imperialism, the "huge task" of overcoming the reification of the colonized subject must ultimately involve "re-introducing mankind into the world, the whole of mankind."[142] Such "reintroduction" necessitates both anticolonial opposition and colonial self-reflection, spe-cifically, on the part of the European proletariat who have too often "rallied behind the position of our common masters on colonial issues."[143] "European masses," in Fanon's words, "must first of all decide to wake up, put on their thinking caps and stop playing the irresponsible game of Sleeping Beauty."[144] As Said puts it in "Representing the Colonized," despite (or because) of its emphasis on anticolonial nationalism, the "whole point of Fanon's work is to force the European metropolis to think its history *together with* the history of colonies awakening from the cruel stupor and absurd immobility of imperial domination."[145]

For the same reason, Said is drawn to the connective logic at work in Aimé Césaire's *Discourse on Colonialism*, a text written in 1950 as, in part, a reflection on the relationship between imperial violence and World War II. On the one hand, Césaire insists on both the *irredeemability* of a European culture that has debased itself completely and on the imperative to *redeem* the ethics and politics of non-exploitative, precolonial cultures in Africa and throughout the colonized world. On the other hand, *Discourse on Colonialism* is also a book about human connection that reimagines differently shared futures through what Said might call a "technique of trouble."[146] Césaire's alternative explanation of the Scramble for Africa, for instance, starts by challenging the developmental and civilizational narratives that drive the ideological juggernaut of imperialism. The "great historical tragedy of Africa," he argues, is not "that it was too late in making contact with the rest of the world" but rather the "manner in which that contact was brought about."[147] In other words, connection is not the problem; imperial capitalism is the problem. Or, as Césaire continues, when Europe stretched out its hand to grasp at Africa, it did so precisely at a moment when the "most unscrupulous financiers and captains of industry" were in charge of its civilization. "Our misfortune," he continues, was "to encounter that particular Europe on our path," a Europe that is "responsible before the human community for the highest heap of corpses in history."[148]

One can see in Césaire's criticism a stylistic form that Said replicates in *Culture and Imperialism*. Césaire, like Said, takes on the leading intellectuals of his day who are engaged in what seems to be—from an academic standpoint—obviously distorted thinking. Why does Césaire spend pages analyzing Roger Caillois's theory of Western scientific and ethnographic superiority, for instance, given the clearly compromised quality of his argument? Because just as Said tackles the facile scholarship of Bernard Lewis and other modern-day Orientalists, Césaire similarly insists that, while not wanting to "overestimate to any degree" the intrinsic value of Caillois's logically thin "philosophy," as it "wallows so voluptuously in clichés," his work is "significant" because it reflects the "state of mind of thousands upon thousands of Europeans." At the same time, Césaire continues in the next sentence, it is significant because it reveals that, at the very historical moment when the word *humanism* is most frequently on the lips of Europeans, the "West has never been further from being able to live a true humanism—a humanism made to the measure of the world."[149] "True humanism," for Césaire, would hold the contradictions of the colonizing and the colonized together, in all their fullness, in all of humanity's ranging dimensions. The world, in this sense, is more than the action sphere of the colonizer. As Robyn Kelly puts it in his revealing introduction to *Discourse*, Césaire "had practically given up on Europe and the old humanism and its claims of universality, opting instead to re-define the 'universal' in a way that did not privilege Europe."[150] Or, as Said puts it, Césaire's response to what he calls "pseudo-humanism" was to insist that Africa and Europe, colonized and colonizer, are "part of the *same* history."[151]

Ultimately, Said is drawn to the writings of Césaire and Fanon because these writings combine counternarrative readings of anticolonial culture and struggle with humanist readings of the imperial ensemble, forging both into a critical practice of resistance. By breaking out of the linear, spatially clogged, "compartmentalized terms" in which imperial history and culture are read, Said's interpretation shines a bright light on the "contradictory energies" of a global environment—in the past and in the present—framed by both imperial conquest and anticolonial resistance.[152] His contrapuntal reading of Césaire's and Fanon's "voyage in" thus opens the door to a "more integrative view of human community and human liberation" and a richer appreciation of both the multiplicity of resistances and the "atonal ensemble" that is the world.[153]

## THE CONTRAPUNTAL ENSEMBLE: IMPERIAL DIVIDE AND SHARED EXPERIENCE

Said concludes *Culture and Imperialism* by returning to a place he so often returns in his work: to the connections between historical and contemporary imperialism. "Imperialism did not end," he argues at the beginning of this final section; it "did not suddenly become 'past,' once decolonization had set in motion the dismantling of the classical empires." Rather, Said continues, a "legacy of connections still binds countries like Algeria and India to France and Britain respectively."[154] The most salient features of today's "re-presentation of the old imperial inequities," he argues, lie in the persistence of those seemingly intransigent hierarchies and inequalities that structure global power politics and sustain the enormous disparity between "poor and rich states."[155] Evolving right alongside—enabling and structuring this postcolonial, post-imperial "re-presentation" of imperial inequalities—is the United States, a global behemoth whose military/economic/political power works primarily to sustain the same international resource privileges, the same power imbalances, and the same patterns of capital distribution established during the heyday of European imperialism.

And yet, America today remains a country inhabited by people who recoil in horror at the idea that they live in an empire, who prefer to imagine the role of America in the world as that of an innocent bystander, a victim, or a benevolent democratic partner only reluctantly drawn into leadership. Said notes that intellectuals in the United States—foreign policy experts, historians, political scientists—often compound this unseeing with words like *world responsibility, leadership,* and *exceptionalism.*[156] In key ways, then, the United States today resembles Said's cultural formulation of classical imperialism but on steroids. Ours is not only a culture that, like nineteenth-century British and French imperial culture, "works very effectively to make invisible and even 'impossible' the actual *affiliations*" at work within narratives of American primacy—narratives that rationalize vast inequalities of power and resources between formerly colonized and formerly colonizing peoples—but also an imperial culture heavily invested in denying the affiliation between American power and the violence, inequalities, and instabilities generated by that power.[157]

Said's response to this contemporary unseeing is to insist (as he does throughout *Culture and Imperialism)* on the need to reintegrate the experiences of the colonized and the colonizers, historically and today. Approaching the world contrapuntally, for Said, is one way to punch through these walls of deflection, denial, and disavowal that consistently work to isolate "Western" culture from historical processes of imperialism, from the material and cultural connection between "the West" and the experiences of men and women throughout the formerly colonized world, and between global politics today and the continuity of resistance. Reading the history of imperialism contrapuntally, bringing "the West" and "the non-West" into the same frame, serves as a constant reminder of the interactions, confrontations, imbrications, violations, erasures, and uprisings that went into making the world what it is. This is the "atonal ensemble," the "complex and uneven topography," of a world that is both post-imperial and not post-imperial. It is also an infinitely richer world—containing infinitely more knotty forms of domination, injustice, resistance, and shared experience—than Enlightenment cosmopolitanism can envision or describe.[158]

And yet, while Said insists that the histories of the "Indian and British, Indochinese and French, American and Native American" were "interdependent" and their legacies of shared experience complex, approaching these histories contrapuntally emphatically *does not* mean avoiding the reality of imperial domination.[159] Indeed, even during those moments when Said's arguments are most focused on overlapping relationships within the global ensemble, he always insists (sometimes within the same paragraph, even the same sentence) on interrogating the "enabling rift between [B]lack and [w]hite, between imperial authority and natives" that both made imperial expansion possible and created the conditions for today's radically inegalitarian world.[160] In his 2003 review essay "Always on Top," for instance, Said both lingers on moments of artistic connection forged through empire and simultaneously rails against pundits like Niall Ferguson, who insist that the failure of developing states to thrive has nothing to do with the legacy of empire.[161] "Who decides," Said demands to know, "when (and if) the influence of imperialism ended?"[162] There is nothing Pollyannish or cloyingly multicultural about Said's emphasis here and elsewhere on connection, polyphony, hybridity, and shared history, nothing that shirks or hides slavery, violence, dispossession, occupation, and extraction. The world simply *is* the product of connection, domination, and resistance. "The problem," he continues, "is to keep in mind two ideas that are in many ways antithetical—the fact of the imperial divide, on the one hand, and the notion of shared experiences, on the other—without diminishing the force of either."[163]

The next chapter looks more closely at two related, critical intuitions that Said brought to bear on his analysis of imperialism: worldliness and humanism. Together, these impulses seek to break down the wall of unseeing that currently obscures both American imperial domination on the one hand and the connected, contrapuntal ensemble on the other. Like counterpoint, both intuitions look toward the "intertwined and overlapping histories" of the West and the non-West, toward a vision of liberation that is radically deconstructive and reconstructive, simultaneously critical and hopeful, oriented toward both imperialism's "enabling rift" *and* the possibility of a shared future.[164] The worldly humanist political project at the heart of Said's contrapuntal strategy thus pulls the colonized and the colonizer back into the same historical and political frame. And it is in this ordered/disordered space—between music and sound—that another world is possible.

# Bridge

To be clear, my exile was/is not literal. I have never, in Said's words, "experienced the ravages" of what it means to be forced from my homeland, to live with physical insecurity, to make my home in a place that is not, to never return, to speak a language everyday that is not my own.[1] Nor have I personally experienced the ravages of military violence or the deprivation of political upheaval. Rather, as a White, middle-class American, I have, since childhood, inhabited a zone of race and class security. I cannot even claim that the misogyny I have encountered in my life has been significantly worse than that experienced by any other woman of my demographic. From all these vantage points, my life appears deeply—unquestioningly—settled.

The exile I experience is both metaphorical in Said's sense and actual but of a different order. I am the mother of a fetal-alcohol-affected son. I did not birth my son, but I have held him—physically and emotionally—since he was two days old. My son was/is an unusually compelling personality, a fiery-strange mind, a huge laugher who brims over with boundless generosity and inexhaustible love for the people in his life. My son was/is sometimes crushing to be around, chaos producing, unstable, bottomless in his needs, threatening when dysregulated, and sometimes dangerous to the people in his life and himself. My son is both. And I have held him since he was two days old. And I also do not.

(Just writing that paragraph is a radical departure from the way I have always written, the way I have learned to write as a scholar, a political theorist, a polemicist, a politically prickly personality in a world riven with daily and systemic injustices. Just writing that paragraph feels self-indulgent in a way that violates every single liberation-theology-social-justice-Catholic dictums of self-denial with which I was raised. Just writing that paragraph plunges me into a space that is at odds with the modus operandi of my scholarship for the last eighteen years: to serve as an escape from the daily grief of watching my child struggle, briefly thrive, and relentlessly devolve. A bulwark against despair. A strategy for deflection.)

The unfolding story of my son's young life can be explained with clinical references to trauma—his and ours—or through the facile, stingingly mean-spirited language of behavioral psychology and the disciplining desire of the entire medical establishment for a diagnosis to determine treatment: fetal-alcohol-affected spectrum disorder, oppositional defiant disorder, conduct disorder, autism, bipolar disorder. Biologically, my son suffers from the "Swiss cheese" brain wrought by uterine alcohol exposure, damaged in some places and coherently thriving in others, such that some days he is more than capable of self-reflection, self-control, self-discipline—all those "selfs" we require of autonomous subjects in a world teeming with other people. And other days, he seems singularly incapable of controlling his desire to consume the world around him, of reflecting on his behavior, of regulating his emotions, of linking action to reaction and cause to effect, of guiding his body through the crowded space around him in ways that don't cause harm.

The unfolding story of my son's young life can be marked on a chronology of conflict and cobbled-together responses: babysitter explosions, preschool and primary school crises, social skills training, therapy, individual education plans, meetings of specialists and teachers, hospitalizations, treatment teams, and the goodwill of a parade of professionals who ultimately—to a one—threw up their hands in frustration before washing them of him. The unfolding story of my son's young life can be marked by a series of encirclings, enclosures, and expulsions: from classroom to behavior room, from behavior room to home school, from home school to emergency room, from emergency room to the "Behavioral Medicine Unit" and the sucking click of the hospital doors behind him/me. On the other side lies my kicking, ground-thrashing son, pinned down by staff, screaming and screaming like the ten-year-old two-year-old that he is. On my side of the door, the ground lurches. On my side of the door, I fall down.

Finally, when it became too much for our family to bear—when my husband and I sat shell-shocked yet again in the emergency room of the small town in eastern Washington where we lived while our son was stitched up from the wounds he'd accrued breaking yet another window, and we begged the social worker to tell us what, if anything, could be done for a ten-year-old boy who was a danger to himself and others, and he looked at us with pity and said "foster care and probably eventually prison," and we decided *no*, that is *not* what would happen to the boy we had held since he was two days old—we spent our entire savings, borrowed from friends and family, and sent our son to residential care. And ever since that day, he has been in, and he has been out. And ever since that day, I hold him. And I do not.

Years into this seesaw existence of expulsions, hospitalizations, relocations, and attempted reunifications, our son seemed ready to come "home" permanently. But "home" could not be the small town where we lived, given the absence of resources for a now-gigantic fifteen-year-old with his challenges. And so I moved. I took a leave of absence from the small liberal arts college where my husband and I worked as professors, went to Seattle, found a small place to live, a suitable school, therapy resources, doctors who specialized in adoption-related health challenges, a psychiatrist to manage medications—all the privileged resources of parents who can afford them and are savvy enough to navigate the system in a desperate attempt to prevent what inevitably happens in America to most children like my son from happening to their children. Then my husband (who continued to teach at the small liberal arts school and commute four and a half hours to Seattle every weekend) and I saw our daughter off to college on the East Coast and, three weeks later, brought our son "home," where we settled down to find each other again. And for a brief, indescribably glorious moment, we did just that, and my son—brimming with possibility and all the love and intensity he brings to the world that inspires love and intensity in others—settled into himself.

And then the golden time faded. My son decompensated. By the end of three months, he had assaulted me in a dark parking lot, and the cycle of hospitalization, relocations, return, and ultimately residential treatment began all over again.

So did my exile begin to take shape. I was left to this strange in-between life away from my academic home, my professional future uncertain, rattling around a house meant for my son without my son, writing a book about Said from which I felt both alienated and unworthy. Every day I would pass by my son's empty bedroom and stand at the door, stare at the stain on the carpet left from the day he had cut his wrists, and I would see him crouched there on the floor, looking up at me in vacant agony. And I would wonder all over again the same thing I had wondered every day since he first went away: Who is holding him tonight? What am I meant to do/be if I can't hold him? I couldn't work up the courage to actually enter the room—to come face-to-face with the enormity of that loss—and so I would just hover at the door until his absence blocked out the sun. And I would walk away.

I was gripped by rage and resentment. I hated my son's birth mother—poor, Texana, abused, drug addicted, vacillating between homelessness and prison in that border town in that border world—for what she had consumed, almost as much as I hated the pious hordes of antiabortion activists who demanded that children like my son be born only so they could abandon them in that instant and smugly condemn them for their antisocial behavior down the line. I raged at a system where insurance companies guide treatment decisions, where poor children meet their first counselor in prison and privileged children meet their first prison in counseling, where thirty-year-old interns teach glassy-eyed parents how best to hide the knives in the house, where liberal politicians wave banners of multiculturalism with one hand and defund social services with the other, where kids of color with undocumented disabilities are incarcerated to satisfy the ceaseless need of White America to prove its racial status, where "wraparound services" replace group homes and "coping skills" stand in place of empathy. And I knew intimately what Said meant when he called exile a "jealous state." "Exiles look at non exiles with resentment," he observes. "*They* belong in their surroundings, you feel, whereas an exile is always out of place."[2] Everyday I had to bite back the resentment I felt toward people with "normal" children, children to whom they could be actual (not epistolary) parents, children they could raise without fear, and I longed to hunker down with my community to the exclusion of all others, with that tribe who spoke my language of disability and special education and trauma and resources and "Have you heard about this treatment? What is the latest on his IEP? How do we take care of ourselves? Who *are* we now?"

And through it all, I kept reading works by and about Said, feeling unworthy and alienated, mourning the loss, nursing my wounds, writing my son letters, stopping by my son's bedroom, standing at the door, staring at the stain, walking away, reading works by and about Said, feeling unworthy and alienated. As I circled, I kept coming back to Said's essay on intellectual exile and getting stuck where I always got stuck: on the idea of exile as metaphor. Because whereas Said sometimes wrote about the pathos of exile as a tangible, clawing thing that one is born or forced into, he also insists that exile is a perspective necessary for the world that can be adopted by intellectuals committed to radical criticism. In Said's words, while exile is an "*actual* condition," it is also "for my purposes a *metaphorical* condition." In this sense, exile is an act of will that the intellectual performs in order to stand outside the familiar and the comfortable embrace of home or nation, a disposition likely, in Said's words, "to be a source not of acculturation and adjustment, but rather of volatility and instability." "You cannot go back to some earlier and perhaps more stable condition of being at home," he continues, "and alas you can never fully arrive, be at one with your new home or situation."[3]

As an intellectual who tends toward the dyspeptic and the perennially pissed off, I was spontaneously sympathetic to this way of thinking and to the idea that I, too, could be a source of volatility and instability. But I didn't actually believe it was possible. If we can all be exiles, then what is so unique about the experience? And if there isn't anything terribly unique about it, then why doesn't everyone write/critique thus?

Everyone doesn't write/critique thus, it seemed to me as I circled, because it is an astonishingly bloody-hard thing to do. How the hell is anyone—much less someone traumatized by the loss of their homeland and the insecurity of their present existence—supposed to gather together the internal resources necessary to stop sitting, in Said's words, "on the sidelines nursing a wound."[4] If, as he insists, there are "things to be learned" from exile, then how does one ever break out of the cycle of despair long enough to learn them? Here I was, in Seattle, an adult who had never known the ravages of exile as an "*actual* condition," and even I couldn't stop nursing my wounds. I couldn't work up the energy to make coffee in the morning, much less occupy the position of intellectual exile and transform it into a jaunty form of unstable criticism capable of engaging a world ravaged by imperialism and violence and racism and war and expulsion.

And so I wandered the house everyday, stopping at the door to my son's bedroom, moving on, reading Said, raging at a racist world that had no solutions for a child born into poverty and precarity—even when adopted by privileged, educated, loving parents—permanently altered by what his pregnant birth mother had done to herself on her tragically drunken blitz through West Texas. Crippled by my always unfolding and never unfolded loss. Stopping at the door. Moving on. Holding my son. And always again. Not.

# 4

# Reading You in Your Presence

## *Political Interpretation and Worldly Humanism*

In September 2000, Edward Said presented a lecture for a conference at Oxford entitled "The Public Role of Writers and Intellectuals" that would eventually become the basis both for his September 2001 article for the *Nation* and the final chapter in his last collection of essays, *Humanism and Democratic Criticism*. Later revised in light of both the events of September 11 and the political climate leading up to America's illegal invasion of Iraq in March 2003, the piece articulates some struggles of the contemporary era that Said believed public intellectuals were well placed to elucidate, individually and as a "common project."[1] First, Said argues, intellectuals can help "protect against and forestall the disappearance of the past" at a time when political events and discourses are hurtling precipitously toward invasion while the rationale for entering into the conflict changes from minute to minute, speaker to speaker.[2] Second, he maintains, intellectuals can participate in constructing "fields of coexistence rather than fields of battle" at a moment in history when many participants in the public media are actively helping propel the imperial state to war.[3]

Said finds the political/cultural/philosophical inspiration for both critical gestures in Giambattista Vico's insistence that the human mind "can re-examine its own history from the point of view of the maker."[4] Inhabiting this reimagined subjectivity, he argues, opens to the door to a critical practice that reintegrates the past with the present while seeking fields of coexistence. In the context of the looming Iraq War, he argues, the best way to begin this epistemological shift is to "imagine the person whom you are discussing—in this case, the person on whom the bombs will fall—reading you in your presence."[5] This chapter explores the intellectual and political orientation made possible by this humble epistemological shift.

93

In what follows, I explore the critical rhythm of that worldly humanism—the swing between recovering the past and constructing fields of coexistence—as it beats its steady way through Said's scholarly and political work toward the goal he articulates in the final pages of *Culture and Imperialism*: "to think concretely and sympathetically, contrapuntally, about others" rather than "only about 'us.'"[6] As separate terms, *worldliness* and *humanism* are each crucially related to Said's contrapuntal approach to history, text, and politics. *Worldliness*, for Said, captures a way of reading text and context that is opposed to metahistorical interpretations and is, as with counterpoint, explicitly committed to incorporating imperialism's literal world making into its interpretive frame. *Humanism*, from Said's perspective, suggests ways of transforming the world of human creation—the reading and the *being* read—into a politics of outward-facing coexistence rather than a politics of indwelling attention to a "people," no matter how creatively or democratically defined. Worldly humanism swings between these two impulses in a way that both exposes forgotten and suppressed histories and suggests ways of transforming these histories into disclosive—rather than retractive—visions of political life.

The chapter begins with an exposition of Said's approach, first to worldliness then humanism. These two sections follow the development of both terms from some of his earliest texts through his last, comparing his approach to that of the Cambridge School and the "humanist" thinkers associated with the "turn to ethics" in political philosophy. The third section examines how the combination of these two critical intuitions resists the "disappearance of the past," focusing again on the critical pace of Said's analysis through a comparison with both the self-proclaimed "humble humanism" of Michael Ignatieff and the "thin universalism" of Michael Walzer. It contrasts Said's vision of the "world"—grounded in cultivating outward-looking "fields of coexistence"—with both Hannah Arendt's approach to the "loss of the world" (in the wake of the Holocaust) and to some contemporary liberal and left political theoretical responses to the election of Donald Trump and the rise of global authoritarianism. I conclude with a few thoughts on the political and interpretive promise of Said's approach and the deep frustrations it can elicit. I argue that despite these frustrations, worldly humanism should be read as both an essential complement and a fundamental challenge to the broad tendency within much of political theory to contain the past and enclose political life precisely at a moment when we should be questioning the role of imperialism in constructing such closures in the first place.

## WORLDLINESS

Said's attachment to the concept of worldliness predates both *Orientalism* and his fuller explication of the term in 1979's "The World, the Text, and the Critic."[7] In a 1976 interview in *Diacritics*, for instance, Said argued against an approach to literary criticism that "tries to reify a) the critic, b) the text, c) criticism." "To treat each of those as if detachable from the others and from society and history," he continued, "is to impose on them a status they have only in their weakest and most rarefied form."[8] For Said, criticism is at its most powerful when it engages the political/cultural/social environment surrounding texts and their production. In essence, texts are "produced and live on in the historical realm," leavened by the "insinuations, the imbrications of power," and the multiplicity of cultural and political expressions woven into the experience of the world in which they are produced.[9] To write and to criticize in the sense Said describes is to interact with—and act on—the world.

Said developed this particular reading of worldliness, text, and criticism out of his engagement with debates taking place between structuralists and poststructuralists in literary criticism during the 1970s. For structuralist critics like Roland Barthes, textuality—the internal relationship between forms, grammar, meaning—circulates in a realm distinct from the author's intention. A text, Barthes argues in *The Death of the Author*, is "not a line of words (the message of the Author-God)" but rather a "multidimensional space in which a variety of writings, none of them original, blend and clash."[10] Moreover, Barthes continues, the context in which the text was written had no bearing on its interpretation. A text in this sense is simply a "tissue of quotations, drawn from the innumerable centers of culture."[11] Poststructuralists and deconstructionist critics like Jacques Derrida and Julia Kristeva later challenged Barthes's sense that meaning could be interpreted through the assumed-to-be stable relationships between signs and signifiers, arguing that such an interpretation continued to privilege a transcendental sense of meaning. Rather, the "literary word," as Kristeva puts it, is an "intersection of textual surfaces" rather than a "fixed meaning."[12] At the same time, Derrida and Kristeva largely agree with Barthes that both the author and the cultural context in which a text is produced are less important than the "intertextual" or "logocentric" world in which the text circulates.[13]

From early on, Said—a scholar with explicit political interests, who thought about his own writing in connection to his identity as a critic and an exile and who concerned himself with the relationship between discourse and the political/material project of imperialism—was uncomfortable with this jettisoning of author and context. At what point, he asks in 1973's "On Originality," "does an author's text begin and where does it end: is a postcard or a laundry list written by Nietzsche a sequence within his integral text or not?"[14] At the same time, with the poststructuralists, Said agrees that texts themselves play a reproductive role within disciplinary systems of knowledge that sustain domination. He also contends that discourse circulates in ways that do not always add up to linear coherence—between description and truth, signs and signifiers, author and intention. The point, he notes in "The World, the Text, and the Critic," is

> that texts have a way of existing that even in their most rarefied form are always enmeshed in circumstance, time, place, and society—in short, they are always in the world and hence worldly. Whether a text is preserved or put aside for a period, whether it is on a library shelf or not, whether it is considered danger-ous or not: these matters have to do with a text's being in the world, which is a more complicated matter than the private process of reading. The same implica-tions are undoubtedly true of critics in their capacities as readers and writers in the world.[15]

Said's worldly approach foregrounds this enmeshment in circumstances, acknowledging both the excessive nature of textual productions (the way they spill over and disseminate in the world) and the tangled relationship between texts and context—the way texts produced *in* the world interact *with* the world. The key, for Said, is to remember that texts are "not finished objects."[16]

Political theorists may note some similarities here between Said's insis-tence on reading texts as "enmeshed in circumstance, time, place, and soci-ety" and the contextualist approach to intellectual history developed, most notably, in the 1970s by scholars associated with the Cambridge School. For such early Cambridge School thinkers as J. G. A. Pocock and Quentin Skinner, studying the history of political thought entails pulling the discur-sive/political context behind canonical texts like Hobbes's *Leviathan* and Locke's *Second Treatise* back into the center of analysis and resituating these thinkers within the rich universe of interlocutors and ideological debates that shaped their ideas.[17] Both reflecting and furthering the "linguistic turn" in intellectual history, Cambridge School thinkers treat texts as rhetorical and discursive "speech-acts" that transform and expropriate inherited linguistic frameworks and patterns of meaning.[18] They thus problematize hegemonic interpretations of canonical texts in the past and present, pushing back against the largely ahistorical framing of the "history of political thought" as it is usu-ally taught. They do this by widening the historical scope of inquiry around canonical texts while introducing new categories of discursive and rhetorical material for reinterpretation while reintegrating this material back into the story of modern European political thought.

Much of Said's work is certainly in sympathy with that of Cambridge School thinkers and dovetails particularly well—as Tully, Dabashi, and Abbas Manoochehri all note—with Skinner's contextualist hermeneutics.[19] His concept of worldliness differs from Cambridge School approaches, however, in a few key ways. First, for all that their work has challenged the sacralizing of the political theory canon (by plucking ideas from the realm of metaphysical conversation and placing them back into the rough and tumble of historical politics), the majority of Cambridge School–inspired thinkers are still largely interested in the Western canon itself, choosing to study those texts associated with a tradition that has decided to study them or, in Pocock's words, that have "grown up in the course of our historical experience."[20] Rather than locating and recuperating scholars and intellectual traditions whose work may have fallen out of canonical favor, for instance, or who wrote from cultural contexts beyond Europe, Cambridge School thinkers often concentrate their methodological efforts on significantly enriching our understanding of the discursive environment *around* canonical thinkers. In this sense, the historical map of European political theory drawn by the likes of Skinner and Pocock looks largely like a series of set points—fixed on a particular cluster of thinkers—out of which radiate multiple paths of rhetorical and textual inquiry, rather like spokes on wheels. The spokes surrounding these canonical thinkers may proliferate and overlap, but the number of centers remains familiar and constant. Thus, in its most narrow and literal of forms, there is always a danger that the Cambridge School approach will, as Ian Hall puts it, transform "ever narrower, syncretic histories of texts, into antiquarianism."[21]

Second, this means that until fairly recently, contextualist intellectual historians have largely ignored non-European thought. While this is certainly changing, and while the number of researchers interested in non-Western political thought who consider themselves influenced by an "ideas in context" approach is increasing, these scholars remain in the minority.[22] This tendency to privilege Western thinkers has also influenced the way many Cambridge-inspired, contextualist scholars have read the intersection of imperialism and the history of political thought, despite the fact that some of the most innovative studies of these entanglements have been conducted by these same scholars. In essence, David Armitage, Sankar Muthu, and Jennifer Pitts have all produced field-transforming works that highlight ideas about imperial governance, property, civilization, slavery, and democracy at work in the political writings of canonical European thinkers and, more broadly, within the evolving disciplines of international law and international relations.[23] Duncan Bell and Karuna Mantena have significantly expanded this "imperial ideas in context" approach to also include a wide variety of noncanonical thinkers and public intellectuals.[24] And yet—again, until recently—these interrogations of imperialism have largely remained focused on analyzing the impact of imperialism on the scholarship of *European* thinkers rather than on the political thought of the colonized.

This focus on European and canonical thinkers is gradually changing, and indeed, some of the most exciting new work on non-Western and anticolonial thought is being produced by the very same Cambridge School–inspired thinkers (e.g., Bell, Mantena, and Pitts) whose work on imperialism was so crucial to the "turn to empire" in the first place.[25] The innovation of Said's worldliness, therefore, isn't just that it expands the ambit of contextually focused scholarly inquiry beyond the usual suspects associated with the Western canon. Rather, what sets Said's worldly approach apart is his insistence on making the contrapuntal ensemble of imperialism and resistance *the* contextual site for analysis. Approaching texts in a worldly manner means situating them within the globe-spanning, discursive universe of transnational contexts oriented toward justifying, naturalizing, spacializing, and resisting imperialism, a context that was neither "invisible" to European authors, Said argues, nor concealing of "its worldly affiliations and interests," even as it strove to render those affiliations both invisible and "impossible."[26] Worldly inquiry means following the contrapuntal flow of ideas from the periphery to the core and back again, from the fugal reception of ideas in colonial contexts to the multiple creative utterances that emerge out of these contexts. Said's worldliness thus differs from comparative approaches (such as those of Leigh Jenco and Dallmayr) that take a theoretically derived, "dialogic" notion of encounter as their methodological entrée into investigations of non-Western theory.[27] By contrast, for Said, the *world itself*—the actual tangles and ligaments and efflorescing connections that flow from actual imperial encounters—provide both the context and the content of critique.

Ultimately, however, what most differentiates Said's worldliness from either a Cambridge contextualist or dialogic approach is his insistence on self-reflection and on troubling and unsettling the critic's relationship to the world. As he explained in a 1998 interview, worldliness as he originally intended it "meant to me, at any rate, some location of oneself or one's work, or the work itself, the literary work, the text, and so on, in the world, as opposed to some extra-worldly, private, ethereal context."[28] Worldliness thus necessarily entails a "very strong sense of what it means to do scholarship" in context and in one's own context: one's relationship to the world, identity, politics, culture, and interpretation.[29] Not for nothing was Said drawn to the writings of Samuel Johnson and Giambattista Vico, two thinkers both exquisitely self-aware of the environments in which they wrote and the fact that these environments "made claims on them culturally and systematically." More importantly for Said, both Johnson and Vico were not merely aware that they were "materially bound to their time"; they were simultaneously committed to resisting the pressures of their cultural/political eras "in every-thing they did."[30]

As this last sentence implies, Said's insistence on the self-awareness of the worldly critic is more than academic; it's political. He believes that inter-rogating one's own critical relationship to text and context helps unsettle the very idea that particular texts *belong* to particular cultures. For Said, worldly writers like Johnson and Vico knew themselves to be situated in the world and understood that the process of writing belongs "to a system of utterances that has all sorts of affiliative, often constricting relationships" to nations, civili-zations, and empires.[31] A worldly, self-aware perspective on writing, on text, and on contexts unsettles the putative fixedness of certain ideas with certain cultures, shining a bright light on the human-made, affiliative connections between people and nation, culture and right, civilization and domination. As Ashcroft and Ahluwalia argue, for Said, worldliness is the "guarantee of the invalidity of the text's ownership by nation or community or religion, how-ever powerful those filiative connections might be."[32] A self-aware, worldly orientation reveals the multiplicity of influences and power networks that course through the assumed "integrity and inviolability" of Western "cultural masterpieces": the centrality of India to John Stuart Mill's conception of lib-erty, the through line of Antigua in the narrative of *Mansfield Park*.[33] When one acknowledges one's own worldly relationship to text and context, one helps to unsettle and bring to light the already "hybrid, mixed, impure" qual-ity of that text and context, revealing the fact that ideas are "produced and live on in the historical realm" while resituating cultural productions in that realm.

Said once suggested that worldliness is, in some ways, a "rather crude and bludgeon like term to enforce the location of cultural practices back in the mundane, the quotidian, and the secular."[34] In this sense, the point of worldli-ness is to prize open, adze-like, the veneer of the text or theory or cultural artifact, exposing the deeply secular (rather than metaphysical or divine) links within. Always set in opposition to "being other worldly," this emphasis on secularism—this insistence on a human-made world open to change—is a consistent feature of Said's scholarly and political writings over the course of his career.[35] Rajagopalan Radhakrishnan argues that Said's secularism is best understood as "profoundly anti-essentialist," an impulse that at every turn resists fixing human beings in discursive, political, national, cultural, or reli-gious categories.[36] For Said, secularism reminds us of the fact that national, cultural, and religious identities "are constructions, not God-given nor natural artifacts."[37]

Not surprisingly, Said's secularism has, over the years, been a source of lively and often-sympathetic disagreement (particularly among postcolonial scholars), and I briefly touch on some of these arguments in chapter 5. For now, my primary concern is to emphasize how his commitment to secularism relates to worldliness, relates to an approach that understands philosophies and cultural productions as neither hallowed objects nor the product of civilizationally inspired geniuses who then communicate with each other across a metaphysical plain. Art, history, and politics, Said stresses, turning again to Vico, are not "divine or sacred" conflagrations burning with the heat of their own internal cultural fires. They are "made by men and women" in the world, and we can only really understand them when we interrogate the "way they are made."[38] And it is precisely here, in his reading of human world making, that we catch the fullest glimpse of the flip side of Said's worldliness: his humanism.

## HUMANISM

Said's interest in something he calls humanism is evident in his earliest writings, particularly in his reflections on Vico. In 1967's "Vico: Autodidact and Humanist," for instance, Said contrasts Vico's theory of perception as secular creation with the "intellectual positivism" and "universal systematizing" of his age.[39] In 1975's *Beginnings*, he continues to explore Vico's thought through an investigation of the difference between "origins" and "beginnings," a difference, he argues, between essence and making. For Vico, Said explains, texts, culture, philosophy, and politics are all the products of human action, human endeavor, and human invention. To write, in Vico's words, is "to 'know' what at the outset cannot be known except by inventing it, exactly, intentionally, autodidactically."[40] Said returns to this aspect of Vico's thought repeatedly in his writing. From the high-water mark of his Foucauldianism in *Orientalism*, to his turn toward a contrapuntal analysis of resistance in the 1980s, to his writings on public intellectuals throughout the 1990s, this aspect of Vico's interpretive theory remains the cornerstone of Said's approach to humanism, an approach that he varyingly calls (among other things) a "usable praxis for intellectuals", a "kind of scrupulosity", and "about transitions from one realm, one area of human experience to another."[41] However he describes it, the thread that ties together all Said's writings about humanism remains this basic, Vico-inspired commitment to reading human beings as makers of history and history as made by human beings.

Not surprisingly, given his profoundly influential critique of Eurocentrism and the "universalizing habit by which a system of thought is believed to account for everything," Said's humanism has remained a controversial subject among his sympathetic critics.[42] This controversy grew louder after he gave a series of lectures in 2000, published posthumously in 2003 as *Humanism and Democratic Criticism*.[43] As Stathis Gourgouris observes in his compelling essay on Said's late style, the lectures on humanism "were met, practically everywhere in American universities, with a sense of betrayal by those who had been counted among his allies in the humanities during the 1970s and 1980s, and a sense of triumphalism by various adversaries, who had once inaugurated themselves as the defenders of Anglo-American humanist principles against the foreign onslaught."[44] People who were sympathetic to Said's often-deconstructive method of proceeding in *Orientalism* and elsewhere experienced this explicit articulation of his ideas about humanism as a terrible about-face, despite the fact that Said had been writing about humanism for years. Detractors, however, either felt vindicated or accused Said of doing with this book what they believed he did with all his scholarship: politicize spaces and ideas that should be free from the ranting bias of the likes of him. In *Humanism and Democratic Criticism*, James Pannero sneers, Said wields humanism as a weapon of indoctrination, an excuse to bend the fragile minds of American undergraduates. "The classroom is the battleground" for Said, argues Pannero, "the lectern is the soapbox, and the instructor is a committed agent of social change." In Said's humanist vision, according to Pannero, "this is the responsibility of the engaged intellectual."[45]

*Humanism and Democratic Criticism*, however, as Gourgouris notes, confounds all sides of this argument. As his 1995 reflections on *Orientalism*'s reception suggest, Said was well aware of the tensions his work embodied.[46] Indeed, he begins the first essay of *Humanism and Democratic Criticism*, "Humanism's Sphere," by recalling James Clifford's 1980 review of *Orientalism*, in which Clifford notes a serious conflict between Said's "avowed and unmistakable humanistic bias" and the "antihumanism" of his Foucauldian approach to his subject.[47] In his reflections on Clifford's review, Said focuses on the assumption that there is something "fundamentally discordant" between humanism and an "advanced theory" committed to analyzing "systems of thinking" and power. His response to this assumption reflects the argument he had been developing—in various forms, through various texts, in various ways—throughout the decades leading up to the publication of *Humanism and Democratic Criticism*: "Although I was one of the first critics to engage with and discuss French theory in the American university, Clifford correctly saw that I somehow remained unaffected by that theory's ideological anti-humanism, mainly, I think, because I did not (and still do not) see in humanism only the kind of totalizing and essentializing trends that Clifford identified."[48] Rather, Said thought it possible "to be critical of humanism in the name of humanism." If one is "schooled in its abuses by the experience of Eurocentrism and empire," he continues, "one could fashion a different kind of humanism" that is both "cosmopolitan" and "text and language bound" and that remains attuned to "emergent voices," many of them "exilic, extraterritorial, and unhoused."[49]

For Said, the key to fostering a humanism able to escape the sucking black hole of Eurocentrism—always poised to swallow up difference through reason, to reinsert divisions between low and high culture, to hide behind the skirts of a canon while claiming to be broadly representative of human culture, to use concepts like "human rights" and "democracy" as excuses to invade and bomb—is to keep its conceptual assumptions narrow. In other words, rather than nesting his attachment to the category of "human" in some ideal moral theory or a long, singing-to-the-sky list of human attributes cobbled together from European culture, Said returns, as always, to Vico's contention "that the historical world is made by men and women and not by God."[50] For Vico, Said explains, human beings are fundamentally makers of history, and human beings "know what we make," or rather, "we know how to see it from the point of view of its human maker."[51] Limiting humanism's definitional reach to "making history" in this Vician manner—an approach that also bares a distinct resemblance to Marx's thought in *The Economic and Philosophical Manuscripts*—frees it from the expansive set of specific requirements attached to Enlightenment conceptions of human reason or to the long litany of Western cultural achievements curated for coherence and exclusion by the likes of Allan Bloom, Donald Kagan, and Steven Ozment.[52]

Moreover, for Said, understanding that human beings are united in their shared "capacity to make knowledge" resists the poststructuralist tendency to imagine people as inescapably bamboozled by power, capable primarily, in his words, of "passively, reactively, and dully" absorbing its weight. Additionally, the flip side of this definition—that we know how to see what we make from the point of view of another because we understand each other as makers—opens up humanistic practice to more expansively generous forms of reading and politics enabled by the "holding and crossing over" between imperialism, postcolonialism, and resistance.[53]

At the same time that Said champions this "common enterprise shared with others," he is also fascinated with, unsettled by, and committed to interrogating the roles of, location, affiliation, and identity in shaping human subjects, in moving discourse, and in enabling both domination and resistance.[54] He is compelled, for instance, by the way Palestinian artist Mona Hatoum wrestles with place and identity through her installations, presenting an identity "unable to identify with itself, but nevertheless grappling the notion (perhaps only the ghost) of identity to itself."[55] Hatoum's discordant, disturbing installations—half-empty houses, doors hanging on hinges, dishes left in the drying rack—replicate the disquietingly abandoned spaces of Palestinian homes, a theme that Said himself returns to in his own ruminations on home and family. Throughout his work, Said twins such ruminations on the feeling of home and the loss of connection with the belief that there is sometimes, as he argues in 1991's "The Politics of Knowledge," something "salutary and necessary" about the politics of nationalism as "resistance to imperialism."[56] And yet, in almost the same breath, Said couples this recognition with a deep skepticism about both nationalism and the politics of identity more generally.

Said thus approaches the politics of identity as a complicated, Janus-faced phenomenon, mobilized by both the oppressor and the oppressed. The "politics of identity that informed imperialism in its global phase," he argues, was steeped in developmentalist narratives of civilization that played a crucial role in fixing "racial or geographical" distinctions between the colonizer and the colonized other.[57] Said is thus particularly attuned to the exclusions and violent impulses of national identities when harnessed to statist expansionism. At the same time, his exilic sympathies compel him toward a Fanonian recognition of nationalism's sometimes necessity, a necessity that coexists alongside its capacity for danger. Said's complicated relationship to nationalism and identity thus consistently urges his thinking toward humanist forms of liberation that both acknowledged identity's pull while troubling its political expression. "The world we live in," he argues in 1994's "Identity, Authority, Freedom," is "made up of numerous identities interacting, sometimes harmoniously, sometimes antithetically."[58] This is the "whole" that he found in the anticolonial humanism of Fanon, Césaire, and James, a conception of a world framed in both opposition to the dispossession and oppression created by imperialism's "enabling rift between [B]lack and [w]hite, between imperial authority and natives" and in the "joint discovery of self and Other."[59] This is a humanism, in other words, grounded in the worldly belief that the connections sewn throughout the long history of colonialism can be transformed, with human effort, into a humanism made, in Césaire's words, "to the measure of the world."[60]

This self-aware coupling—of the pain that accompanies exilic homelessness and imperial dispossession with a radical anti-essentialism and a joyful openness to the complicated, riotous world of human making and human connection—is what most differentiates Said's humanism from those of other contemporary thinkers who have similarly attempted to locate their approaches to ethics and politics in a limited claim on the human experience. For instance, scholars associated with what has sometimes been referred to as the "turn to ethics"—a diverse group of thinkers united primarily, as Ella Myers argues, by the "conviction that ethics constitutes that missing something that can help cure what ails democratic life"—similarly champion a narrow conception of humanism.[61] Thus, advocates of "new humanism," like Judith Butler and Emmanuel Levinas ground their ethical theories in a relatively bare-bones conception of shared humanity. Butler, for example, locates her notion of humanism in the "corporeal vulnerability" of all human beings.[62] Levinas, by contrast, emphasizes a theologically derived commitment to the "irreducible dignity of humans" that is related to a "suffering for the suffering—be it inexorable—of someone else."[63]

There is, however, nothing terribly generative or transformative about a politics grounded in corporeal vulnerability, dignity, or the suffering we experience when we witness the suffering of others. Indeed, there isn't anything really *political* about mortality, dignity, or suffering at all, something both Myers and Bonnie Honig argue about both the new humanism and the "turn to ethics" in general. As Honig points out, Butler's grounding of humanism in the "ontological fact of mortality" has the potential to eschew politics altogether for a moribund performance of permanent mourning.[64] The concept of "dignity," as Michael Goodhart so clearly argues, similarly sidelines politics, particularly in the context of human rights discourse. When treated either as the foundation for human rights claims or as a term explicitly "conjoined" with human rights claims, the idea of "dignity," Goodhart maintains, can and does obscure the power politics that shape notions of human rights in the first place while also sidelining the political possibilities of human rights as "emancipatory practice."[65]

More troubling, notions of humanism grounded in suffering not only have the potential to avoid politics, but they also fit well into the deflective logic that plays such a historical and ongoing role in the language of liberal internationalism/liberal imperialism, or, as it is often framed today, support for something called the "American-led liberal world order." The liberal internationalist/imperialist public intellectual Michael Ignatieff, for instance, argues that his approach to international political ethics flows from a "humble humanism" rooted in a common "capacity to imagine the pain of others."[66] This "capacity," he maintains, enables people from liberal societies to empathize with people from illiberal societies whom they might otherwise consider unworthy of toleration. And yet, there is nothing inherent in the "capacity to imagine the pain of others" that inspires empathy toward those others. In other words, a "capacity to imagine" the pain experienced by people in various parts of the illiberal world can happily coexist—as it does in Ignatieff's work—with a willingness to rationalize that pain. There is nothing reflective about this "capacity," nothing that necessarily prods conscience toward self-scrutiny or that might prompt a member of a liberal society to pause for longer than the minute it takes to "imagine" pain. Moreover, there is nothing about the capacity to imagine pain that invites reflection on the long, imperial history behind Ignatieff's neat division of the world into liberal and non-liberal spheres. Indeed, there is nothing about Ignatieff's humanism that invites *thought* at all.

In practice, Ignatieff's combination of ethical hand wringing with spine-stiffening exhortations to bomb, invade, or commit to policies of "enhanced interrogation" specifically meant to amplify the pain of others is the most consistent rhetorical feature of his writing on human rights and foreign policy. "Humble humanism," in Ignatieff's case, gives rise not to an ethics of care or sympathy or reflection but to an ethics of liberal self-righteousness that allows pundits like himself to feel terribly bad about supporting the awful thing that must be done in the name of a "responsibility to protect" and then—having engaged in that performative act of feeling terribly bad—move on to accept the awful thing that must be done, affirmed of his own depth of feeling.[67] In the final analysis, imagining the victims of drone strikes or bombings or invasions as bodies capable of experiencing pain may prick Ignatieff's conscience—it may cause him to consider the size and intensity of the mission, it may provoke public expressions of guilt or crocodile tears—but it does nothing to alter the surety of his faith that drone strikes or bombings or invasions are necessary.

Nowhere is Said's approach to humanism better illustrated than in the explicit comparison he draws between his approach and Ignatieff's, a comparison that frames the passage that begins this chapter. Again, in "The Public Role of Writers and Intellectuals," Said argues,

> It takes a good deal more courage, work and knowledge to dissolve words like "war" and "peace" into their elements, recovering what has been left out of peace processes that have been determined by the powerful, and then placing that missing actuality back in the center of things, than it does to write prescriptive articles for "liberals," à la Michael Ignatieff, that urge more destruction and death for distant civilians. The intellectual can be perhaps a kind of counter-memory, putting forth its own counterdiscourse that will not allow conscience to look away or fall asleep. The best corrective is, as Dr. Johnson said, to imagine the person whom you are discussing—in this case the person on whom the bombs will fall—reading you in your presence.[68]

Imagining the person on whom the bombs will fall not merely as a body capable of experiencing pain—someone whose life Ignatieff might consider sadly before moving on to the real business of bombing with a resigned sigh—but as a reader, critic, and thinker who is actively analyzing *you* shifts the intellectual authority away from the policy makers at Harvard, Princeton, and the Council on Foreign Relations to the person being discussed. Suddenly, the object of inquiry becomes a maker of history, a person who looks on you with potential openness and potential scorn. This person has counterhistories and counternarratives to relate and—because they are also readers, makers, and thinkers who read your prescriptions back at you—has different solutions to offer. Understanding this thinking person as *like you*—equally able to make history, equally able to read you—and yet as someone who potentially reads/theorizes/imagines history and the world *differently* from you facilitates a sense of counterpoint: of familiarity and remoteness, nearness and distance. In this in-between space does worldly humanism unfold.

At the heart of Said's unfolding humanism sits the thinking subject, the maker of history and knowledge, both reader and read. Said never imagines this subject to be unaltered by power, nor does he believe that the process of human inquiry runs unidirectionally—from the mind to the world. For Said, individuals and groups—and the texts and discourses they generate—are always "in the world and subject to its numerous heterogeneous realities." Such worldliness, in Said's words, "assured contamination." Said also argues, with Vico, that human knowledge is permanently undermined by the "indefinite nature of the human mind," so there is "always something radically incomplete, insufficient, provisional, disputable, and arguable" about it.[69] Thus, the critical subjects of Said's humanism approach the world from within the world—from within the connections forged through the long history and contemporary practices of imperialism, for instance—rather than from a metaphysical position of disembodied reason, or what Inés Valdez calls "unworldly" Eurocentrism.[70]

This incomplete, provisional, disputable form of humanist criticism also, according to Said, expresses itself as a "continuous practice of questioning and of accumulating knowledge that is open to, rather than in denial of, the constituent historical realities of the post–Cold War world, its early colonial formation, and the frighteningly global reach of the last remaining superpower today."[71] The twinned impulses of worldliness and humanism thus meet in this "continuous" critical practice aimed at re-engaging history and reintegrating power knowledge back into the global context of contemporary imperialism. And it does this by first resisting the disappearance of the past.

## AGAINST THE DISAPPEARANCE OF THE PAST

In a short piece on populism in the age of COVID-19 published on the London School of Economics Public Policy Review website in July 2020, Michael Ignatieff explains to his audience that "our" expectations "of 'normality'—expectations of stasis and equilibrium—make it difficult for us to identify when liberal democracy is truly in crisis."[72] This admission of opacity—of the possibility that denizens of liberal democracies might not immediately be able to recognize a rupture in the normal fabric of life when they see it, given the sheer volume of events—is interesting for a man who has spent the entirety of his career fretting over clear and present dangers. In January 2016, for instance, Ignatieff gave a lecture at Central European University in Budapest (of which he would soon become president) entitled "The Right to Have Rights: Migrants, Refugees and the Duties of States." "You are at the very center of a world historical event," Ignatieff warned his audience, "an unprecedented crisis."[73] Two years earlier, in "The New World Disorder," written for the *New York Review of Books*, Ignatieff implored his readers to accept the fact that Putin's invasion of Ukraine, the downing of flight MH17, and the ongoing violence in Syria had given rise to a "new world," one profoundly off-kilter from the long peace and prosperity brought about by the liberal order of the postwar era.[74] Even earlier, in 2003, confidently parroting what we now know to be false Bush administration intelligence, Ignatieff argued in "American Empire: The Burden" that a full-blown, US invasion of Iraq was absolutely necessary because "Iraq represents the first in a series of struggles to contain the proliferation of weapons of mass destruction, the first attempt to shut off the potential supply of lethal technologies to a global terrorist network."[75] In a 2002 article, Ignatieff insisted that our "contemporary situation in global politics has no precedent since the age of the later Roman emperors."[76] Going back even further, throughout the 1990s, Ignatieff's scholarly and quasi-scholarly writings on nationalism, human rights, and humanitarian intervention rely similarly on the assertion and reassertion of crises and turning-point moments.

Ignatieff appears, in each of these instance, as the sage, scholarly observer—perennially dragging Harvard behind his name like a golden ball on a chain—who stands on the doorstep and opines about the world historical events unfolding around him: the "crisis of human rights," the failure of the postcolonial project of self-determination, the "chaos" that followed the end of the Cold War.[77] Indeed, given the persistence with which Ignatieff declares that liberal democracy and the entire global order sit on the precipice of nonexistence, it is almost as easy to poke fun at his world historical pronouncements as it is to mimic the world historical pronouncements of the similarly dumbstruck Thomas Friedman.[78] And yet behind Ignatieff's histrionics—behind his perennially innocent hand wringing, his "oh what to do with this crisis?" proclamations—lie real consequences and real violence. Such proclamations are inevitably followed by prescriptive arguments that, in Said's words, "urge more destruction and death for distant civilians" living in what Ignatieff terms "postcolonial zones" where state failure and chaos reign supreme.[79]

Ignatieff's response to the crises in Syria and Ukraine in 2014 illustrates this addiction to crisis particularly well. Since 2012, he had been gently insisting that the United States ought to intervene in Syria for humanitarian reasons, even as he expressed reluctant satisfaction with the way Obama sought and failed to attract both domestic and international support for the use of force, arguing that when "democracy becomes the venue for testing the legitimacy of force, the bar of justification is set high."[80] By the summer of 2014, however, Ignatieff's worries had shifted from mild fear to the kind of full-on panic that he experienced just before the war with Iraq, when he insisted that the current situation in world politics was almost entirely unprecedented.[81] In "The New World Disorder," written in the summer of that year, Ignatieff implores his readers to understand that, in the new dysfunctional world brought on by the Syrian conflict and Russian expansionism, intervention must happen in Syria, and it must happen now. As in the early days of the new millennium, Ignatieff hammers home the case for increased US intervention by arguing that the contemporary circumstances were and without precedent.[82] "With the proclamation of a terrorist caliphate in the borderlands of Syria and Iraq," he argues, "the dissolution of the state order created by Mr. Sykes and Monsieur Picot in their treaty of 1916 is proceeding to a fiery denouement."[83]

Of course, as anyone with the slightest familiarity with the history of the Middle East knows, the Sykes-Picot Agreement was a treaty brokered in secret by Britain and France during the First World War, in which the two empires agreed to divide the former Ottoman territories between themselves, despite the fact that they had promised independence to the Arabs who fought with them in the war. The resulting mandated territories of the Middle East were administered by Britain and France with the sanction of the League of Nations, often through tactics of divide and rule or (in the case of Britain) through the novel use of chemical weapons.[84] The states that emerged from the mandatory period were rarely stable and were often purposely destabilized by France, Britain, and the United States throughout the coming century.[85] The order the agreement secured served the purposes of those global world powers intent on oil extraction and the antidemocratic leaders they supported, and the kind of Arab nationalism it engendered could be state centered and militaristic. And yet, for Ignatieff, the betrayal, chaos, and violence that followed in the immediate aftermath of Sykes-Picot and continues—in varying degrees—up to today, simply falls out of the picture when it comes to the current crisis. It is as if, for Ignatieff, the disorder of the present is frozen permanently in the looming, imperiled moment: urgent, frantic, desperately requiring military intervention. Nothing before contributed to the now, and nothing before deserves our "humble" humanistic consideration.

Said's humanist criticism provides us with two responses to the broader gesture Ignatieff's rhetoric typifies, a gesture that makes invisible and even impossible the historical and contemporary affiliations between European and American imperialism and the global disorder that so terrifies pundits of Ignatieff's ilk. The first response focuses on time and speed; the second, on counternarrative. Thus, in a 1991 interview he gave around the time of the First Gulf War, Said argues that there are "generally two time frames" that concerned intellectuals have to work with. The first, he maintains, is "immediate," and the other requires time. Said calls this latter approach "slow politics," an idea that he later expands in a 2003 essay he wrote in response to the buildup of another war with Iraq.[86] Reflecting on insights he develops in *Orientalism, Said argues in this essay that one of his main goals in writing Orientalism* had been to "use humanistic critique to open up the fields of struggle, to introduce a longer sequence of thought and analysis to replace the short bursts of polemical, thought-stopping fury that so imprison us."[87] Said thus understands his "slow politics" as a countermethod to the fast-paced, evolving, and often-quixotic logic for invasion proffered by the Bush administration and flowing from the pens of such imperialist public intellectuals as Bernard Lewis, Fouad Ajami, and Ignatieff himself.[88]

Hence, for Said, the work of protecting against and forestalling the disappearance of the past entails slowing analysis down, even in the midst of so-called crises. In other words, Said's humanistic resistance requires what he calls "slow but rational" criticism. It demands that inquiry pause, refuse to vomit out instantaneous solutions to "acts of terror" or "escalating violence," and instead engage in the careful (always-time-consuming) work of filling in the historical and discursive holes left by the linguistic and political bulldozer of the powerful—the space, for instance, between Sykes-Pico and the present. Homi Bhabha beautifully describes Said's approach here as the "slow narrative of humanistic critique," a "deliberative measure of ethical and political reflection that maintains tension rather than resolves it."[89] For Bhabha, Said's "slow reflection" resists the kinds of snap judgments and processes of totalization through which aesthetic schools and universalizing philosophies dispense with ambiguity and, instead, rushes from the event/text to the realm of transcendental value. And while Bhabha's emphasis here is on the aesthetic, Said himself clearly understood "slow reflection" in political terms as an antidote to the "polemical, thought stopping fury" that too often accompanies calls for invasion, regime change, sanctions, and so-called "targeted" drone strikes that belch forth from the world's global hegemon.[90]

The pace of Said's humanism enables deeper and more detailed historical inquiries into contemporary politics and, through these inquiries, constructions of counternarratives that challenge the excision of history—the muting of alternative voices—from narrative framings of the political present. Against the discursive-academic world of political science—where international relations (IR) scholars and foreign policy experts exert most authority over analyses of global politics and where these experts consistently evacuate global politics of any historical connection to imperialism—Said's method of slow, humanist inquiry patiently but insistently demands that we re-world these conversations. Critics do this by focusing inquiry on "what has been left out" (which histories, which voices) of the current object of fixation—the site for invasion, the civil war, the unrepentant terrorist, the "stateless" society, the rogue regime, the nuclear outlaw, the crowd of refugees—and then reading these absences against the dominating discourse. The idea is, again, to place these missing actualities "back in the center of things."[91]

The counternarrative strategy that Said employs most often in his scholarly and political (and scholarly-political) writings is a form of historical reorientation and re-placement. This practice begins with a heightened awareness of silence and utterance, a fine-grained attention to rhetoric and language grounded, as he puts it in "The Return to Philology," in a "lifelong attentiveness to the words and rhetorics by which language is used by human beings who exist in history."[92] This mode of critique drills into the space between words and silence to reveal the holes where narrating subjects should be, subjects like the majority of Palestinians who, despite their rhetorical invisibility, still experience the daily joys and trials of life and the material violence of a world that refuses to acknowledge them or create the space for them to represent themselves. As Said puts it in *Representations of the Intellectual, when the Western media pays attention to Palestinians, it is usually to emphasize their "terror or immoderation." Within this discursive environment, he continues, the rule of thumb is that "you renounce them soundly and go on to praise Israeli democracy." Then, he continues, "you must say something good about peace."*[93] The absence of Palestinian perspectives uttered by Palestinians is meant to go unnoticed beneath the speeding train of linked signifiers: democracy, peace, Israel, Palestine, terror.

From a Said-inspired perspective, the good we say about peace should always be read in the context of absence, in the shadow of the silence where voices connected to other, material existences should be. This begins with an investigation of the discursive strategies that enable unhearing and unseeing. In "Permission to Narrate," for instance, Said does this by excavating the rhetorical economy surrounding the 1982 Israeli invasion of Lebanon that made it so impossible for "policy makers, the media, and the liberal intelligentsia" in the United States and Europe to acknowledge the suffering of Palestinian people and the death of nearly 20,000 civilians.[94] He begins by focusing on the reception of a 1984 report (authored by an international commission of six jurists) entitled *Israel in Lebanon*. Written in the wake of the 1982 invasion, the report (which came out in Britain but failed to find a publisher in the United States) claims that Israel was guilty of acts of aggression contrary to international law, that it made use "of forbidden methods and weapons," and that it deliberately and recklessly bombed civilian targets.[95] Again, Said's critical goal here is to interrogate why policy makers in Israel, the United States, and Europe were so incapable of hearing these criticisms. The "political question of the moment," he argues, "is why, rather than fundamentally altering the Western view of Israel, the events of the summer of 1982 have been accommodated in all but a few places in the public realm to the view that prevailed before those events: that since Israel is in effect a civilized, democratic country constitutionally incapable of barbaric practices against Palestinians . . . its invasion of Lebanon was *ipso facto* justified."[96]

The rhetorical sleight of hand here is teleological, oriented toward deflecting attention away from Israeli state violence through assertions of Israeli state character. The noise and clatter of these character claims preemptively mute the embodied experiences and political articulations of Palestinians. Assertions about terrorism and terrorist violence—contrasted with democracy—stand in where collective and individual narration should be and make it impossible for "policy makers, the media, and the liberal intelligentsia" to, by Said's lights, make necessary connections; draw different, more nuanced conclusions; and, at base, recognize historical facts.[97]

The focus of Said's criticism here, however, is not just the media and foreign policy intelligentsia but also sympathetic, leftist intellectuals who believe that research, exposure, and an encyclopedic recitation of the facts on their own can make a difference. For instance, while tremendously sympathetic to Noam Chomsky's careful documentation of the long, complicated relationship between Israel, the United States, and the Palestinians in 1983's *The Fateful Triangle*, Said was not convinced that this compiled mass of evidence alone could percolate through the layers of narrative deflection that encase Western publics, who must be convinced in order to demand change from the Israeli state. "Facts," in his words, "do not speak for themselves, but require a socially acceptable narrative to absorb, sustain, and circulate them."[98] In the absence of Palestinian voices and the looming din of arguments about Israeli democratic character, alternative narratives cannot penetrate, and facts cannot be recognized as such.

In this discursive universe, bombings, apartheid, displacement, the struggle for water, the struggle to move freely, the artistic expressions, the cultural revivals, the stories of triumph, the stories of suffering, the stories of survival, the stories of protest—the stuff of historical/everyday Palestinian life—simply cannot stick to the edifice of a state "incapable of barbaric practices."[99] The invisibility of the Palestinian experience—in all its complexity—means that "policy makers, the media, and the liberal intelligentsia" can simply continue to make blanket statements about that experience even in the face of obvious and excessive Israeli state violence. For instance, only four months after a 2014 Israeli bombing campaign in Gaza that killed two thousand people (including five hundred children), Dennis Ross wrote in a *New York Times* op-ed that Israel was being too soft on terrorism and that it was "time to make it costly for [Palestinians] to focus on symbols rather than substance."[100] Only a massive deflective edifice and a gaping chasm between rhetoric and reality made it possible for this former director of policy planning in the State Department under George Bush—special advisor on the Middle East and Southwest Asia for both Bill Clinton and Secretary of State Hillary

Clinton—to overlook the deaths of five hundred children, as if their bodies lay scattered in a separate universe from the one he describes with such chilling calm.[101] Interrogating this thickening silence requires, for Said, a worldly "theory of perception, a theory of intellectual activity" that he identifies as the very essence of humanist practice. This oppositional mode of analysis remains hyperattentive to history, to power, and to the rhetorical elisions that dwell "between the space of words."[102]

Another example of this probing "between the space of words" in Said's political writings can be found in a 1989 article he wrote for the *Nation* entitled "Mideast Elections Agenda: Sanctum of the Strong," in which he looks closely at emerging plans to hold elections in Palestine as an alternative to the intifada and Israel's violent response. The Israeli prime minister and Bush administration officials alike, argues Said, refused to discuss "whatever might give substance" to the idea of elections, what leaders from both countries dismissed as "details" to be worked out later. Behind this caginess, Said identifies an Israeli and American rhetorical desire to have their cake and eat it, too, to engage in a political performance that looked and sounded like democracy but that never actually acknowledged the existence of the *demos*—the Palestinian people. Said goes on to interrogate this phenomenon through a careful exegesis of an interview Prime Minister Shamir gave to the *Jerusalem Post* that year that went largely ignored by US media. In the interview, Shamir made it clear that he had no interest in discussing the "details" of the election, including details regarding the shape of the electorate itself. The reporter continually pressed him on this:

> Q: "What if, after elections, the Palestinian representatives declare themselves a government?" "No," answers Shamir, "there has to be prior agreement on the process as a whole." Q: "But agreement by whom?" A: "By the body with whom we will negotiate before the election." Q: "So the agreement won't come before the elections?" A: "It must come before the elections." Q: "But before the elections no one has been elected. So who will agree?" A: " . . . Elections will be held only after agreement with a body which is going with us to the negotiations." Q: "But who is this body?" A: "It will have to be a Palestinian body."[103]

Said's analysis of this quotation guides us toward the obvious object missing from Shamir's discursive response: any recognition of the Palestinian people as a discrete nation—preexisting the Nakba and forged under conditions of exile, apartheid, and dispossession—who can be neither seen nor heard by the American and Israeli states, the Western media, and the countless liberal public intellectuals and political actors now insisting that elections take place. Said's analysis thus pulls out of the space between words the levels of evasion and deflection that stand in for where the *demos* should be.

This is a mode of "humanistic critique" devoted to opening up a "longer sequence of thought" that runs throughout the corpus of Said's scholarly and popular—and literary and political—work. Much of *Orientalism*, for instance, is devoted to the purposeful exposition of Orientalism's silences, probing the way silences circulate through the discursive universe of imperialism. We see this in his interrogation of eighteenth-century Europe's fascination with *The Bacchae* and with the play's generative gulf between Europe and the Orient, that "silent and dangerous space beyond familiar boundaries."[104] We see it also in his exploration of the early-twentieth-century Scottish historian H. A. R. Gibb's writings about Islam and the silences that surround Gibb's object of inquiry. For Gibb, and for other Orientalists, Said argues, the "one thing the Orient could not do was to represent itself."[105] Again and again, in *Orientalism*, Said excavates this lack of representation, the voices that filled its absence, the actual people who inhabited these spaces, and the various discursive strategies by which their silence was assured.

Alongside his efforts to expose silences, Said orients his worldly, humanist critique toward first dissolving "words like 'war' and 'peace' into their elements," then "recovering" what has been left out of dominant political and cultural narratives, finally "placing that missing actuality back in the center of things."[106] The process of "recovering" what has been left out of imperialist discourses—like those surrounding "peace processes" ordained by dominant states that circulate through American exceptionalist understandings of democratic governance at home and abroad—begins with a slow, measured self-reflection that moves in precisely the opposite direction from Ignatieff's rush to diagnose, contain, evade, and prescribe. Slow humanism demands an alternative accounting of the very crises and political phenomena that keep Ignatieff awake at night: the volatility of "rogue" regimes, the rise of ethnic violence, the insecurity of failed states, the threat of terrorism. It thus opens our interpretive horizons to both alternative accounts of the past and alternative visions for the future.

In many of his writings on Palestine-Israel, for instance, Said insists on slowing down inquiry to build up a counternarrative engagement with that conflict's imperial origins, origins that almost always go unseen or denied by mainstream accounts of the founding of the Israeli state.[107] In 1992's *The Question of Palestine*, for instance, Said begins by focusing on the period of intense Zionist planning for the state of Israel (during and after World War I) and on the emergence of an increasing popular, Orientalist discourse in Europe that imagined this future state rising from the ashes of an older, enfeebled, and rapidly disappearing Arab Palestine. Said maintains that this discourse mirrored conceptions crucial to "high European imperialism": the idea of the lazy native who was also passing into obscurity; the need to bring Western ingenuity to make an otherwise-fallow desert bloom; the descriptions of a near *terra nullius*, a landscape dotted with only a few—largely ruined—villages.[108] The Balfour Declaration of 1917, in which the British (soon to be the mandatory power in Palestine) declared that they "view with favor the establishment in Palestine of a national home for the Jewish people" was, Said argues, similarly imperialist in its logic and execution.[109] In this text and elsewhere, Said braids these historical acts of dispossession, disclosure, occupation, and disappearance with analyses of the way Palestinians are routinely erased from whatever iteration of the "peace process" are currently being discussed by mainstream Western media outlets or foreign policy think tanks.

Slow humanism thus entails writing back to the naturalized, densely skeined, discursive landscape that was and is the affiliative weave between the history of modern Western imperialism and contemporary culture; in Palestine-Israel, in the Middle East, in Latin America, in Asia, in Europe, in Africa, and within the settler societies of the United States, Australia, New Zealand, and Canada. For Said, this "work of theory, of criticism, demystification, deconsecration, and decentralization" is "never finished." Rather, theory must necessarily overflow its own banks in the same way as does imperialism, moving "beyond its confinements," unsettled and exilic, demanding the time it takes to link contemporary questions of justice, coexistence, and democracy to the past, the present, and the future.[110] The critical subject engaged in this analysis is self-aware of their own attachments and simultaneously willing to emigrate and theorize beyond those attachments. Such an analysis itself relies on no short cuts but instead questions the cultural signifiers that are accepted as common sense. And such an analysis reintegrates history, politics, and culture with the world rather than reading today's dominant institutions or the canonical texts of the "Western heritage" as vehicles through which "to see yourself, your people, society, and tradition in their best lights" and, in the process, to make a firm distinction between "us" and "them."[111]

All this makes Said's worldly humanism a particularly useful mode of interpretation for challenging the spaces of silence, eruptions of amnesia, willed "ignorance" (in Charles Mills's sense), and modes of unseeing that can work their way through political theories that claim some affiliation with particular ethical traditions, no matter how loose these affiliations.[112] Said's review of Michael Walzer's *Exodus and Revolution* offers a particularly productive glimpse into this interpretive disposition at work. Walzer has always styled himself a liberal communitarian of sorts, a moral philosopher who works within a tradition that attempts to puzzle through the relationship between a "practical" realism and a modest form of pacifism. His broadly catholic approach rejects Kantian and Rawlsian accounts of justice and maintains instead that we can identify "thin," ethical convergences emanating from "thick," local sites of normative agreement about human rights and/or conduct in war. These sites of convergence, Walzer argues, constitute what he refers to as "thin universalism."[113] Walzer's methodological deployment of these overlaps has remained remarkably consistent throughout his career, from 1972's "Dirty Hands," to 1977's *Just and Unjust Wars*, to 1999's *On Toleration*, to 2015's *The Paradox of Liberation*. His method thus pulls together insights from a number of transhistorical figures and schools, links this cluster of ideas together as a series of overlapping affiliations, and then draws from them a modest narrative meant to provide "practical" insights into the problems of peace and justice for the contemporary world.[114] Whether it be about terrorism or democratic tolerance, Walzer's often-breezy style and simple but effective rendering of complex ideas (through comparison to simplified representations of other complex ideas) makes him the ideal public intellectual for ethics- and foreign-policy-oriented think tanks and liberal publications eager for digestible bits of normative thinking that never stray too far from the status quo.[115]

Said's worldly, humanistic approach is, from the outset, the inverse of Walzer's methodology in a number of ways. The most telling of these differences—as is evident from the immense intellectual effort he brings to bear on his review of Walzer's extraordinarily slim book—is his enormous concern for slow, historically oriented arguments. While Said's frequent forays into the realm of public intellectualizing often entailed making bold statements, his academic work—no matter how interdisciplinary and "unsystematic"—is most often concerned with critically assessing cultural detail and assembling historical examples and secondary sources to buttress his arguments about power and discourse. Said brings a forensic zeal to his review of *Exodus and Revolution*, weaving his argument through both that text and the broad corpus of Walzer's work. Indeed, a perusal of his papers (housed in the Columbia University archives) reveal a massive folder bursting at the seams with primary and secondary literature written by and about Walzer.[116] Indeed, Walzer himself notes in his response to Said's review, "His materials are my own books and articles and everything I have written, in fact, since the watershed year of 1967."[117] For Walzer, Said's intense investigation into the breadth of his work can only be read as a form of character assassination, and in his astonishingly petty response to the review published in *Grande Street*, he elides every one of Said's substantive arguments, reiterating his assertion (with increasingly wounded intensity) that Said's motives were personal, his critique a reflection of his damaged and enraged soul. "People don't always get the enemies they want," he opines. "Edward Said seems particularly unsatisfied in this respect, and so he has set out to make up his enemies to suit himself."[118]

Walzer's harrumphing aside, Said's actual argument (as opposed to Walzer's caricature of that argument) is remarkably thorough, as is obvious from the very title, "Michael Walzer's 'Exodus and Revolution': A Canaanite Reading." In other words, Said's approach to the narrative Walzer develops in the book is to slow down its whimsical, fast-paced compilation of a liberationist tradition (from Exodus through the civil rights movement) and instead demand that Walzer take into account the myriad silent voices and historical experiences ("Canaanite" voices and experiences) over which his narrative simply bulldozes. As Said makes clear at the outset, he would have had very few quibbles with Walzer's argument had Walzer chosen to write the book "as a poetic or metaphoric excursus through an Old Testament text."[119] But that is not the book Walzer wrote. Instead, *Exodus and Revolution* claims to trace a "continuous history from the Exodus to the radical politics of our own time," a history that conveniently elides (among many other histories) the existence of all the other ancient and contemporary occupants of Israel who are not included in this messianic narrative.[120]

For Said, Walzer's non-metaphorical story of exile represents the worst of two worlds: a fantastical, whitewashed account of an exiled people on the one hand and a brutal silence with regard to Palestinian existence on the other, a silence that erases entirely the settler-colonial history of Israel and the contemporary conflicts to which it has given rise. What is so arresting about this book, Said claims, are the stunning intricacies of this silence. As a reader, he argues, "what bothers you is the world of Walzer's discourse, the verbal space in which his discussions and analyses take place, as well as the political locale isolated by him for reflection and hypothesis."[121] The Exodus story is an "imaginative geography," for Walzer, a platform on which he spins a narrative with a moral, a history, and an ethical conclusion that appears completely coherent on its own terms. As you read this story, Said continues, "you begin to notice how many extremely severe excisions and restrictions have occurred in order to produce the calmly civilized world of Walzer's Exodus."[122] Of course, he argues, this "strategy of decoupage" is not entirely avoidable; in the process of making an argument, every author of nonfiction does some "cutting and delimiting in order to manage his or her subject."[123] These cuttings tend to occur "offstage," Said continues, but not too far offstage, or the argument that the author makes necessarily exits the world of historical reality. The problem with *Exodus and Revolution* is that the excisions occur so far offstage and are so profoundly total in their expurgation that they begin to take on a life of their own, occasionally peaking above the waves of Walzer's prose like periscopes on a flotilla of silent submarines.

The result is a form of historical decoupage that excises Canaanite "others" from the "founding act" of people-making-through-exile that pumps life into Walzer's Exodus story.[124] Walzer frames this "founding act" as the template for both a Jewish state (now and in antiquity) as well as for *the* "radical politics of our time," a politics embraced historically, he argues, by groups as diverse as the English Puritans, the South African Boers, the African National Congress, Black civil rights leaders in United States, and supporters of liberation theology in Latin America.[125] From Said's perspective, the speedy exuberance of Walzer's excisions (and the affiliative story that these excisions make possible) has the double effect of transforming Exodus into the ur-history of contemporary social change and the contemporary history of Zionism into an unconflicted story of liberal progress. Ultimately, through its strategic silences, Walzer's narrative manages to conflate the history of liberation with the history of Zionism while presenting this history as both entirely "linear" and absolutely "clear."[126]

More disturbingly, and somewhat tragically, Said believes, *Exodus and Revolution* also has the effect of eviscerating any notion of belonging that includes historical and future coexistence. Indeed, he notes, the ultimate lesson the book seems to teach is that "you cannot both 'belong' and concern yourself with Canaanites who do not belong."[127] Said makes this point by contrasting the argument in the book with Walzer's 1984 essay on Camus's "intimate criticism." He sees in Walzer's praise for Camus's affiliation with "a people"—that is, *his* people, the "colonizing *pied-noirs* of Algeria"—a troubling rejection of precisely the critical distance he believes necessary to write the kind of "continuous history" Walzer claims to write in *Exodus and Revolution*.[128] In other words, Said finds that Walzer's unwillingness to reflect deeply on his own relationship to Zionism blinds him to a more complicated, post-1967 reality, in which it "became difficult to portray the Israeli occupation armies in Gaza, the West Bank, Sinai and the Golan Heights as furthering a great social experiment."[129]

Could it be, Said asks more forcefully in the bitter exchange of letters following Walzer's angry response to his review, that Walzer's "brand of 'connected' criticism, which had already rehabilitated Camus' refusal to condemn French colonialism," was now being used to expropriate Exodus as an "in-house community text" in order to "excuse Israel's ideology of ethnic or religious separation and systematic oppression of the Palestinian people entailed by that ideology?"[130] The problem with Walzer's "intimate criticism," for Said, is not that it is intimate. Intimacy—awareness of long and often-troublingly complicated connections to one's own people—is the bread and butter of Said's own understanding of exile. Rather, for Said, the problem lies first with Walzer's treatment of the Exodus story as universally applicable in the grand sweep of history and then with his subsequent unwillingness to trouble his intimate connection to a movement that, since 1967, has become increasingly violent, oppressive, nationalist, and unjust. Just as Walzer's

Camus essay fails to acknowledge that there is a significant normative distinction between the critic who is intimately connected to a society of oppressors and the critic "whose connection is to an *oppressed*," Walzer's failure to pause even for the briefest moment and reflect on his association with what is now—post-1967—an often-oppressive political movement associated with illegal settlements and right-wing extremism, is troubling to Said.[131] *Exodus and Revolution* is, at the end of the day, not a book about exile, history, or liberation, he argues, but a book about a narrative in search of liberatory validation. It obscures both the history and suffering of the Palestinian people while at the same time drawing a tight circle around a transhistorical, moral community whose existence is alluded to through myriad references to "us" and "ours."

The overall discursive impulse of Walzer's historical decoupage—which he is still conducting to this day—does yeoman's work for a species of identity politics in America that imagines liberalism as transhistorically connected to a long-standing agenda of peace, justice, and civil rights. In reality, that agenda is almost entirely blanched of detail and uncomfortable truths, blind to alternative narratives about how the present became what it is or how the commonsense liberal "we" became "us." Walzer's vituperous overreaction to Said's review—presuming, as it does, that Said's primary purpose is not to make a legitimate argument but to challenge Walzer's liberal/radical bona fides—highlights the fragility of this identity structure. It is a reaction formation, a profound act of projection that says far more about Walzer's tortured sense of political identity than it does about the quality or fairness of Said's argument.

To this day, that fragility drives Walzer to respond with disproportionate ire to any criticism of his work, no matter how gentle or respectful.[132] In an ironic mirroring of Donald Trump's defensive reaction to the mere mention of racism in the United States—as if simply uttering the word somehow implicated *him*—Walzer continues to bristle at the possibility that there are ways of approaching the politics of race and protest that differ from his own oft-rehearsed narratives about race and protest. In June 2020, for instance, he chided Black Lives Matter protestors for failing to grasp the importance of the racial "unity necessary to win" and, in July of that year, complained that the phrase *racial capitalism* was confusing and divisive.[133] "Do the writers who use it have some idea about what it means?" he groused. "Or are they just against racial capitalism, whatever it means?"[134] Of course, as Olúfẹ́mi O. Táíwò and Liam Kofi Bright argue in their polite response to Walzer's query, if Walzer had really wanted to know what the scholars and activists using the term meant by *racial capitalism*, then "[h]e could have just asked."[135] People would have explained to him that the term originated in the work of Eric Williams in the 1940s, that it has been developed over the years by such scholars Cedrick Robinson, Ruth Wilson Gilmore, Robyn Kelly, and others, and that its goal is to suggest the co-constituting—rather than exclusionary—entanglement of racism and capitalism.

But it would never occur to Walzer to ask such a thing because to ask would imply that the story he has so carefully constructed over the years about liberation, ethics, and "thin universalism" might not, in fact, be the whole story. To ask such a thing would suggest that the "us" of whom he speaks—liberal people of goodwill linked to a history of progress since Exodus—might themselves be affiliated with historical acts of violence, oppression, and exclusion that Walzer cannot—*will not*—see. Such questions would require acknowledgment, self-awareness, and, as Said insists, "compassion and atonement," feelings that do not come easily to a certain deflective kind of liberal. Ignatieff, for instance, and an entire generation of liberal foreign policy experts who participated in ginning up the ideological environment that rationalized the 2003 war in Iraq, have similarly been unable to express an ounce of compassion for the 2.4 million Iraqi dead, nor have they properly atoned for their complicity in providing the moral, political, and juridical justification for the invasion.[136] Looking at, acknowledging, and atoning for this complicity is impossible for liberal pundits like Ignatieff because the histories they tell are not meant to elicit reflection but to prevent other narratives from rising to the surface.

From this perspective, even when talking heads like Ignatieff claim to be considering the impact of history, they can only do so through elision, through amnesia, and through modes of speech so deflective that facts bounce of them like rocks off the windshield of a speeding car. By way of example, at a panel discussion on military involvement in Syria and Iraq held at Harvard in the summer of 2014, Ignatieff took a moment to consider the "lessons" of an invasion he had wholeheartedly and publicly supported in 2003. "I think the United States is in the middle of a very difficult re-evaluation of its role in the world consequent upon Iraq," he noted.

> Part of the challenge of thinking about the Middle East is to learn from the lessons of failure. Clearly invading a large and proud Arab country with a lot of troops and trying in a very short period of time to build stable institutions and then coming home didn't work very well at all. But the alternative, which is to give a lot of speeches and walk away, seems to me to draw the wrong lesson from failure.[137]

Even in the very moment of "re-evaluation," Ignatieff's memory won't allow him to fill in the details that led up to the war with anything other than a blank, "large and proud" Arab nation stripped of imperial history, recent and remote. Against such blankness, the only lessons to be learned are about "us" and "our" capacity to act boldly or to dither. In the end, with Walzer, every time Ignatieff speaks, he not only draws a curtain over the richness of the past—he not only bolsters a narrative in which "facts do not speak for themselves"—but he also forecloses any alternative understandings of connection, of a political life based not on decoupage and elision and the space between words but on the whole, worldly cloth of coexistence.

## RATHER THAN FIELDS OF BATTLE

The election of Donald Trump did more than offer America a terrifying glimpse of a racist, postdemocratic future. It also ushered in a new era of liberal panegyrics. In the pages of popular and semipopular academic journals, cable news, social media—any communicative space that would cozen their anguished howls—liberal public intellectuals struggled to come to terms with the election of a commander-in-chief who was willing to simply say things aloud that, for years, his more self-controlled predecessors had kept on the down low. In the context of foreign policy alone, Trump's racist references to "shithole countries," his glib asides about the size of his "nuclear button," and his cavalier willingness to ask foreign governments to interfere in American elections (thus accidentally revealing the extent to which the United States has interfered in the elections of states around the globe since the end of the Second World War) relentlessly exposed the fragility of America's enlightened self-perception.

Such utterances have driven some of the most mainstream liberal public intellectuals and political theorists to suddenly become fascinated by the politics of populism, identity, and—in the words of Rogers Smith—the "stories we tell ourselves" about "who we are."[138] For thinkers like Walzer, this has meant explicit hand wringing about what liberalism means "for us" in the context of a country in which nearly half of Americans want a White nationalist autocrat to be their president.[139] Liberal thinkers and pundits worry about the "dangers" they didn't see coming from the placid flow of American culture, dangers lurking behind our current moment.[140] Similarly, Trump's election compelled supporters of the "American-led liberal world order" like John Ikenberry to clutch their pearls in horror at the "hostile revisionist power" who sat in the Oval Office, scheming to overthrow everything good about that world order—"trade, alliances, international law, multilateralism, environmental protection, torture, and human rights."[141] In all, liberal public intellectuals have responded to Trump by turning inward and perseverating on "who we are" while mourning the loss of the liberal world.

Not surprisingly, given that Trump often presents like a character out of central casting for a film about the rise of Hitler or Mussolini, a number of these thinkers have turned toward investigations of Nazi Germany in an effort both to theorize the potential populist dangers flowing like toxins through the liberal body politic and to interrogate the aesthetic qualities of what William Connolly calls Trump's "aspirational fascism."[142] From early journalistic fixations with Trump's seeming passion for *Mein Kampf* to the subsequent explosion of cross-disciplinary literature on right-wing populism, scholars and public intellectuals have sought historical lessons in the rise of the Third Reich and in the Frankfurt School's account of the authoritarian personality.[143] In an indication of just how deeply the similarity between Trumpism and Nazism seemed to cut, in the week after Trump's inauguration, so many people rushed out to buy Hannah Arendt's classic text *The Origins of Totalitarianism* that Amazon completely sold out of copies.[144]

This turn to Arendt is simultaneously both deeply understandable and more than a bit ironic. It makes sense given that, in her historical moment, Arendt was similarly trying to explain the emergence of totalitarianism from within a "liberal democratic" context. It is ironic in that, unlike nearly all other public intellectual and political theoretical inquiries into the rise of right-wing populism—historically and today—it offers the reader a prolonged glimpse into the relationship between totalitarianism in Europe and European imperialism; that is, between the liberal polity whose transformation she sought to explain and the illiberal acts of that polity in the world. Again, for Arendt, the origins of early-twentieth-century totalitarianism—the way it rendered entire populations capable of embracing, as she puts it in *Eichmann in Jerusalem*, the "fearsome, word-and-thought-defying banality of evil"—must be understood in terms that are not confined to a sui generous anti-Semitism flowing from changes in Europe's political economy and the nation-state form.[145] Rather, her analysis also stresses the political and economic expansion of European power *outside* Europe and the transformation of scientific racism in a colonial context into a political force that boomerangs back onto the homeland.[146]

And yet, Arendt's boomerang thesis is not only extraordinarily enlightening for what it tells us about the rise of totalitarianism in Europe via European totalitarianism in the colonies, but also for what it tells us about Arendt's sense of what has been lost in the process. In other words, for Arendt, the modern era more generally is distinguished by the seepage of managerial thinking (which she associates with the "housekeeping" activities of the private sphere) into the public realm.[147] The metastasizing tyranny of the *oikos* over the *polis*, she argues, created a vacuum in Europe that only nationalism and then imperialism could fill, and once unhitched from the restraining bonds of the state, these dominating impulses rebounded, creating the ethical conditions both for Nazism and for the annihilation of the public. Writing in the 1950s, in the wake of the Holocaust and out of the starkness of her own exile, Arendt describes this new reality as the "loss of the world."[148]

In *The Human Condition*, Arendt explains that what makes this loss so unsettling is the absence of anything to mediate the political/ethical space that has now opened up between "us": the denizens of that etiolated husk that used to be the public sphere. Arendt continues, "The weirdness of this situation . . . resembles a spiritualistic seance where a number of people gathered around a table might suddenly, through some magic trick, see the table vanish from their midst, so that two persons sitting opposite each other were no longer separated but also would be entirely unrelated to each other by anything tangible."[149] The tangibility of the world, for Arendt, the ethical/philosophical/political/cultural structures that connect "us" to each other, have disappeared from the modernity-wrecked landscape, and we find ourselves in free-floating limbo, unable to meaningfully communicate or find common ground.

Interestingly, for a critic of imperialism who spent so much time thinking about European actions outside Europe, Arendt's political-theoretical response to this evaporation of the public sphere—and the crisis of political identity and political culture engendered by modernity—entails virtually no engagement at all with non-Europeans. Again, as Arendt puts it later in her *Denktagebuch*, the "real tragedy" of imperialism was not imperialism itself but rather the fact that imperialism became the only way for Europe to solve "national problems that had become insoluble."[150] Hence, theorizing the rise of totalitarianism through the unhinged and unbounded expressions of power and domination that came to fruition in a colonial context requires, for Arendt, no sustained rumination on imperialism as a specific form of domination with its own forms of knowledge or on the specificities of the imperial context for non-Europeans. In other words, Arendt found it unnecessary to dwell on the long-term impact of European resource extraction, land dispossession, and racial violence on the colonies, nor was she the least interested in the modes of life on the African continent that were disrupted by colonialism. The pre-European experience of the "natives" fails to grasp Arendt's attention in *Origins* because her interest begins and ends with the experience of European imperialists in Africa. Thus, while she is peripherally concerned with the Boers, she relegates Africans themselves to the shadowy dreamworld before civilized time, a somnambulant historical space where inhabitants "vegetated for thousands of years."[151]

Hence, while Arendt believed that political life in Europe had stumbled (with the evisceration of the public sphere) and then fallen (first into imperialism then into totalitarianism), she never considered that the philosophical traditions associated with Europe might need to be supplemented, in some way, by engagement with the world beyond Europe. Her philosophical response to the lost world of public culture was to turn inward, toward a novel reengagement with older European traditions. Arendt describes this need for reengagement in the absence of familiar normative guidelines as the process of negotiating a world without "banisters." Under normal conditions, she argues, "as you go up and down the stairs you can always hold on to the banister so that you won't fall down," but now, "we have lost this banister."[152] For Arendt, "thinking without a banister" entails abandoning the flawed principles of modernity and steering critical subjects toward creative reinterpretations of normative ideals.[153] She found philosophical means of resisting the conflation of the private and public spheres, for instance, in a reinterpretation of the Athenian *polis*, in Aristotle's commitment to *zoon politikon*, and in the tradition of Greek thought she finds "throughout Occidental antiquity."[154] Confronting the world that is lost then, for Arendt, means using the tools of hermeneutics to look critically at the ur-phenomena that have been lost from sight: to look, with eyes "undistorted by any tradition, with a directness which has disappeared from Occidental reading and hearing ever since Roman civilization submitted to the authority of Greek thought."[155]

In essence, Arendt never imagines that a European crisis of modernity (first realized in the violence of imperialism and then in the catastrophic violence of the Holocaust) requires anything other than a culturally insular, "Occidental" response, despite the fact that this crisis quickened in the womb of Europe's engagement with the colonial world. In noting this internal response, I am not implying that Arendt's reaction to the loss of her world is nearly as facile as so much of the American public intellectualizing in the face of Trumpism and the loss of "our" liberal values. These nostrums are largely nostalgic, oriented toward a return to what makes us "us" in the first place. "Thinking without a banister" is more complicated than this, more self-reflective, and it can ultimately give rise to a distinct approach to political ethics that Myers describes as "care for the world."[156]

At the same time, while Arendt may have been horrified by imperialism, the Holocaust, and the deracinating effects of modernity on the public sphere, her philosophical response is ultimately—despite its bold, "banister-less" character—about *return*, about re-creating the new polis from the ashes of the old. Nothing suggests this more strongly than the metaphors she uses to describe the loss of the world and its re-creation. For a woman who was so intensely critical of the bourgeois private sphere and "housekeeping," these metaphors are notably domestic and contained, internal to the house or the *oikos*: the table, the banister, the "four walls of one's private property."[157] This house/world is blind to sites beyond its conceptual purview except insofar as what happens in those sites affects the home front. This house/world is self-haunted, maimed by the long-term impact of touching—and never being touched by—the colonized other. Rebuilding the new house/world without banisters implies no reckoning with the excessive violence of imperialism, no compassion, no atonement, no acknowledgment. All the needful items for its reimagination can be found within. The doors of this house/world remain closed against the possibility that conceptual resources for fighting totalitarianism and forging new collective life worlds in our age might be found elsewhere: in other cultures, other politics, and the fraught points of connection forged through imperialism and a shared global history.

By contrast, when Said, like Arendt, slips into domestic metaphors, he tends not to emphasize the furniture nor the walls but rather the passages in and out of the house: doorsteps, doorways, windowsills.[158] For Said, it is precisely in these passages in and out, in the critical practices of a mobile, "unhoused," exilic anticolonialism—practices "born in the resistance and opposition to the confinements and ravages of imperialism"—that we find disruptive, decentered forms of culture, theory, and politics.[159] This is the exilic space "between domains, between forms, between homes, and between languages," and it is here, again in the works of anticolonial thinkers, that Said identifies the liberatory, critical energies necessary to establish and foster "fields of coexistence."[160] A worldly humanist response to the "loss of the world" that Trump's appearance on the political scene portends would be more likely to confront rather than avoid the decimating impact of settler colonialism and slavery on contemporary American politics, the terror engendered by seventy years of US anti-insurgency policies abroad, and the deaths of countless Black men and women at the hands of a militarized police force at home.

Likewise, a worldly humanist response to the global crisis of liberal democracy would entail neither retrenchment nor a reaffirmation of "who we are"—no matter how banister-less the affirmation. Rather, for Said, the world itself *is already* contaminated by the "holding and crossing over" between colonialism in the past and the politics of today.[161] We cannot undo this past, and therefore the stuff we need to reimagine the world lies not in imaginary, self-contained spheres of tradition, doctrine, identity, "complete theories," or canons. Rather, we can only find it in the "hybrid counter-energies" and hints of "collective human existence" that spring from the experiences of exile and the overlapping histories of imperialism. We can only find it, in other words, in the connections we build as we come and go through, in Said's words, the "large, many-windowed house of human culture as a whole."[162]

Said locates these collective, hybrid counter-energies in myriad historical, cultural, political spaces, most of them arising *out of* the contested and joint experiences of the colonized and the colonizer. The "overlapping experience of Westerners and Orientals," he argues in *Culture and Imperialism*, and the "interdependence of cultural terrains in which colonizer and colonized co-existed and battled each other through projections as well as rival geographies, narratives, and histories" provide the raw material for theorizing and imagining different, more capacious, potentially more just forms of human comity.[163] Said once described imperialism as a "vast ocean of human effort in which the official culture exists like an archipelago."[164] In the currents and countercurrents that mix and flow around and against this archipelago, he discovers sites for coexistence: in the "multicultural, multiethnic, multireligious" history of Palestine, in the "potential for an emergent non-coercive culture" in the writings of revolutionary Iranian writer Ali Shariati, in the "alternative communities all across the world" that sprang up in protest before the war in Iraq.[165] Over the years, numerous Said-inspired scholars have taken this insight and used it to explore the "repressed or resistant" histories of overlap and human culture-making within communities of crossover and resistance that thrive throughout the archipelago: in Maroon settlements in Jamaica, in the Creole "intimacies" of Black, Chinese, and Indian laborers in the British West Indies, in the globe-spanning, anticolonial resistance movements that animated the mid-twentieth century.[166] For Said, imperialism brings people together through practices of domination and discourses of hierarchical ordering while simultaneously engendering new modes of interaction, new cultures of resistance, and new forms of connection.

Again, for Said, there is nothing facile or overly optimistic about these connections, no easy acceptance of an indwelling culture of coexistence that we can ferret out if we just look close enough, deep enough into the past. I am not, Said insists in "The Changing Bases of Humanistic Study and Practice," "speaking of domestication, of tokenism, or polite civility." This is not, he continues, a "laissez-faire or feel-good multiculturalism."[167] Rather, the kind of "humanistic culture as co-existence" that he envisions throughout *Humanism and Democratic Criticism* and elsewhere requires human effort and human envisioning precisely because the contradictions, tensions, and necessary complexities involved in the broad, historical reach of imperialism generates communities that are themselves often at cross-purposes. As Paul Bové puts it in his sensitive review of Said's *Culture and Imperialism*, nationalisms "form communities against imperial occupation; yet nationalisms threaten division and separatism."[168] This is why Said continually turns to examples of people working from within an anticolonial framework who were committed to challenging nationalism, not by rejecting its resistant energies, but by both troubling its limitations and "deconsecrating" and "demystifying" the metropole. Fanon, Said maintains, believed that a "new system of mobile relationships must replace the hierarchies inherited from imperialism." Through a combination of political philosophy, poetry, and drama, Said continues, Fanon made a case for liberation as "consciousness of self 'not the closing of a door to communication' but a never-ending process of 'discovery and encouragement' leading to true national self-liberation and to universalism."[169] "Liberation" and human coexistence, for Said, thus emerge out of a practice of both opening up—of being "saturated with worldly concerns"—and of self-reflection, or "consciousness of self."[170]

In the context of dominant and imperial societies, this twinned impulse necessarily entails confronting the material co-constitution of the global North and the global South, confronting, that is, the extent to which "liberal democracies"—whose very existence is now endangered by the autocrats, populists, and [w]hite nationalists that send liberals into paroxysms of fear and doubt—are themselves the products of imperialism. As Gurminder Bambra argues, today's European welfare states developed within the context of long-standing, historical patterns of wealth accumulation and racialized immigration policies first normalized within an imperial context. These same states developed labor markets grounded in racist forms of domination and exclusion. In postwar Britain, for instance, the "apparently domestically inclusive welfare state regime" depended on a political economy "of Imperial and (subsequently) Commonwealth preferences which was designed to enrich the British state while restricting the rights extended to subjects throughout its territories."[171] Likewise, in the context of the United States, the racist and militarized police practices that came to be the focus of so much protest in the summer of 2020 cannot themselves be completely understood in the absence of what Stuart Schrader calls a "frenzied, to-and-fro itinerary" between racist policing at home and a history of American counterintelligence practices abroad.[172] In other words, the politics and policies that frequently strike the liberal imagination as uniquely new and troubling have, in reality, long imperial histories.

Along with what he describes as Fanon's, James's, and Césaire's conscious efforts to "enter into the discourse of Europe and the West" by forcing it to "acknowledge marginalized or suppressed or forgotten histories," Said insists that engagement with suppressed and constituent histories plays an essential role in the process of opening up humanistic fields of coexistence.[173] Where Arendt's "world" circles inward toward a house without banisters, Said's worldliness moves between inside and out, between acknowledgment and shared futures. Any plans for peace, any visions of human coexistence, for Said, *must* entail grappling with the imperial past (recent and remote) and with the fact that these pasts still structure the inequalities of the present—a fact that remains unchanged despite the formal equality of nations. "The major task," he thus argues in a 1988 interview with Bruce Robbins, "of the American or the Palestinian or the Israeli intellectual of the Left is to reveal the disparity between the so-called two sides, which appear rhetorically and ideologically to be in perfect balance but are not in fact."[174] In reality, he continues, "there is an oppressed and oppressor," and no vision of the future is possible in the absence of this recognition.

Said's insistence on this point ultimately became another point of contention in his long-standing disagreement with Walzer, a disagreement on full display in a public confrontation that took place during a 1988 debate. Said later recalled,

> At one point, Walzer said to me: "Alright, listen. You've recognized Israel. You obviously have or can have your own state. But don't keep speaking about the past. Let's talk about the future." This is very often said to me by my critics; that I always talk about the past, that I dwell too much on the injustices done to Palestinians, and so on and so forth. The audience was, I would say, about 99% Jewish. When he said it, my mouth hung open but I didn't say anything because a woman in the audience . . . got up and started vociferously attacking Walzer. She said: "How dare you say that to a Palestinian? How dare you say that to anybody? Because of all the people in the world, we ask the world to remember our past. And you're telling a Palestinian to forget the past? How dare you." It was an extraordinary thing.[175]

Walzer's irritation at Said, his insistence that Said move on and stop talking about the past, is understandable, given that most of his work treats history as a necessary backdrop against which one develops practical theories with thin universal value. For Said, by contrast, the "disruptive detail" of history, as he puts it in *Orientalism*, cannot be suppressed for the convenience of the theorist but must be actively engaged, while in the political realm, inequalities and past injustices must be actively rectified.[176] Thus, in the case of Palestine-Israel, anyone actually interested in "peace" has to begin with a frank acknowledgment that the "idea of inequality between Jews and Arabs" was "built into British, and subsequently Israeli and United States, policy from the start."[177] This is the precursor, for Said, to any discussion about peace.

Rather than running in a single direction, this envisioning requires people within overlapping communities to creatively engage the lived, historical facticity of each other's existence. Indeed, if there is one theme that consistently reemerges throughout Said's work, it is the danger of separation, of partition, of *disengagement,* all of which lead, he argues, to political solipsism and the fetishization of identity. Thus, Said consistently champions the kind of engagements that flow from both acknowledgment of history and the sympathies, insights, and affiliations forged through the "hybrid energies" of exile, with its "crossing of barriers" and "accommodation with various cultures." For Said, the exilic realm makes possible both the "interplay" between "memory, place, and invention" and the active reimagination of "liberation and coexistence."[178]

To provide a "concrete example" of this kind of imagining, Said turns again to Palestine-Israel. Israelis and Palestinians, he argues in 2000's "Invention,

Memory, and Place," are now "so intertwined through history, geography, and political actuality that it seems to me absolute folly to try and plan the future of one without that of the other."[179] The problem, he thus argues, with the American-sponsored Oslo Accords, was that it assumed separation and partition, which, more than anything, "closed these two unequal communities of suffering to each other" so that the kinds of real recognition necessary for coexistence were hidden from sight. New forms of community, new possibilities for human coexistence, for Said, had to be creatively reimagined from the realm of overlap, from the very fact that "everywhere one looks in the territory of historical Palestine, Jews and Palestinians live together."[180] The "liberation and coexistence" that Said prefers start "once we grant that Palestinians and Israelis are there to stay."[181] Or, as Judith Butler puts it in her comparison of Said and Martin Buber, once we grant that "Israel and Palestine are parts rather than antagonists of each other's history and underlying reality."[182] At its core, recognition of this "part-ness" entails seeing "the other" as someone who—like you—criticizes, creates, and makes the world—and reads you in your presence. Worldly humanistic practice, at the end of the day, must begin from acknowledgment of shared history, shared territory, and shared humanity. Only then can one move on to imagining coexistence.

And yet even in the moment of reaching for this coexistence, Said acknowledges that the tensions and "disruptive detail" of history never disappear and the various conflicting experiences to which they give rise can never be entirely resolved. Indeed, as I discuss in chapter 2, such attempts at philosophical and/or political resolution frequently efface and repress alternative—often-conflicting—interpretations of both the past and the present. Thus, unresolved tensions will always remain in Palestine-Israel, Said insists, given the historical realities that constitute the current situation. The struggle over Palestine, Said continues, cannot "be simply resolved by a technical and ultimately janitorial rearrangement of geography allowing dispossessed Palestinians the right (such as it is) to live in about 20 percent of their land." Nor, he continues, "would it be morally acceptable to demand that Israelis should retreat from the whole of former Palestine, now Israel" essentially becoming refugees all over again, like the Palestinians. "No matter how much I have searched for a resolution to this impasse," he concludes, "I cannot find one for this is not a facile case of right versus wrong."[183]

This does not, however, mean that Said believes those seeking to construct fields of coexistence rather than fields of battle should simply abandon this endeavor altogether. Rather, the key to worldly humanism is the frank acknowledgment that total reconciliation is impossible. Overlapping yet irreconcilable experiences demand, Said insists, the "courage to say *that* is what is before us."[184] This is a method for thinking about coexistence that remains radically open to the irreconcilable. As Said put it in another 1999 lecture, "Humanism is disclosure; it is agency; it is immersing oneself in the element of history; it is recovering what Vico calls the topics of mind from the turbulent actualities of human life."[185] There can be no reconciliation, but there can be overlap, and there can be coexistence, and there can, he insists, be more just, less dominative forms of political life. The point, he insists, is to think through disclosure to better understand the unbelievable difficulty involved with constructing spheres of coexistence. And then to commit oneself to this effort anyway.

Said's humanism here stands in exquisite contrast to Arendt's thinking without a banister. Her response to the "loss of the world" is similar in some ways to that of many liberals as they struggled to come to terms with Trump's election and the spike in [w]hite nationalism that this election heralded around the world. She circles in. She concentrates on the furniture. And while it is no doubt unfair to compare the reactions of Walzer and Ikenberry to Arendt's more sophisticated and creative reimagining through antiquity, the political-theoretical impulse—the turning inward, the fascination with what makes "us" us—remains the same.

Even for a left populist like Chantal Mouffe, the rise of fascism in Europe and America requires a similar circling in what remains ignorant of the "turbulent actualities" of history and, in particular, of imperial or settler-colonial history as it pertains to the founding of the very "people" with whom she is concerned. Rather than falling back on ethnic or nationalist assumptions about what constitutes a "people," Mouffe insists in 2018's *For a Left Populism*, that the process through which a people is/are constituted ought to involve democratic contestation.[186] She never interrogates, however, the way this "people" also just happens to cohere to the nation-state, and this coherence has—in the context of the United Kingdom, France, and Belgium—an imperial history. In this sense, Mouffe responds to the rise of right populism by doing what she always does: acknowledging the "paradox" of liberal democracy (the tension between the bounded nature of the polity and the freedom of the liberal individual) and then accepting that the "logic of democracy" implies a "moment of closure which is required by the very process of constituting the 'people.'"[187] There is, for Mouffe, an outer edge to critique that holds "us" together, and this "us" is foundational; it precedes politics even as it is meant to be the subject of democratic contestation.[188] The *demos*, for Mouffe, is conditioned from the very outset by its boundaries.

Said, by contrast, begins with disclosure, with "irreconcilable experiences," and then moves back and forth between these paradoxes and moments of overlap and coexistence. His conception of the "world" remains open to glimmers of connective resources in the past and present and creative reimaginings of political life in the future. It thus begins by de-exceptionalizing the current moment and the current polity rather than nostalgically insisting that it be reinvigorated through return (e.g., Walzer and Ikenberry) or through banister-less reengagement with an "Occidental" tradition (e.g., Arendt) or through a "left populism" that remains committed to the fixity of the "people" (e.g., Mouffe). And it begins, as Said makes clear in his early support for Rushdie's *Satanic Verses*, by holding two ideas in tension: that there is no "pure, unsullied, unmixed essence to which some of us can return" and that "although it contains many spheres, the contemporary world of men and women is one world."[189]

## HUMANISM IN THE WORLD

The internal rhythm of Said's worldly humanism—the movement between forestalling against the disappearance of the past and constructing fields of coexistence rather than battle—serves as an important corrective to some impulses in political theory that tend toward closure and toward a reading of history that strips it of "disruptive detail." In this sense, worldly humanism helps prize open political imagination to voices that have been denied permission to narrate and to tension-filled moments of connection in both the past and the present that can serve as sites for sustained political engagement. For this reason, it is hardly surprising that those few political theorists over the years who have looked seriously to Said as a source of inspiration have been thinkers like Tully who also have capacious, humanistic interests in "deparochializing" dialogue and exposing the multiplicity of "different *practices* of citizenship in the West and non-West" that have circulated, and continue to circulate, through the global "contrapuntal ensemble."[190]

At the same time, Said's insistence on remaining in the "precarious exilic realm" and his resistance to closure can also be objectively, frustratingly, and maddeningly vague for political theorists of a variety of stripes. On the one hand, normative theorists and analytical philosophers who are interested in developing moral and philosophical frameworks for "transitional justice" or multicultural democracy are never going to be satisfied with Said's approach. Said, for instance, used words like *justice* and *peace*, but he remained resolutely uninterested in *theorizing them* or in subjecting these terms to modes of analysis that removed them from imperial context. On the other hand, Said's worldly humanism also presents problems for critical theorists interested in constructing counterhegemonic projects. In this sense, for all that Said was drawn to and inspired by Gramsci's interpretation of public intellectuals, his writings on common sense and hegemony, and his "explicitly geographical model" of culture and power, he was less interested in Gramsci's positive theorizing about how to foster a "national popular collective will."[191] We get very little in the way of strategy from Said, very little about building counter-hegemonies or movement politics or organizing.

This does not mean, however, that Said didn't demand better, more just, more pluralistic and democratic political futures. Indeed, for Said, humanism is the "only and I would go so far as saying the final resistance we have against the inhuman practices and injustices that disfigure human history."[192] His primary concern, however, and the impulse of his political project, is not to theorize the details of that "final resistance" nor the shape of the world to come. In fact, the very act of theorizing such details entails precisely the kinds of abstract, otherworldly thinking that, he argues, can blinker political options, silence alternative voices, and hasten the disappearance of the past. And again, this can be enormously frustrating for anyone interested in theorizing movement politics, for instance, or democratic participation. But if one can accept worldly humanism for what it is—a mode of "oppositional analysis" that does not dwell in the pain or "dignity" of others nor tell inspirational stories about the ahistorical emergence of justice traditions over time but instead opens up spaces of connection and coexistence—it can be enormously generative for politics and thinking politics. Humanism in this mode is a disposition toward slowing down, digging "between the space of words," and embracing the reflective possibilities of reading and being read. Humanism, as Said puts it in the last line of "The Return to Philology," takes the search for justice, knowledge, and liberation to the "ground of daily life and history and hopes."[193] The ground, you might say, where critique and solidarity come face-to-face.

# 5

# The Honeypots of Our Minds

## *Public Intellectuals in an Imperial World*

In 1987, Edward Said delivered a paper at the annual meeting of the American Anthropological Association in Chicago that would form the basis of his influential 1989 article "Representing the Colonized: Anthropology's Interlocutors." Written roughly ten years after the publication of *Orientalism*, Said explained to his audience of academic anthropologists that one of the things he had tried to do in that field-transforming text was investigate the role that scholars and intellectuals play in sustaining and challenging imperial discourse, both from within imperialist societies themselves and from within the colonized world. In both settings, he maintains, these figures can be roughly divided into two categories: powerful and/or "compliant" interlocutors whose intellectual inquiry furthers the goals of the imperial society, and noncompliant interlocutors who adopt a "radically antagonistic" mode of interlocution with imperial power.[1]

Said then proceeds to think through what these categories of interlocutors mean in the context of America today: that is, in the context of an imperial state supported by an imperial culture, both of which insistently refuse to acknowledge themselves as such. At stake, he argues, is the

> deep, the profoundly perturbed and perturbing question of our relationship to others—other cultures, other states, other histories, other experiences, traditions, peoples, and destinies. The difficulty with the question is that there is no vantage outside the actuality of relationships between cultures, between unequal imperial and nonimperial powers, between different Others, a vantage that might allow one the epistemological privilege of somehow judging, evaluating, and interpreting free of the encumbering interests, emotions, and engagements of the ongoing relationships themselves. When we consider the connections between the United States and the rest of the world, we are so to speak *of* the connections,

133

not outside and beyond them. It therefore behooves us as intellectuals, humanists, and secular critics to grasp the role of the United States in the world of
nations and of power, from *within* the actuality, and as participants in it, not
as detached outside observers who, like Oliver Goldsmith in Yeats' marvelous
phrase, deliberately sip at the honeypots of our minds.[2]

For Said, there is no neutral vantage point within the belly of the beast, no
"outside and beyond" that enables "epistemological privilege" free from the
"ongoing relationship" between America and its various "others." American
intellectuals, he insists, are *of* the connections between the United States and
the rest of the world. Rather than turning inward and sipping at the honeypots
of our minds, he insists, "intellectuals, humanists, and secular critics" must
begin their analyses by reflecting on and confronting both these connections
themselves and the role intellectuals play in sustaining them through popular
and scholarly elaborations of both the "other" and "*our* culture."[3] Such work
entails speaking back to the lingering, layered modes of silence that consistently diminish the audible roar of American power abroad and at home. It
also means challenging both those anodyne, exceptionalist discourses *and* the
neutral, academic "we" voice that supports these silences. In Said's words,
"writing and speaking to silence" is nothing less than the "functional idiom
of the intellectual vocation."[4]

Said elaborates on this vocation later in the introduction to 1994's
*Representations of the Intellectual, turning to James Baldwin and Malcolm X
as examples of thinkers who "most influenced my representation of the intellectual's consciousness," a consciousness gripped by what he describes as a
"spirit in opposition rather than accommodation."*[5] Such a spirit relentlessly
upends the subjective surety of mainstream intellectual culture in the global
North (particularly the United States) and demands a different orientation
toward politics, culture, and knowledge, one Said unflinchingly links to both
the disorientation of exile and the history of anticolonial struggle. "What
Fanon and Césaire required of their own partisans," he argues, "even during the heat of struggle, was to abandon fixed ideas of settled identity and
culturally authorized definition" and instead to remain perennially alert to
the ways identity and inclusion can silence and exclude.[6] So, too, he argues,
must "intellectuals, humanists, and secular critics" who speak and theorize
from within or adjacent to the American academy call into question their use
of the nominally inclusive "we" voice. Rather, as Joseph Masad puts it, Said
always believed the "life of an intellectual should be that of a migrant and
an exile," perennially unsettled and disruptive, acknowledging and forging
affiliations, and always drawing attention to the halting quietude and smooth
silences that obscure and rationalize domination.[7] Throughout his career, he

spent a considerable amount of time elaborating on what it means to be an intellectual who thinks, writes, speaks, and acts as an exile.

This chapter begins with a closer look at Said's understanding of the relationship between public intellectuals and political power, paying particular attention to his treatment of those figures associated most closely with quasi-scholarly accounts of both the "other" and "our culture" that function to legitimate imperial power. I also speculate further about why it is that so many political theorists are reluctant to engage the writings and utterances of public intellectuals like Said, whom they consider *too* political. The next section analyzes more closely Said's reading of the oppositional and exilic intellectual, focusing on his understanding of exile as a "metaphysical" condition, his rigorous excavation of pronoun politics, and his insistence that American intellectuals understand themselves as "*of* the connections" between the United States and the rest of the world. The third section offers some extensive reflections on criticisms of Said's approach, paying particular attention both to reactionary and liberal mischaracterizations of his "rage" and to sympathetic criticisms that highlight both the problems and promises of his thinking. The chapter concludes with a return to Said's call for an intellectual orientation that locates itself within imperial connections and the rest of the world and suggests that such an orientation provides political theorists with a productive set of lenses through which to critically engage the historically protracted entanglements between liberalism and imperialism.

## INTELLECTUAL POWER

In 1992, Said was invited by the BBC to give the following year's Reith Lectures. Founded in 1948 by Bertrand Russell, the Reith Lecture series invites important figures of the day to give several public talks that advance "public understanding and debate about significant issues of contemporary interest."[8] These lectures are recorded in front of live audiences in various locations and are ultimately broadcast on BBC Radio 4 and the BBC World Service. From Robert Oppenheimer to Jonathan Sturgeon, these (still predominantly White and male) speakers are often prominent figures in the realm of politics and public culture. Said was a controversial speaker from the outset, not because of the topics he raised but, by contrast, because of who he was. Almost from the moment the lectures were announced, he later reflected, "there was a persistent, albeit small chorus of criticism" directed at the BBC for inviting him. "I was accused of being active in the battle for Palestinian rights," he recalled, "and thus disqualified for any sober or respectable platform at all."[9]

Said chose to embrace the platform he was given, not by lecturing on the politics of Palestine or on culture and imperialism, literature, and/or historical interpretation more broadly. Rather, he chose to focus his series of lectures on what it meant to *be* a public intellectual. And while his dismissive critics might have been surprised by this choice of topics, no one familiar with Said's political and scholarly writings and activism over the years would have been. On the one hand, Said simply was and nearly always had been a public intellectual, a status he embraced early in his career, when he decided to write about the contemporary situation in Palestine for both scholarly and popular/media outlets. That status was only amplified after *Orientalism* burst on the scene, thrusting him into the spotlight as both a widely acclaimed cultural and literary critic and an outspoken partisan who, in Ned Curthoys and Debjani Ganguly's words, "kept the truth of Palestine alive."[10] On the other hand, throughout his career, Said also committed himself to what Timothy Brennan describes as a "deliberate and studiously repetitive elaboration of *how* to write and speak as a public person." For Brennan, Said never simply argues that being a public intellectual is a "good thing," but rather, consistently engages in a "prolonged and minute inquiry into the mechanics of being so."[11]

Said's Reith Lectures—later collected in *Representations of the Intellectual*—synthesize many of the ideas about power, criticism, and intellectual engagement that had intrigued him for decades. In his first lecture, "Representations of the Intellectual," he begins by articulating what he clearly understood to be the essential *publicness* of the intellectual vocation, arguing with Gramsci that all intellectuals are attached in some fashion (and whether they like it or not) to a public. "I want to insist," Said notes, "that the intellectual is an individual with a specific public role in society."[12] Indeed, what most differentiates Gramsci from Foucault, argues Said, is that he was "always trying to change the political situation." Said continued to amplify this specific public role for intellectuals to the end of his life, even as he acknowledged that the then still pre-social-media-internet landscape had substantially changed the texture of the public sphere itself, expanding it so much "as to be virtually without borders."[13] Despite the broad dispersion of the "public" realm, he maintains, and despite the "spate of books and articles saying that intellectuals no longer exist" in our neoliberal age of commodified media and commercialized education, Said was convinced intellectuals still exercise considerable influence over the discursive environments in which they participate as gadflies, opponents or creators, and enablers. The crush of intellectuals who came out both in support of and in opposition to the 2003 Iraq War is testament, to his mind, of the enduringly significance of this intellectual power.[14]

Said's lifelong engagement with the work of public intellectuals, his insistence on theorizing the role public intellectuals play in society, and his

explicit commitment to *being* a partisan public intellectual with political affiliations may also help explain why his work has remained so opaque for many
political theorists. Political theorists frequently think of themselves as engaging in a different level of philosophical rigor than do most public intellectuals
who often straddle the worlds of academia, media culture, activism, and/or
policy making. There is a long tradition in critical theory, for instance—from
Kant through Horkheimer and Adorno, Rawls and Habermas—of eschewing
"instrumental reason" and its circulation through both state institutions and
the rationalizing exclusions of bourgeois culture. For figures associated with
this Enlightenment tradition, theorizing about democracy, communication,
and critique largely occurs alongside theorizing about a robust public sphere,
a sphere that remains—to various degrees—autonomous from both the
specificities of the "life world" and technical reason of the state.[15] Latter-day
thinkers in this mode—notably, Rawlsians and contemporary critical theorists
like Rainer Forst—remain committed to promoting ideal theories of nonin-
strumental, democratic speech and have tended to cast a wary eye on public
expression that is too partisan, too political, speech that resembles what
Habermas calls "distorted communication."[16]

Exacerbated by an internally focused yet ironically colonizing, academic
industry that feeds off Rawls's deeply apolitical "veil of ignorance" and
Habermas's "ideal speech situation," this general aversion within the field to
"distorted communication" or "ideological" speech has grown over the years,
resulting in the somewhat ironic situation where a sizable group of scholars
associated with an academic subdiscipline devoted to theorizing politics often
ignore the theorizing or scholarship of anyone who seems *too* political. Said
was explicitly political and also spent a considerable amount of time arguing
with, and engaging the work of, influential public intellectuals like Bernard
Lewis, Fouad Ajami, Thomas Friedman, and Samuel Huntington, men whose
work was often instrumental on its face, ideologically driven, intellectually
compromised, even unsavory. These are people whose public utterances
sometimes lag, as Michael Freeden puts it in his seminal work on the relationship between ideology and political theory, "in the status stakes behind the
high prestige of political philosophy, whether analytical or critical."[17]

This emphatically does *not* mean that all political theorists today remain
uninterested in the study of ideologies and rhetoricians. From Freeden's
"morphological analysis" of ideology as a "genre," to Richard Shorten's reading of reactionary thought, to Ernesto Laclau's approach to discourse, many
political theorists have found inquiry into the discursive world of decidedly
non-high theory to be worthy of inquiry.[18] But overall, the general thrust of
the subdiscipline is to avoid what Freeden calls the "bad theory" that takes
place in "public spaces."[19] Or, as one political theory colleague said to me

while I was in the process of writing my last book, "Why would you want to write about Niall Ferguson? Everyone knows he's just an imperialist hack."

Edward Said engaged the utterances of imperialist hacks (and many other similarly compromised intellectuals) because he knew that they were influential and that their ideas mattered, an assumption that flowed directly from the critical approach to culture, imperialism, history, and power that he developed over the course of his career. In *Orientalism* and elsewhere, Said argues that understanding the mechanism through which Europe maintained its imperial power for hundreds of years entailed sustained analyses of the thick constellation of knowledge *about* the "other." "Knowing vocabularies," culture motifs, and "imaginative geographies" developed during the eighteenth and nineteenth centuries by professional and amateur Orientalists, for instance, collectively flattened living realities in Asia and the Middle East, stripping them of historical specificity and internal diversity. This static system of "synchronic essentialism," Said maintains, froze the East in time and reduced it to an infinitely knowable (and yet always elusive) object of inquiry and fascination for those European scholars and intellectual dabblers circulating through both high and popular culture, disseminating their increasingly taxonomical accounts of the Orient via "works of literature, political tracts, journalistic texts, travel books, religious and philological studies."[20] Said's hybridist method traces, connects, and critiques the connections between power, intellectuals, and publics. Orientalism is, by necessity, broadly historical, "worldly and circumstantial," interdisciplinary, and committed to following thinkers and texts from one historical context to the next and "from genre to genre."[21] Finally, as Said puts it, *Orientalism* itself is oriented toward both a "theoretical constituency" and a "political constituency."[22]

Thus, Said's interdisciplinary approach in *Orientalism* and elsewhere entails close engagement with intellectuals who help instantiate and popularize this expansive system of knowledge about the East. It thus entails close engagement with thinkers of all stripes, both those who pass the high-culture sniff test and those whose work appears deeply instrumental, popular, and compromised. And as early as 1976, he described this methodological engagement with public intellectuals and the universe of ideas they helped keep in circulation in explicitly political terms. *Orientalism*, he reflected in an interview with *Diacritics*, interrogates a "family of ideas" (e.g., "Oriental despotism, Oriental sensuality, Oriental modes of production, and Oriental splendor") that have emerged and reemerged in different historical iterations over time, through the "rhetoric of Cromer, Balfour, Kissinger, and other statesmen."[23] For Said, the fabric of Orientalist knowledge, woven over the centuries by numerous intellectuals, is by its nature, complex, catalytic, and connected to power. Orientalist ideas contribute to systems of exclusions and prohibitions that are "directly projected onto a colonial administration."[24]

These same kinds of direct projections, Said continues, still circulate through American academic discourse today, as well as in the "conduct of U.S. decision-making and foreign policy."[25] Throughout his career, Said refused to stick to his lane when it came to analyzing the relationship between a discursive/scholarly world of Orientalist inquiry and the machinations of contemporary foreign policy making and discourse. "Perhaps you might say," he mused during a lecture on Orientalism and the Iraq War in 2003, "that I am making too many abrupt transitions between humanistic interpretation on the one hand and foreign policy on the other."[26] Said immediately rejects this suggestion. In a world dominated by the insulating, technocratic language of Donald Rumsfeld and his minions, he insists, it is absolutely necessary to link the technologies of war and violence to the history and contemporary circulation of Orientalist narratives now mouthed by the intellectual enablers who make war happen.

Indeed, as Said argues in *Covering Islam*, there seems to have been a "strange revival of canonical, though previously discredited, Orientalist ideas" about non-White and Muslim people circulating within the foreign policy and media spheres, ideas that have achieved "startling prominence" at a historical moment when explicit religious and racial stereotyping of other cultural groups was neither tolerated nor "circulated with such impunity."[27] This "simplified view" of Arabs reached a fever pitch, for Said, in the many arguments marshalled by intellectual supporters of the Iraq invasion.[28] Thus, despite its obviously compromised reasoning, he continues, "its lamentable jargon, its scarcely concealed racism, its paper-thin intellectual apparatus," the "family ideas" that made sense out of eighteenth- and nineteenth-century imperial domination flourishes today in the ideological hothouse where the American academy and American foreign policy meet.[29]

As Said argues in the introduction to 1988's *Blaming the Victims*, if one is to adequately grasp the complex relationship between American foreign policy and the politics of the Middle East today, then one must take into account both the languages that inform policy "on the ground" as well as the "ideological, political and cultural terms" that circulate through the media, popular culture, and scholarship.[30] For this reason, Said was drawn to analyze the obviously biased writings of academic and academic-adjacent intellectuals who exercise outside influence on American foreign policy today, thinkers that Robert Vitalis calls "intellectual middlemen"; scholars, journalists, professional diplomats, and policy experts skilled in "getting ideas across to non-academic audiences in Washington, New York, and beyond."[31] Despite the dubious quality of some of their work, Said brings to his analysis of compromised thinkers the same critical/genealogical zeal he brings to his study of Orientalism historically. This "spurious scholarship," he argues, doesn't emerge in a vacuum; it is connected to a tradition of Orientalist thinking that is validated in multiple institutional and academic locations through the work of actual people: intellectual middlemen, compliant interlocutors, and public intellectuals who participate in sewing together the affiliative fabric that makes sense out of imperialism. In other words, Said refuses to speak about Orientalism in the past tense or the passive voice. Domination has a scholarly face, and he spent his career exposing that face, no matter the backlash. Rashid Khalidi describes this aspect of Said's approach as a fearless refusal to go silent in the face of that "babble of conventional political and media consensus in blind support of the destructive vagaries of American policy in the Middle East."[32] For Said, the job of the principled intellectual is to consistently and relentlessly remind people of the actual "density and interdependence of human life" occluded by robust forms of public Orientalism and intellectual warmongering.[33]

Said thus not only spent a considerable amount of time speaking back to the "babble" of conventional wisdom regarding the Middle East that flowed from the pens of public intellectuals, he also thought critically and expansively about what he describes in "Representing the Colonized" as the "immense network" of cultural, political-intelligence and policy-making relationships that sustained American imperialism and American hegemony.[34] Sometimes these connections are extremely direct and instrumental. For instance, powerful public intellectuals—like the liberal, academic manque Michael Ignatieff—will often participate in international conversations that write policy language for conventions that then have enormous political impact on the lives of people throughout the formerly colonized world. In the late 1990s, for instance, Ignatieff sat on the United Nations' International Commission on Intervention and State Sovereignty and helped provide the language for the Responsibility to Protect doctrine (R2P).[35] Notoriously controversial, R2P has been invoked by the UN General Assembly multiple times, including to permit the use of air strikes in Libya in 2011.[36] For many critics, the logic of R2P provides a rationale for the continuation of American and Western domination in a post-colonial and post–Cold War environment, recasting that domination as necessary for the stabilization, in Jessica Whyte's words, "of a global, neoliberal order."[37]

Domestically, American hegemony is rationalized, theorized, and sustained by what Said describes as "armies and armies of scholars" working in both a formal and informal capacity.[38] On the one hand, some of these thinkers serve the simple and direct function of in-house experts for the US military. The US Department of Defense (DoD), for instance, runs its own Language Training Center (LTC) Program, which is aimed at leveraging the "expertise and infrastructure of institutions of higher education to train DoD personnel in language, culture, and regional area studies" so that they might better pursue US security interests in those regions.[39] On the other hand, some of these affiliations are more auxiliary but still directly tie academics to the State Department, the military, and the president. Hence, through their multiple and often-overlapping connections to the RAND corporation, the Aspen Institute, the Council on Foreign Relations, and various other policy think tanks (and through the publications of these think tanks), "intellectual middlemen" associated with the foreign policy establishment (famously nicknamed "the Blob" by former Obama advisor Benjamin Rhodes) exercise considerable influence over presidential administrations hungry for security expertise.[40]

Individuals associated with these think tanks can influence policy in ways sometimes subtle and sometimes extraordinarily direct. As an example, take the career of Bernard Lewis, a man with, in Said's words, an "extraordinary capacity for getting everything wrong."[41] Lewis's academic work on the Middle East surfaces throughout the documents of important think tanks associated loosely with policy making. The Aspen Institute's 2004 report on developing an American "grand strategy" in the Middle East, for instance, refers broadly to Lewis's "expertly conveyed" characterization of the main struggles in the Middle East today.[42] But he also served in more explicit advisory roles. During the buildup to the invasion of Iraq, for instance, officials from the Bush administration reached out directly to Lewis, bringing him into their most intimate war-planning sessions, inviting him to give, in the words of Michael Hirsch, "spine-stiffening lectures to Dick Cheney over dinner."[43] Thus, through both their academic work and their direct access to power, public intellectuals like Lewis give imperial domination, according to Said, a "veneer of omniscient tranquil authority."[44] When both he and Ignatieff threw the weight of that authority behind the 2003 invasion of Iraq—an invasion we now know to have been predicated on ginned-up military intelligence—they did so with the imprimaturs of their academic institutions: Princeton and Harvard.

The particular stories that intellectual supporters of American imperial hegemony like Lewis and Ignatieff tell are appealing to policy makers committed to US global primacy for two additional reasons that have to do with the Janus-faced nature of Orientalism itself and the way narratives about imperial culture tend to circulate within the metropole. The first is the more obvious. Scholars like Lewis and Huntington consistently make connections "between foreign policy and 'the other'" by inscribing and reinscribing the differences between "Western culture" and Islam, by emphasizing the opaqueness and irrationality of Arabs, and by distilling all the complexities of imperialism to the palliative simplicity of a "clash of civilizations" narrative.[45] These so-called experts on Arabs and the Islamic world, Said maintains, give American military hawks a language for imagining this difference: the "Arab mind" or notions of a "centuries-old Islamic decline which only

American power could reverse."[46] This is a cultural and political language in which the "other" is and always has been different in essence from "us."

The reverse side of this persistent othering is an equally persistent (and equally ideological) narrative about who "we" are. As Said explains, the dense cultural formation that has developed around essentializing the "other" for foreign policy discourse is always accompanied by another, equally dense cultural formation fixed on articulating, energizing, and reinforcing the uniqueness of America and of Western culture more generally. The powerful swathe America cuts through the world, Said reflected in the mid-1980s, is "not merely the result of one Reagan and a couple of Kirkpatricks" (or, from the perspective of the early 2020s, one Biden and a couple of Samantha Powers). Rather, "it is also heavily dependent on cultural discourse, on the knowledge industry, on the production and dissemination of texts and textuality, in short, not on 'culture' as a general anthropological realm . . . but quite specifically on *our* culture."[47] In other words, the discursive binds tying the United States to a foreign policy that relies on America's global hegemony requires more than the ceaselessly rearticulated threat of an Orientalized "other." It also requires copacetic narratives that cogitate on who "we" are as a people and culture: a democratic-liberal "us" set in permanent opposition to a despotic, violent, fundamentalist "them." As Ignatieff put it in 2004, our "best defense" against the "hatred of those who want to destroy us" is "to stay true to who we are."[48]

It is precisely at the intersection between American narratives about the "other" and American narratives about "who we are" that much contemporary foreign policy discourse in the United States resides and finds both validation and cover. It is also precisely against the "reinforcing overlap" between these two identity narratives that Said aims the powerful force of his public intellectualizing: an alternative mode of intellectual engagement *contra* Lewis, Huntington, Ignatieff (and so many others), that is committed to unsettling rather than reinforcing the narrative identity structures that sustain domination.

## THE EXILIC PUBLIC INTELLECTUAL

Said begins *Representations of the Intellectual* by agreeing with Gramsci that in any society, intellectuals comprise a large and internally diverse social body and that they play a variety of roles in relation to various class and social movements.[49] Said's affinity for Gramsci also relates to Gramsci's own obvious affiliations and political commitments and his sense that, in "trying to take stock of the situation," intellectuals played an important role in political change and political organization.[50] Intellectuals in this embedded and affiliated Gramscian sense, Said thus continues in *Representations*, are "endowed with a faculty for representing, embodying, articulating a message, a view, an attitude, philosophy or opinion."[51] There is thus, for Said, an inherently representational quality to the work of intellectuals who, by nature of what they do, articulate worldviews and arguments "to, as well as for, a public."[52]

Somewhat uniquely, Said combines this embedded political conception of the Gramscian intellectual—emeshed within a system of representation shaped by cultural and political relationships, always affiliated with social movements and constituencies—with a much more individualist reading of the intellectual that he gleans from the conservative French philosopher Julien Benda.[53] Said admits the somewhat-paradoxical quality of his attraction to Benda's elitist vision, a vision in which individuals form a "tiny band of super-gifted and morally endowed philosopher-kings who constitute the conscience of mankind."[54] Said rejects Benda's politics and his assumptions about super-gifted "philosopher-kings" but is intrigued by Benda's belief that intellectuals ought to be able to retain a certain distance from the exclusionary impulses of nationalism and that they have a particular public role to play. *Representations* thus reflects Said's unique coupling of a Gramscian-inspired, socially embedded, politically situated, "representing, embodying, articulating" public intellectual with Benda's aesthetic and ethical vision. The intellectual to emerge from this pairing is thus both socially aware and individually attuned, able to imagine the "conscience of mankind" while also disrupting the siren's song of "our" culture and "our" nation. Much like the figure of the exile for Said, the intellectual in this vein is always both/and: both attached to and somewhat detached from, the political/cultural environment that shapes them.

Throughout the 1970s and '80s, Said confected this idea of the intellectual alongside—and in active conversation with—his work on culture, criticism, and politics. The public intellectual he envisions plays a "specific public role in society" that cannot be "reduced simply to being a faceless professional" occupying a "service or management role" in the culture industry.[55] Here, in "The Future of Criticism" and elsewhere, Said opposes what he calls the "professional intellectual" who approaches scholarship as "something you do for a living, between the hours of nine and five" in order to make "yourself marketable and above all presentable, hence uncontroversial and unpolitical and 'objective.'"[56] Rather, the kind of intellectual with whom Said most identifies is dispositionally opposed to the "guild" logic of "certified experts," resists accommodation, and raises nettling questions about power and domination.[57] Or, as he puts it in 1996's "On Defiance and Taking Positions," the role of the intellectual is "not to consolidate authority, but to understand, interpret and question it."[58] Said understood intellectuals in this vein as field-transcending interlopers, scrappy and pugnacious, self-aware products of the world in which they remain invested. Their resistance to domination is so relentless and needling that their stylistic self-representation can seem like "curmudgeonly disagreeableness" sometimes "bordering on dyspepsia."[59]

Intellectuals who critique in a style influenced by Said thus embrace a particular "vocation" for what he calls the "art of *representing*" through scholarship, teaching, public speaking, and writing, a vocation that entails "commitment and risk, boldness and vulnerability."[60] Said's mode of intellectualizing has an "edge to it," and one cannot engage in its rhythms and flows unless one has a sense of oneself as the person in the room who publicly raises "embarrassing questions" and confronts (rather than produces) "orthodoxy and dogma."[61] Most of all, he maintains, this type of intellectual's capacity for representation is oriented toward people who are *unrepresented,* marginalized, silenced, and oppressed, people whose concerns and ways of life are too often ignored or "swept under the rug."[62] Such an intellectual, he continues, is "neither a pacifier nor a consensus-builder" but someone "whose whole being is staked on a critical sense, a sense of being unwilling to accept easy formulas, or ready-made cliches, or the smooth, ever-so accommodating confirmations of what the powerful or conventional have to say, and what they do."[63] To enter into the public sphere in this way, Said insists, requires abandoning the fear of making controversial claims. There is nothing more maddening, as he puts it, "than people who say, 'Oh no, no, that's controversial; I don't want to do it . . . because I mean, you know, I may disturb matters and people may think the wrong thing about me.'"[64]

From early on, Said locates the core of this fearless and disruptive intellectualizing in the generative uncertainties and insecurities of exile. In his third Reith Lecture (which appears as chapter 3, "Intellectual Exile: Expatriates and Marginals," in *Representations of the Intellectual*), Said argues that the intellectual "who considers him or herself to be part of a more general condition affecting the displaced national community" is likely not to be a source "of acculturation and adjustment, but rather of volatility and instability."[65] These are people, rather, whose very presence complicates the "presumed homogeneity" of the societies in which they now live and whose capacity to effectively see double—to see the nuances of both the home that was and the new home that is and is not home—making them especially disposed toward disruptive critique. And yet, as with his thinking on exile more generally, Said was under no illusion that public intellectuals who embrace this "undomesticated" and marginal status were ever loosed completely from feelings of connections to nations and localities to which they no longer have access. No one, he argues, is entirely "free floating," without "attachments and sentiments."[66] At the same time, he maintains, public intellectuals whose subjective attachments and sentiments are enduringly troubled by the uncertainty of their status are *more likely* to call the often-obfuscating and abusive certainties of identity into question than are those intellectuals whose attachments and sentiments remain resolutely untroubled. They are more open to feeling sympathy with outsiders and with the victims of injustice. The strength of the exilic position, he argues, is "that being defeated and 'outside,' you can perhaps more easily feel compassion, more easily call injustice injustice, more easily speak directly and plainly of all oppression, and with less difficulty try to understand (rather than mystify or occlude) history and equality."[67] Intellectuals resonating in this exilic key are thus, for Said, "unusually responsive" to the marginalized, the excluded, and the forgotten.[68]

Said values this "unusually responsive" exilic sensibility to such a degree that he argues it be voluntarily adopted by intellectuals within settled communities who are not exiles in material terms. Exile, he continues, is an "*actual* condition," but it is also "for my purposes a *metaphorical* condition."[69] And while Said insists that his approach to the intellectual in exile is derived from the experiences and histories of migration, dislocation, and expulsion, it is "not limited" to them. Rather, even intellectuals who are entrenched, lifelong members of a society can be divided into what he identifies as insiders and outsiders, "yeasayers" and "naysayers." These individuals are

> at odds with their society and therefore outsiders and exiles so far as privileges, power, and honor are concerned. . . . Exile for the intellectual in this metaphysical sense is restlessness, movement, constantly being unsettled and unsettling others. You cannot go back to some earlier and perhaps more stable condition of being at home; and alas you can never fully arrive, be at one with your new home or situation.[70]

Settled intellectuals can thus, Said argues, embrace the metaphorical (or metaphysical) lifeworld of exile by rejecting the affiliative, commonsense comforts associated with place. This means calling into question the kinds of dominant narratives that make sense out of home and people by choosing to stand on the side of the naysayers and by consistently "being unsettled and unsettling others." Said describes this aporetic public intellectual as a "ranting Thersites" who is temperamentally disruptive rather than accommodationist and professional. The intellectual exile by choice stands outside the halls of power, in solidarity with the excluded, and turns the full weight of their critical engagement against domination by persistently calling its smooth logic into question, even when they would seem to clearly benefit from it. In the process, through their "faculty for representing, embodying, articulating a message," these intellectual exiles draw our attention to precisely those voices that dominant discourses seek to silence.[71]

It is hardly surprising, given all the personality traits he associates with being an exilic critic, that Said is drawn to the portrait of the intellectual painted by Adorno in *Minima Moralia*, a text Adorno wrote while living in exile in America during the war. With Adorno, Said agrees that it is "part of morality not to be at home in one's home" and that public intellectuals speaking in exilic tones should commit themselves to "dodging both the old and the new with equal dexterity."[72] In other words, with Adorno, Said urges intellectuals to embrace the experiential discomfort of living in exile as an appropriate political/ethical response to a world wracked with systemic violence and injustice. The point, Said and Adorno both agree, is for intellectuals to remain perennially uncomfortable with such a world.

Said parts company with Adorno, however, over what he describes as the exilic intellectual's "special duty" to actively *resist* this world both intellectually and politically. Again, for Said, the fact that exile is "terrible to experience" did not vitiate the "positive things" that can be gained from it: trenchant modes of seeing and critiquing that offer, to Said's mind, unique insight into the affiliative connections between power, culture, and politics.[73] But he also believes that the incisiveness of the exilic gaze gives rise to an ethical obligation on the part of the intellectual to "address the constituted and authorized powers" at work in contemporary forms of domination.[74] Exilic critique and political engagement are coinstantaneous phenomena, argues Said, and this is particularly true for those exilic intellectuals who find their academic homes *within* imperializing and formerly imperializing societies. In other words, exilic intellectuals who work from "within the actuality" of the transnational, imperial relationships—cultural, political, social, and economic—that sustain our radically unequal and unjust world, have an added obligation to both critique those unequal relationships and oppose those injustices.[75] Those of us who benefit from the protected academic environments made possible by the contemporary global reach of American power are not "detached outside observers" of these connections, blandly making pronouncements while sipping at the honeypots of our minds. We are *of* the connections; they make "us" possible. And thus, from a Said-oriented perspective, we have a choice: say nothing and remain complicit with imperialism or challenge it from the inside out.

The goal, therefore, of the exilic intellectual is to be a noncompliant interlocutor who rejects the perspective of the detached observer—who rejects, for instance, the liberal-democratic "we" that public intellectuals like Ignatieff, Lewis, Niall Ferguson, and John Ikenberry routinely evoke with such relish when they discuss American foreign policy. This "we" prescribes solutions and policies for the rest of the world as if "we" had no skin in the game, had no blood on "our" hands. Said counters by politicizing Adorno's "gloomy and unyielding" portrait of the intellectual. He turns the gaze of the exilic critic both inward toward reflection on the "we" and outward toward interrogation of the "them." He thus transforms the moral imperative to not be at home in one's home into a moral imperative to query identity and expose domination. The movement of Said's exilic method—captured in the swing between attachment and detachment, inward and outward, "us" and "them"— thus demands that intellectuals do more than settle comfortably back into the warm embrace of "who we are," writing prescriptive articles for liberals.

Because of this mobile orientation, Said's exilic intellectual is studiously self-aware of the contemporary politics of pronouns, although that politics looks different from the "he/his," "she/her," "they/them" discussions that are so important for transgender politics in the early 2020's. Said's attention to pronouns calls on intellectuals to explore their own complicated relationship to scholarship, academia, power, status, and politics and then transform that self-reflection into a mode of disruption. In other words, as he argues in "On Defiance and Taking Positions," the majority of intellectuals are in fact "affiliated with things": universities, departments, professional organizations, political and artistic communities, nation-states.[76] For intellectuals who are interested in disrupting the "centralizing powers of our society," he continues, it is essential to acknowledge and query these affiliative links and the relationships they forge between identity and domination. This means that Said's intellectual is hyperaware of the various ways that pronouns—"we," "them," "us"—attach themselves to the corpuscular shell of the academic and popular languages of expertise, culture, and imperial power.

Interrogating the "we," "them," and "us" is particularly important, Said argues, for intellectuals within the global North (and particularly in the American academy), given our embeddedness in the overlapping sets of power connections that enable imperialism. For Said, excavating and reflecting on this situatedness requires "making an inventory" of one's own subject position, a conceptual innovation he found, again, in the work of Gramsci. Thus, as Said explains in a 1999 interview, when he first read *The Prison Notebooks*, he found that he was particularly drawn to a passage in which Gramsci suggests that "history is deposited as an infinity of traces in you without leaving an inventory."[77] Unfortunately, Said continues, the Quintin Hoare translation (which is still the most widely available English translation of *The Prison Notebooks* today) abruptly expurgates what Gramsci goes on to say next: that it is therefore "necessary *to make* an inventory." This is, Said argues, "quite a different thing than to say that it leaves us with an infinity of traces *without* an inventory."[78] Gramsci's point here, according to Said, is not to suggest that we can *never* know any of the historical traces that crisscross our own subject positions because they have left no inventory. Rather, because they have left no inventory, it is our job to *make* one. One makes an inventory by engaging in contrapuntal criticism and constructing unsettled accounts of one's own affiliations and through a hyperawareness of the context through which subjectivity comes into being.

Making an inventory of these connections and troubling the affiliative "we" from within the midst of empire does not, however, mean that one ceases to theorize from a position of "we" altogether. Again, Said insists that everyone—all "we's"—are affiliated with culture and power and this is not something we can reverse-engineer or escape. What Said's intellectual orientation demonstrates and demands again and again is self-reflection on what that "we" is doing for "us" and for an imperial culture whose very expansiveness makes it impossible to identify as imperial. The "deafening, repetitive frequency" of this American "we" mantra—"We are number 1," "We are bound to lead," "We stand for freedom and order"—resonates with the rhetorical chorus of European imperialism while simultaneously claiming to be "exceptional, not imperial."[79] In essence, in an imperial context that refuses to recognize itself as such, every "we" is overdetermined; every "we" points toward different instances of connection; every "we" draws us closer to uncomfortable affiliations with power or structures of domination that exclude even as they unite, that acknowledge even as they deflect and disavow, and for which "we" must make an inventory.

Attached and detached, the exilic intellectual brings awareness of this fraught relationship to the "we" that theorizes, pontificates, collectivizes, and colonizes while consistently troubling their own relationship to that "we." Sometimes this takes the shape of an explicit attempt to affiliate the "we"— the "us" and "our"—with either the dominant community or with voices of resistance within that community and outside it. For instance, as Said argues in his second Reith Lecture, an American columnist "writing during the Vietnam War" who uses the "word 'us' and 'our' has appropriated neutral pronouns and affiliated them consciously *either* with that criminal invasion of a distant Southeast Asian nation, *or*, a much more difficult alternative, with those lonely voices of dissent for whom the American war was both unwise and unjust."[80] It is the intellectual's task, Said continues, to be attentive to subtleties of language, the way pronouns mask some identities while constructing others. The national "we," he insists, is not an organic designation but a "constructed manufactured, even in some cases invented object, with a history of struggle and conquest behind it that is important to analyze and, sometimes, to represent."[81] Said thus twins the imperative to think in more complicated ways about all that lurks behind the effortless assertion of a "we" with a political imperative to represent that "we" otherwise.

Said's own prose style is shot through with this braided self-awareness and counterpractice of pronouns. Sometimes this takes the form of a performative slippage in and out of the "we" voice in ways that are simultaneously playful and deadly serious. In a 1991 *New York Times* op-ed called "The Tragic

Convergence," for instance, Said refers to "we Americans" who are "insulated by our wealth and power."[82] That same year, in a piece for the *Nation*, he pivots toward a discussion of "we Arabs" hooked "into dependency and consumerism, cultural vassalage and technological secondariness, without much active volition on our part," and then switches halfway through the article to embrace the position of "we Palestinians."[83] The net effect of this mobile "we"—vivified by Said's own experience as an exile—is profound and arresting. It catches the reader offguard and forces them to pause, shift perspectives midstream, and in the process, call into question their own, unconscious situatedness in a particular "we," emanating from a particular cultural or political location.

At other times, Said's attentiveness toward pronouns entails a perspicuous account of the way they circulate in political/national culture. In "Nationalism, Human Rights, and Interpretation," for instance, he punctuates his observations about wartime rhetoric and the public sphere with strategically placed quotation marks. On an occasion like the Gulf War, he writes, there is a

> fantastic jump to be observed in the public sphere from the humdrum facts to astonishingly large and finally destructive idealizations of what "we" are all about as a nation. Gone are "our" aggressions in Panama and elsewhere, as well as "our" record of nonpayment of UN dues—to say nothing of flouting Security Council Resolutions that "we" have voted for—and in are trundled the orotund pieties about how "we" must draw a line in the sand and reverse aggression, no matter the cost.[84]

Unflinchingly, Said's quotation marks highlight the fantastical-ness of this jump, how a small set of facts become a "we" at war, an "us" at one with a massive military state acting in "our" name. He brings this same attentiveness to his reflections on subjectivity and scholarly authority. *Culture and Imperialism*, for instance, is replete with intentional and performative "we's" and "ours": from the sympathetic, scholarly "we" that profits from "our" reading of hitherto ignored texts, to observations about the New World Order politics that "we" see happening in the late-twentieth century, to the final exalted line of the book, wherein the reader is encouraged to think differently about "our" culture.[85]

The exilic intellectual—the noncompliant interlocutor who destabilizes their own complex connection to the "we" of imperial power—also pushes critique outward in the "spirit of opposition, rather than accommodation."[86] Again, as examples of intellectuals in this spirit, Said turns to figures like Malcolm X, Aimé Césaire, and James Baldwin, intellectuals who were outside-inside the empire, racial and ethnic minorities, exiles, or foreigners excluded from that "overwhelmingly powerful network of social authorities—the media, the government and corporations, etc.—who crowd out the possibilities for achieving any change."[87] Neither pacifiers nor consensus builders, he argues, they resisted the dominant/imperial culture's attempts to sew up the world in its own exclusive rationality by writing and speaking back to the totality of this knowledge network, exposing its contradictions, giving voice to its studied silences, and painting the affiliative dots between high culture and violence.

At times, Said maintains, intellectuals writing in this mode focus on scalpel-like excavations of the imperial or racial subtexts that work their way through hegemonic accounts of the world. Césaire's interrogations, for instance, of the "very distinguished, very humanistic" European citizen illuminate the internal violence lurking within this benign figure.[88] At other times, Said continues, noncompliant interlocutors are constrained in their capacity to "effect direct change" and instead, like Baldwin, actively inhabit the "role of witness," testifying to the "horror otherwise unrecorded."[89] But whether through exposition or witness, the "kind of work that has most influenced my representations of the intellectual's consciousness," Said explains, is *oppositional* at its core, unsettling intellectual life through dissent, resisting the status quo by denaturalizing the logic of imperialism and racial hierarchy, and dragging the struggles of disadvantaged, underrepresented, and marginalized peoples from the periphery to the center of the world's attention.[90]

Said values the "spirit of opposition" not merely for opposition's sake—not merely because the world always needs a ranting Thersites or a hectoring Socrates to challenge fixed belief. Rather, he believes that cultivating a spirit of opposition is the only way to wrest the mainstream academic and public culture that dominates so much of our public life in the global North today—the culture that sustains and propels an un-selfconscious "we"—from its blithe insouciance and its ongoing enabling, rationalizing, and unseeing of racism and imperial violence. For Said, there is no innocent academic "we" and no neutral position divested of interest. In essence, his writings on public intellectuals extend the critical impulse he had developed throughout his career—to shatter the placid Enlightenment "we"—outward, into the world.

Said thus insists that American academics and all intellectuals writing from within the "liberal democracies" of the world—states that are "literally" (in Fanon's terms) the products of colonialism—understand themselves to be *of* the connections between the United States and the rest of the world rather than "outside and beyond" those connections.[91] The spheres American academics inhabit—from the university to the think tank to the foreign policy establishment to the White House—are complicit in strengthening and amplifying the most abusive characteristics of these connections. They are also caught up in the very knowledge industry that implicitly and explicitly supports common sense about "*our* culture." Linked assertions about who "we" are—"We are number 1," "We are bound to lead," "We stand for freedom and order"—circulate in a discursive universe alongside and in support of those other less explicit assertions that cohabitate the worlds of philosophical argumentation, knowledge, and expertise: "We" theorize; "we" know; "we" reason; "we" have intuitions about justice.

Importantly, Said never calls on intellectuals to abandon the "we" voice. Indeed, the centrality of identity and place in this work, coupled with his critical orientation toward both domination and resistance, highlights his commitment to the critical subject. But this subject, he insists, must be intentional, grounded in an awareness of connection, complicity, and responsibility rather than closure, innocence, and exception. In other words, Said's "we" is self-consciously "*of* the connections" between the dominant power and the other. Being an exilic intellectual in an imperial society, he thus argues, entails the "absolute necessity to connect oneself, to affiliate oneself, to align oneself" with ongoing, anticolonial processes of struggle and liberation.[92] Through these self-conscious acts of affiliation, "we" create, inspire, and participate in communities of critique, solidarity, and resistance.

Not surprisingly, Said's partisan mode of *being* an exilic intellectual—his insistence on intentionality and affiliation—was/is the source of considerable controversy among his many critics. Often, however, as the next section explores, these criticisms emerge from very different places and suggest very different things about the problems and promises of Said's approach.

## THE MANY FACES OF CRITIQUE

Much of the criticism that has been directed at Said's work on public intellectuals over the course of his career has involved criticisms of both the political content of that work and his style. Indeed, content and style are frequently inextricably linked for many of these critics in ways that, predictably, replicate the racial narratives of civility and comportment common to imperialist readings of the "other." Commentators who explicitly oppose Said's policy positions on the Middle East and Palestine-Israel, for instance, often frame that opposition in relation to Said's supposed excessiveness and his anger. For these critics, the manner in which Said performed public intellectual expression was simply unbecoming for a scholar. He was too emotionally attached to its subject, too hyperbolic and rageful to be reasonable, a man whose way of being exceeded the invisible lines of civility and reason meant to constrain the comportment of a well-behaved professor of literature. Edward Alexander, for instance, who famously dubbed Said "Professor of Terror" in a 1989 article for *Commentary* magazine, repeatedly castigated him, not only for his then affiliation with the PLO, but also for his "double career as literary scholar and ideologue of terrorism." Alexander sneeringly suggests that Said's career as a scholar provided a "potent argument against those who believe in the corrective power of humanistic values."[93]

Other critics similarly camouflage their political disagreement with Said through feigned horror at his intellectual inappropriateness. Here was a professor of comparative literature and literary theory, with a focus on the eighteenth and nineteenth centuries, who had the audacity to comment in a public way on the contemporary politics of race, imperialism/foreign policy, and the dispossession of the Palestinian people. It is clear, for example, from Joshua Muravchik's deeply facile engagement with *Orientalism* in "Enough Said: The False Scholarship of Edward Said" that what drives him to distraction about Said is not the "travesty" of his scholarship but Said's engagement with left politics. "What made the book electrifying," Muravchik insists, is not that Said had developed a fundamentally new, contrapuntal way of reading the history of the West through imperial culture but rather "that Said had found a new way to condemn the West for its most grievous sins: racism and the subjugation of others."[94] Throughout the article, Muravchik swings effortlessly between his stylistic discomfort with what he describes as Said's "oeuvre"—his "deviousness and posturing" and his "ineffable vanity"—and his disdain for Said's politics. For Muravchik, this politics is perfectly encapsulated in Said's choice to cast "Arabs and Muslims as the moral equivalent of [B]lacks" and "Israel as the racist [w]hite oppressor."[95]

Said's liberal detractors often frame their objections to Said's politics in the same terms as reactionary critics like Muravchik: as objections to his style. In his reaction to Said's review of *Exodus and Revolution*, for instance, Walzer sidesteps each of Said's substantive criticisms of the exclusionary politics the book smuggles in under the cover of liberation.[96] Instead, Walzer devotes the bulk of his prickly response to painting an artful caricature of Said as a man compelled "to make up his enemies to suit himself," as if Said were truculent by nature, moved by a dispositional anger rather than legitimate critique. In his peevish exchange with Said, Walzer claims to be affronted not by Said's politics themselves but by his polemics, by his politically motivated fury that clearly exceeds the boundaries of reasonable academic exchange.[97] "For Jewish supporters of Israel," Walzer opines, "there is only one politics, and we cannot design it for ourselves; Said designs it for us in the image of his rage."[98]

This characterization of Said's comportment—by liberals and reactionaries alike—is perhaps best captured in the firestorm of reactions to the publication of an image in 2000 of Said symbolically hurling a stone from Lebanon over a barbed-wire border fence into Israel.[99] As Bill Mullen puts it, the "stone that Said threw that July day hit nothing," and yet, "it shattered a shallow public myth that academe is a genteel retreat where disruptive ideas are never consecrated as actions, even symbolic ones."[100] The ensuing controversy that followed the publication of this photograph may have been more sustained and overblown than previous reactions to Said's activism on behalf of the Palestinians, but it continued an earlier trend of painting Said as singularly unhinged and—perhaps more importantly—as someone who inappropriately disrupts the fiction of academia as a "genteel retreat" from politics. That Said's own prose has, over the years, often been praised for (as Brennan puts it) its "unusual balance" and "its basic generosity, its candid and unguarded self-criticism" has little to no impact on a particular mainstream discourse bent on remembering him as "Hezbollah's philosopher."[101] While scholars like Donald Kagan, Allan Bloom, and a cadre of angry, partisan conservatives responded to student activism and political change over the years by creating explicitly political think tanks like the Project for a New American Century, and founding university programs in "Great Books" and "Grand Strategy," they have rarely been pilloried in the pages of the *New York Times* in the way that Said was throughout his career.[102] At the end of the day, it was and is the *content* of Said's political critique—rather than the manner in which he expressed that content while he was alive—that truly drove (and continues to drive) his detractors to distraction.

And yet, criticisms of Said's approach to public intellectualizing are not limited to his liberal and right detractors. Otherwise-sympathetic readers of Said's work and politics have expressed reservations about several aspects of his thinking in this regard, beginning with his assertion that public intellectuals who are longtime members of politically and economically dominant societies (but who care about opposing domination) can effectively choose to become like exiles. The argument is, on its face, rather confusing, even tautological. It is never really clear, for instance, how much agency is involved in approaching exile as a "metaphorical condition." On the one hand, Said seems to suggest that naysayers (people who are "lifelong members of a society" but "at odds" with this society) are exiles by dint of their refusal to go with the flow. They are like exiles *because of* their dispositions. On the other hand, Said clearly believes that taking up the mantle of exile is also a vocation, an intentionally chosen way of life.

It's slippages like these—between exile as a choice or as a forced condition, exile as a metaphysical or a material state of being—that both sympathetic and hostile critics have found discomforting, indeed a little maddening. It is difficult, as Bill Ashcroft and Pal Ahluwalia put it in their 1999 overview of Said's work, "to see how far the idea of metaphoricity can be taken without dissolving the concept of exile altogether."[103] This confusion harkens back to the paradox at the very heart of the exilic experience as Said explains it: At what point does treating exile as a "compelling" thing to think about minimize or mute the fact that it is also a "terrible"—real, material, potentially horrific and violent—thing to experience? Unlike Adorno, Said sets himself up for this line of questioning not only by politicizing exile as a mode of critique able to confront contemporary domination but also by actively championing its positive, even "pleasurable" characteristics.[104]

Said's commitment to both the actual and metaphorical exilic perspective has, with good reason, struck some otherwise-sympathetic readers as potentially out of touch with the lived, material experience of volatility that exile brings. They argue that Said's primary concern with the concept lies in its conceptual utility for an elite circle of academics rather than with the people for whom statelessness means permanent and unwanted material deprivation and political disenfranchisement. "The choice to live in a metaphorical exile," as Ian Buruma puts it, "is in fact already a form of privilege, something only people who face no real danger can afford."[105] Sean Scalmer, who is otherwise extremely sympathetic to Said's overall critical project, similarly argues that his approach to exile as metaphor is elitist, embedded in an "over-identification with the university" as the principal site of free intellectual work, which has the unintended effect of marginalizing "those who pursue truth outside its borders."[106]

While I don't agree with Scalmer's conclusion that Said's reading of intellectual work necessarily marginalized those who "pursued truth" outside the university, I don't think he is wrong about Said's rose-tinted attitude toward the university itself—an attitude that persisted throughout his career, despite the neoliberalization of the academy that had already begun by the 1990s and despite his long-standing critique of market-driven education. As Dabashi points out, Said consistently underestimated the silencing impact of those professional pressures associated with the neoliberal university. "By the time the tenure process is over," Dabashi argues, "bending over backward to accommodate power and being compromising and appeasing become almost second nature to the junior faculty."[107] In fact, from the perspective of anyone working in the Shock Doctrine environment of higher education today—an environment particularly harsh in the United States and the United Kingdom, in which faculty are pitted against one another in the race to secure grant money and where the freedom of speech once attached to tenure is increasingly a thing of the past—Said's thoughts about the status of the university as a "protected space" and a site for radical inquiry can seem almost quaintly naïve.[108] Throughout his career, Said continued to insist that the university itself did/could/ought to provide this protected space in which the kinds of radical inquiry he most valued could flourish.[109] That he insisted on this even as his own activism became the subject of hostile recrimination from some students, alumni, and academic administrators at Columbia is a testament to how strongly he believed in the university's special status.[110]

The critique of Said as an elitist is compounded by the fact that Said often just genuinely *was* an elitist. As Walter Armbrust argues, Said was "fairly typical in his disdain for cultural artifacts produced outside the languages of metropolitan societies."[111] A classically trained pianist, Said could be notoriously dismissive of popular music, a studied blindness that some scholars believe led him to undervalue "its politically subversive potential."[112] Neil Lazarus takes these points further, arguing that Said's elitism and occasional tone-deaf insistence on the "pleasures of exile" not only underplay the real impact of power, violence, and systemic hierarchy on exiled populations, but also romanticizes the figure of the individual intellectual—lonely, brooding, and removed—and actively vitiates the possibility of developing criticism out of communal and solidaristic practices.[113] Ahmad is even more cutting in his critique of Said's insistence on the representational burden carried by individual intellectuals. This elitist emphasis on *speaking for*—for the voiceless, the marginalize, the dispossessed—smacks of hubris, Ahmad maintains, as if it were solely thanks to Said's rhetorical interventions that "Palestinians will never be lost to history."[114]

Thus, Said's cultural tastes, his commitment to the academy as a privileged space, his sense that individual intellectuals have some unique and important role to play in society, and his insistence that the experience of exile is capturable by members of settled societies for metaphorical purposes can all be read as elitist, a quality that, as Darwish's poem suggests, even his most loving friends acknowledged. But the conclusion to which this leads some of his critics—that Said was closed to popular expressions of solidarity, that he did not value life beyond the academy, that he was dismissive of the material reality of exilic life, or that he believed only intellectuals were capable of representing the oppressed—is unnecessarily dismissive and forecloses a number of generative and genuinely complex ways of reading Said's understanding of the relationship between exilic intellectuals and the world.

First, nothing in Said's approach to the politics of intellectual engagement precludes activist politics and the forging of solidaristic links beyond the academy. Indeed, many scholar-activists whose work with protest groups sometimes, as Jules Boykoff puts it, "involves hitting the streets with them" have long taken inspiration from Said's conviction that intellectual and political work are mutually reinforcing and that the role of the public intellectual has an "edge to it."[115] In terms of his own personal commitments, the huge number of letters in Said's papers from Palestinian activists, Indigenous activists, members of the African National Congress, and many more, all clearly indicate that people outside academia were and continue to be inspired by Said's work and public interventions.[116] Indeed, even the briefest perusal of Said's collected papers makes clear that he truly believed in his own insistence that there is an "absolute necessity to connect oneself, to affiliate oneself, to align oneself with an ongoing process or contest of some sort" that takes place beyond the walls of the university.[117] Said took the relationship between scholarship and activism extremely seriously, and while he was not directly involved in activism to the extent that many of his supporters would have liked, he devoted much of his professional life to forging connections between the two worlds, committing enormous amounts of time to corresponding with Palestinian activists as well as activists from the African National Congress, the Palestinian Aid Society, the Jewish Committee on the Middle East, and many other organizations and individuals. He constantly spoke at events, attended demonstrations, and worked with political artists, even as he was undergoing chemotherapy for his recurrent battle with leukemia.[118] Said clearly did believe that when it came to making targeted interventions in America's media landscape, "individuals" (in solidarity with political movements) "make the difference," but this never stopped him from becoming involved with multiple, overlapping forms of collective action aimed at similarly changing that landscape through political practices of organization and demonstration.[119]

Likewise, Said's famous exhortation "never solidarity before criticism"—first articulated in "Secular Criticism" and later in *Representations of the Intellectual*—isn't meant to permanently privilege criticism at the expense of solidarity, nor is it meant to elevate the elite realm of the university above the realm of political struggle.[120] Rather, Said uses the phrase to critique schools of thought and approaches to politics he believes leave identity uninterrogated. This does not mean, as he makes perfectly clear in "Secular Criticism," that one does not take sides on issues of justice or that one does not fight, tooth and nail, with one's compatriots for these causes. Much of his own activism, for example, was oriented toward expanding and deepening global solidarity with the Palestinian cause.[121] But it does mean, he argues, that even in the "midst of a battle in which one is unmistakably on one side against another, there should be criticism."[122]

Said's "elitism" similarly complicates simplistic dismissals at nearly every level of analysis. Take the tense relationship between his affinity for the academic discourse emanating from universities—a position from which he both spoke and for which he advocated—and the violence, instability, and unseeing that haunts the daily experiences of so many exiles and refugees. Again, Said addresses this discordance not by attempting to resolve it but by drawing attention to it. He thus asks intellectuals to effectively *become* exilic in their orientation (in a "metaphysical sense") and, at the same time, warns his readers against uncritically embracing the romantic metaphor of exile by both remembering the "unnacountable masses for whom UN agencies have been created" *and* those intellectuals in physical exile who, as he put it in a 2003 interview, "used words where geography was cruel."[123] Here, as elsewhere in his work, Said leaves the tensions that accrue to elitism and distance unreconciled, as if the very point of the unanswered questions—those consistent, thrumming ruptures—was to generate more questions. In essence, while he may never have resolved the tensions of exile, he never flinched from making them the object of analysis.[124]

Said's approach here (his insistence on letting the obvious friction between exile as an intellectual metaphor and exile as a lived experience simply stand) reflects his baseline belief that the relationship between exile and metaphor (as with the relationship between exile and nationhood) is always both/and. Thus, Said was well aware that the attachments to "home" experienced by many people in the Palestinian diaspora who had never been to Nazareth or Ramallah were effectively—and intergenerationally—"metaphorical." At the same time, as he explained in a 1997 interview with Jacqueline Rose, simply saying to a Palestinian living in the West Bank or Lebanon whose identity has been declared "unconfirmed or indeterminate" that their experience of attachment is "just metaphorical" is nonsensical because for them, that metaphor is real. The "refugee's piece of paper" gives it substance: "it's lived."[125] Here, as elsewhere, Said thinks through exile to draw our attention to the constructed nature of national belonging—the affiliative connections that are the product of culture, politics, ideology, and collective memory—while never once diminishing the suffering of people for whom the absence of a legal homeland has very real and painful material consequences. For this reason, he vocally supported a Palestinian "right of return" as a necessary part of rectifying the historic and contemporary injustice of Palestinian displacement and statelessness.[126] Thus, even as he enjoins us all to *be* exiles, he demands a better life *for* exiles, in part by insisting that the metaphorical homeland be made real, all the while calling into question the affiliations of homelands more generally.

Said's elitism here is thus not only difficult to characterize, but it also pulls in several different directions at once. In other words, just because Said is interested in elite forms of political or intellectual expression does not mean that this expression is necessarily hostile to liberation or that it will always, with quiet determination, express itself the same way. In his work on Said's fascination with the upward mobility narratives at the core of the anticolonial "voyage in," Bruce Robbins argues that charges of elitism leveled at Said fail to take into account the actual content of these elite themes. Thus, Robbins argues convincingly, the power of many anti-elitist arguments—such as Richard Rorty's denunciation of "rootless cosmopolitans"—lies not in their refusal of upward mobility narratives but in their rejection of the idea that these narratives must always mean the same thing. Said's journey with James, Césaire, and Fanon from periphery to metropole to resistance similarly focuses on elite narratives, but it should also be read, according to Robbins, "as a courageous and well-timed effort" to "take back" these narratives and to use them in an alternative "sharing out" of intellectual authority.[127] In essence, for Robbins, Said's contrapuntal reading simultaneously radicalizes and democratizes elite narratives.

In a similar way, critics who focus on Said's "privileged" position in academia tend to read privilege as always and definitively meaning the same thing: smugness, distance, unfamiliarity. They thus accuse Said of being *too* privileged and *too* distant and therefore *too* removed from the very political movements he was working to support and amplify. For Scalmer, this removes Said from the kinds of "activist wisdom" "confirmed by swelling crowds and political victories rather than by the receipt of fresh publications or the distribution of academic laurels."[128] For James Clifford, Said is overly attached to a model of critic as "outsider and participant observer," a "familiar modern topos"—detached, rational, committed to a conception of "humanist cosmopolitanism" and "personal integrity."[129] But these criticisms fail to identify, I argue, the way that Said's own understanding of exilic distance *as* privilege circulates somewhat differently from these if-a-then-b formulations. For instance, Said's critique of Adorno's approach to exile in *Minima Moralia* stems from his disagreement with Adorno's unwillingness, as Said sees it, to embrace the "privileges" of exile. Thus, he argues, "while it is true to say that exile is the condition that characterizes the intellectual as someone who stands as a marginal figure outside the comforts of privilege, power, being-at-homeness . . . it is also very important to stress that that condition carries with it certain rewards and, yes, even privileges."[130] These "privileges" include, for Said, the potential capacity to see differently and articulate differently those affiliative connections rendered all but invisible by hegemonic narratives of civilization, security, global order, domination, Orientalism, national identity, and so on. At the same time, even as Said draws attention to this form of privilege, he rejects the idea that exile is primarily a "privileged site for individual self-reflection."[131] "Privilege" in this sense invites both self-reflection *and* external criticism; it is necessarily individual *and* connected to the humanity of others *and* to the reality of life for so many in an age "of migrants, curfews, identity cards, refugees, exiles, massacres, camps and fleeing civilians."[132]

Said's argument with Adorno thus stems precisely from this sense that the internal complexities of privilege ought to compel public intellectuals toward political investment. In contrast to Adorno's discomfort with political activism, Said's exilic intellectual acts on their *privilege* by becoming "unusually responsive" to the marginalized and the voiceless while working with others to actively challenge the "authoritatively given *status quo*."[133] In Said's sense of the word, *privilege* moves in precisely the opposite direction from the now common use of the word in liberal identity parlance, a usage heard far more frequently in the years since Said's death in 2003. *Privilege* in this sense is a marker of insufferable, insurmountable, unearned power that adheres to certain identities and bodies and that requires admission and "checking" and whose political translation—*allyship*—is frequently refigured by conservatives as befuddled resentment and by liberals as immobilizing shame.

*New York Times*' columnist Jillian Steinhauer's 2019 reaction to Risa Puno's public art project *The Privilege of Escape* describes this liberal orientation to privilege perfectly. Puno's installation uses the concept of the escape room to demonstrate—in real time—how structural inequality affects the ability of groups or individuals to navigate life or, in this case, to navigate the game. *The Privilege of Escape*, Steinhauer notes, is a beautifully designed and executed demonstration of the frustrations and baffling unfairness built into systems of power. At the same time, the way the lesson of the game is ultimately revealed to the participants, she argues, feels like more of a "gotcha moment than a prompt for reflection or action." "When I found out that my team had been given an advantage," Steinhauer continues, "I felt guilty, as if we had cheated—not an unreasonable reaction, but not a constructive one either, and the facilitated discussion that followed didn't push me to consider the experience more deeply or critically."[134] Privilege, in this sense, is a status that one is either aware of or not. When one is made aware of it, one can feel bad about it and potentially even reject it. But after that moment of reveal, there doesn't seem to be much to be gained upon reflection. One "checks" one's privilege, or one is a failed liberal.

By contrast, Said's much more complicated approach to privilege from this exilic intellectual perspective removes it from either the realm of *noblesse oblige* or a finger-wagging command to "leave it at the door." Privilege, in Said's work, is not an identity but a set of power relations and circumstances that generates complex forms of reflection and political and intellectual choices. The "privilege" of exile is a complicated, reflective predicament, simultaneously internally variegated, the product of power and enabling of insight into power, whose political translation is not "checking" or shame but a heightened responsiveness. In this sense, Said's impulse is always to query identity, status, and situatedness but then to move outward toward critique and connection. Acknowledgment of privilege, in all its complexities, is not the end of the intellectual journey, the place where awareness meets stultifying shame. It is, rather, always the beginning.

Said's sensibilities here reflect his commitment to an oppositional mode of analysis that is radically anti-essentialist and that refuses to be lodged in one place—in one particular identity, philosophy, or worldview. His criticism of academic Marxism, for instance, springs precisely from this reluctance to be limited by a particular methodology or school of thought. As he puts it in "Secular Criticism," "I have been more influenced by Marxists than by Marxism or any other *ism*."[135] Thus, just as Said constantly challenges both academic identity politics and the way "popular metaphors for 'us' and 'them'" stand in for critique and reflection, so, too, does he also oppose over-affiliation with one particular way of reading the world. To affiliate thus, he argues, potentially substitutes connection for critical consciousness, which can lead to the *unconscious* creation of zones of inclusion and exclusion, "doctrinal walls" that preclude alternative interpretations. In contrast, Said calls not for the systemwide maintenance of "theoretical machines" but for a criticism that remains resolutely, unabashedly oppositional, perennially suspicious of "rigidly enforced disciplinary divisions" and the "customary way of doing things."[136]

In this sense, it is possible to read Said's sympathetic critique of academic Marxism very differently from the way it has been read by some academic Marxists, who, like Ahmad, tend to interpret Said's approach in *Orientalism* and elsewhere as another totalizing methodology in disguise. Thus, Said argues, despite their commitment to structural analyses that are explicitly dialectical and that are concerned, on a political level, with destabilizing the foundations of capitalism, Marxist theorists like Terry Eagleton and Frederick Jameson still all too frequently structure their own political approaches through an intellectual language grounded in a self-rationalizing, metaphysical logic and motivated by an unwillingness to challenge Marx's own elitism.[137] Said wasn't just troubled by this orthodoxy for analytical reasons; he also believed it had political consequences insofar as it left the "extra-academic world outside" prey to the discursive, ideological, and material machinations of the political Right.[138] For Said, proclaiming oneself *to be* a Marxist is an identity claim, and this claim can effectively silo theory that—in the context of a phenomenon as densely imbricated, overlapping, and complex as imperialism—has the unfortunate effect of circumscribing criticism itself. As he puts it somewhat controversially, "criticism modified in advance by labels like 'Marxism' or 'liberalism' is, in my view oxymoronic."[139] To stake these kinds of claims, Said maintains, is to place oneself "outside a great many things going on in the world, so to speak, and in other kinds of criticism."[140]

Many people have, over the years, been particularly dissatisfied with this aspect of Said's approach both to Marxism *and* to the work of the intellectual more generally, focusing their criticisms on his belief in an independent, secular, detached, oppositional subjectivity able to unsystematically glean insight from multiple interpretive locations. For some critics, this smacks of precisely the kind of the universal Enlightenment rationality against which Said's own work has consistently pushed. As Wael Hallaq puts it in his brilliant and sympathetic rethinking of *Orientalism*, Said's "epistemic self-confidence" throughout the book stands in stark contrast to the reflective, critical impulses of the text itself.[141] Hallaq argues that Said's secularist insistence on "traditional rational inquiry" can express itself in ways that silence rival approaches to politics, culture, and the world, approaches emerging from spiritual or theological traditions and/or alternative ways of knowing that might provide new resources for tackling today's global problems (e.g., the enormity of environmental crisis and the ongoing violence inspired by sovereignty). Robert Tally also thinks that Said's method of intellectual inquiry limns too close for comfort to the traditions he criticizes, arguing that his criticisms of academic Marxism have the unfortunate effect of echoing "liberal and conservative critics in dismissing Marxism as a pseudo-religion, a merely academic exercise in theory, and an utterly irrelevant discourse."[142]

And yet, it is a testament to the power of Said's approach that a great many of his sympathetic methodological critics—as opposed to those who disagree with his politics but disguise that disagreement as methodological critique—have developed extraordinarily novel and creative ways of reading Said's approach to intellectual subjectivity that expand that approach beyond what they identify as its limitations. Hallaq's argument in *Restating Orientalism*, for instance, urges the reader to accept Said's challenge in *Orientalism*, to begin "with a due consideration of the Other," and then to push this challenge in political and philosophical directions that confront the ironclad logic of Enlightenment sovereignty and an academic orthodoxy that "thinks the state, and the world, through the state."[143] In a similarly sensitive expansion of Said's thought, Khaled Furani combines an analysis of what he sees as Said's mirroring of "European Enlightenment's critique of religion" with a methodological orientation toward the "other" that he gleans from Said's own work. Thus, he argues, scholars can approach Orientalism in history not simply as a dominating discourse that distorts other cultures but also in light of the way it produces a myriad of complicated identities—"confused, anxious, forgotten, dominating"—that often find themselves "living the schism between faith and reason, belief and science, and criticism and tradition."[144] Likewise, Tally argues that Said's own critique of Marxism can't be reduced to a simple form of rejectionism but has to be understood within the context of Said's own explicit borrowing from a Lukács, Gramsci, Adorno and other twentieth-century Marxists, particularly the extent to which these theories encouraged his own "spatial turn" in *Orientalism*.[145]

In other words, it is not only possible but also clearly common to develop Said's own insights beyond what different scholars identify as his various blind spots. This is particularly true of Said's unwavering commitment to secularism, which many of these same sympathetic scholars read as a residual attachment to the epistemological certainties of the Enlightenment, certainties that press against the grain of Said's critique. During Said's lifetime, sympathetic critics like Rajagopalan Radhakrishnan pushed him to leave more room "for a position which is decidedly pro-secular, politically speaking, and is yet a critique of secularism, epistemologically speaking."[146] Said would often push back—as he did in an exchange with Radhakrishnan—by both agreeing with the epistemological critique and yet still arguing that, in practice, the secular "at least gives one the opportunity to present, to talk, to discuss, and to change, which is the most important thing."[147] My point here is not that Said's approaches to Marxism, secularism, or critique can always be read fruitfully against his own conceptual limitations but rather that Said's methodological capaciousness—his willingness to travel with his own theory—creates opportunities for doing precisely this.

## LIBERALISM, DOMINATION, AND
## INTELLECTUAL EXILE

Said's approach to inhabiting the role of the intellectual originates in his conviction that, in a world shaped by imperialism, intellectuals play a role in maintaining domination. In order to be the kind of intellectual who opposes that domination, one must be willing to submit the utterances of public and popular intellectuals to the same kind of scrupulous critique to which one submits theory and high culture. One must also be willing to link that critique to the persistence of narratives that both reify the "other" and, simultaneously, sew a husk of common sense around *our* culture." Making these kinds of interventions, Said insists, requires that intellectuals in the global North, for instance, understand themselves as *of* the connections created by imperialism, not outside or beyond these connections. This entails, he argues, reflection, self-awareness, and a willingness to think beyond the "honeypots" of our minds and reimagine the complex circulation of the generative, enabling "we" that sustains domination. Said found the genesis of that critical orientation in both the actual and "metaphorical" condition of exile, a perspective that interrogates identity while remaining attuned to both the necessity of identity itself and the need to purposely and creatively unsettle and refigure the "we" that critiques and theorizes and works in solidarity with others.

Legitimate criticisms—as opposed to purely political attacks posing as intellectual disagreement—have been made of Said's often-maddening contradictions, his tendency toward elitism, and his unapologetic secularism. I am sympathetic to many of these critical interventions. I do, however, object strenuously to the suggestion—made most strongly by Ahmad and others—that Said was an unreconstructed liberal. In this interpretation, Said's interest in the individual subject, his commitment to humanism, and his faith in secular criticism suggest that he was unable to think, in E. San Juan Jr.'s words, "beyond the limits of a liberal, even libertarian, mentality."[148] Making this claim, I argue, involves more than a distortion of Said's work. It also entails a very limited conception of what constitutes liberalism. If, on the one hand, we define *liberalism* in terms of an immediately recognizable list of fixed and transparently obvious and uncontested "values" that represent the same things through time (and identify anyone who espouses any of these values at any time to be a liberal), then the moniker makes sense: Said is a liberal. As is anyone who has ever uttered the words *secular* or *humanist* or who believes individuals can have an impact on the world. But if we understand liberalism as an actually existing ideology that operates in relation to a far more complex discursive universe that can all too frequently sustain domination and imperialism, then not only is Said *not* a liberal, but his approach also offers political theorists a number of invaluable tools for analyzing liberalism in our age.

In the next and final chapter, I explore how Said's methodological intuitions, combined with his engagement of public intellectuals and his inhabitation of that role, provides political theorists with a novel point of entry for interrogating liberalism as it circulates ideologically in the world. That approach to liberalism begins, again, with the demand that American intellectuals understand their own critical subjectivity as located "*within* the actuality" of the connections between the United States and the rest of the world. This awareness wrests intellectual engagement from the "honeypots of our minds"—from that unattached, unaffiliated space from whence scholars cast a cool eye on American foreign policy or make sage philosophical observations about "our" moral intuitions—and reweaves it back into the dense affiliative landscape of imperialism. In "Representing the Colonized," Said accepts that it would be difficult to convince intellectuals who were either ignorant of or embarrassed by this "imperial setting" to accept such an epistemological orientation. But, he continues,

> there is no way that I know of apprehending the world from within our culture (a culture by the way with a whole history of exterminism and incorporation behind it) without also apprehending the imperial context itself. . . . The real problem remains to haunt us: the relationship between anthropology as an ongoing enterprise and, on the other hand, empire as an ongoing concern.[149]

My goal, throughout this book, is to argue similarly that the real problem that remains to haunt us as political theorists and scholars of politics is the relationship between political theory as an "ongoing enterprise" and imperialism as an "ongoing concern." Nowhere, I argue in this next chapter, is that relationship more obvious than in the affiliative universe that links that "ongoing concern" to liberalism.

# The Treason of the Intellectuals

## *Reading Said against Liberal Narcissism*

In June 1999, Said penned a short piece for *Al-Ahram Weekly* entitled "The Treason of the Intellectuals," a reference to Julien Benda's 1927 short book of the same title. Benda's book excoriated nineteenth- and twentieth-century philosophers, artists, and "men of science" for first remaining "attached to their nations," even when those nations engaged in egregious acts of military and imperial violence, and then rationalizing that violence in the name of civilization.[1] Said's essay does something similar. Reflecting on the NATO bombing campaign against Serbia that had begun in March of that year, Said focuses on how liberal intellectuals—particularly in the United States—justified, rationalized, and deflected attention away from the sheer amount of violence, dislocation, and civilian death being carried out in the name of a humanitarian intervention. "[L]iberal columnists and intellectuals," Said argues, "whose war in a sense this was, simply looked away from the destruction of Serbia's infrastructure (estimated at $136 billion) in their enthusiasm for the idea that 'we' were doing something to stop ethnic cleansing."[2] *Treason* is a strong word, but Said, like Benda, means it. It implies betrayal, not of a nation or a state, but of the putative ideals for which these liberal intellectuals stand. It also implies responsibility, a responsibility for aiding and abetting imperialism that Said observed liberal intellectuals deflecting through the relentless drumbeat of "who we are": "We," who are doing something to stop ethnic cleansing. "We," who are leading the free world. "We," who are the champions of human rights.

Said's decision to wade into this particular foreign policy debate is typical of his absolute determination to expose connections between imperial history, imperial culture, and the writings and utterances of public intellectuals today: "liberals á la Michael Ignatieff" who make it their business to write "prescriptive articles" demanding US intervention. This refusal to stick to his disciplinary lane, however, is yet another possible explanation for why Said's work has remained so illegible for political theorists, who usually steer clear of foreign policy. Indeed, the reluctance to comment on contemporary international politics persists today even among scholars whose work explores the relationship between liberalism and imperialism. Jennifer Pitts wonders about precisely this lack of engagement in her 2010 review essay on theories of empire and imperialism, describing it as a failure on the part of political theorists to address the "critical demands of the present" while retaining a "deeply informed historical sense" of the past.[3] This failure is particularly odd, Pitts suggests, given that many of the theorists who were initially involved in the "turn to empire" were, in part, inspired to explore the entanglements of liberalism and imperialism by the foreign policy debates that surrounded the invasions of Afghanistan and Iraq, debates that seemed aimed at justifying, in Pitts's words, "unaccountable imperial rule."[4]

And yet, despite that initial spur to action, very few political theorists have gone on to connect liberalism's historical entanglements with imperialism to analyses of contemporary American foreign policy, however unaccountable and imperial that policy may be. This reluctance can be attributed to a variety of factors: the structural division between international relations (IR) and the rest of the discipline, the widespread avoidance by theorists of "intellectual middlemen" whose work often dominates foreign policy debates, and/or legitimate contextualist fears about making historical generalizations. Whatever the reason, in practical terms, most political theorists today avoid venturing onto the landscape of contemporary foreign policy debates. Ultimately, unless they are global justice scholars speaking largely to each other in a very particular philosophical vernacular, political theorists leave analyses of contemporary "liberalism" on the global stage to IR scholars, liberal internationalists, and those "liberal columnists and intellectuals" who periodically urge the country to war.

Throughout his career, Said refused to cede foreign policy analysis to the foreign policy establishment. He thus firmly rejected the idea that foreign policy within complex modern societies with massive militaries must, by necessity, "be commanded by formidable technical-policy experts like Donald Rumsfeld and Richard Perle."[5] In a 2003 lecture, "Orientalism Once More," Said also objected vigorously to the limiting truism that scholars must stick to either "humanistic interpretation" or "foreign policy" critique, fixing his sights instead on the *connection* between these two realms—the overlap between discourse and foreign policy—as the primary conceptual portal through which to analyze culture and politics. His approach refuses to let the distinction between both domestic and international politics and between interpretive and policy analyses limit criticism. Instead, his work often bridges these conceptual realms by interrogating the web of relation-ships between rhetorical constructions of the "other" and rhetorical construc-tions of "who we are" as liberal, democratic peoples. Additionally for Said, because they are *of* the connections between the United States and the rest of the world, American intellectuals have a particular responsibility to make an inventory of affiliations between political discourse and imperial domination. They do this not by snobbishly dismissing the Ignatieffs of the world for their obvious lack of academic rigor but by actively engaging public intellectuals who speak, as he puts it, with "breathtaking insouciance" in the "name of for-eign policy."[6] In essence, Said's critical intuitions bridge the divide between high and low culture, humanistic inquiry and policy analysis, and foreign and domestic politics by dragging imperial affiliations from the periphery to the center. He then demands that "we" look these affiliations straight in the face and begin to think about them otherwise.

I argue in this chapter that, for all these reasons, Said's critical orientation provides political theorists with a uniquely fertile approach for transforming their increasingly robust critiques of liberalism and imperialism into equally robust critiques of how liberalism circulates in contemporary American for-eign policy discourse. *Liberalism* here and throughout this chapter refers to both a discrete wing of political philosophy *and* to a complicated universe of signs and signifiers that disseminates through a number of popular and schol-arly (domestic and international) discourses. Approaching foreign policy utterances in this fashion, I maintain, exposes the reliance of liberal inter-nationalists, in particular, on identity narratives about "our" liberal values. Ultimately, the identity work done by these narratives obscures the myriad historical and contemporary entanglements between global liberalism and imperial politics, both historical and ongoing. And while one would think that the election of Donald Trump and the rise of xenophobic, racist, and White nationalist movements around the world would have led supporters of what is known as the "American-led, liberal world order" to reflect more critically—and with a bit more humility—on these imperial entanglements, the responses of prominent liberal internationalists have tended quite starkly toward retrenchment, hubris, and a fixation with "who we are" as liberal peoples. These responses are often so vociferous and so self-justifying that they border on a malign form of liberal narcissism.

By contrast, a Said-inspired approach challenges that narcissism by reject-ing liberal paeans. Rather than beginning with an investigation of liberal philosophy or a liberal "tradition" or even a liberal "urge" to exclude or colonize, it begins with a worldly probing of the historical and contempo-rary affiliations between liberal discourse, liberal policies, and imperialism. Taking these affiliations as its critical compass, a Said-influenced perspective refuses to allow liberals to muscle their way to the front of an overcrowded political field and demand that we take them seriously on their own, self-regarding terms. Rather, Said's mode of critique approaches liberalism as it is: a densely conflicted, always-already-affiliated bundle of intertwined ideas, commitments, and values that has interfaced productively with imperialism since people first began referring to themselves as liberals. Moreover, Said understood that any investigation of imperialism was always a both/and proposition. In other words, for Said, imperialism was *both* a complicated, internally diverse, and discordant amalgamation of ideas, thinkers, and institutional connections that expressed itself in particular historical contexts *and* a discursive universe in which similar ideas, tropes, and rhetorical strategies reemerge over time. Approaching the connection between liberalism and imperialism in this both/and manner enables scholars to identify imperializing moments within global liberalism without feeding liberal narcissism; that is, without reducing questions about liberalism to questions of inherency and/or identity.

This chapter makes this argument by first looking more closely at contemporary political theoretical approaches to the study of liberalism, focusing on the distinction between studies of liberalism as a political philosophy and those inquiries that have become more common since the "turn to empire" in the field: studies of liberalism as a historical ideology. The chapter then pivots to an analysis of contemporary liberal internationalism in foreign policy discourse, concentrating on the work of scholars best known for their impassioned endorsements of the "American-led, liberal world order." It then lays out a Said-inspired critique of liberal internationalism, insisting on a methodological straddling of political theory and foreign policy analysis. I argue that Said's both/and approach to imperialism provides political theorists with the tools necessary to tie contemporary liberal foreign policy to imperialism while avoiding the siren's song of the "we" narrative. It also suggests ways that critics can resist popular liberal reframings of global politics as existential crises, reframings that freeze policy analysis in time, foreclose on possibilities for reflection, and shut down novel forms of reinterpretation. I end with some thoughts on the "treason" of the intellectuals in a post-Trump world and some final reflections on a Said-inspired critical reimagination of that world.

## LIBERALISM AND POLITICAL THEORY

Within the field of political theory today, approaches to something called liberalism tend to be split between the study of political philosophy and the study of ideology, between political theoretical and what Barry Hindress calls "actually existing" liberalism.[7] In the North American and British academies, most self-described liberal theorists tend to have been schooled in the tradition established by John Rawls in the 1970s and carried on by his sympathetic acolytes. The majority of these scholars continue to treat liberalism exclusively as a species of moral philosophy, unburdened by the historical relationship between liberal ideas and actual politics.

Liberal theorists thus often read the overarching goal of political theory in general as the theorization and achievement of liberal tasks conceived of through an analytical framework that constrains the goals of theory from the outset. For instance, at the beginning of *Justice as Fairness*, Rawls confirms what roles political philosophy "may have" as "part of society's public political culture."[8] There are, he argues, precisely four of them, and they all refer to restraining and clarifying the shape and functioning of the polity, from the practical settlement of disputes, to the validation of institutions, to the ring-fencing of political vision within the boundaries of what Rawls considers to be "realistically utopian." The questions Rawlsian political philosophers often ask are similarly contained. Of what does a reasonable pluralism consist?[9] How do "we" conceptualize a fair relationship between equality and autonomy?[10] How can "we" theorize a fairer basic structure? The goal of such questions, thought experiments, and expositions is to craft conceptually tight theories of political justice that are as impenetrable to philosophical scrutiny as possible; that is, to fashion philosophical positions that, as Rawls puts it in the first few paragraphs of *A Theory of Justice*, resist "obvious objections" from other philosophers.[11]

At the same time, Rawls always maintains that the liberalism he theorized had a connection to what Said would call worldly politics, despite the fact that his mode of argumentation took place almost entirely in an analytical register. He thus insists that, while it is possible to work out the problems of politics primarily at the level of abstraction, the foundations of this abstraction—the "tradition" to which he refers—are historical. His approach to "justice as fairness," he argues, is "political not metaphysical," grounded on principles of toleration that have been worked up out of the "social and historical conditions" associated with liberal democratic states in Europe since the "Wars of Religion following the Reformation."[12] And yet, after that brief historical gesture, we never hear another word about context from Rawls, largely because the point of the gesture is to situate, rather than inform, theory. In effect, the Wars of Religion in Rawls's work serve as deep background only. They provide his analytical system with a distant anchor in politics that then allows him to proceed as if history and context don't matter.

Likewise, Rawls maintains in *The Law of Peoples* (his only attempt to theorize international politics "out of a liberal idea of justice") that his ideas are also "realistically utopian" because they are grounded in "familiar and largely traditional principles I took from the history and usages of international law and practice."[13] And yet, aside from this nod toward history and practice, Rawls makes little attempt in *The Law of Peoples* to engage the substance of international law and practice in any detail, much less discuss the historical entanglements of international law with imperialism and colonial governance.[14] Indeed, rather than talk about the historically and politically charged challenges of developing a liberal, "law of peoples" approach to actually existing states in the Middle East whose governments might be dominated by religious conservatives, Rawls works up a theory aimed at accommodating both "reasonable liberal peoples" and "decent hierarchical peoples" through an elaborate exploration of an entirely fictitious Islamic nation he calls "Kazanistan."[15]

Thus, while Rawls and those liberal theorists following in Rawls's footsteps may gesture toward moments of worldly grounding, the vast majority of their theorizing assumes that the conceptual framework for justice as fairness they develop and employ is meant to influence and respond *to* the world rather than be shaped *by* the world. In 2013's *Justice and Foreign Policy*, for instance, Michael Blake develops an approach to international liberalism that he similarly links to the history of international law. Describing this approach as "something that Rawls might have developed out of his own work," Blake argues that international law provides a thin form of deep justification—a residual "part" of the overall guidance—for a more robust, analytical theory of how "already committed" liberal states can develop moral approaches to foreign policy.[16] Ultimately, however, Blake's vision of what counts as "liberalism"—something "already committed" liberal people are meant to intuitively recognize—bears little resemblance to ideological liberalism as it has expressed itself through the actual history of global/imperial power politics. Historical liberalism's "disruptive details"—as Said might call them—aren't important for Blake's theorizing because the point of history is simply to enable that theorizing. In other words, history is useful for Blake insofar as it provides a stage for his mind, a suitably hazy, legitimating foundation on which he can build liberal, theoretical castles.

Scholars like Hindress who study liberalism as a "powerful historical phenomenon" argue that it circulates in a manner frequently at odds with how it is theorized by philosophers like Rawls or Blake.[17] Today, thanks to the work of Michael Freeden, Richard Bellamy, Duncan Bell, and others, there is considerably more work in political theory devoted to exploring that historical phenomenon. Rather than approach liberalism as an internally consistent political philosophy, these scholars treat liberalism as a roughly two-hundred-year-old constellation of ideas, symbolic gestures, and political visions, evoked in different contexts and under different circumstances by a diverse cadre of thinkers, politicians, political activists, public intellectuals, pundits, citizens, organizations, lobbyists, reading groups, and think tanks.

These studies tend to read liberalism as, in Freeden's words, a "semantic field," a "plastic, changing thing, shaped and reshaped by the thought-practices of individuals and groups."[18] Scholars like Freeden are, therefore, less interested in the familiar philosophers' questions that continue to dominate debates among contemporary liberal theorists (global and domestic) and their communitarian, feminist, socialist, and conservative critics, questions such as: What is more important, rights or community? Is a liberal system of justice possible in the international realm? Is fairness compatible with inequality? Rather, contextual readers of liberalism suggest that scholars ought to be subjecting something called the "liberal tradition" to historical interrogation rather than simply theorizing either *as* liberals or as critics *of* liberalism, as if liberalism were a coherent object on whose characteristics we can all agree. They thus focus their inquiries on crafting historical excavations of those sets of interests and rhetorical incoherences that have given rise to something called "liberalism" in Britain and America in the nineteenth and twentieth centuries.

To be fair, casting a historical eye on the contextual development of European liberalism is hardly a new phenomenon. Such prewar intellectuals as Harold Laski and his students (most notably C. B. Macpherson) were less likely than many of today's political theorists to treat liberalism as a coherent body of thought with only a thin connection to the historical outcome of the Wars of Religion or a set of intuitions about international law. In 1936's *The Rise of European Liberalism*, Laski maintains that the success of liberalism as a political ideology simply can't be chalked up to zeitgeist or a single "conscious and persistent search" for individual freedom moving through the ages.[19] Rather, he insists, whatever it is that we call liberalism today must be seen as the gradual accretion of economic, social, and political forces coalescing over time into an ideology strong enough to first challenge and then become the existing social order. Those political actors and intellectuals engaged in articulating this unfolding vision did so within a political milieu that required them to respond and adjust their vision to a variety of political, historical, and economic facts. "Into the development of liberalism," observes Laski, "there have entered winds of doctrine so diverse in their origin as to make clarity difficult, and precision perhaps unattainable."[20] Laski's goal in this text is to follow the paths of these diverse doctrines back to their origins, not to make them cohere, but rather to disrupt what appears on the surface to be ideological cohesion.

As John Gunnel and Bell both argue, the transformation of liberalism into a coherent political theory with a supposed tradition occurred after Laski's death in 1950. In other words, liberal theory only became the "liberal tradition" during the postwar period largely through the professionalization and structural transformation of the discipline of political science in Britain and North America. In Bell's words, despite some differences, British and American narratives about liberalism "converged during the ideological battles of the middle decades of the twentieth century, creating the expansive vision of liberalism that dominates scholarly discourse today."[21] In this environment, Laski-like explorations of something called "liberalism's" diverse origins were replaced with increasingly prima facie and common sense assumptions about a coherent tradition developed over time, from Locke, through Kant and Mill, to Rawls. Against this common sense today, intellectual historians and scholars of the history of political thought like Bell are subjecting liberalism to genealogical scrutiny, focusing on the "way in which the liberal tradition is understood" rather than simply assuming that everybody understands that tradition in the same way.[22]

For Bell, liberalism is best contextualized as a "universe of languages," a complex ideological constellation with a complex history attached to global and local forms of politics and discourse. Liberalism, in Bell's sense, is not a coherent theory that has shifted slightly over time but is rather the "sum of the arguments that have been classified as liberal and recognized as such by other self-proclaimed liberals across time and space."[23] The point of this approach—also embraced by such intellectual historians as Samuel Moyn and Katrina Forrester—is not only to broaden our understanding of what counts as liberalism in history but also to trouble the surface-calm waters of liberal philosophy's self-perception today.[24] This entails querying how, for instance, a theory as divorced from actual politics as Rawls's came to have the kind of predominance that it did. As Forrester maintains, it is remarkable that, a mere decade after its publication, *A Theory of Justice* had become so omnipresent in the field that "one bibliography listed 2,512 books and articles" in conversation with it. "It is no understatement," she continues, "to say that over the course of the 1970s political philosophy was remade in his [Rawls's] image."[25] Both Forrester and Moyn note that Rawls and Rawlsianism (in both its domestic and "global varieties") came to predominance approximately at the same moment in the early 1970s, when calls for greater global economic redistribution were on the rise throughout the recently decolonized world. The response of analytical liberalism, Forrester continues, to demands made by "theorists of the New International Economic Order for the overhaul of relations between Global North and South" was, in Brian Barry's words, to "domesticate" those demands and shut out possibilities for more radical forms of criticism.[26]

This recent movement to push analyses of liberalism in increasingly critical and historical directions is also connected to the field's "turn to empire" in the early 2000s. In the global moment of reckoning that followed the American government's response to the events of September 11—the invasion of Afghanistan, the 2003 Iraq War, and the invention of a "war on terror" without end—a growing number of political theorists began to look with skepticism at Francis Fukuyama's ebullient claim that the "universalization of Western liberal democracy as the final form of human government" was now upon us.[27] As Jennifer Pitts notes, the "combination of overwhelming and unaccountable power" exercised by the United States in Afghanistan and Iraq cast into stark relief the disconnect between expressions of liberal democracy and state domination.[28] More political theorists began to critically reevaluate the historical relationship between the two; that is, between state and corporate practices of occupation, violence, and resource extraction and an ideological worldview committed to freedom, equality, and sovereign autonomy that developed right alongside those practices. Uday Mehta describes this in *Liberalism and Empire* as the tension between "self-consciously" universal theories expressed by the likes of Mill and Mill's full-throated support for the imposition of "undemocratic and non-representative structures" on people he considered civilizationally stunted.[29] Many scholars involved in this "turn to empire" in political theory, such as Mehta, Pitts, and Muthu, began exploring liberalism and imperialism as *co-constituting* historical discourses. They did this through close, historical engagement with particular thinkers in context, focusing primarily on canonical figures in the history of political thought (e.g., Kant, Mill, Tocqueville) who advanced their ideas about liberalism in relation to imperialism, colonial governance, and the global politics of the age.

Other scholars interested in the complex history of liberalism, such as Helena Rosenblatt, Mantena, and Bell, have, by contrast, focused less on canonical thinkers than on the shifting terrain of liberal arguments, practices, narratives, and claims evoked by various figures "in the context of their time."[30] For Bell, this means treating liberalism as an "actor's category" embraced by a variety of "thinkers, ideas, and movements that were regarded as liberal" in their day.[31] This approach has led Bell to focus on lesser-known, pro-imperial thinkers who happened to identify as liberals. He argues that it is through engagement with this diverse universe of public intellectuals, historians, philosophers, artists, journalists, and novelists—some now barely remembered—that we gain essential insight into the deeply capacious and frequently unstable character of liberalism as a political ideology concerned, at different historical moments, with ruling and ordering the world. For Bell, it is only "by recovering the political concerns, languages, anxieties, and fantasies" of the "motley cast of characters" associated with schemes for expanding and strengthening imperial union, for instance, that "we begin to apprehend the content and complexity of imperial political thought at the apogee of the largest empire in history" and the relationship of this thought to something these characters called "liberalism."[32]

But regardless of whether their studies focus on canonical or noncanonical thinkers, for many political theorists and intellectual historians interested in exploring the relationship between liberalism as philosophy and liberalism as a political language, imperialism is the wedge issue that cracks open narratives about liberalism as a political philosophy and/or political orientation to the complexities and contradictions of its own history. Often, scholars writing in this vein refer specifically to *Orientalism* when they introduce the idea of imperialism as worthy of historical inquiry in the first place. As Andrew Fitzmaurice notes in the first line of his 2012 article on liberalism, imperialism, and international law, "Since the publication of Edward Said's *Orientalism*, historians have exposed liberalism's complicity in empire."[33] Likewise, Pitts identifies the publication of *Orientalism* in 1978 as inaugurating an academic moment when a significant number of scholars (outside of political theory) became interested in imperialism.[34] Hindress also mentions Said several times in his article on "actually existing liberalism," although somewhat unusually, he does so by referring to a question Said raises in 1992's "Nationalism, Human Rights, and Interpretation" rather than to *Orientalism* more generally. In this article, Said notes that Great Powers "babble on about how really moral they are," immediately before they launch into doing "some particularly gangsterish things" on the global stage. "The question I am addressing," Said continues, "is how there is an appeal for liberals in such a rhetoric—from Tocqueville's to George Bush's."[35]

Thus, in 1992, before the "turn to empire" in political theory, Said was exploring a contradiction within historical liberalism that would become the focal point for much political theory inquiry into the subject just a few years later: the disconnect between liberals' stated commitments to freedom, equality, and sovereign autonomy on the one hand and their willingness to invade, occupy, and generally engage in "gangsterish things" on the other. And yet, Said's phrasing of this contradiction reflects an orientation toward imperialism and liberalism that makes his approach markedly different from that of many political theorists. Specifically, he queries not just how it has expressed itself historically, but he also links this same contradiction to foreign policy discourse—from Tocqueville to George Bush. And it is precisely this impulse, I suggest, that makes Said's approach to imperialism different from the majority of political theorists exploring the imbricated history of liberalism and imperialism today. Because while Pitts argues that it may have been September 11 and the Iraq War that drove political theorists to study the historical relationship between liberalism and European imperialism in the first place, virtually none of those theorists connected these historical studies to a critique of contemporary, American imperialism. There are, thus, very few models in political theory today of scholars who attend, in Pitts's words, to the "critical demands of the present" while retaining a "deeply informed historical sense" of liberalism's and imperialism's braided past.[36]

Since Pitts's article was published in 2010, more work has been done at the intersection of political theory and the history of international thought to link the historical entanglements of imperialism and liberalism to contemporary politics. In her own 2018 book *Boundaries of the International*, for instance, Pitts specifically understands her analysis of imperialism and international law in the eighteenth and nineteenth centuries as part of an effort to "illuminate continuing uses of ideas of international law and human rights to obscure dynamics of domination by the Global North over the Global South."[37] I also try to do something similar in my 2014 book *Empires without Imperialism* by examining the rhetorical similarities between British liberal imperialists at the beginning of the twentieth century and contemporary liberal imperialists in the United States today.[38] It remains the case, however, that political theorists still generally avoid linking historical analyses of liberalism and imperialism to contemporary expressions of liberalism in American foreign policy, no matter whether they are interested in canonical or noncanonical thinkers, in liberalism as a transcendent theory, or in liberalism as a completely contextual phenomenon. In other words, political theorists tend to avoid writing about rhetorical expressions of liberalism that support and rationalize today's empire: the global military hegemon that is the United States.

Said, by contrast, has little patience with theoretical orientations toward philosophy, culture, and politics that refuse to bring historical criticisms linking liberalism and imperialism to bear on contemporary global politics. In the spirit of that impatience, the next section takes a deep dive into the discursive universe of liberal internationalism, a scholarly and policy orientation toward global politics that makes sense out of American imperialism largely by deflecting attention away from its illiberal actions. The purpose of this Said-inspired mode of inquiry, I argue, is to daylight the historical and discursive affiliations between "liberal global order" narratives and imperialism and, in the process, explore some of the key rhetorical strategies by which this worldview constricts inquiry and silences debate by perseverating on liberalism itself.

## LIBERAL INTERNATIONALISM, LIBERAL NARCISSISM

As a school of thought, contemporary liberal internationalism is closely associated with IR scholars like John Ikenberry and Daniel Deudney, international legal scholars like Anne-Marie Slaughter, liberal philosophers like Michael Blake, academic-adjacent public intellectuals like Michael Ignatieff, former foreign service professionals like Ivo Daalder, and other thinkers and pundits connected to such high-powered policy institutes as the Princeton Project on National Security, Harvard's Kennedy School, and the Chicago Council on Global Affairs.[39] They tend to have extensive connections with international organizations and committees like the Canadian-sponsored International Commission on Intervention and State Sovereignty, which drafted the original language for the United Nations' "Responsibility to Protect" (R2P) principle.[40] They also are frequently connected to think tanks like the Council on Foreign Relations and the Carnegie Endowment for International Peace. Liberal internationalists thus straddle the worlds of academia, government agencies, and the foreign policy establishment, forming a powerful policy wing of that congeries known as "the Blob."[41]

Liberal inhabitants of the Blobosphere like Ikenberry and Slaughter have described themselves as "neo-Wilsonians" who belong to a tradition of IR thought first associated with the ideas behind the League of Nations, which, according to this narrative, were successfully brought to fruition following World War II, when the United States emerged as "first citizen" of a collection of liberal-minded states.[42] This "Western liberal order," according to Ikenberry, was constructed by the "United States and its partners" after the war and is organized around "free-world values," such as "basic economic openness, multilateral institutions, security cooperation and democratic solidarity."[43] These thinkers largely believe, with Ikenberry, that there is a necessary connection between the survival of this "liberal order" and the "hegemonic leadership" of the United States.[44] That maintaining this international order in the name of stated liberal ends can sometimes entail the "use of dangerous tools" (Blake's euphemistic term for war, violence, coercion, bombing, invasion, and occupation) is an unfortunate but necessary fact of life for liberal internationalists and not something on which they prefer to dwell.[45]

Supporters of the liberal world order often claim that their approach to foreign policy bears no resemblance to the hawkish interventionism of neo-conservatives like Paul Wolfowitz, Donald Kagan, and Max Boot, who rose to prominence in the George W. Bush administration and helped engineer the catastrophic Iraq invasion of 2003.[46] And yet, as Michael Desch argues, their vehement protestations often sound a bit "too much like the Queen in Shakespeare's *Hamlet*" to accept at face value.[47] In truth, there is often substantively very little difference between neoconservative and liberal internationalist ideas. Both groups of thinkers are committed, according to Inderjeet Parmar, to a "historically effective ideology of global intervention."[48] This consensus concretized after September 11, 2001, through what he terms an "effective fusion" of two key foreign policy developments: the increasing influence of conservative think tanks like the Heritage Foundation in foreign policy circles during the 1990s and the development since the late 1980s of a "robust, crusading and theoretically confident liberal interventionism" grounded in "democratic transition" theory.[49] The fact that so many liberal internationalists rose so easily to prominence after Obama's 2008 election—and then, once again, slipped smoothly into place in the Biden administration as though they'd never left—suggests that they offer nothing significantly different from the *longue durée* of American foreign policy.[50]

Moreover, while Ikenberry and Slaughter may insist that the political vision of their patron saint, Woodrow Wilson, bears no resemblance to the interventionist agenda of the neoconservatives, they have historically forgotten that Wilson himself was essential to furthering the development of an interventionist and racialized international order—a form of global Jim Crow—that formed the basis for the secularized racism and American exceptionalism after World War II that has remained essential to mainstream Republican and Democratic foreign policy arguments in the United States ever since.[51] Today's "Neo-Wilsonians"—despite the fact that they doth protest too much—are clearly linked to a tradition that transformed racial superiority into democracy promotion and hitched America's military and political primacy to the preservation of liberal democracy worldwide.[52] Moreover, the very international power formation they champion has contributed time and time again to ensuring that, despite formal decolonization in the post-war period, most of the world's resources continue to flow in the same direction that they did during three hundred years of European imperialism: from the global South to the global North.[53] Advocates of the liberal world order thus play a key role in maintaining the rhetorical edifice of a form of American global domination that is imperialist in all but name while actively ignoring, deflecting, or explaining away the racist and imperial origins of that domination and of their own tradition.

Because supporters of the liberal world order are committed to the belief that American military hegemony is not imperial, they are constantly engaged (on an almost micrological level) in rhetorical practices that frantically try to square the circle between liberalism and domination; that is, between a rhetoric of liberal equality, democracy, and sovereign autonomy on the one hand and a hierarchical world system that has historically been (and continues to be) maintained through racist violence or threat of racist violence on the other. They often thread this needle by combining liberalism with more anodyne titles for global power other than empire, such as "primacy," "hegemony," and "liberal world order" itself, a term that reveals some of the deepest tensions inherent in the liberal internationalist project more generally. This rhetorical twinning of "liberal" and "order" has the effect of softening and occluding the actual power politics involved in "ordering" the world, thus erasing, as Patrick Porter puts it, the "memory of violence, coercion, and compromise that also marked post-war diplomatic history."[54] "While liberalism and liberal projects existed," during this era, he continues, "such 'order' as existed rested on the imperial prerogatives of a superpower that attempted to impose order by stepping outside rules and accommodating *illiberal* forces."[55] In this sense, the "liberal world order" that emerged after World War II is really, as Hedley Bull once observed, just "imperialism with good manners."[56]

Perhaps even more obfuscating and unstable, however, is Ikenberry's other term of choice: "liberal hegemony."[57] Assuming that liberalism in an international context implies (at bare minimum) some commitment to freedom of movement, human rights, formal equality, the rule of law, sovereign autonomy, constitutional government, and free trade, it hardly seems compatible with the way most IR scholars have traditionally conceived of hegemony in terms of a great power's capacity to shape the international system through the exercise of coercive and noncoercive (economic, political, cultural) power.[58] Of course, the contradiction inherent in the term *liberal hegemony* is hardly uncommon in the history of liberal governance, on either a domestic or global scale. In many ways, that contradiction reflects the underlying unfreedom of liberal governments historically: their dependence on coercive/disciplining forms of sovereignty and capitalism and their long, coterminous, and constitutive relationship to European imperialism.[59] In other words, in its various historical iterations and contexts, the developing ideology and set of political and economic practices we have come to associate with something called liberalism and liberal governance has routinely attached notions of freedom to territorial expansion, to the undemocratic coercion of entire populations, and to the marginalization, enslavement, and subordination of peoples considered incapable of appreciating liberal freedom both within the colonies and within the metropole.[60]

Additionally, the key canonical figures associated with the liberal tradition have not only been keenly interested in imperialism, but they also have often engaged in rhetorical practices that exclude particular groups of undesirables in order to circumscribe liberalism's barbarian outside. Key thinkers in the European liberal tradition, as well as liberal public intellectuals and administrators associated with European imperialism, often did this by employing what Mehta and Mantena have referred to as rhetorical "strategies of exclusion." These include, for example, Locke's exception for the "quarrelsome and contentious", Tocqueville's excision of Black slaves and Indigenous people (or, in a French imperial context, Algerian Arabs and Berbers) from humanity, and Mill's contempt for those "states of society in which the race itself may be considered as in its nonage."[61] When read in this light, "liberal hegemony" appears simply as a transparent nod to a long tradition in liberal thought of pairing the benefits of liberal government with the political annihilation, enslavement, dispossession, and domination of entire populations in the name of freedom.

What differentiates contemporary liberal internationalists from nineteenth-century liberal imperialists like Tocqueville and Mill, however, is that they can't actually use the word *empire* in reference to American power, and they can't voice their "strategies of exclusion" in a language that entails explicit reference to racial superiority or even the triumph of Western civilization. They therefore tend to rely more heavily on what I refer to elsewhere as "strategies of deflection": arguments, utterances, and rhetorical gestures whose ultimate effect is to first acknowledge and then immediately draw attention away from the tension between liberalism's explicitly articulated universal values, the hierarchical nature of the liberal world order, and the structural domination of the United States.[62]

Sometimes liberal internationalists approach this deflective challenge through the strategic use of realpolitik; that is, through an overreliance on examples of those instances when (sadly, unfortunately, and reluctantly) "we" must make illiberal foreign policy decisions in the name of the liberal world order. Ignatieff, for instance, relies heavily on this rhetorical sleight of hand when he differentiates between what he calls the realm of "professional ethicists" and the hard zone of "realist" policy making. He argues that people and institutions embedded in the real world—policy makers, NGOs, governments, and, one assumes, liberal public intellectuals like himself—are often forced to confront what Ignatieff calls "contradictions" between the reality of what they need to do to support the American-led world order and what universal norms of justice would seem to require. Ignatieff describes this conflict as a clash between the "view from somewhere" and the "view from nowhere."[63] "Professional ethicists" interested in abstract theories of human rights and global justice "have a job to do," Ignatieff concedes, but it is clearly subsidiary to the work of active, engaged public intellectuals like himself, people invested in the push and pull of international politics. Hence, "professional ethicists" concerned with universal principles are relevant insofar as their theories illuminate contradictions between different ethical values in a manner that "will help us to negotiate them in practical politics."[64]

The ethical position Ignatieff advances here treats liberal principles not as *essential* but potentially *auxiliary* to the project of the liberal world ordering. Liberalism itself, in this view, is thus nothing more than a loose bundle of principles that can be violated when the reality of politics necessitates. On its face, this approach is fraught with certain rhetorical perils for liberal internationalists. If liberal values can be picked up and put down by Great Powers at will, what then makes the order they maintain "liberal"? Liberal internationalists who want us to believe that both America and the order it leads are essentially liberal sometimes get tangled in precisely this contradiction and end up simply saying different things at different times. For instance, in 2009's "Liberal Internationalism 3.0," Ikenberry declares, "Liberal international order—both in its ideas and real-world political formations—is not embodied in a fixed set of principles or practices" but rather flows in an ongoing way from those institutions and norms that have "made appearances in various combinations and changing ways over the decades."[65] By contrast, in 2014 he associated the liberal world order with a "fixed set of principles" that included "support for the rule of law, open and reciprocal trade, and a commitment to democratic government and human rights."[66] By 2017, Ikenberry was arguing that these "fair-minded rules and norms of the order" were essential features of the liberal world order throughout the postwar era and were (and had always been) readily apparent to any state that wanted to align themselves with the growing club.[67] In 2018, however, he had backtracked a bit, insisting that the liberal world order was merely a "complex and multilayered political formation with liberal characteristics" rather than a global order guided by liberal principles.[68]

When not saying different things at different times, supporters of the American-led liberal world order tend to fall back on two modes of argumentation that help them establish the consistent liberal character of America's primacy, even when the United States behaves in ways that appear patently illiberal. The first mode is similar in form to the way Rawls and Rawlsians treat history as deep background for their analytical theorizing. For instance, just as Rawls grounds his "realistically utopian" approach to the "law of peoples" in the "familiar and largely traditional principles I took from the history and usages of international law and practice," so do liberal internationalists sometimes gesture toward a distant, equally vague, historical grounding that serves as deep background for their contemporary assertions. Ignatieff, for instance, insists that the foundations of the "global ethics" he articulates are to be found in the tradition of European natural law established by international lawyers "from Hugo Grotius onward," whose norms are now "enshrined in the structure of existing international law" and in its "principle institutional pillars," such as the UN Charter, the Universal Declaration of Human Rights, and the Geneva Conventions.[69]

The second, more common approach adopted by liberal internationalists is to simply insist that the American-led liberal international order doesn't just *usually* try to apply liberal principles but that it is *already* always liberal in essence, even when its hegemon acts illiberally. In other words, the words *liberal* and *liberalism* for these thinkers imply more than a collection of chosen principles, such as respect for human rights, equality under the law, international governance, sovereign autonomy, and democracy. Rather, these words circulate throughout the discursive universe of liberal internationalism as signifiers of *identity*: cultural markers that relate to the underlying character traits of both the United States, its citizens, and its liberal democratic allies. Simply put, for liberal internationalists, liberalism is the ur-identity, the foundational essence that makes us "who we are" such that "we" can never be anything else.

This means that not only do liberal internationalists have a fraught relationship to the liberal principles they instrumentally employ, but they also have a fraught relationship with reality. As liberals, these thinkers reject empire as an illiberal, "extreme form of hierarchical order in international relations."[70] They acknowledge that the "United States has dominated the post-war international order" and that this order is "hierarchical" and "built on asymmetries of power" but simultaneously insist that "it is not an imperial system."[71] Rather, it is only through the continued military, political, and economic primacy of the United States and its liberal allies that we are able to "safeguard liberty under law."[72] In this tautological vision, America must act like an empire but is not an empire—nor should it ever be understood thus—because "we" are not imperial people.

Liberal internationalists thus often respond to the possibility that what they are suggesting is illiberal or imperial by recentering liberal identity narratives about themselves and the liberal world order, an order they insist is anti-imperial but whose hegemon must sometimes act coercively in a manner that may—incidentally and sadly—sometimes resemble imperialism. Navigating this rhetorical tension requires supporters of the liberal world order to privilege what Slaughter calls the "idea" of America over the actuality of America. The United States, Slaughter thus argues, is simultaneously the "indispensable nation" without whom "nothing gets done" and an aspirational nation, constantly striving to live up to the "fixed stars" of its core values—"liberty, democracy, equality, justice, toleration, humility, and faith"—even when it fails to do so in policy practice.[73] Slaughter's framing here is fairly typical of the way supporters of the liberal world order perennially ask us to believe that what matters most about American hegemony is not what America actually *does* with its power but what it understands itself to always be *trying to do*. They insist that the United States be judged by its intentions, by "our" continual "striving to improve ourselves, to advance, to live up to our ideals" rather than by the actual impact of "our" foreign policy on the world or whether "we" ever live up to these ideals or not.[74] Slaughter and her like-minded colleagues thus tend to talk about the United States as if it/we were an exuberant teenager just trying to adhere to the goodness within itself/ourselves and not always hitting the mark. The fact that this well-intentioned teenager also happens to be the most powerful nation on earth—with a grotesquely metastasizing, nearly trillion-dollar-a-year security budget, a massive nuclear arsenal, and more military bases around the world than, in David Vine's words, "any other people, nation, or empire in history"—is ultimately not the point.[75] The point is that "we" strive to get it right next time.

Thus, for all that its champions may present themselves as a happy medium between idealism and clear-eyed realism—the "view from nowhere" and the "view from somewhere"—the *Weltanschauung* on which the liberal world order rests is fundamentally a species of what Carl Schmitt calls "political theology."[76] As Porter accurately observes, for the most influential members of the foreign policy elite in Washington, American primacy is not merely one option among many but an unshakeable "article of faith."[77] That US military dominance often entails violence—that its interventionist and belligerent behavior throughout the postwar period often bears an eerie resemblance to the most abusive aspects of European imperialism—is again incidental to its inherent liberalism. That the contemporary liberal world order itself has its roots in the imperialist strategizing of Wilson, Jan Smuts, and other leading statesmen in Europe and America who played a key role in the formation of the League of Nations, the Royal Institute of International Affairs, and the Council on Foreign Relations is, again, not worth noticing and incidental to the bigger project.[78]

This means that sometimes—for instance, when Ikenberry argues that the liberal world order is "not really American or Western even if, for historical reasons, it initially appeared that way" or when Daniel Deudney and Ikenberry insist that although it "emerged in the West" the "values" of this order "have become universal"—these thinkers simply ask us *not* to accept the idea that historical facts matter.[79] More important than the liberal world order's historical links to imperialism and imperial law, to their minds, is the fact that in the decades following World War II, the United States "stepped forward," in Ikenberry's words, "as the hegemonic world leader, taking on the privileges and responsibilities of organizing and running the system." In this scenario, America was simply more able and capable than the other Great Powers at that crucial moment in history, boldly stepping up to its natural hegemony, eventually presiding over what Ikenberry has sometimes (in his less ebullient moments) referred to as a "hierarchical order with liberal characteristics."[80]

When explaining why other states (particularly states in the non-West or the global South, many well into the process of decolonization) would accept this "hierarchical order with liberal characteristics," Ikenberry refers not to the existing historical record but rather to an origins story that he takes from Hobbes's *Leviathan*. Significantly, Ikenberry chooses to focus on the story Hobbes tells, not about international politics, but about the imaginary transition from the state of nature to the commonwealth, a moment when hypothetical consenting individuals agreed to hand over all their power—including power over their own lives—to the Leviathan. Ikenberry argues that, after World War II, "other countries, particularly in Western Europe and later in

East Asia, handed the reins of power to Washington, just as Hobbes' individuals in the state of nature construct and hand over power to the Leviathan."[81] The result, he argues, is a "liberal" Leviathan, a "hierarchical" world order led by the United States, grounded in the "virtues of liberal internationalism."[82]

At first glance, Ikenberry's choice of a Hobbesian metaphor to help him narrate his story isn't entirely surprising, given that there aren't many characters in the history of European political thought to whom IR scholars routinely turn for inspiration beyond the trifecta identified by the field in the first half of the twentieth century: Thucydides, Machiavelli, and Hobbes. Upon closer inspection, however, Ikenberry's particular use of a Hobbesian framework to explain the foundation of the liberal international order, in terms of decisions made by consenting *state* subjects to escape global insecurity through voluntary submission to the United States, is actually quite jarring. In *The Leviathan*, Hobbes is concerned with theorizing a reasonable (in his words, "geometrical") solution to the problem of civil instability that he envisions through the creation of the great Leviathan, or commonwealth, a solution he explicitly warns is inappropriate to the international realm. Realists have historically been drawn to Hobbes's work precisely because of this. In total agreement with his belief that human beings are moved primarily by the desire for power, they read Hobbes's refusal to imagine an international commonwealth as proof that he understood relationships between commonwealths themselves to be largely ungoverned and the extrastate realm to be comprised of both "zones of conflict" and "zones of peace" between entities who remain in a permanent state of nature with each other.[83] English School rationalists like Hedley Bull, however, tend to think that Hobbes simply didn't understand the domestic and the international to be analogous spaces requiring similar political solutions.[84] For Bull, the realist account of Hobbes fails to appreciate "how deeply pacific Hobbes' approach to international relations was, at least in the values from which it sprang."[85] Their disagreements aside, however, Bull and the realists both agree that Hobbes *did not* think it was possible to build an international Leviathan.

So, what then does Ikenberry get out of extending a metaphor that was never meant for the international to the inception of an international order? First and foremost, he gets the benefit of Hobbes's fundamental sleight of hand without acknowledging its existence. In other words, in *The Leviathan*, Hobbes identifies two ways in which a commonwealth can be inaugurated: "by Institution" (when "men agree amongst themselves to submit to some Man or Assembly") or "by Acquisition" (when a man "by Warre subdueth his enemies").[86] Hobbes baldly admits that the second mode of commonwealth creation is historically far more common than the first but that this distinction doesn't really matter because the "rights and consequences" that inhere in the sovereign Leviathan, are the "same in both" cases. In Hobbes's words,

His power cannot, without his consent, be Transferred to another; He cannot
Forfeit it; He cannot be Accused by any of his Subjects of Injury; He cannot
be Punished by them; He is Judge of what is necessary for Peace, and Judge of
Doctrines; He is Sole Legislator; and Supreme Judge of Controversies and of
the Times, and Occasions of Warre and Peace.[87]

If the end results of commonwealth by acquisition and commonwealth by
institution—the lodging of total sovereignty in the person of the Leviathan—
are not only identical but also equally desirable, why then does Hobbes spend
so much time talking about a hypothetical process by which consenting subjects submit themselves to a sovereign?

For Philip Pettit, Hobbes engages in this extensive counterfactual exercise for pedagogical reasons. In other words, thinking about how the extant
commonwealth *could* have been generated through consent provides us with
important insight into the nature of the commonwealth more generally, "in the
same way Economics 101 explains what money is by showing how it could
have emerged from a barter economy."[88] A less sanguine interpretation suggests that Hobbes simply prefers the idea of a total sovereign who "cannot
be accused" by his subjects and the point of *The Leviathan* is to retroactively
justify this position by demonstrating how free subjects might once have
*agreed* to their submission, even if we have no idea when this might have
been or if it actually occurred. Thus, not only does Hobbes twin consent
and coercion on a philosophical level throughout *The Leviathan*, but he also
deflects his readers' attention away from the more common, violent moment
of acquisition by tilting the majority of his argument toward institution. You
may not like what the sovereign is doing to you right now, the overall thrust
of *The Leviathan* suggests, but at some historical moment, your progenitors
might very well have consented to be governed thus.

Ikenberry, like Hobbes, is a thinker for whom the *idea* of consent matters.
Borrowing Hobbes's origins story allows him to cast the institution of a world
order in which the United States is "Judge of what is necessary for Peace" as
a choice made by consenting states who are, in this story, also individual consenting subjects. The difference, of course, is that Hobbes situates his moment
of Leviathan formation in the distant past, back in the ether of history before
written time, so that no evidence remains to prove or disprove commonwealth by institution. The same cannot be said of Ikenberry, whose "Liberal
Leviathan" was established and then consistently reestablished during
moments of historical record. And yet, it doesn't seem to matter to Ikenberry
that we can actually look to the decades following the postwar period and
identify time after time when colonized peoples and states were dragged
involuntarily into the American orbit through various forms of military, economic, and political pressure, which, during the Cold War, took a variety of

stick-and-carrot-type shapes.[89] From the first CIA-orchestrated coup in Syria in 1949, the United States attempted to overthrow or successfully overthrew governments in Albania, Iran, Guatemala, Costa Rica, Egypt, Indonesia, British Guiana, Iraq, Vietnam, Cambodia, Laos, Ecuador, the Congo, Brazil, the Dominican Republic, Cuba, Bolivia, Ghana, Chile, Greece, Australia, Angola, Portugal, Jamaica, the Seychelles, Chad, Grenada, South Yemen, Suriname, Fiji, Libya, Nicaragua, Panama, Afghanistan, Somalia, Yugoslavia, Venezuela, Haiti, and Honduras.[90] It seems simply not to matter to Ikenberry, in other words, that we can actually look to recent history and identify numerous instances when the instantiation and reinstantiation of a global order by acquisition—*not* a global order by institution—was the norm.

Recent documented history doesn't matter for Ikenberry, I suggest, because his worldview functions through a different logic, one in which liberalism as an idea and a metahistorical category matter more than the actual application of liberal principles. Indeed, Ikenberry's decision to dub the international order he describes a "liberal" Leviathan says everything about the status of something called liberalism in both his thinking and the thinking of most liberal internationalists. Again, as Ikenberry's consistent hedging on its actual content as an ideology would suggest, liberalism for liberal internationalists is, first and foremost, what Ignatieff terms a "fighting creed": a set of signifiers not located in specific and consistently applied policy practices but in an *identity* that is simultaneously meant to be universal and associated with specific nations and peoples in the global North.[91] Once this identity is taken for granted, American imperialism is transformed into liberal order by virtue of association. States that oppose this order—for whatever reasons—become, by default, existential threats that must be controlled and/or contained. The chilling matter-of-fact-ness by which the authors of the *Report of the Princeton Project on National Security* (including Ikenberry, Thomas Wright, and Francis Fukuyama) discuss the "use of preventive force against rogue states" is illustrative in this regard. Through the alchemy of liberal identity, states who challenge the norms of the American-led international order—whatever their historical experiences of that order might be—are transmuted into "rogue" states, and therefore the "limited collateral damage" associated with bringing them to heel is "clearly proportional."[92] In other words, a world order whose "moral grace notes are all liberal and democratic," as Ignatieff described it in 2003, cannot be otherwise.[93] Hence, its opponents must hate liberalism.

Liberalism as an identity, a category to differentiate between states and peoples, plays a not insignificant role in justifying the continuation of imperial practices that liberal internationalists insist ended with the decline of European power after World War II and the rise of the American hegemony. As public intellectuals and members of the foreign policy establishment, they play an essential role in perpetuating the belief in Washington that the global primacy of the United States must remain completely unchallenged. They thus help foster a policy environment in which American military hegemony remains the only game in town—a more-than-seventy-year-old "habit," in Porter's terms, grounded in "axiomatic choices made from unexamined assumptions"—that has extended across multiple Republican and Democratic administrations.[94] That a president who received the Nobel Peace Prize in 2009 for ostensibly creating a "new climate in international politics" (Barack Obama) and a president who declared in a 2016 Twitter rant that he would "make our Military so big, powerful & strong that no one will mess with us" (Donald Trump) would both commit more than half of their country's discretionary spending to maintaining its absolute military supremacy says volumes about how "unexamined" those assumptions truly are.[95] That the military budget Biden proposed in the spring of 2021 not only preserved Trump's huge spending hikes but also expanded them—from $740 billion to $753 billion—further hammers home the extent to which narratives of liberal identity deflect attention away from the material reality of the international order.[96] Liberal internationalists are thus deeply complicit in sustaining a foreign policy environment grounded neither in history nor in contemporary reality but in a fantasy realm where "who we are" always matters more than "what we do," no matter the cost, foreign or domestic.

Thus, at the end of the day, liberal internationalism sits atop a rhetorical rupture. On the one hand, as an ideological worldview, it is connected historically to imperialism and to ongoing forms of imperial power. On the other hand, its most faithful proponents refuse to engage this connection or this power in a sustained way and remain deeply committed to deflecting critical inquiry through the habitual turn to liberal identity narratives. Anyone approaching this rupture from a Said-inspired perspective will be immediately struck not just by its centrality but by the "we's" strung like signifying pearls on a string between one American presidential administration and another: "We are number 1; we are bound to lead; we stand for freedom and order."[97] These "we's" constitute the backbone of liberalism in its contemporary foreign policy iteration. They provide the terrain on which any discussion of American power *as* imperial is meant to wither on the vine because "we" are not an imperial people. And it is on this terrain—this space between imperial practice and liberal identity assertions—that the bulk of political-theoretical approaches to historical and contemporary liberalism fear to tread. And it is on this terrain that Said's approach stakes its claim and opens its doors.

## AMERICAN FOREIGN POLICY AND THE
## BOTH/AND OF LIBERAL IMPERIALISM

A key element of Said's critical orientation toward politics and culture is his persistent centering of imperialism. In other words, throughout the corpus of his scholarship, Said takes the internally fluctuating structure of discursive power—what Freeden might call a "semantic field" and Tully might call a "contested field"—that has sustained imperialism since the eighteenth century as his primary object of analysis.[98] This imperial system expresses itself through policy, through violence, through culture, through media, through text, and through the writings and public utterances of a variety of intellectual types who are often connected to each other through a dense web of affiliations that make sense out of the extant and ongoing domination of others. This scalar vision of the world changes over time and expresses itself differently in changing imperial contexts: from the self-confident crowing of nineteenth-century imperial administrators, to the British Round Table Society's softened vision of imperial commonwealth just before World War I, to George H. W. Bush's late-twentieth-century proclamations of a "New World Order." There are, however, discursive features of modern imperialism (e.g., Orientalist framings of the "other," narratives of civilization, mechanisms of occlusion, strategies of deflection) that consistently reassert themselves in different historical epochs and whose visibility make it possible to trace commonalities, as Said puts it, in the "rhetoric of Cromer, Balfour, Kissinger, and other statesmen."[99] By its sprawling nature, imperialism is thus always both/and. It is *both* historically and contextually specific, *and* there are similarities that scholars can identify in its rhetorical and material expressions that emerge and reemerge through the narratives of public intellectuals—popular and scholarly—over time.

An analysis of liberalism's entanglements with imperialism that forefronts this both/and quality of imperialism allows us as political theorists to do two things. First, it decenters questions about liberalism *as* liberalism and instead treats the connection *between* imperialism and liberalism as the primary site of inquiry. This is contrary to the way most of us, raised in the political theory tradition as it is taught in graduate schools (particularly in Britain and North America) are used to approaching liberalism and the questions generated by its relationship to empire. Thus, investigations of liberalism and imperialism often begin, as does Mehta's influential *Liberalism and Empire,* *by foregrounding liberal theory and then scrutinizing it "through the mirror that reflects its association with the British Empire."*[100] Mehta thus frames his queries in the book as queries *about* the limitations and possibilities of liberalism. And Mehta is not alone. I often frame my own inquiries into liberalism and imperialism thus, suggesting, for instance, that the goal of my first book is to "journey down the road that connects liberalism with its antithesis, to explore one of the most philosophically interesting moments when liberal thinkers and activists engaged in the politics of hierarchy and paternalism."[101] In effect, because political theorists have for so long been taught to envisage liberalism as a discrete and coherent tradition within our field and because we have only relatively recently decided that imperialism is a phenomenon worthy of our attention, it makes sense that so many investigations into the relationship between the two would be oriented toward discovering what imperialism can tell us *about* liberalism.

But framing interrogations of liberalism's connections to imperialism in this way—and again, I have been as guilty of this as anyone—can have the effect of transforming those interrogations into debates about inherency. Thus, when we take what seems to be the obvious philosophical contradiction between liberal universalism and imperial domination as our starting point, the central questions we inevitably ask assume that there *is* a contradiction and that it can be explained at the levels of ideas alone. Is there something, for instance, about liberalism as a school of political thought that makes it philosophically more likely to enable and/or support imperialism? Mehta, for instance, frames his intervention as an examination of those "reasons internal to liberalism" that compel advocates of a universal theory to respond to the unfamiliar with exclusion and domination.[102] His analyses of the work of John Locke and that of James and John Stuart Mill thus concentrate on the various "strategies of exclusion" that he believes play a major role in their liberal imaginations, strategies that ultimately manifest themselves in the internal "urge to dominate the world."[103] He then finds a theoretical antidote to this way of thinking in Burke's writings on India. Mehta's framing of the question, however, exacerbates the sense that these are debates about liberalism's internal world, about its soul.

Whether we agree with Mehta, framing the question thus—*Is* liberalism imperialist, or is it not?—has the unfortunate effect of transforming all questions about liberalism's connections to imperialism into questions of inherency. And this presents scholars interested in interrogating these connections with a twofold problem. First, if we decide with Mehta that liberalism is inherently imperial, how do we explain those myriad historical examples of times when its self-described adherents were decidedly not? How, for instance, do we explain what Fitzmaurice describes as the "depth of liberal opposition to empire" throughout the nineteenth century?[104] Mehta's work doesn't provide us with any answers.

Second, for scholars interested in the links between liberalism, imperialism, and American foreign policy, the inherency framing has the effect of privileging liberalism as the object of analysis, a privileging that then has the knock-on effect of reinforcing the profound self-absorption of actually existing liberals. In other words, as the huge body of literature and public intellectualizing associated with the liberal world order demonstrates, "liberalism" is not just the dominant political philosophy of our age; it is also hegemonic common sense, the lingua franca of much contemporary public discourse in America about America. From Ikenberry to Ignatieff, Bernard Lewis to Samuel Huntington, Niall Ferguson to Anne-Marie Slaughter, some of the most powerful public intellectuals of our age understand their societies *to be* liberal and democratic in their essence. Actually existing liberalism thus circulates through the public discourse of the world's most emphatically imperializing and formerly imperializing states in a way that is capaciously and ebblessly narcissistic. If not our mode of liberal hegemony, asks Ikenberry, then whose? Would you prefer those "rising powers," like China, Russia, or India?[105] If not us, ask mainstream liberal Democrats in America or New Labour in Britain, then who? Would you rather Donald Trump? Jeremy Corbyn? As Jeffrey Isaac put it shortly before the election in 2016, the choice for America was clear: either "Clinton or barbarism."[106] No other possibilities could ever exist, now or in the future. Political-theoretical inquiries into liberalism *as* liberalism—as a coherent, discrete, intellectual, philosophical, and political tradition—can end up reinforcing the very exceptionalist qualities that liberal public intellectuals often ascribe to their ideological universe. At the center of this universe sits liberalism, shining so bright it casts all other political options into shadow.

Perhaps nothing better exemplifies this narcissism than the stunted attempts at reflection one finds in Ikenberry's decades-long engagement with a liberal world order in "crisis." It is thus not an exaggeration to say that Ikenberry uses the word *crisis* more than any other IR scholar writing today, exceeding even Ignatieff's catastrophizing wolf-crying. From 2007's, *The Crisis of American Foreign Policy: Wilsonianism in the Twenty-first Century*, to 2008's *The End of the West? Crisis and Change in the Atlantic Order*, to 2012's *Liberal Leviathan: The Origins, Crisis, and Transformation of the American World Order*, to 2019's *The Crisis of Liberal Internationalism*, Ikenberry's conceptual modus operandi has been to assume that the liberal world order exists in a constant state of peril.[107] Ikenberry's conviction in this regard has only increased since he first began framing his arguments in these terms in the 1990s, reaching fever pitch in the wake of 2016 and the election of Donald Trump. For example, prior to Trump's election, Ikenberry tended to imagine that threats to the liberal world order came from geographic locations outside the United States. Thus, he argues in *Liberal Leviathan*, the *"American-led liberal hegemonic order is now in crisis" because there are "pressures for change" in the organization of that order that threaten its "underlying foundations" and jeopardize peace, security, freedom, and the global rule of law.*[108] These pressures for change emanated largely from "non-Western rising states such as China and India" and from an aspirational Russia.[109] After Trump's election, Ikenberry turned his sights inward to the halls of power in Washington. "Today," he argued in 2018, the "liberal international order is in crisis" because, "for the first time since the 1930s, the United States has elected a president who is actively hostile to liberal internationalism."[110]

Despite the difference in location, however, the crisis Ikenberry identifies is much the same whether it originates from without or within the United States. Thus, in 2011, he argued that the "recent global economic slow-down" has "bolstered this narrative of liberal international decline," and in 2017 he similarly insisted that the liberal world order is "increasingly seen as a neoliberal project aimed at facilitating the transactions of globetrotting capitalists."[111] The problem in both 2011 and 2017, for Ikenberry, was one of perception and reputation; increasingly, events were conspiring to convince people around the world that the American-led liberal world order is not working in their interest. The only difference between these two moments was that, in 2017, the president of the United States himself failed to appreciate the benefits of this order. Thus, at the core of Ikenberry's perceived crisis lurks a deep fear about loss of faith: specifically, loss of faith in the "grand project" of liberal order. As he puts it in his 2020 book-length investigation of the subject, *A World Safe for Democracy*, today's crisis is "most profoundly manifest in a lost confidence in collective solutions to common problems."[112]

Throughout the corpus of his work, Ikenberry looks at the historical and contemporary diversity of world politics—the wars, invasions, humanitarian crises, global economic downturns, the rise in authoritarianism, failed and successful coups, drone strikes, bombings, mass forced migrations—and concludes that the myriad problems associated with liberalism on a global scale can largely be chalked up to a loss of confidence and a failure to believe. Only rarely does Ikenberry stop to consider the historical developments that might have contributed to this loss of faith. In other words, the crisis of the liberal world order for Ikenberry may prompt us to consider the imperial origins of that order, it may cause us to reflect briefly on the relationship between that order and neoliberalism, and it may even necessitate some engagement with America's long history of forced regime change. But at the end of the day, those issues never stay the focus of our inquiry for very long because, almost immediately after referring to them, he returns to the question that interests him most: What do these external realities say *about* the liberal world order? Every crisis is an existential crisis, an invitation to look in the mirror and ask the same, self-serving questions. Like a salmon retracing its journey back up its natal river, Ikenberry relentlessly returns to questions of inherency. "Are liberal states inherently revisionist?" he asks. "Is liberalism inherently expansionist and self-destructive?" "Is the American liberal tradition inherently interventionist?"[113]

This constant looking in the mirror without actually seeing deflects attention away from anything outside its all-consuming orbit. We find this even in a book like *A World Safe for Democracy*, in which Ikenberry not only explicitly acknowledges but also actively engages some of the work that has been done by scholars of imperialism and liberalism for the last two decades. In this book, Ikenberry admits that liberal internationalism has "dirty hands," that it was "brought into the 20th century on the back of European empire."[114] And yet, despite this engagement, he ends up concluding, as he always does, that this history simply doesn't (and can't) outweigh the good liberalism *has* and *can do*. Thus, even though liberal internationalism, according to Ikenberry, has been "implicated in almost constant military interventions during the era of American global dominance," these interventions are always the exceptions that prove the rule. Every single occupation for Ikenberry, every instance of overreach, every moment of violence, every neoliberal austerity package only reconfirms that faith.[115] "The most telling critique of liberal internationalism," he thus maintains toward the end of a chapter entitled "Liberalism and Empire," is not to be found in any "urge for empire" or in "policies of coercive regime-change." Rather, for Ikenberry, it is the exact opposite. Crises in the liberal world order ultimately reveal that "liberal internationalism is too often weak and easily co-opted by other agendas."[116] In other words, for the last one hundred years, liberal internationalism has not failed; it has simply been prevented from being its best self by global forces beyond its control.

By contrast, an approach to liberalism and imperialism inspired by Said shifts the historical gaze away from that constant, nagging, self-absorbed question—*Is* liberalism necessarily imperial?—toward the actual historical and contemporary *connections* between liberalism and imperialism. For Said, these worldly entanglements are the stuff of inquiry rather than philosophical and ethical puzzles to be solved in the process of deciding whether liberalism is inherently imperial. The questions become not: *How* has liberalism writ large been compromised or enhanced by imperialism? and *How* have liberal intellectuals negotiated this intersection? Rather, a contrapuntal perspective that takes imperial connection as its point of entry asks: What can we learn about the complicated apparatus of imperialism from its historical entanglements with liberalism? What do liberal intellectuals—from Mill to Ikenberry—get out of this relationship? What alternative approaches to politics and culture—both domestic and global—are silenced by the frantic back-and-forth between liberalism and empire? What historical narratives

have been lost, and what might we want to reengage? By elevating the affiliation between liberalism and imperialism to the center of our vision, this critical orientation both resists deflection and de-essentializes liberalism as the
ur-theory writ large that always sucks up all the oxygen in the room.

The opposite conceptual problem, however, may be the case with
approaches to liberalism and imperialism that seek to *over-de-essentialize*
and decenter liberalism by treating something called "liberalism" not as a
transcendent worldview but, in Bell's words, as an "actor's category" with
very specific, local, and temporal characteristics voiced through a "motley
cast of characters." Bell and similarly minded contextualists, for instance,
reject approaches that treat liberalism as a coherent ideology with coherent
traits recognizable over time because this approach can lead to "sweeping
generalisations" that "typically mislead more than they inform."[117] The point,
for thinkers like Bell, is not to use liberalism's relationship to imperialism as
a means through which to understand some inherent "urge" to empire that
runs through liberal philosophy as a whole over time but instead to explore
how liberal*isms* circulate in their historical contexts as culturally and rhetorically diffuse and distinct, discursive phenomena evoked by various historical
actors in support of or against empire.

The problem with this approach is that, while it avoids the overdetermined
quality of treating liberalism as a coherent bundle of ideas that are consistent
throughout the ages, it presents challenges for political theorists interested in
pairing a "deeply informed historical sense" with the "critical demands of the
present."[118] In other words, this approach makes it difficult (or even impossible) to make any consistent observations about liberalism's entanglements
with imperialism historically and then to identify similarities in liberal strategies over time in ways that might deepen our understanding of the present.

By contrast, if we take Said's both/and orientation to heart, then we can
approach the imperialism-liberalism nexus as a complicated and internally
diverse and discordant amalgamation of ideas, thinkers, and institutional connections and identify those aspects of this affiliative universe that reemerge,
fairly consistently, throughout the *longue durée* of modern imperialism.
Thus, for Said, imperial ideology works on two levels simultaneously: at the
level of individual expression, unique to particular thinkers, and at the level
of expansive—narratively sprawling—imaginative geographies that naturalize and sustain European and American cultural, political, economic, and
military imperialism over time. While it is too simplistic and reductive, he
maintains in *Culture and Imperialism*, to argue "that everything in Europe or
American culture . . . prepares for or consolidates the grand idea of empire,"
it is also "historically inaccurate to ignore these tendencies—whether in narrative, political theory, or pictorial technique—that enabled, encouraged, and

otherwise assured the West's readiness to assume and enjoy the experience of empire."[119]

This readiness has remained consistent over the last three centuries, *even as* particular modes of imperializing have changed: from formal to informal, from colonial to neocolonial, from European to American. As Said puts it, each "great metropolitan center that aspired to global dominance has said, and alas done, many of the same things."[120] One can thus identify rhetorical themes, narratives, and rationalizations about both the West and its "other" that persist over the centuries, even when these take on distinct characteristics, such as the "family of ideas" associated with Orientalism—"Oriental despotism, Oriental splendor, cruelty, sensuality."[121] His treatment of Orientalism is, from this perspective, not unlike Bell's sense of liberalism as an "actor's category" in that, with Bell, Said's worldly orientation draws him toward close readings of these ideas in context. At the same time, he also explores the way these ideas create frameworks for thinking about expansion, intervention, and occupation that remain internally consistent through modern imperial epochs. Moreover, his expansive understanding of public intellectuals as worthy of critical inquiry means that Said extends his exploration of these frameworks for thinking—again, both historically and today—to the rhetorical universe occupied by scholars, politicians, and intellectual middlemen, from Austin to Cromer, Conrad to Kissinger, Bush to Lewis.[122] In its various expressions, Said argues, Orientalist rhetoric has been "directly projected onto a colonial administration" and in turn "converted directly into a system of rules, exclusions, prohibitions placed upon Orientals in the Orient." Reflections of these same direct projections are present today, he continues, in the "government and the academy in the U.S." and "in the conduct of U.S. decision-making and foreign policy." For instance, they persist in the "simplified view" of Arabs marshaled by supporters of the Iraq War to justify "terror, pre-emptive war, and unilateral regime change."[123]

In essence, Said's approach to imperialism identifies distinct resemblances between the contemporary language of foreign policy and the "family of ideas" he associates with imperialism without equating, for instance, the high Orientalism of the nineteenth century and today's "clash of civilizations" rhetoric. This same sensibility clearly works as a way of approaching liberalism. Again, as I argue vigorously in my last book, a fruitful comparison can be drawn between the popular rhetoric and scholarly ideas of self-described liberal supporters of the British Empire in the early days of the twentieth century and those of contemporary liberal supporters of US hegemony today. In both periods, public intellectuals obsessed with what they believed to be the imminent decline of their empires turned to the "family of ideas" associated with the rhetoric of liberal democracy to construct extraordinarily similar metanarratives about their imperializing societies that naturalized the putatively anti-imperial qualities of both Britain and America while deflecting attention away from the violence and illiberalism of both imperial states.[124] While historically and discursively distinctive, the myriad languages of liberalism in both these instances smooth over the reality of global inequality, racial hierarchy, and state-sanctioned violence.

There are a variety of deflective moves that liberal internationalists make today that bear a distinct and eerie resemblance to those made by earlier imperialists. Take, for instance, recent liberal internationalist efforts to acknowledge the complicity of liberalism with a history of racial domination. In 2018, dismayed by Trump's lack of commitment to the liberal world order, Ikenberry and Daniel Deudney responded by both extolling the virtues of that order and reflecting on its flaws. They couch this criticism, however, in a very particular and rhetorically circumscribed way that returns, almost immediately, to liberalism's "overall" character. "Overall," Ikenberry and Deudney argue, despite its faults,

> liberalism remains perennially and universally appealing because it rests on a commitment to the dignity and freedom of individuals. It enshrines the idea of tolerance, which will be needed in spades as the world becomes increasingly interactive and diverse. Although the ideology emerged in the West, its values have become universal, and its champions have extended to encompass Mahatma Gandhi, Mikhail Gorbachev, and Nelson Mandela. And even though imperialism, slavery, and racism have marred Western history, liberalism has always been at the forefront of efforts—both peaceful and militant—to reform and end these practices. To the extent that the long arc of history does bend toward justice, it does so thanks to the activism and moral commitment of liberals and their allies.[125]

For anyone approaching this statement with even a vague sense of the historical entanglements between liberalism and "imperialism, slavery, and racism," Ikenberry and Deudney's gesture of first acknowledging liberalism's historical complicity and then, almost in the same breath, stressing its efforts "to reform and end these practices" might appear simply tone-deaf, maybe a bit crass and self-serving. The gesture itself is clearly aimed at tying something essential about liberalism to the "long arc of history" in a manner that nods to and then dismisses the historical misdeeds of liberals—and, by extension, the American-led liberal world order.

But history's arc bends in a far more complex direction than Ikenberry and Deudney's prose reveals. If liberals have "always been at the forefront of efforts" for justice, then they have also "always been at the forefront of efforts" to use rhetoric about the "forefront of efforts" to deflect attention away from liberalism's history of *injustice.* In other words, the claim that what matters most about liberalism is how hard it tried to correct its own failures is as familiar to liberalism as imperialism. For instance, in his 1915 magnum opus, *The Commonwealth of Nations*, Lionel Curtis (one of early-twentieth-century Britain's most influential liberal supporters of empire) seeks to distance British imperialism from its historical complicity with the Atlantic slave trade in almost the exact same manner as Ikenberry and Deudney. Written over nearly a decade and in close consultation with his colleagues at the Round Table Society, Curtis's tome tells the metahistorical narrative of a liberal empire with origins in the Athenian polis, whose ultimate goal was always to spread freedom and the rule of law around the globe. In the midst of this five-hundred-page book, Curtis pauses for precisely a paragraph to acknowledge that the British had been involved with the Atlantic slave trade. Simultaneous to this admission, however, Curtis insists that the "question of real importance" regarding British slavery was just how quickly Britons "were able to purge themselves of the poison and rise to a higher realization of their duty towards races that they were called by the claims of their own superior civilizations to protect."[126] Thus, like Ikenberry and Deudney, Curtis can't dismiss Britain's historical involvement with slavery, but he can deflect attention away from that involvement by shifting the emphasis to the "question of real importance": how fast the Empire *disentangled* itself, how quickly it realized its "higher duties."

Curtis's argument about the British Empire and Ikenberry and Deudney's account of global liberalism both erase the agency of colonized people in ending precisely the forms of racist, imperial domination that liberal agents of empire had been instrumental in establishing in the first place. There are no slave revolts, for instance, in Curtis's brief, paragraph-long account of British slavery and no mention of the enormous, albeit indirect impact of Toussaint Louverture and the Haitian revolution on Britain's slave-owning future.[127] This erasure is even more egregious in Ikenberry and Deudney's case. Yes, the "activism and moral commitment of liberals and their allies" played a role in the decolonization movements of the twentieth century. But it is equally clear that, despite all the good intentions of the American-led liberal order, the United States and its allies also *opposed* these same anticolonial movements. Indeed, in 1960, when national members of the General Assembly brought Resolution 1514, the Declaration on the Granting of Independence to Colonial Countries and Peoples, to the floor of the United Nations, that resolution *was opposed by* the United States, Australia, Belgium, the Dominican Republic, France, Portugal, Spain, the Union of South Africa, and the United Kingdom.[128] In essence, independence for most colonial states didn't happen because liberals and leaders of liberal democracies suddenly woke up one morning gripped by their own liberal sensibilities. We live today in a (formally) post-imperial world because the formerly colonized people of the world *made it so* through revolution and protest. Indeed, we live in a post-imperial world despite, not because of, liberalism.

Furthermore, the way Ikenberry and Deudney's framing hides this fact in plain sight—or, rather, deflects attention away from it—also flattens the reception of liberalism and liberal ideas in the global South. Certainly, individuals like Gandhi and Mandela marshaled the rhetorical resources of liberalism for anticolonial causes and fights against racial injustice. This does not mean that Gandhi and Mandela considered themselves liberals per se or that their use of liberal concepts didn't take on distinct characteristics that transformed the original ideas in ways that, as Said puts it in "Traveling Theory Reconsidered," sometimes reshaped the "fiery core" of the original ideas beyond recognition.[129] Gandhi's adamant insistence in *Hind Swaraj*, for instance, that the national liberation he wanted entailed more than liberal nationalism—more than the "tiger's nature" without the tiger—demonstrates creative borrowing, transformation, and rejection of liberalism, all at the same time.[130] Ikenberry and Deudney's account erases the richness and diversity of this historical invention in a manner that not only deflects attention away from the illiberalism of the United States but also transforms something we call "liberalism" into an essence, an identity category that remains constant across time.

A methodology that forefronts the both/and quality of historical and contemporary imperialism provides us with a lens through which to de-essentialize liberalism and simultaneously identify reoccurring patterns of deflection and disavowal that have plagued global liberalism throughout its history as an "actor's category." This enables critics to link their observations about the present to discursive strategies from the past, not to make claims about something essential to liberalism, but rather to notice patterns in rhetorical framing that liberals have historically used to deflect the observations of anticolonial critics. It makes it possible, for example, to resist the essentializing impulse implicit in Ikenberry and Deudney's presentation of liberalism as a worldview whose most important attribute is its "overall" commitment to fight oppression while at the same time linking this essentializing impulse to earlier forms of liberal imperialist deflection.

Finally, approaching liberal internationalism through Said's both/and orientation toward imperialism draws the attention of the reader to the identity narratives that undergird this vision of global order. Thus, when Said sets about unpacking what "appeal for liberals" there might be in the soaring morality tales of democracy and freedom inevitably trotted out by imperial states before they rain violence down on other societies, he does so in part through an investigation of the identity work that imperialist discourse does for liberals and the identity work that liberal discourse does for empire.[131]

Said was interested, for instance, in the way disclaimer narratives uttered by nineteenth-century European imperialists and advocates of American hegemony alike (e.g., "'We' are exceptional, not imperial"; "We" brought the Third World democracy, so why can't "they appreciate us, after what we did for them?") often work to distance liberals from the actions of their own states, distance liberal states from their own actions, and distance essentially liberal peoples from the essentially illiberal peoples that they colonize or once colonized.[132]

On the one hand, as with his argument against NATO's Serbian campaign, Said's focus on disclaimer narratives highlights the extent to which these narratives allow liberal public intellectuals to "simply look away" from bombings and destruction in their enthusiasm for policies and rhetorics that strengthened their own sense of themselves as liberal human rights crusaders taking a stand against, in that case, "ethnic cleansing." On the other hand, such narratives reinforce the long-standing imperial claim that Western and non-Western states and peoples are fundamentally different from one another, that liberal democracies today are sui generis, that nothing they do for the formerly colonized world or "failed states" is ever appreciated or recognized, and therefore that they bear no historical responsibility for creating the massive inequalities and enduring insecurities of today's global environment. For Said, the complex reality of those historical and ongoing connections that have been sewn over the centuries between the colonizer and the colonized simply disappear behind these disclaimer narratives, these inward-looking paeans about "us" and "our values" and who "we" have always been in relation to "them."

Disclaimer narratives express themselves most forcefully today, Said argues, in the endlessly recycled, "strident journalistic debates about decolonization" and its impact, debates that predictably appear whenever some new "crisis" appears to raise its head on the global horizon.[133] Ferguson encapsulates the finger-wagging tone of these missives in his 2005 book *Colossus*:

> Colonialism was not all good, of course, and independence has not been all bad. But it is not convincing (though it is certainly convenient for the likes of the Zimbabwean despot Robert Mugabe) to blame all the problems of the developing world today on the malign after-effects of colonial rule. . . . The experience of much of Africa and the Middle East since 1945, as well as large parts of Asia, makes it clear that Roosevelt's faith in decolonization was misplaced.[134]

With Ferguson, the reaction of liberal intellectuals to global inequality is often to blame the problems of the postcolonial world on the formerly colonized themselves, on the internal failures of their societies, rather than, in Said's words, the "malign after-effects of colonial rule."[135] For Said, the true malignancy in such arguments lies in their hubristic surety. The underlying message, he paraphrases, is thus: "[Y]ou are what you are because of us; when we left, you returned to your deplorable state." Further, because "we" are liberal democratic peoples in our essence and you are not, "there is little to be known about imperialism that might help either you or us in the present."[136]

Through their repeated claims to liberal consistency—often channeled through confidently self-assured statements about the "fixed stars" of "our" liberal values and intentions—liberal internationalists consistently dismiss what might be known about imperialism that could help us in the present. That "we" has become a rhetorical tic for liberal internationalists, a spasm of ideological common sense that tolerates no self-inquiry because it never takes its eyes off itself. For thinkers like Slaughter, Ikenberry, and Ignatieff, the American-led liberal world order is simply always the only game in town, always the only grownup in the room, always preening in front of its own reflection, always the only thing standing between chaos and order.

Liberalism in this narcissistic, global iteration thus mirrors the muted nineteenth-century narratives of Western civilization to which it is related and that still flow through contemporary discussions of American primacy and the need for military intervention. Again, unlike their more self-confident imperial predecessors, advocates of American power today cannot outright call White culture superior or link the foreign policy of the United States to racial hierarchy because to do so would be to violate the stated liberal norms of racial equality. And yet, as with earlier, more explicit forms of imperial discourse, today's rhetoric of liberal interventionism similarly assumes what Said calls the "primacy and even the complete centrality of the West," even as it cloaks itself in the language of liberal diversity. The thing to notice about the way this discourse operates today, Said continues, is "how totalizing is its form, how all-enveloping its attitudes and gestures, how much it shuts out even as it includes, compresses, and consolidates."[137]

Scholars of political theory who would like to extend their critiques of liberalism and imperialism into the international arena would, I argue, benefit from thinking more broadly about the work of the totalizing "we" voice in contemporary liberal discourse, the way it shuts out, includes, compresses, and consolidates the world. Adopting a critical orientation influenced by Said prompts critics to ask probing questions about liberal identity more generally, not just about those pronouns that parade through Ignatieff's, Slaughter's, and Ikenberry's cool assertions of "our values," but also about liberal political theory's own breezy subjectivity. Thus, where global justice scholars theorize about what "we" might owe the global poor or speculate about "our" moral intuitions, Said-inspired political theorists query which constituencies, ways of knowing, alternative histories, and visions of the future are being shut out, included, compressed, and consolidated. Where Blake argues that "we" have "good reasons to be extremely careful" in how "we" interact with "illiberal societies," Said-inspired political theorists look beneath this comfortable surety about "our" liberality and instead ask: What histories of illiberal violence fall out of Blake's picture? What future collateral damage lurks behind that seemingly effortless assertion that "we" know "we" are liberal and "we" know "they" are not? In essence, what identity work does *imperialism* do for liberal philosophers like Blake? And conversely, what identity work does *liberalism* do for Blake's not-so-philosophical support for American imperialism?

## BEYOND DEFLECTION: READING AND BEING READ

The election of Donald Trump in 2016 and the long, surreal four years that followed had the ironic effect of exposing the perennial rigidity of the liberal "we" that beats at the heart of American foreign policy. Throughout the postwar period, all presidents, regardless of party, have stuck to the same general script regarding American primacy, American exceptionalism, and the status of the United States as a liberal, anti-imperial world power whose goals are ultimately to secure the world for freedom and democracy. As Obama once gushed during a 2014 speech on foreign policy, "I believe in American exceptionalism with every fiber of my being."[138] Trump echoed this language and frequently—particularly on those rare occasions when he spoke from a teleprompter—even uttered phrases familiar to mainstream foreign policy analysis.[139] But these nods to convention sat uncomfortably alongside references to "shithole countries" and intimations that American power is—for all intents and purposes—imperial, racist, and without restraint.[140]

And yet, it was precisely Trump's inability to play by the rules—his unwillingness *not* to say terrible things aloud—that consistently drew the very logic of an American-led liberal order hard up against the shores of its own contradictions. The foreign policy discourse, for instance, that renders a phenomenon as patently insane as nuclear proliferation into a practical policy of "deterrence" requires everyone in the world to know, in their heart of hearts, that the president of the United States could authorize the use of nuclear weapons if he felt moved. But by convention, no one—particularly the president with that power—is supposed to actually say this. Trump audibly sputtered and tweeted such things, threatening the "obliteration" of Iran and mockingly comparing Kim Jong-un's "nuclear button" to his "bigger and more powerful one."[141] In unhinged tweets and off-the-cuff remarks, he constantly revealed that the language of liberal freedom, mutuality, order, and restraint—what Ikenberry refers to as the "rule-based character of the post-war system"—is a brittle shell whose integrity can be undermined at any time if the world's most powerful nation just happens to elect a commander in chief with a pathological lack of decorum.[142] When he approved and then abruptly canceled military strikes on targets in the Middle East, he exposed the uncomfortable fact that we live in a world where the American president has access not only to the most titanic military industrial complex in history but also, as commander in chief, to an undemocratic mode of demagogic choice making and unmaking that sets him outside of political restraint. Trump acted like an emperor because, in the context of foreign policy, he *was* an emperor, not because of *whom* he resembled aesthetically or stylistically— Mussolini-like strutting aside—but because America is an imperial state and there is nothing to *prevent* a Trump from becoming commander in chief aside from an unquenchable faith in "our" liberal bona fides—a faith that often exists alongside obvious facts to the contrary. Trump was the exception, not because he was exceptional, but because he made the implicit obvious: that an imperial system grounded in its own unseeing can always produce a Trump, and no amount of demanding that we see it otherwise can make it untrue. Or, as Trump put it in a 2017 interview with Bill O'Reilly when asked why he supported Putin "even though he is a killer": "There are a lot of killers. You think our country's so innocent?"[143]

Trump's constant lying, coupled with those moments when shockingly uncomfortable truths just erupted from his mouth, exposes precisely the connection between something we call the liberal world order and a historical and contemporary practice of American imperialism. Because, of course, America has never been "innocent." But from the perspective of a liberal "we"—where the imperial actions of the United States can only be seen as unfortunate deviations from "our values" and where "overall" liberals have stood at the forefront of efforts to end imperialism—Trump's utterances are nearly incomprehensible. The response of many liberal internationalist supporters of the liberal world order when confronted with this unsettling reality has been to blame Trump for undermining a system that depends on nudges and winks. In Ikenberry's sorrowful words, the liberal world order was not *supposed* to end this way: "The great threats were supposed to come from hostile revisionist powers seeking to overturn the postwar order. The United States and Europe were supposed to stand shoulder to shoulder to protect the gains reaped from 70 years of cooperation. Instead, the world's most powerful state has begun to sabotage the order it created."[144]

We have thus reached a crucial moment in American and world history where the emperor's lack of clothing has been accidentally revealed by a crass opportunist-cum-president. And yet, a sizable number of liberal public intellectuals have responded to Trump by first deflecting attention away from the broken imperial system his election made visible and then by treating his presidency as an existential crisis, a threat to "our" way of life. "You can't say that aloud," they insist, "because that can't be us."

As I argue throughout this book, Said's attitude toward the rhetorical politics of the "we" voice—and all the affiliations and power dynamics that it occludes and enables—is never to insist that we stop speaking in this voice, that we deny our political and intellectual affiliations, or that we reject the solidaristic groups and communities with whom (and sometimes for whom) we speak. Rather, Said insists that any "we" be reflective rather than deflective and that, even in the midst of struggle, any invocation of identity—any subject position with authority behind it—must be intentional. For public intellectuals from the global North whose academic, professional, and intellectual lives fall under the penumbra of America's global power but who are committed to disrupting the logic of that power, this means situating our criticism in relation to imperial affiliation. Beginning from a Said-influenced place of intention means locating our analyses of liberalism and imperialism at the point of connection between the two rather than from the perspective of liberalism—either as pristine political philosophy or as a lingering question about inherency. It also means thinking, writing, and speaking with an awareness that we are *of* these connections, not "detached outside observers."

Throughout his long career, Said maintained that American intellectuals needed to reflect honestly on American imperialism, particularly when the wall of unseeing looms large and every deflective strategy in the liberal imperial arsenal is set to obscure that power. As he put it in 1989, as "citizens and intellectuals in the United States we have a particular responsibility for what goes on between the United States and the rest of the world," a responsibility that cannot be "discharged or fulfilled" by such disclaimer narratives as "the Soviet Union is worse."[145] This notion of connection and responsibility resists the identity-driven narcissism of the liberal internationalists who are so invested in eliding the affiliations between liberalism and American imperialism that they return, with relentless repetition, to increasingly more poisonous and unacceptable alternatives that seem to loom ever closer to home: If not us, then who? The Russians? China? Trump?

Now, more than ever, political theorists who interrogate the long-standing entanglements between liberalism and imperialism need to shift our attention toward interrogating those entanglements in the present. This means overcoming the reluctance of our field to analyze liberalism in contemporary foreign policy and instead to privilege "what goes on between the United States and the rest of the world" in our theorizing. Such a reorientation, as Said puts it in "The Treason of the Intellectuals," requires us to "demystify the debased language and images used to justify American practices and hypocrisy."[146] Indeed, for Said, American scholars and anyone who benefits from the primacy of the United States have a responsibility to reveal imperial connections and demystify the verbiage thrown up by liberals to deflect attention from the violence that hides behind the innocent "we": the military budgets that go unquestioned, the anti-insurgency practices that ricochet back and forth between American cities and foreign sites of conflict, the civilians killed in supposedly bloodless drone strikes, the years of instability wreaked by "humanitarian intervention." In other words, political theorists writing about liberalism and imperialism have a duty to expose and interrogate the self-absorption of liberal foreign policy discourse, to link this self-absorption to liberal imperialism in the past and present, and to call it what it is: a form of intellectual "treason," in Said's and Benda's sense. A willful refusal to take responsibility. A narcissistic form of unseeing.

Beyond this oppositional mode of criticism, Said's insistence on highlighting imperial connection also encourages a self-aware mode of political and intellectual engagement that refuses, in his words, "to look away or fall asleep."[147] Again, Said argues that the best corrective to the insouciance of "'liberals,' á la Michael Ignatieff" who inveigle the American state toward "more destruction and death for distant civilians" is to "imagine the person whom you are discussing—in this case the person on whom the bombs will fall—reading you in your presence."[148] Rather than allowing liberal foreign policy experts and intellectuals to dominate all the public space and insist that bombings—or drone strikes, assassinations, regime changes—are necessary to bring about liberal ends, this mode of proceeding demands radical humility. It demands not only that political theorists make connections between liberalism, foreign policy, and contemporary imperialism but also that those theorizing from empire's core root our thinking about politics in that unsettling, vulnerable place where those human subjects-cum-objects of American foreign policy read "us."

\*

In May 2021, the violent suppression of Palestinian protests by Israeli police and the subsequent occupation of the al-Aqsa Mosque prompted Hamas to launch rockets into Israel, which then prompted Israel to launch air strikes against Gaza. By the time a cease-fire had been reached after eight days, 13 Israelis (including 2 children) and 256 Palestinians (including 66 children) had been killed.[149] Among the many disturbing and powerful images to emerge from both the days of protest and the subsequent week of disproportionate violence, perhaps none was more arresting than the short video clip of a young Palestinian woman named Maryam Al-Afifi. The video shows police dragging Al-Afifi—who had been protesting the forced evacuation of Palestinians from their homes in East Jerusalem—by her red hijab, forcing her to the ground, and clapping her in handcuffs. Bur rather than hang her head or look afraid as one might in such a moment, Al-Afifi looks straight across the police barricade at the camera and flashes a radiant, triumphant smile, as if to say, "You little men—you have no power here."[150]

The camera then stays briefly with Al-Afifi as she sits handcuffed on the ground, talking to the Israeli soldier who looms silently next to her. "How do you feel?" she asks. "I know that you are human and that maybe you have a family. . . . Do you want your kids to grow up and grow old . . . defending the oppressors?" Al-Afifi then asks the soldier in an exasperated tone, "This is what you wanted to be when you were young?" The soldier, standing in the shadows, says nothing.

This video went viral for a variety of reasons. Because it captures a moment of violence and injustice. Because it captures a moment of irrepressible spirit in the face of that violence and injustice, a determination to be, and to be OK, even in the midst. And because it captures a moment of human connection that could have been, had the soldier Al-Afifi questioned been open to being read by the other: How do you feel? Is this what you want? The video also quite rightly raises international interest in a young woman who could smile with such composure at her captors and then ask them probing, ethical questions in the middle of a war zone.

It soon emerged that Al-Afifi is a member of the Palestinian Youth Orchestra, an ensemble created by the Edward Said National Music Conservatory. Formerly the National Conservatory of Music in Ramallah, the school changed its name after Said's death "as a tribute to the invaluable intellectual and cultural contributions to humanity of the late Dr. Edward Said, an honorary member of the Board."[151] Founded in 2004, the same year the conservatory changed its name, the Palestinian Youth Orchestra is exilic in its very construction, bringing together young Palestinians "residing around the world" to perform work by Palestinian and Arab composers "alongside well-known standards of the Western symphonic repertoire."[152] Perhaps not surprisingly, in her calm, triumphant smile and in her bold, humanizing questions, Al-Afifi beautifully captures Said's contrapuntal practice, giving voice to his demand that Palestinians be allowed to narrate their own experiences and his insistence that Palestinians—and all those "on whom the bombs will fall"—be understood as fully knowing subjects.

"I would like to think," Said notes in the final lines of *After the Last Sky*, "that we are not just the people seen or looked at in these photographs; We are also looking at our observers." "We Palestinians sometimes forget," he continues, "we too are looking, we too are scrutinizing, assessing, judging. We do more than stand passively in front of whoever, for whatever reason, has wanted to look at us. If you cannot finally see this about us, we will not allow ourselves to believe that the failure has been entirely ours. Not any more."[153] Said's uncompromising call for full Palestinian agency here sits alongside his equally uncompromising call for an approach to politics and the world that puts reflection and thinking "concretely and sympathetically, contrapuntally, about others" rather than "only about 'us,'" at the heart of what it means to be a critic and a public intellectual. This approach is simultaneously excoriating—taking both "liberals *á la* Michael Ignatieff" and silent Israeli soldiers to task for their unseeing—*and* connective, dwelling in connections rather than assertions, questions rather than answers, reflection rather than narcissism.

In this spirit, Said returns in the final pages of *Culture and Imperialism* to the loss of exile and finds in it a way of destabilizing fixed, dominant identity formations furnished by illusion and dogma, "whether deriving from pride in one's heritage or from certainty about who 'we' are."[154] Throughout his work, Said never gives up on the idea that once one has destabilized these certainties, it becomes possible to "just hold" contrasting political realities without resolving them. One can strive to make justice and nondomination a reality, even while critiquing liberal narratives of improvement. One can seek out moments of sympathy in connection, even while interrogating the imperial roots of that connection. One can acknowledge the power of national identity, even while resisting national identity's power. One can refuse to let "who we are" stand in for "what we do." One can tell the story of our deflective imperial age differently. And ultimately, one can sing a different, contrapuntal song about the world we share.

# Coda

And then, in the midst of the circling—in the midst of the cogitating on exile as an actual and metaphorical condition, the turning inward toward resentment, the worrying about my unsettled professional future, the hovering at my son's bedroom door, the raging at his birth mother and the legions of pro-lifers who seemed to occupy the same frozen, unforgivable space in my mind—I was stopped in my tracks by the passage from Darwish's poem that begins the introduction to this book. In this passage, Said also hovers at a door, fretting about seeing and being seen, wondering if the current occupants will tell him there is no place for two dreams in one bedroom. And for some inexplicable reason, in that moment, I was overcome by two blindingly obvious, crucial aspects of Said's relationship to loss that I had previously—in my frantic perambulating—failed to grasp. Soon, these insights would transform my own relationship to loss and to the writing of this book.

First, it is painfully difficult to look across the threshold and meet loss face-to-face when loss *has* a face. Exile is not putting the past to rest—it is not death or finitude or final goodbyes—because the past is always present; it is always right there in front of you, out of reach and yet demanding recognition. In the process of longing for it, raging about it, and reconstructing it in your mind, you see all the things that go into affiliation: into the making of a natural homeland and the making of an expulsion, the stories nations tell, the racist narratives of place and not place, the setting and resetting of borders, the dispossession and extraction, the gutting of lives and cultures from one generation to the next, the thriving despite and at a distance, the beauty and the unanticipated connections. And the terror. Seeing through loss in this way is different from the experience of mourning because there is no foreseeable end to it, the door is never fully closed, and so both the wound and the possibility for change stay open. This is the essence of what Said means when he insists that what is true of all exile is "not that home and love of home are lost, but that loss is inherent in the very existence of both."[1]

Second, despite the hesitation and the fear, the truly astonishing thing about the actual, not poetical, Said is that, throughout his life, he routinely walked into that bedroom, confronted the loss, and demanded a place for two dreams. Demanded that we just hold them together. Said lived in, worked in, fought in, laughed in, wrote in, was mad as hell in the unsettling tension between dreams, between longing for home and loss of home, between community and intellectual solitude, between difference and human comity, between multiplicity and universality, between imperial violence and imperial connection, between discipline and resistance, between the victims and the victims' victims. Said never resolved these tensions. He simply painted richer, more complicated portraits of the whole while simultaneously looking loss in the face and demanding a better world.

Said, I decided, would have had absolutely no truck with the kind of avoidance that moved me to stop, stare at the stain on the carpet, and move on. Rather, his work invites everyone who inhabits loss to look deeply into that pool—into the unhealable rift between then and now, home and lived life—and not to reconcile these tensions but just to hold them together. Over and over again, Said's work says to all of us: "Don't run. You, worldly intellectual, stay put. Live in the out of place. Occupy the unsettled. Experience what it means for loss not to be the place where the soul goes to die but where the mind of winter goes in search of summer, however remote."

This book is intended to be about many things, but it is, at base, about honoring Said's vision by reading through loss to critique and hope. In the process of writing, I've stopped sitting on the sidelines and avoiding my son's bedroom. I've stopped standing at the door like a beggar. Every day I walk into this now metaphorical space with the stain on the carpet, and I demand that it accommodate the victim and the victim's victim—my son's birth mother and my son—and all the irreconcilable connections that flow from encounters at borders, abroad and within. I choose to enter with full awareness of my son's soaring moments of grace and his plunges into the abyss—to embrace without reconciling his negatives and positives—and to make that imperfect, maddeningly unstable space filled with loss and love a site from which to see the world. In this space, I hold him together even when I cannot hold him. Because I choose to believe, at least for now, that there is room in there for two dreams.

# Notes

## SERIES EDITOR'S INTRODUCTION

1. Steven Johnston, *Lincoln: The Ambiguous Icon* (Lanham, MD: Rowman & Littlefield, 2018); J. Donald Moon, *John Rawls: Liberalism and the Challenges of Late Modernity* (Lanham, MD: Rowman & Littlefield, 2014); Jason Frank, *Publius and Political Imagination* (Lanham, MD: Rowman & Littlefield, 2013); Davide Panagia, *Impressions of Hume* (Lanham, MD: Rowman & Littlefield, 2013).

2. William E. Connolly, *The Augustinian Imperative: A Reflection on the Politics of Morality* (Lanham, MD: Rowman & Littlefield, 2002); Richard E. Flathman, *Thomas Hobbes: Skepticism, Individuality, and Chastened Politics* (Lanham, MD: Rowman & Littlefield, 2002); Stephen K. White, *Edmund Burke: Modernity, Politics, and Aesthetics* (Lanham, MD: Rowman & Littlefield, 2002); George Kateb, *Emerson and Self-Reliance* (Lanham, MD: Rowman & Littlefield, 2002); Tracy B. Strong, *Jean-Jacques Rousseau: The Politics of the Ordinary* (Lanham, MD: Rowman & Littlefield, 2002); Jane Bennett, *Thoreau's Nature: Ethics, Politics, and the Wild* (Lanham, MD: Rowman & Littlefield, 2002); Michael J. Shapiro, *Reading "Adam Smith": Desire, History, and Value* (Lanham, MD: Rowman & Littlefield, 2002); Thomas L. Dumm, *Michel Foucault and the Politics of Freedom* (Lanham, MD: Rowman & Littlefield, 2002); Fred Dallmayr, *G. W. F. Hegel: Modernity and Politics* (Lanham, MD: Rowman & Littlefield, 2002); Seyla Benhabib, *The Reluctant Modernism of Hannah Arendt* (Lanham, MD: Rowman & Littlefield, 2003); Kennan Ferguson, *William James: Politics in the Pluriverse* (Lanham, MD: Rowman & Littlefield, 2007); Diana Coole, *Merleau-Ponty and Modern Politics After Anti-Humanism* (Lanham, MD: Rowman & Littlefield, 2007); Shadia Drury, *Aquinas and Modernity: The Lost Promise of Natural Law* (Lanham, MD: Rowman & Littlefield, 2008); Nicholas Tampio, *Deleuze's Political Vision* (Lanham, MD: Rowman & Littlefield, 2015); Kam Shapiro, *Carl Schmitt and the Intensification of Politics* (Lanham, MD: Rowman & Littlefield, 2009).

3. Jeanne Morefield, *Covenants Without Swords: Idealist Liberalism and the Spirit of Empire* (Princeton, NJ: Princeton University Press, 2005); *Empires without*

*Imperialism: Anglo-American Decline and the Politics of Deflection* (Oxford, UK: Oxford University Press, 2014).

4. Frantz Fanon, *Black Skin, White Masks*, trans. Charles Lam Markmann (New York: Grove Press, 1967); Frantz Fanon, *The Wretched of the Earth*, trans. Constance Farrington (New York: Grove Press, 1963); Uday Singh Mehta, *Liberalism and Empire: A Study in Nineteenth-Century British Liberal Thought* (Chicago: University of Chicago Press, 1999).

5. Morefield, *Empires without Imperialism*, 28.

6. Morefield, *Empires without Imperialism*, 57.

7. Morefield, *Empires without Imperialism*, 150.

## PRELUDE

1. From 1992 interview with Bonnie Marranca, Marc Robinson, and Una Chaudhuri, "Criticism, Culture, and Performance," in Gauri Viswanathan (ed), *Power, Politics, and Culture* (New York: Vintage Books, 2002), 99.

2. Te-hsing Shan, "An Interview With Edward Said," in *Interviews With Edward W. Said*, ed. Amritjit Singh and Bruce G. Johnson, Conversations With Public Intellectuals series (Jackson, MS: University Press of Mississippi, 2004), 131.

3. Viswanathan, "Introduction," *Power, Politics, and Culture*, xi. For recent reflections on Said and his life, see Timothy Brennan's important new biography *Places of Mind: A Life of Edward Said* (London: Bloomsbury, 2021), and Hamid Dabashi, *On Edward Said: Remembrances of Things Past* (New York: Haymarket, 2020).

## INTRODUCTION

1. Mahmoud Darwish, "Edward Said: A Contrapuntal Reading," trans. Mona Anis, *Cultural Critique*, 67 (2007), 176.

2. Edward Said, "Palestine, Then and Now," *Harper's Magazine* (December 1992), 50.

3. Darwish, "Edward Said," 180.

4. Edward Said, "Afterword to the 1995 Edition," *Orientalism* (New York: Penguin, 1995), 339.

5. Edward Said, "Reflections on Exile," in *Reflections on Exile and Other Essays* (Cambridge, MA: Harvard University Press, 2000), 186.

6. Edward Said, "Intellectual Exile: Expatriates and Marginals," in *Representations of the Intellectual: The 1993 Reith Lectures* (New York: Vintage Books, 1996), 53.

7. Edward Said, "Representing the Colonized: Anthropology's Interlocutors," *Critical Inquiry*, 15.2 (1989), 217.

8. Eqbal Ahmad, Introduction to the 1994 Edition, in David Barsamian (ed.), *The Pen and the Sword: Conversations With Edward Said* (New York: Haymarket, 2010).

9. For a glimpse into the world of scholarly luminaries who continue to engage Said's work, see Rosi Braidotti and Paul Gilroy (eds.), *Conflicting Humanities* (London: Bloomsbury, 2016). Braidotti and Gilroy's collection includes contributions by Gayatri Spivak, Akeel Bilgrami, Judith Butler, and Etienne Balibar.

10. For more on Said's key role in introducing Foucault to the American academy, see Mai Al-Nakib, "Deleuze and Race and Middle East Studies," *Postcolonial Studies*, 18.3 (2015), 313–19; Karlis Racevskis, "Edward Said and Michel Foucault: Affinities and Dissonances," *Research in African Literatures*, 36.3 (2005), 83–97; and Viswanathan (ed.), Introduction, *Power, Politics, and Culture*. Recent examples of works dedicated to Said and the ideas he inspired include (among others) Brennan, *Places of Mind*; Dabashi, *On Edward Said*; and Wael Hallaq, *Restating Orientalism: A Critique of Modern Knowledge* (New York: Columbia University Press, 2018).

11. Rashid Khalidi, "Edward Said and the American Public Sphere: Speaking Truth to Power," *Edward Said and the Work of the Critic: Speaking Truth to Power*, ed. Paul A. Bové (Durham, NC: Duke University Press, 2000), 155, 153.

12. David Harmon, "Edward Said," *Prospect*, November 20, 2003, https://www.prospectmagazine.co.uk/magazine/edwardsaid. Last accessed March 28, 2022.

13. An extremely incomplete list of such works includes Duncan Bell, *The Idea of Greater Britain* (Princeton, NJ: Princeton University Press, 2009); Karuna Mantena, *Alibis of Empire: Henry Maine and the Ends of Liberal Imperialism* (Princeton, NJ: Princeton University Press, 2009); Uday Mehta, *Liberalism and Empire* (Chicago: University of Chicago Press, 1999); Jeanne Morefield, *Covenants Without Swords: Idealist Liberalism and the Spirit of Empire* (Princeton, NJ: Princeton University Press, 2005); Sankar Muthu, *Enlightenment Against Empire* (Princeton, NJ: Princeton University Press, 2003); Jennifer Pitts, *A Turn to Empire: The Rise of Imperial Liberalism in Britain and France* (Princeton, NJ: Princeton University Press, 2005); James Tully, *Public Philosophy in a New Key* (Cambridge, UK: Cambridge University Press, 2009); and James Tully, *Strange Multiplicity: Constitutionalism in the Age of Diversity* (Cambridge, UK: Cambridge University Press, 1995).

14. Another extremely list of such works includes Lawrie Balfour, *The Evidence of Things Not Said: James Baldwin and the Promise of American Democracy* (Ithaca, NY: Cornell University Press, 2000); Glen Coulthard, *Red Skin, White Masks: Rejecting the Colonial Politics of Recognition* (Minneapolis, MN: University of Minnesota Press, 2014); Jane Gordon, *Creolizing Political Theory: Reading Rousseau Through Fanon* (New York: Fordham University Press, 2014); Juliet Hooker, *Theorizing Race in the Americas: Douglass, Sarmiento, Du Bois, and Vasconcelos* (Oxford, UK: Oxford University Press, 2017); Murad Idris, *War for Peace: Genealogies of a Violent Ideal in Western and Islamic Thought* (Oxford, UK: Oxford University Press, 2018); Andrew March, *Islam and Liberal Citizenship: The Search for an Overlapping Consensus* (Oxford, UK: Oxford University Press, 2011); Robert Nichols, *Theft Is Property! Dispossession and Critical Theory* (Durham, NC: Duke University Press, 2019); Aziz Rana, *The Two Faces of American Freedom* (Cambridge, MA: Harvard University Press, 2014); Neil Roberts, *Freedom as Marronage* (Chicago, IL: University of Chicago Press, 2015); Inés Valdez, *Transnational Cosmopolitanism: Kant, Du Bois, and Justice as Political Craft* (Cambridge, UK: Cambridge University

Press, 2019); and Lorenzo Veracini, *Settler Colonialism: A Theoretical Overview* (New York: Palgrave MacMillan, 2010).

15. See Burke Hendrix and Deborah Baumgold (eds.), *Colonial Exchanges and the Agency of the Colonized* (Manchester, UK: Manchester University Press, 2017); Leigh K. Jenco, Murad Idris, and Megan C. Thomas, Introduction, *The Oxford Handbook of Comparative Political Theory* (New York: Oxford University Press, 2020); and Andrew March, "What Is Comparative Political Theory?" *Review of Politics*, 7.14 (2009), 531–65, for different perspectives on what political theorists mean by "comparative political theory."

16. Leela Gandhi, *Postcolonial Theory: A Critical Introduction* (New York: Columbia University Press, 1998), 4.

17. Imre Salusinszky, "Edward Said," in *Criticism in Society: Interviews with Jacques Derrida, Northrop Frye, Harold Bloom, Geoffrey Hartman, Frank Kermode, Edward Said, Barbara Johnson, Frank Lentricchia, and J. Hillis Miller* (New York: Routledge, 1987), 128.

18. Edward Said, *Out of Place: A Memoir* (New York: Viking, 1999), 5.

19. See Peter Osborne and Anne Beezer's interview with Said, "Orientalism and After," *Radical Philosophy*, 063 (Spring 1993).

20. Said, *Out of Place*, 140.

21. Edward Said, "The Arab Portrayed," in *The Arab Israeli Confrontation of 1967*, ed. Ibrahim Abu-Lughod (Evanston, IL: Northwestern University Press, 1970).

22. Edward Said, *Orientalism* (New York: Vintage Books, 1978), 2. For Said's ruminations on this moment, see his last interview, conducted by Charles Glass in 2002, in Charles Glass, "The Last Interview," https://icarusfilms.com/if-said. Last accessed March 28, 2022.

23. Edward Said, *Culture and Imperialism* (New York: Vintage Books, 1994), 8, 6.

24. Said, *Orientalism*, chap. 1, pt. 2.

25. Said, *Orientalism*, 250.

26. Said, *Orientalism*, 205.

27. Said, *Orientalism*, 240.

28. Edward Said, "Secular Criticism," in *The World, the Text, and the Critic* (Cambridge, MA: Harvard University Press, 1983), 3.

29. Edward Said, "Orientalism 25 Years Later: Worldly Humanism v. the Empire-Builders," *Counterpunch*, August 3, 2003, http://www.counterpunch.org/2003/08/05/orientalism

30. Said, *Orientalism*, 204.

31. Gandhi, *Postcolonial Theory*, 68.

32. Edward Said, "Intellectuals in the Post-Colonial World," *Salmagundi*, 70-71 (1986), 59.

33. Edward Said, "Michel Foucault as an Intellectual Imagination," *Boundary* 2: *A Journal of Postmodern Literature* (1972), 1–36. (1972); Erich Auerbach, "Philology and *Weltliteratur*," trans. Maire Said and Edward Said, *The Centennial Review*, 13.1 (1969), 1-17. For his thoughts on teaching Gramsci at Columbia, see Neeladri Bhattacharya, Suvir Kaul, and Ania Loomba, "Edward Said: In Conversation with

Neeladri Bhattacharya, Suvir Kaul, and Ania Loomba, New Delhi, 16 December 1997," *Interventions: International Journal of Postcolonial Studies*, 1.1 (1998), 91.

34. See Said's thoughts on these debates in 1973's "On Originality," *The World, the Text, and The Critic*, 130 [originally, "On Originality," in *Uses of Literature*, ed. Monroe Engel (Cambridge, MA: Harvard University Press, 1973), 49–65].

35. Edward Said, "Interview With Edward Said," *Diacritics*, 6.3 (1976), 30–47.

36. Said, "Arab Portrayed," 8.

37. Edward Said, *Covering Islam: How the Media and the Experts Determine How We See the Rest of the World* (New York: Vintage Books, 1997), xi.

38. See Edward Said, "Traveling Theory," *The World, the Text, and the Critic*, 244 [originally, "Traveling Theory," *Raritan*, 1.3 (1982), 41–67], and Edward Said, "Traveling Theory Reconsidered," *Reflections on Exile and Other Essays*, 436–52.

39. Said, *Culture and Imperialism*, 279.

40. Rosi Braidotti, "The Contested Post-Humanities," in *Conflicting Humanities*, 18.

41. Edward Said, "The Politics of Knowledge," *Raritan*, 11.1 (1991).

42. Said, "Reflections on Exile," 186.

43. Partha Chatterjee, cited in S. N. Balagangadhara, *Reconceptualizing Indian Studies* (Oxford, UK: Oxford University Press, 2012), 35.

44. Ardi Imseis, "Speaking Truth to Power: On Edward Said and the Palestinian Freedom Struggle," in *Edward Said: A Legacy of Emancipation and Representation*, eds. Adel Iskandar, Hakem Rustom (Berkeley, CA: University of California Press, 2010), 248; Edward Said, "Permission to Narrate (1984)," in *The Politics of Dispossession: The Struggle for Palestinian Self-Determination, 1969–1994* (New York: Vintage Books, 1995), 247–48.

45. Edward Said, "Introduction," *The Politics of Dispossession*, xi.

46. Imseis, "Speaking Truth to Power," 248.

47. See Zarefa Ali, *A Narration Without an End: Palestine and the Continuing Nakba* (Birzeit, Palestine: Ibrahim Abu-Lughod Institute of International Studies, Birzeit University, 2013).

48. Indeed, as Haidar Eid put it in 2020, "Relying on what he called 'common sense,'" Said "predicted the tragic situation that unraveled after 1993; nothing more, nothing less." Salah D. Hassan, "Passing Away: Despair, Eulogies, and Millennial Palestine," *Biography*, 36.1 (2013), 34.

49. Haidar Eid, "Edward Said's Spectre and the End of Oslo," *Al Jazeera*, June 6, 2020, https://www.aljazeera.com/opinions/2020/6/6/edward-saids-spectre-and-the-end-of-oslo. Last accessed March 28, 2022.

50. Joseph Masad, "Affiliating With Edward Said," in *Edward Said: A Legacy of Emancipation and Representation*, 35.

51. Imseis, "Speaking Truth to Power," 271–72.

52. Edward Said, "Truth and Reconciliation," *Al-Ahram Weekly*, 412, January 20, 1999, http://weekly.ahram.org.eg/Archive/1999/412/op2.htm. Last accessed March 22, 2022.

53. Edward Said, "Between Worlds: Edward Said Makes Sense of His Life," *London Review of Books*, 29.9 (1998), https://www.lrb.co.uk/the-paper/v20/n09/edward-said/between-worlds

54. Joseph Masad, "The Intellectual Life of Edward Said," *Journal of Palestine Studies*, 33.3 (2004), 14.

55. Alexander Coburn, "The FBI and Edward Said," *Nation*, January 12, 2006, https://www.thenation.com/article/archive/fbi-and-edward-said/

56. David Price, "How the FBI Spied on Edward Said," *Counterpunch*, January 13, 2006, https://www.counterpunch.org/2006/01/13/how-the-fbi-spied-on-edward-said/

57. See Said's description of death threats in "Between Worlds." See also Edward Alexander, "Professor of Terror," *Commentary*, August 1989, https://www.commentarymagazine.com/articles/professor-of-terror/

58. Edward Said, "On Palestinian Identity: A Conversation With Salman Rushdie," *New Left Review*, 160 (November 1, 1986), 68.

59. See Said's description of this event in his interview with Rushdie.

60. A. Naomi Paik, "Education and Empire, Old and New: HR 3077 and the Resurgence of the US University," *Cultural Dynamics*, 25.1 (2013), 4.

61. "Testimony of Stanley Kurtz Before the House Subcommittee on Select Education for Hearings on International Education and Questions of Bias," *Campus Watch*, June 19, 2003, https://www.meforum.org/campus-watch/8470/testimony-of-stanley-kurtz-before-the-house

62. Jennifer Pitts, "Political Theory of Empire and Imperialism," *Annual Review of Political Science*, 13 (2010), 212, 213.

63. Pitts, "Political Theory," 226.

64. See Robert Vitalis on these associations and the "intellectual middlemen" – skilled at "getting ideas across to nonacademic audiences in Washington, New York, and points beyond" – who straddled these academic and foreign policy worlds. In, Robert Vitalis, *White World Order, Black Power Politics* (Cornell University Press, 2017), 4. See also Patrick Porter's important article on the relationship between professional IR and the U.S. foreign policy establishment, "Why America's Grand Strategy Has Not Changed: Power, Habit, and the U.S. Foreign Policy Establishment," *International Security*, 42.4 (2018).

65. The first professor of international politics in the world, for instance, was an Oxford-trained classicist named Alfred Zimmern. See Morefield, *Covenants Without Swords*, and Jeanne Morefield, *Empires without Imperialism* (Oxford, UK: Oxford University Press, 2014). For more on the intellectual and disciplinary openness of international thought before World War II, see Ian Hall and Lisa Hill (eds.), *British International Thinkers From Hobbes to Namier* (London: Palgrave, 2009), and David Long and Peter Wilson, *Thinkers of the Twenty Years Crisis* (Oxford, UK: Oxford University Press, 1995).

66. Duncan Bell, "Political Realism and International Relations," *Philosophy Compass*, 12.2 (2017), 12.

67. Martin Wight, "Why Is There No International Theory?" *International Relations*, 2.1 (1960), 35.

68. See Charles Beitz, *Political Theory and International Relations* (Princeton, NJ: Princeton University Press, 1999), and Henry Shue, *Basic Rights: Subsistence, Affluence, and U.S. Foreign Policy*, 2nd ed. (Princeton, NJ: Princeton University Press, 1996).

69. Hans Morgenthau, quoted in Nicolas Guilhot, *After the Enlightenment: Political Realism and International Relations in the Mid-Twentieth Century* (Cambridge, UK: Cambridge University Press, 2017), 28, 31. See also Or Rosenboim, *The Emergence of Globalism: Visions of World Order in Britain and the United States, 1939–1950* (Princeton, NJ: Princeton University Press, 2017).

70. See, for instance, Morgenthau's discussion of sovereignty and Thucydides, in particular, his insistence that the centrality of state interest is "indeed of the essence of politics and is unaffected by the circumstances of time and place." Hans Morgenthau, *Politics Among Nations*, 7th ed. (New York: McGraw-Hill, 2005), 10.

71. David Armitage, *Foundations of Modern International Thought* (Cambridge, UK: Cambridge University Press, 2013), 13.

72. David Armitage, "The International Turn in Intellectual History," in *Rethinking Modern European Intellectual History*, ed. Darrin M. McMahon and Samuel Moyn (Oxford, UK: Oxford University Press, 2014), 239. From Armitage's perspective, the question scholars of the history of international thought should be asking today is not "how did 'we'—whoever 'we' are—come to acquire the concept of the state" but rather "how did 'we'—all of us in the world—come to imagine that we inhabit a world of states?" Armitage, *Foundations*, 13.

73. See, among other texts on this subject, John M. Hobson, *The Eurocentric Conception of Politics: Western International Theory, 1760–2010* (Cambridge, UK: Cambridge University Press, 2012), and Vitalis, *White World Order*.

74. Vitalis, *White World Order*, 7.

75. Jodi Byrd, "Silence Will Fall: The Cultural Politics of Colonial Agnosia," unpublished manuscript, last modified 2014, 13, quoted in Grant Ardnt, "Settler Agnosia in the Field: Indigenous Action, Functional Ignorance, and the Origins of Ethnographic Entrapment," *American Ethnologist*, 43.3 (2016), 466.

76. Much of Vitalis's book is devoted not only to demonstrating that many of the earliest scholars of international politics (from the late nineteenth century onward) were White supremacists concerned with the demographics of race and imperialism but also to exploring the work of Black scholars of international politics in America who actually *did* write critically about imperialism well into the 1950s.

77. See, among many other important texts, Geeta Chowdhury and Sheila Nair, *Power, Postcolonialism and International Relations: Reading Race, Gender and Class* (London: Routledge, 2002); Robbie Shilliam, *The Black Pacific: Anti-Colonial Struggles and Oceanic Connections* (London: Bloomsbury, 2015); and Sanjay Seth, *Subject Lessons: The Western Education of Colonial India* (Durham, NC: Duke University Press, 2007).

78. Michael Doyle, *Empires* (Ithaca, NY: Cornell University Press, 1986), 45 (italics mine).

79. Paul Kramer, "Power and Connection: Imperial Histories of the United States in the World," *American Historical Review*, 116.5 (2011), 1350.

80. John J. Mearsheimer and Stephen M. Walt, "The Case for Offshore Balancing," *Foreign Affairs*, 95.4 (2016), 72.

81. G. John Ikenberry, *Liberal Leviathan, The Origins, Crisis, and Transformation of the American World Order* (Princeton, NJ: Princeton University Press, 2012), 10.

82. Morgenthau, *Politics Among Nations*, 24.

83. See, for instance, Richard Ned Lebow and Simon Reich, *Goodbye Hegemony: Power and Influence in the Global System* (Princeton, NJ: Princeton University Press, 2014), and my critical exchange with the authors in *Perspectives on Politics*, 12.4 (December 2014).

84. As a sign that this is changing, see Duncan Bell (ed.), *Empire, Race, and Global Justice* (Cambridge, UK: Cambridge University Press, 2019), and Catherine Lu, *Justice and Reconciliation in World Politics* (Cambridge, UK: Cambridge University Press, 2017).

85. See Nancy Fraser and Rahel Jaeggi, *Capitalism: A Conversation* (New York: Polity, 2018).

86. See Gurminder Bhambra's crucial critique of Fraser in "Colonial Global Economy: Towards a Theoretical Reorientation of Political Economy," Review of International Political Economy, 28.2 (2021).

87. Wendy Brown, *Edgework: Critical Essays on Knowledge and Politics* (Princeton, NJ: Princeton University Press, 2005), 66.

88. C. Delisle Burns, Bertrand Russell, and G. D. H. Cole, "Symposium: Nature of the State in View of Its External Relations," *Proceedings of the Aristotelian Society*, 16 (1915–1916), 290–335.

89. Edward Said, "Zionism From the Standpoint of Its Victims," *Social Text*, 1 (1979), 25.

90. Said, "Representing the Colonized," 215. See also Craig Calhoun, Frederick Cooper, and Kevin Moore (eds.), *Lessons of Empire: Imperial Histories and American Power* (New York: New Press, 2006), for more on Saidian-inspired, contrapuntal approaches imperialism.

91. Kramer, "Power and Connection," 1349 (italics mine).

92. See James Tully, "Lineages of Contemporary Imperialism," in *Lineages of Empire*, ed. Duncan Kelly (Oxford, UK: Oxford University Press, 2009), 5.

93. Charles Mills, *Black Rights, White Wrongs: The Critique of Racial Liberalism* (Oxford, UK: Oxford University Press, 2017), 49–71.

94. Brown, *Edgework*, 65.

95. See, Duncan Bell, "What Is Liberalism?" *Political Theory*, 42.6 (2014); John Gunnell, "Dislocated Rhetoric: The Anomaly of Political Theory," *Journal of Politics*, 68.4 (2006), 777; Jeanne Morefield, "Urgent History: The Sovereignty Debates and Political Theory's Lost Voice," *Political Theory*, 45.2 (2017), 164–91.

96. Thomas Hobbes, *Leviathan*, (Oxford, UK: Clarendon Press, 1909), 268.

97. Wendy Brown, *Walled States, Waning Sovereignty* (Princeton, NJ: Princeton University Press, 2010), 73–74.

98. Said, *Culture and Imperialism*, 178, quoted in Amy Allen, *The End of Progress: Decolonizing the Normative Foundations of Critical Theory* (New York: Columbia University Press, 2016), 1.

99. Aside from quoting (briefly) *Culture and Imperialism* and gesturing toward (without engaging) *Orientalism* and 1989's "Representing the Colonized," the entire corpus of Said's work—the lifetime of essays, articles, interviews, books—is missing from Allen's analysis.

100. Fred Dallmayr, *Beyond Orientalism: Essays on Cross Cultural Encounter* (Albany, NY: State University of New York Press, 1996), xi.

101. Joshua Muravchik, "Enough Said: The False Scholarship of Edward Said," *World Affairs*, 175.6 (2013), 16.

102. Caroline Glick, "Edward Said, Prophet of Political Violence in America; Opinion," *Newsweek*, July 7, 2020, https://www.newsweek.com/edward-said-prophet-political-violence-america-opinion-1515770. Last accessed March 28, 2022.

103. Edward Said, "Opponents, Audiences, Constituencies, and Communities," *Critical Inquiry*, 9.1 (1982), 17.

104. Said, *Culture and Imperialism*, 13.

105. Conor McCarthy, *The Cambridge Introduction to Edward Said* (Cambridge, UK: Cambridge University Press, 2010), 14.

106. See Edward Said, "Professionals and Amateurs," in *Representations of the Intellectual*, 73–83.

107. Edward Said, quoted in Te-hsing, "An Interview With Edward Said (1997)," in *Interviews With Edward W. Said*, 131.

108. Adel Iskandar and Hakem Rustom, eds. *Edward Said: A Legacy of Emancipation and Representation* (Berkeley: University of California Press, 2010), 5.

109. Said, *Orientalism*, 339.

110. John S. Dryzek, Bonnie Honig, and Anne Phillips, "Overview of Political Theory," in *The Oxford Handbook of Political Science* (Oxford, UK: Oxford University Press, 2013), 62.

111. See Hannah Arendt, "Zionism Reconsidered," in *The Jew as Pariah* (New York: Random House, 1978). See also Margaret Canovan's thoughtful treatment of Arendt's relationship with Zionism in *Hannah Arendt: A Reinterpretation of Her Thought* (Cambridge, UK: Cambridge University Press, 1994).

112. Seyla Benhabib, "Hannah Arendt and the Redemptive Power of Narrative," *Social Research*, 57.1 (1990), 173.

113. Hannah Arendt, *The Origins of Totalitarianism* (New York: Meridian Books, 1958), 131.

114. Arendt, *Origins of Totalitarianism*, 136–37.

115. Arendt, *Origins of Totalitarianism*, 160–61.

116. Arendt, *Origins of Totalitarianism*, 123.

117. Edmund Burke, "Speech on the Impeachment of Warren Hastings," in *The Works of Edmund Burke* (London: Little, Brown, 1839), 283.

118. Harold Laski, "The Economic Foundations of Peace," in *The Intelligent Man's Way to Prevent War*, ed. Leonard Woolf (London: Camelot Press, 1933), 527, and Harold Laski, *Karl Marx: An Essay* (London: The Fabian Society and Allen and Unwin, 1922), 38.

119. This is precisely Aimé Césaire's point in *Discourse on Colonialism* (which I explore in subsequent chapters). See also Andrew Sartori's discussion in Andrew Sartori, *Liberalism in Empire: An Alternative History* (Oakland: University of California Press, 2014), 15, 7, 128, of the way "anticapitalist trajectories" within Locke's political thought were uniquely transformed in the context of nineteenth-century legal disputes between landowners and tenants in Bengal, transformations

that then circulated within Bengali legal and political discourse in ways that would ultimately influence twentieth-century Muslim nationalism in India.

120. See Michiel Bot's translation of this entry, entitled "The National Principle," *The Hannah Arendt Center for Politics and Humanities*, https://hac.bard.edu/amor-mundi/the-nation-principle-2014-11-24.

121. Arendt, *Origins of Totalitarianism*, 79.

122. Hannah Arendt, "Reflections on Little Rock," *Dissent*, 6.1 (1959), 46. See also Patricia Owens, "Racism in the Theory Canon: Hannah Arendt and 'The One Great Crime in Which America Was Never Involved,'" *Millennium*, 45.3 (2017), 403–24.

123. Kwame Nkrumah, *Neo-Colonialism: The Last Stage of Imperialism* (New York: International, 1965), ix.

124. Aimé Césaire, *Discourse on Colonialism* (New York: Monthly Review Press, 2000); W. E. B. Du Bois, "The African Roots of the War," *Atlantic Monthly*, 115 (May 1915).

125. See Rashid Khalidi, *Resurrecting Empire: Western Footprints and America's Perilous Path in the Middle East* (Boston: Beacon Press, 2004); Keith Wattenpaugh, "The Guiding Principles and the U.S. 'Mandate' for Iraq: 20th Century Colonialism and America's New Empire," *Logos*, 2 (2003), 26–37.

126. Said, *Culture and Imperialism*, 51.

127. Edward Said, "Culture and Imperialism," in David Barsamian (ed.), *The Pen and the Sword: Conversations With Edward Said* (New York: Haymarket, 2010), 77–78.

128. Tammer El-Sheikh looked closely at Said's correspondences with publishers, now located in the Said Papers at Columbia. His observations on these correspondences appear as a lengthy footnote in his PhD thesis, "Strategies of Refusal: Art and Cultural Politics in the Work of Edward W. Said and Hassan Khan" (Quebec, Canada: McGill University, 2013), 99.

129. Jurgen Habermas, *Knowledge and Human Interests* (London: Heinemann, 1972), 9; Michael Freeden, *Ideologies and Political Theory: A Conceptual Approach* (Oxford: Clarendon Press, 1996), 1.

130. See Michael Walzer's reaction to Said's review in "An Exchange: 'Exodus and Revolution,'" *Grand Street*, 5.4 (1986), 246.

131. Walzer, "Exchange," 249.

132. See "A Case for Discussing BDS at APSA, Or: What Really Happened at the Foundations Meeting in D.C.," Oct. 7, 2019 https://mespi.org/2019/10/07/a-case-for-discussing-bds-at-apsa-or-what-really-happened-at-the-foundations-meeting-in-dc/. Michael Walzer has gone on to call supporters of BDS "useful idiots." See "Don't Be Useful Idiots for BDS," *The Third Narrative*, Sept. 9, 2019, https://thirdnarrative.org/bds-does-not-equal-peace-articles/three-substantive-points-against-bds/. Last accessed March 28, 2022..

133. Said, "Representing the Colonized," 220, 210.

134. Edward W. Said, "The Public Role of Writers and Intellectuals," in *Humanism and Democratic Criticism* (New York: Columbia University Press, 2004), 142.

135. James Tully, "On Local and Global Citizenship," in *Public Philosophy in a New Key* (Cambridge, UK: Cambridge University Press, 2009), 290–91.

136. See James Tully, "Dialogue and Decolonization," in *Dialogue and Decolonization*, ed. Monika Kirloskar-Steinbach (London: Bloomsbury, forthcoming, 2023).

137. See, for instance, Mathieu E. Courville, *Edward Said's Rhetoric of the Secular* (London: Bloomsbury, 2009); Aamir R. Mufti, "Auerbach in Istanbul: Edward Said, Secular Criticism, and the Question of Minority Culture," *Critical Inquiry*, 25.1 (1998), 95–125; and Bruce Robbins, "Secularism, Elitism, Progress, and Other Transgressions: On Edward Said's 'Voyage In,'" *Social Text*, 40 (1994), 25–37.

138. For more on Said and subaltern studies, see Said's foreword to Ranajit Guha and Gayatri Chakravorty Spivak, *Selected Subaltern Studies* (Oxford, UK: Oxford Univ. Press, 1988). See also chapter 2, "The Beginnings of Postcolonial History: Writing: Edward Said and Subaltern Studies," in Rochona Majumdar, *Writing Postcolonial History* (London: Bloomsbury, 2010). For an overview of the controversies surrounding the reception of *Orientalism*, see Fred Halliday, "Orientalism and Its Critics," *British Journal of Middle Eastern Studies*, 20.2 (1983), 145–63. See also John M. Mackenzie, "Edward Said and the Historians," *Nineteenth-Century Contexts*, 18.1 (1994).

139. For an important introduction to this IR literature, see the forum on "Edward W. Said and International Relations," in *Millennium*, 36.1 (2007), which includes articles by Raymond Duval, Geeta Chowdhury, Shampa Biswas, and Shelia Nair. An important new political theory investigation of themes about which Said cared deeply (as well as an engagement with Said himself) is Hagar Kotef, *The Colonizing Self: Or Home and Homelessness in Israel Palestine* (Durham, NC: Duke University Press, 2020).

140. Akeel Bilgrami, foreword, in *Humanism and Democratic Criticism*, by Edward W. Said (New York: Columbia University Press, 2004), ix.

141. Said, "Public Role of Writers," 144.

142. Said, *Culture and Imperialism*, 216, 230.

143. Edward Said, "The Future of Criticism," in *Reflections on Exile*, 171.

144. Duncan Bell, *Reordering the World: Essays on Liberalism and Imperialism* (Princeton, NJ: Princeton University Press, 2016), 4.

145. Ikenberry thus devotes an entire chapter of 2020's *A World Safe for Democracy* to an exploration of both these historical connections and to the grander question: Is there a liberal "urge for empire"? G. John Ikenberry, *A World Safe for Democracy: Liberal Internationalism and the Crises of Global Order* (New Haven, CT: Yale University Press, 2020), 231.

146. Cindi Katz and Neil Smith, "An Interview With Edward Said," *Environment and Planning D: Society and Space*, 21 (2003), 635.

147. Said, "Public Role of Writers," 142–43.

148. Dabashi, *Edward Said*, 30.

# 1

1. Edward Said, "Reflections on Exile,", 173.

2. Said, "Reflections on Exile," 185.

3. Edward Said with Jean Mohr, *After the Last Sky: Palestinian Lives* (New York: Columbia University Press, 1998), ix.

4. Said and Mohr, *After the Last Sky*, 130.

5. Bill Ashcroft and Pal Ahluwalia, *Edward Said: The Paradox of Identity* (New York: Routledge, 1999), 3.

6. Ashcroft and Ahluwalia, *Edward Said*, 3.

7. Said, *Out of Place*, 293.

8. Said recalls his father saying, "[Y]ou're a literature professor. . . . [S]tick to that." Said, *Out of Place*, 117.

9. Edward Said, "The Arab Portrayed," in *The Arab Israeli Confrontation of 1967*, ed. Ibrahim Abu-Lughod (Evanston, IL: Northwestern University Press, 1970), 8.

10. Edward Said, "The Mind of Winter: Reflections on a Life in Exile," *Harpers* (September 1984), 49.

11. The cover art for Said's *Reflections on Exile and Other Essays* (Cambridge, MA: Harvard University Press, 2000): a close up of Edward Said

12. Theodore Adorno, *Minima Moralia: Reflections from a Damaged Life* (New York: Verso, 2005), 39.

13. Ian Buruma, "Real Wounds, Unreal Wounds: The Romance of Exile," *New Republic* (February 12, 2001), 34. Said himself was explicitly indebted to a critical tradition in Judaism that focused on exile, so much so that—in the course of an interview for *Ha'aretz* (August 29, 2000) that included his thoughts on both Adorno and a one-state, binational solution—Ari Shavir told Said, "You sound very Jewish." Said responded provocatively, "Of course. I'm the last Jewish intellectual. . . . Let me put it this way: I'm a Jewish-Palestinian." See the interview, "Orientalism, Arab Intellectuals, Marxism, and Myth in Palestinian History," in *Power, Politics, and Culture: Interviews With Edward W. Said*, ed. Gauri Viswanathan (New York: Vintage, 2002), 458.

14. Said, "Reflections on Exile," 186.

15. Said, "Reflections on Exile," 173.

16. Said, "Reflections on Exile," 175.

17. Said, "Reflections on Exile," 174.

18. Said, "Reflections on Exile," 175.

19. Said, "Reflections on Exile," 174, 175.

20. Said, "Reflections on Exile, 175, 181.

21. David Kettler, *The Liquidation of Exile: Studies in the Intellectual Emigration of the 1930s* (New York: Anthem Press, 2011), 6.

22. Kettler, *Liquidation of Exile*, 7.

23. Frederick Luis Aldama, *Why the Humanities Matter: A Commonsense Approach* (Austin: University of Texas Press, 2010), 79.

24. Aldama, *Why the Humanities Matter*, 79.

25. Joseph Masad, "The Intellectual Life of Edward Said," *Journal of Palestine Studies*, 33.3 (2004), 9.

26. Edward Said, "Intellectual Exile: Expatriates and Marginals," in *Representations of the Intellectual: The 1993 Reith Lectures* (New York: Vintage Books, 1996), 48–49.

27. Edward Said, "Secular Criticism," in *The World, the Text, and the Critic* (Cambridge, MA: Harvard University Press, 1983), 8.

28. Said, "Reflections on Exile," 173.

29. Edward Said, *Culture and Imperialism* (New York: Vintage, 1994), 336.

30. Said, "Reflections on Exile," 181.

31. Said, "Reflections on Exile," 178.

32. Said, "Reflections on Exile," 178.

33. Said, "Reflections on Exile," 177.

34. Said, "Reflections on Exile," 177 (emphasis mine).

35. Edward Said, "Criticism, Culture, and Performance (1991)," in *Power, Politics, and Culture*, 99.

36. Said, "Intellectual Exile," 122.

37. Said, *Culture and Imperialism*, 336.

38. Said, "Criticism, Culture, and Performance," 99.

39. Said, "Intellectual Exile," 122.

40. Said, "Secular Criticism," 20.

41. Said, "Secular Criticism," 24, 23.

42. Said, "Secular Criticism," 16.

43. Said, "Secular Criticism," 24.

44. Stuart Hall, "The West and the Rest: Discourse and Power," in *Formations of Modernity*, ed. Bram Gieben and Stuart Hall (Cambridge, UK: Polity Press, 1992), 221.

45. Said, "Secular Criticism," 24.

46. Said, "Secular Criticism," 6, 8.

47. Edward Said, Introduction to Eric Auerbach, *Mimesis*, 50th anniversary ed. (Princeton, NJ: Princeton University Press, 2003), xvii.

48. Said, Introduction to *Mimesis*, x.

49. Said, "Secular Criticism," 24.

50. Said, Introduction to *Mimesis*, x.

51. Edward Said, "Orientalism 25 Years Later: Worldly Humanism v. the Empire-Builders," *Counterpunch*, 2003, http://www.counterpunch.org/2003/08/05/orientalism/. Last accessed March 28, 2022.

52. Edward Said, "The American Left and Literary Criticism," in *The World, the Text, and the Critic*, 174.

53. Edward Said, "Opponents, Audiences, Constituencies, and Community," in *Reflections on Exile*, 119.

54. Said, *Culture and Imperialism*, 336.

55. Said, *Culture and Imperialism*, 336.

56. Said, *Culture and Imperialism*, 336.

57. Said, *Culture and Imperialism*, 336

58. Said, *Culture and Imperialism*, 336.

59. Said, "Reflections on Exile," 184.

60. Said, *Representations of the Intellectual*, 53. Said, "Reflections on Exile," 184. Said, *Culture and Imperialism*, 336.

61. Denise deCaires Narain, "Affiliating Edward Said Closer to Home: Reading Postcolonial Women's Texts," in *Edward Said: A Legacy of Emancipation and Representation*, ed. Adel Iskandar and Hakem Rustom (Berkeley: University of California Press, 2010), 139.

62. Edward Said, *The Question of Palestine* (New York: Vintage Books, 1979), xviii.

63. Masad, "Intellectual Life of Edward Said," 14.

64. Mahmoud Darwish, "The Earth Is Closing in on Us," in *Victims of a Map: A Bilingual Anthology of Arabic Poetry* (London: Al-Saqui Books, 1984).

65. Edward Said, "On Palestinian Identity: A Conversation With Salman Rushdie," *New Left Review* (November 1, 1986), 65.

66. Said and Mohr, *After the Last Sky*, 92.

67. Said and Mohr, *After the Last Sky*, 11.

68. Said and Mohr, *After the Last Sky*, 46.

69. Said and Mohr, *After the Last Sky*, 46.

70. Said and Mohr, *After the Last Sky*, 46.

71. Said and Mohr, *After the Last Sky,* 48.

72. Said and Mohr, *After the Last Sky*, 128.

73. Said and Mohr, *After the Last Sky*, 4.

74. Edward Said, "Permission to Narrate," in *The Politics of Dispossession* (New York: Vintage Books, 1994), 249; Golda Meir, quoted in Edward Said, "How to Answer Palestine's Challenge," *The Politics of Dispossession*, 138. Meir herself clarified this statement in a 1976 op-ed for the *New York Times*: "I have been charged with being rigidly insensitive to the question of the Palestinian Arabs. In evidence of this I am supposed to have said, 'There are no Palestinians.' My actual words were: 'There is no Palestinian people. There are Palestinian refugees.'" "Golda Meir, on the Palestinians," *New York Times*, January 14, 1976. http://graphics8.nytimes.com/packages/pdf/oped40/CONFLICTMeir.pdf. This distinction, while crucial for Meir, was precisely what most worried Said.

75. Said and Mohr, *After the Last Sky*, 149.

76. Said and Mohr, *After the Last Sky*, 34.

77. Said and Mohr, *After the Last Sky*, 92.

78. Said and Mohr, *After the Last Sky*, 93.

79. Said and Mohr, *After the Last Sky*, 94, 96.

80. Said and Mohr, *After the Last Sky*, 20.

81. Said and Mohr, *After the Last Sky*, 129.

82. Said and Mohr, *After the Last Sky*, 129.

83. Said and Mohr, *After the Last Sky*, 34.

84. Said and Mohr, *After the Last Sky*, 20.

85. Said and Mohr, *After the Last Sky*, 5.

86. Said, "Representing the Colonized: Anthropology's Interlocutors," *Critical Inquiry*, 15.2 (1989), 225.

87. Said and Mohr, *After the Last Sky*, 130.

88. Said and Mohr, *After the Last Sky*, 150.

89. Edward Said, "The Art of Displacement: Mona Hatoum's Logic of Irreconcilables," in *Mona Hatoum: The Entire World as a Foreign Land* (London: Tate Gallery, 2000), 110.

90. Said and Mohr, *After the Last Sky*, 34.

91. Said, "Reflections on Exile," 185.

92. Edward Said, *Reflections on Exile and Other Essays* (Cambridge, MA: Harvard University Press, 2000), xxxv.

93. Said, *Reflections on Exile*, xxxv.

94. Said, *Culture and Imperialism*, 336.

95. Edward W. Said, "The Public Role of Writers and Intellectuals," in *Humanism and Democratic Criticism* (New York: Columbia University Press, 2004), 144.

## 2

1. Edward Said, *Out of Place: A Memoir* (New York: Viking, 1999), ix.

2. Said, *Out of Place*, 295.

3. Dallmayr, in particular, acknowledges Said's work as inspirational, dedicating *Beyond Orientalism: Essays on Cross Cultural Encounter* to Said and Gadamer "with respect, gratitude, and admiration." Fred Dallmayr, *Beyond Orientalism* (Albany: State University of New York Press, 1996), xi.

4. Fred Dallmayr, "The Politics of Nonidentity: Adorno, Postmodernism—and Edward Said," *Political Theory*, 25.1 (1997), 33.

5. Dallmayr, "Politics of Nonidentity," 33–34.

6. Dallmayr, "Politics of Nonidentity," 38.

7. Dallmayr, "Politics of Nonidentity," 38.

8. Theodore Adorno, *Negative Dialectics* (New York: Routledge, 2004), 191.

9. Dallmayr, "Politics of Nonidentity," 35.

10. Dallmayr, "Politics of Nonidentity," 51.

11. Said, *Orientalism*, 322.

12. Said, *Culture and Imperialism*, 31.

13. Dallmayr, "Politics of Nonidentity," 50.

14. Dallmayr, "Politics of Nonidentity," 34.

15. Dallmayr, "Politics of Nonidentity," 44.

16. Said, "Permission to Narrate,".

17. See Adrien Whilding's nuanced account of this moment and Adorno's politics in "Pied Pipers and Polymaths: Adorno's Critique of Praxisism," in *Negativity and Revolution Adorno and Political Activism* (New York: Pluto Press, 2009), 28–29.

18. Joan Cocks, "A New Cosmopolitanism? V. S. Naipaul and Edward Said," *Constellations*, 7.1 (2000), 47.

19. For some radical approaches to resistance and anticolonial orientations that explore and challenge this universal-versus-particular configuration, see, for instance, Jakeet Singh's work on "top-down" and "bottom-up" approaches to cultural difference in "Recognition and Self Determination: Approaches from Above and Below," in Avigail Eisenberg, Jeremy Webber, Glen Coulthard, and Andre Boiselle (eds.),

*Recognition v. Self Determination: Dilemmas of Emancipatory Politics* (Vancouver: University of British Columbia Press, 2014), 47–74.

20. See Mathias Risse, *On Global Justice* (Princeton, NJ: Princeton University Press, 2002), and Laura Valentini, *Justice in a Globalized World: A Normative Framework* (Oxford, UK: Oxford University Press, 2011).

21. Nancy Fraser, "Recognition Without Ethics?" *Theory, Culture and Society,* 18:2–3 (2001), 87.

22. Cocks, "New Cosmopolitanism?" 59.

23. Cocks, "New Cosmopolitanism?" 60.

24. Joan Cocks, "Political Predicaments of Exile," in Bashir Abu-Manneh (ed.), *After Said: Postcolonial Literary Studies in the Twenty-First Century* (Cambridge, UK: Cambridge University Press, 2018), 169.

25. Cocks is hardly alone in her critical desire for a space outside the universal and particular divide—a differently configured container for "the political"—nor is she alone in wondering whether such a politics is feasible. In 2017's "The Cosmopolitan Idea and National Sovereignty," for instance, Robert Young similarly asks what a "transnational" cosmopolitanism would look like. Would such an approach, he wonders, be capable of reconciling the "competing and often conflictual claims that cosmopolitanism attempts to mediate today?" See, Robert Young, "The Cosmopolitan Idea and National Sovereignty," in Bruce Robbins and Paulo Lemos Horta (eds.), *Cosmopolitanisms* (New York: New York University Press, 2017), 136.

26. Edward Said, "Overlapping Territories," interview with Gary Hentzi and Anne McClintock, in *Power, Politics, and Culture,* 56.

27. Thomas Nagel, *The View from Nowhere* (Oxford, UK: Oxford University Press, 1989).

28. Said, "Reflections on Exile," in *Reflections on Exile,* 186.

29. Said, "Reflections on Exile," 186.

30. Dallmayr, "Politics of Nonidentity," 33.

31. Said, *Culture and Imperialism,* 108, 50.

32. Dipesh Chakrabarty, *Provincializing Europe: Postcolonial Thought and Historical Difference* (Princeton, NJ: Princeton University Press, 2000), 43.

33. Martha Nussbaum, "Kant and Stoic Cosmopolitanism," *Journal of Political Philosophy,* 5.1 (1997), 3.

34. See John Rawls, *The Law of Peoples* (Cambridge, MA: Harvard University Press, 2001). See also Michael Goodhart's comparison of what he calls "cosmopolitan" and "social" liberals in Michael Goodhart, "Constructing Global Justice: A Critique," *Ethics and Global Politics,* 5.1 (2012), 2.

35. Kwame Anthony Appiah, *Cosmopolitanism* (New York: Penguin, 2007), 106. See also Ulrich Beck's sympathetic but ultimately limited and ahistorical defense of cosmopolitanism in the context of multiculturalism and globalization in Ulrich Beck, "The Cosmopolitan Society and Its Enemies," *Theory Culture Society,* 19.1–2 (2002), 17–44.

36. See, for instance, Gurminder Bhambra, "Cosmopolitanism and Postcolonial Critique," in Maria Rovisco and Magdalena Nowicka (eds.), *The Ashgate Companion to Cosmopolitanism* (New York: Ashgate, 2011), and Vivienne Jabri, "Solidarity and

Spheres of Culture: The Cosmopolitan and the Postcolonial," *Review of International Studies*, 33.4 (2007), 715–28.

37. See, for instance, Babacar M. Baye, *Black Cosmopolitanism and Anticolonialism: Pivotal Moments* (New York: Routledge, 2017); Getachew, *Worldmaking After Empire*; and Valdez, *Transnational Cosmopolitanism*.

38. James Tully, *Dialogue and Decolonisation*, ed. Monika Kirloskar-Steinbach (London: Bloomsbury, forthcoming 2023).

39. Charles Mills, *Black Rights, White Wrongs: The Critique of Racial Liberalism* (Oxford, UK: Oxford University Press, 2017), 71.

40. David Miller, *National Responsibility and Global Justice* (Oxford, UK: Oxford University Press, 2007), 27. Miller argues that, for cosmopolitan global justice scholars, these far-flung others "must count with us when we decide how to act or what institutions to establish."

41. See Mathias Risse, "What We Owe to the Global Poor," *Journal of Ethics*, 9.1 (2005).

42. Alasdair MacIntyre, *After Virtue: A Study in Moral Theory* (Notre Dame, IN: University of Notre Dame Press, 2007), 221.

43. Jack Goldsmith, "Liberal Democracy and Cosmopolitan Duty," *Stanford Law Review*, 55.5 (2003), 1677.

44. Will Kymlicka, "Citizenship in an Era of Globalization," in Garret Brown and David Held (eds.), *The Cosmopolitan Reader* (Cambridge, UK: Polity, 2010), 437.

45. Young, "Cosmopolitan Idea," 137.

46. "To be attached to the subdivision, to love the little platoon we belong to in society, is the first principle (the germ as it were) of public affections. It is the first link in the series by which we proceed towards a love to our country and to mankind." Edmund Burke, *Reflections on the Revolution in France* (Oxford, UK: Oxford University Press, 2009), 47.

47. Said and Mohr, *After the Last Sky: Palestinian Lives*, 34.

48. Said, *Culture and Imperialism*, 336.

49. Said, *Culture and Imperialism*, 336.

50. Thomas Pogge, "Cosmopolitanism and Sovereignty," *Ethics*, 103.1 (1992), 50.

51. Said, *Representations of the Intellectual*, 60.

52. William Spanos, *Exiles in the City: Hannah Arendt and Edward Said in Counterpoint* (Columbus, OH: Ohio State University Press, 2012), 52.

53. Goodhart, "Constructing Global Justice," 2.

54. Michael Goodhart, *Injustice: Political Theory for the Real World* (Oxford, UK: Oxford University Press, 2018), 27.

55. A. John Simmons, "Ideal and Nonideal Theory," *Philosophy and Public Affairs*, 38.1 (2010), 34.

56. Thomas Pogge, "World Poverty and Human Rights," *Ethics International Affairs*, 19.1 (2005), 2.

57. Thomas Pogge, "Priorities of Global Justice," *Metaphilosophy*, 32.1–2 (2001), 6–24; Thomas Pogge, *World Poverty and Human Rights* (Cambridge, UK: Polity Press, 2008).

58. Iris Marion Young, "Self-Determination as Non-domination: Ideals Applied to Palestine-Israel," *Ethnicities*, 5.2 (2005), 150.

59. Young, "Self-Determination as Non-domination," 156.

60. Young, "Self-Determination as Non-domination," 140.

61. Young, "Self-Determination as Non-domination," 154.

62. Young, "Self-Determination as Non-domination," 142.

63. Young, "Self-Determination as Non-domination," 154.

64. Young, "Self-Determination as Non-domination," 140.

65. For more, see Haim Gerber, "Zionism, Orientalism, and the Palestinians," *Journal of Palestine Studies*, 33.1 (2003), 23–41. For more on the image of the disappearing native in America, see Allison McQueen and Burke Hendrix, "Tocqueville in Jacksonian Context: American Expansionism and Discourses of American Indian Nomadism in Democracy in America," *Perspectives on Politics*, 15.3 (2017), 663–77.

66. Said, "Permission to Narrate," 247–68.

67. Said and Mohr, *After the Last Sky*, 94.

68. Cristina Beltrán, *The Trouble With Unity* (Oxford, UK: Oxford University Press, 2010), 61.

69. Beltrán, *Trouble With Unity*, 61.

70. Edward Said, "Identity, Negation, and Violence," in *The Politics of Dispossession: The Struggle for Palestinian Self-Determination, 1969–1994* (New York: Vintage Books, 1995), 355.

71. Said, "Identity, Negation, and Violence," 356.

72. Said, "Identity, Negation, and Violence," 356.

73. Edward Said, "Bases for Coexistence," in *The End of the Peace Process: Oslo and After* (New York: Vintage Books, 2001), 208.

74. Said, "Bases for Coexistence," 209.

75. Said, "Bases for Coexistence," 208.

76. Edward Said, "A Method for Thinking About a Just Peace," in Pierre Allan and Alexis Keller (eds.), *What Is a Just Peace?* (Oxford, UK: Oxford University Press, 2006), 193.

77. Said, *Representations of the Intellectual*, 60.

78. Goodhart, *Injustice*, 9.

79. Pierre Allen and Alexis Keller (eds.), *What Is a Just Peace?* (Oxford, UK: Oxford University Press, 2006), 1.

80. Said, "Method for Thinking,"176, 193.

81. Said, "Method for Thinking," 193.

82. See, for instance, the language of the Oslo treaty itself:

> The Government of the State of Israel and the PLO team . . . agree that it is time to put an end to decades of confrontation and conflict, recognize their mutual legitimate and political rights, and strive to live in peaceful coexistence and mutual dignity and security and achieve a just, lasting and comprehensive peace settlement and historic reconciliation through the agreed political process.

UN General Assembly, Security Council, "Declaration of Principles on Interim Self-Government Arrangements," October 11, 1993, A/48/486 S/26560 (English), 4.

83. Said, "Method for Thinking," 177.

84. Edward W. Said, "Invention, Memory, and Place," *Critical Inquiry* 26.2 (2000), 184.

85. Said, "Bases for Coexistence," 209.

86. Said, "Method for Thinking," 193.

87. Said, "Method for Thinking," 190.

88. Said, "Method for Thinking," 178–79.

89. Said, "Method for Thinking," 179.

90. Said, "Method for Thinking," 193.

91. Said, "Method for Thinking," 193; Edward Said, "The One-State Solution," *New York Times Magazine*, January 10, 1999, https://www.nytimes.com/1999/01/10/magazine/the-one-state-solution.html. Last accessed March 24, 2022.

92. Dallmayr, "Politics of Nonidentity," 34.

93. James Tully, "Integral Nonviolence. Two Lawyers on Nonviolence: Mohandas K. Gandhi and Richard B. Gregg," in James Tully, *To Think and Act Differently*, ed. Alexamder Livingston (New York: Routledge, forthcoming 2022). James Tully, "Dialogue and Decolonization," in *Dialogue and Decolonization*, ed. Monika Kirloskar-Steinbach with Garrick Cooper, Sudipta Kaviraj, Charles W. Mills and Sorhoon Tan (London: Bloomsbury, forthcoming 2023).

94. Said, "Method for Thinking," 194.

95. Said, "Method for Thinking," 194.

96. Said, "Method for Thinking," 179.

97. Said, "One-State Solution." Said's lifetime preference for secular rather than religious identity here—coupled with his commitment to secularism more generally—has been criticized over the years by scholars for failing to acknowledge the potentially liberatory and critical practices of sacred traditions and the intensity of religious affiliation for both Palestinians and Jews. See, for instance, Darren E. Dahl, "Criticizing 'Secular Criticism': Reading Religion in Edward Said and Kathryn Tanner," *Studies in Religion* 31.3–4 (2002), 359–71. See also Bruce Robbins's sympathetic exploration of these issues in "Secularism, Elitism, Progress, and Other Transgressions: On Edward Said's 'Voyage In,'" *Social Text*, 40 (1994), 25–37.

98. Said, "A Method for Thinking About a Just Piece," 193.

99. Said, "Method for Thinking," 194.

100. Young, "Self-Determination as Non-domination," 152.

101. Young, "Self-Determination as Non-domination," 150.

102. Said, "One-State Solution."

103. Said, "Representing the Colonized: Anthropology's Interlocutors," *Critical Inquiry*, 15.2 (1989), 225.

104. Edward Said, "The Future of Criticism," *MLN*, 99.4 (1984), 951.

105. Said, "Method for Thinking," 176.

106. Said, "Future of Criticism," 957.

107. Said, "Reflections on Exile," 184.

108. Hagar Kotef, *The Colonizing Self: Or Home and Homelessness in Israel/Palestine* (Durham NC: Duke University Press, 2020), 51.

109. Said, "Reflections on Exile," 186.

## 3

1. Edward Said, quoted in Cindi Katz and Neil Smith, "An Interview With Edward Said," *Environment and Planning D: Society and Space*, 21.6 (2003), 648. See also, Edward Said, "The Music Itself: Glenn Gould's Contrapuntal Vision," in *Music at the Limits* (New York: Columbia University Press, 2008).

2. Said, quoted in Katz and Smith, "Interview," 648.

3. Said, *Culture and Imperialism*, 5; Said, "Music Itself," 8.

4. Said, "Reflections on Exile,", 186.

5. Said, *Culture and Imperialism*, 259.

6. Said, *Culture and Imperialism*, 51.

7. Edward Said, "Culture and Imperialism," in David Barsamian (ed.), *The Pen and the Sword: Conversations With Edward Said* (New York: Haymarket, 2010), 78.

8. Said, "Culture and Imperialism," 78.

9. Said, *Culture and Imperialism*, 318.

10. Said, *Culture and Imperialism*, xxvii.

11. Said, *Culture and Imperialism*, 54, 279.

12. Said, *Culture and Imperialism*, 216, 230.

13. Edward Said, "The Future of Criticism," in *Reflections on Exile*, 171.

14. Said, *Culture and Imperialism*, 9.

15. Said, *Culture and Imperialism*, 282.

16. Said, *Culture and Imperialism*, 51.

17. Viswanathan, *Power, Politics, and Culture*, xii.

18. Robert Young, *White Mythologies: Writing History and the West* (London: Routledge, 1990), 127.

19. Karlis Racevskis, "Edward Said and Michel Foucault: Affinities and Dissonances," *Research in African Literatures*, 36.3 (2005), 83.

20. Edward Said, "'Abecedarium Culturae': Structuralism, Absence, Writing," *TriQuarterly*, 20 (1971), 60.

21. Edward Said, "Traveling Theory," in *The World, The Text, and the Critic*, 215 [originally Edward Said, "Traveling Theory," *Raritan: A Quarterly Review*, 1.3 (1982)]; Edward Said, "Criticism and the Art of Politics," in *Power, Politics, and Culture*, 138. Foucault did begin to write about resistance in his later work, but his focus remained largely on resistance as a "series of oppositions." See Michel Foucault, "The Subject and Power," *Critical Inquiry*, 8.4 (1982), 780.

22. Edward Said, *Orientalism* (New York: Penguin, 1995), 3.

23. Aijaz Ahmad, *In Theory: Classes, Nations, and Literatures* (London: Verso, 1994), 168.

24. Leela Gandhi, *Postcolonial Theory: A Critical Introduction* (New York: Columbia University Press, 1998), 69.

25. Gandhi, *Postcolonial Theory*, 72.

26. Said, "Traveling Theory," 210.

27. Said, *Culture and Imperialism*, 51.

28. See Said's early reviews of Glen Gould's ability to revel in the "contrapuntal or polyphonic" quality of Bach's music in Edward Said, "The Mind of Winter:

Reflections on Life in Exile," *Harpers*, September 1984, 49–55; Said, "Music Itself," 8 [originally published in John McGreevy (ed.), *Glenn Gould: By Himself and His Friends* (Garden City, NJ: Doubleday, 1983), 45–54]; Edward Said, "Reflections on Exile," *Granta* 13 (1984), 159–74.

29. Said, *Culture and Imperialism*, 51.

30. Said, *Culture and Imperialism*, 51.

31. Said, *Culture and Imperialism*, 259.

32. Said, *Culture and Imperialism*, 259.

33. See chapter 3, section 4, "The Voyage in and the Emergence of Opposition," in Said, *Culture and Imperialism*, 239–61.

34. Said, *Culture and Imperialism*, 191.

35. Said, *Culture and Imperialism*, 81.

36. Said, *Culture and Imperialism*, 87.

37. Said, *Culture and Imperialism*, 95.

38. Said, *Culture and Imperialism*, 95.

39. Said, *Culture and Imperialism*, 33.

40. Said, *Culture and Imperialism*, 32.

41. Said, *Culture and Imperialism*, 149.

42. Said, *Culture and Imperialism*, 175; Michael Walzer, "Commitment and Social Criticism: Camus's Algerian War," *Dissent* (Fall 1984): 424–32.

43. See David Armitage, "John Locke, Carolina, and the Two Treatises of Government," *Political Theory*, 32.5 (2004), 602–27, and Herman Lebovics, "John Locke, Imperialism, and the First Stage of Capitalism," in *Imperialism and the Corruption of Democracies* (Durham, NC: Duke University Press, 2006).

44. Said, *Culture and Imperialism*, 191.

45. Said, *Culture and Imperialism*, 175.

46. This is not unlike Susan Buck-Morss's reading of Rousseau's work alongside the glaring absence of references to *actual* chattel slavery, despite its ubiquity in France and despite the fact that Toussaint Louverture would transform Rousseau's own abstract observations into concrete reality. See Susan Buck-Morss, "Hegel in Haiti," *Critical Inquiry*, 26.4 (2000), 821–65.

47. Said, *Culture and Imperialism*, 259.

48. Here, Said refers to Salman Rushdie's important 1982 essay "The Empire Writes Back With a Vengeance," *Times* (London), July 3, 1982.

49. Said, *Culture and Imperialism*, 54, 216.

50. Said, *Culture and Imperialism*, 244.

51. Said, *Culture and Imperialism*, 242. In another chapter in *Imperialism and the Corruption of Democracy*, "France's Black Venus," Lebovics argues that the modernist protest against time and capital was also influenced by European imperialism and the "discovery" of the East. Artists like Gauguin and Picasso "hated the European admixture to colonial lives" and "painted it out, preferring a "form out of time"—an "imagined pure undiluted original culture" of the native—to the more complicated cultural world in both the colonies and the metropole. Lebovics, *Imperialism and the Corruption*, 86.

52. Said, *Culture and Imperialism*, 244.

53. Said, *Culture and Imperialism*, 242.

54. Lord Milner worried in 1910 about the impact of "alien colored races, even if they be British subjects" on White communities throughout the Empire. Quoted in Bill Schwartz, *The White Man's World* (Oxford, UK: Oxford University Press, 2011), 110. On Black Paris, see Tyler Stovall, "Aimé Césaire and the Making of Black Paris," *French Politics, Culture and Society*, 27.3 (2009), 45. For more on London School of Economics and Indian students, see Brant Moscovitch, "Harold Laski's Indian Students and the Power of Education, 1920–1950," *Contemporary South Asia*, 20.1 (2012), 33–44.

55. Said, *Culture and Imperialism*, 244 (italics mine).

56. Said, *Culture and Imperialism*, 244–45.

57. Said, *Culture and Imperialism*, 248.

58. Said, *Culture and Imperialism*, 248.

59. Said, *Culture and Imperialism*, 252.

60. Said, "Culture and Imperialism," 77–78 (italics mine).

61. See Eric Hobsbawm:

> Virtually all the anti-imperial movements of any significance could be, and in the metropolis generally were, classified under one of these headings: local educated elites imitating European "national self-determination" (as in India), popular anti-Western xenophobia (an all purpose heading widely applied, notably to China), and the national high spirits of martial tribes (as in Morocco or the Arabian deserts).

Eric Hobsbawm, *Nations and Nationalism* (Cambridge, UK: Cambridge University Press, 1990), 151. See also Partha Chatterjee's critique of Benedict Anderson's *Imagined Communities* in *National Thought and the Colonial World: A Derivative Discourse* (Minneapolis: University of Minnesota Press, 1993).

62. Said, *Culture and Imperialism*, xii.

63. Said, *Culture and Imperialism*, 52.

64. Said, *Culture and Imperialism*, 52.

65. See, C. A. Bayly, "Ireland, India and the Empire: 1780–1914," *Transactions of the Royal Historical Society*, 10 (2000).

66. For an overview of Bandung and its legacy, see Luis Eslava, Michael Fakhri, and Vasuki Nesiah (eds.), *Bandung, Global History, and International Law: Critical Pasts and Pending Futures* (Cambridge, UK: Cambridge University Press, 2017). For an important overview of Pan-Africanism see, Hakim Adi, *Pan Africanism: A History* (London: Bloomsbury, 2018).

67. Said, *Culture and Imperialism*, 219.

68. Said, *Culture and Imperialism*, 219.

69. Said, *Culture and Imperialism*, 220.

70. See, for instance, Anthony Pagden, *European Encounters With the New World* (New Haven, CT: Yale University Press, 1993), and many chapters in Anthony Pagden, *The Burdens of Empire: 1539 to the Present* (Cambridge, UK: Cambridge University Press, 2015).

71. The European Union is, Pagden argues, the "one confederacy" that fulfills the "conditions of Kant's 'League of Nations.'" Anthony Pagden, *The Enlightenment and Why It Still Matters* (New York: Random House, 2013), 414.

72. Pagden, *Enlightenment*, 414.

73. In Gurminder Bhambra's words, these "non-European immigrants" in Europe could also be considered "legitimate beneficiaries of the post-war social settlement—emerging from its history of colonialism." Gurminder Bhambra, "Whither Europe? Postcolonial Versus Neocolonial Cosmopolitanism," *Interventions: Journal of Postcolonial Studies*, 18.2 (2016), 188.

74. See Anthony Anghie's important work on the imperial formulation of international law, the imperialist intentions of the mandate system, and the role of colonial resistance in both. Anthony Anghie, *Imperialism, Sovereignty and the Making of International Law* (Cambridge, UK: Cambridge University Press, 2004).

75. Pagden, *Burdens of Empire*, 256. See Jürgen Habermas, *The Divided West* (Cambridge, UK: Polity Press, 2006), 36.

76. Said, *Culture and Imperialism*, 278.

77. Said, "Traveling Theory," 244.

78. Said, "Traveling Theory," 246.

79. Said, "Traveling Theory," 245.

80. Said, "Traveling Theory," 215; Said, "Criticism and the Art of Politics," 138.

81. Said, "Traveling Theory," 247.

82. Said, *Orientalism*, 13.

83. Said, *Orientalism*, 32.

84. Said, "Opponents, Audiences, Constituencies, and Community," in *Reflections on Exile and Other Essays*, 135.

85. Said, *Culture and Imperialism*, 278.

86. Robert Nichols, "Progress, Empire, and Social Theory: Comments on the End of Progress: Decolonizing the Normative Foundations of Critical Theory," *Political Theory*, 46.5 (2018), 782.

87. Nichols, "Progress, Empire," 782.

88. Nichols, "Progress, Empire," 784.

89. Nichols, "Progress, Empire," 784.

90. Said, *Culture and Imperialism*, 8, quoted in Nichols, "Progress, Empire," 784. In his response to Allen in this same symposium, Yves Winter reiterates this materialist critique of Said, arguing that, along with other postcolonial theorists, Said "sidelined" the material conditions of imperialism, transforming the concept of "the West" into a "cultural site." Yves Winter, "Formally Decolonized but Still Neocolonial?" *Political Theory*, 46.5 (2018), 788.

91. Nichols, "Progress, Empire," 782.

92. Ahmad, *In Theory*, 181.

93. Ahmad, *In Theory*, 35.

94. Fred Dallmayr, "The Politics of Nonidentity," 44.

95. Ahmad, *In Theory*, 98.

96. Ahmad, *In Theory*, 208.

97. Ahmad, *In Theory*, 175.

98. Ahmad, *In Theory*, 193.

99. Said, "Culture and Imperialism," 71.

100. Said and Mohr, *After the Last Sky*, 93.

101. Hamid Dabashi, "Edward Said's *Orientalism*," in *On Edward Said: Remembrance of Things Past* (New York: Haymarket, 2020), 192.

102. Edward Said, "Nationalism, Human Rights, and Interpretation," *Reflections on Exile and Other Essays*, 435 [originally "Nationalism, Human Rights, and Interpretation," *Raritan*, 12.3 (1993)].

103. Jonathan Arac, "Edward Said's *Culture and Imperialism*: A Symposium," *Social Text*, 40 (1994), 11.

104. Said, *Culture and Imperialism*, 324.

105. Said, *Culture and Imperialism*, 324.

106. Said, "Future of Criticism," 171.

107. Said, "Culture and Imperialism," 76.

108. Said, "Culture and Imperialism," 77.

109. Edward Said, "Intellectuals in the Post-Colonial World," *Salmagundi*, 70 (1986), 54; Said, *Humanism and Democratic Criticism*, 68.

110. Said, *Culture and Imperialism*, 216.

111. Said, *Culture and Imperialism*, 279.

112. Said, *Culture and Imperialism*, 216.

113. Said, *Culture and Imperialism*, 278.

114. Frantz Fanon, *Wretched of the Earth*, trans. Constance Farrington (New York: Grove Press, 1963), 58.

115. Said, *Culture and Imperialism*, 278.

116. Edward Said, "Michel Foucault, 1927–1984: In Memoriam," in *Reflections on Exile and Other Essays*, 197 [originally "Michel Foucault, 1927–1984: In Memoriam," *Raritan*, 4.2 (1984), 1–11].

117. Foucault, "The Subject and Power," 780.

118. Foucault, "Subject and Power," 789.

119. Said, *Culture and Imperialism*, 278.

120. Edward Said, "Traveling Theory Reconsidered," in *Reflections on Exile and Other Essays*, 447 [originally "Traveling Theory Reconsidered," in Robert M. Polhemus and Roger B. Henkle (eds.), *Critical Reconstructions: The Relationship of Fiction and Life* (Stanford, CA: Stanford University Press, 1994)].

121. Fanon, *Wretched of the Earth*, 5.

122. Said, "Traveling Theory Reconsidered," 448.

123. Said, "Opponents, Audiences," 128. Said's target in this essay is, in large part, new criticism.

124. Said, "Traveling Theory Reconsidered," 452.

125. Said, *Culture and Imperialism*, 216.

126. Said, *Culture and Imperialism*, 216.

127. Chatterjee, *Nationalist Thought*.

128. Mohandas Gandhi, *Hind Swaraj and Other Writings* (Cambridge, UK: Cambridge University Press, 2009), 28.

129. Chatterjee, *Nationalist Thought*, 38.

130. Said, *Culture and Imperialism*, 217.

131. Said, *Culture and Imperialism*, 217.

132. Said, *Culture and Imperialism*, 218.

133. Said, *Culture and Imperialism*, 268.

134. Said, *Culture and Imperialism*, 269.

135. Frantz Fanon, "Letter to the First Minister," in *Toward the African Revolution* (New York: Grove Press, 1994), 53; Fanon, *Wretched of the Earth*, 3.

136. Fanon, *Wretched of the Earth*, 9.

137. Fanon, *Wretched of the Earth*, 12.

138. Said, *Culture and Imperialism*, 270.

139. Fanon, *Wretched of the Earth*, 107, quoted in Said, *Culture and Imperialism*, 272.

140. Said, *Culture and Imperialism*, 273.

141. Fanon, *Wretched of the Earth*, 148, quoted in Said, *Culture and Imperialism*, 273.

142. Fanon, *Wretched of the Earth*, 62, quoted in Said, *Culture and Imperialism*, 269.

143. Fanon, *Wretched of the Earth*, 106.

144. Fanon, *Wretched of the Earth*, 106.

145. Edward Said, "Representing the Colonized: Anthropology's Interlocutors," *Critical Inquiry*, 15.2 (1989), 216.

146. Said, *Culture and Imperialism*, 269.

147. Aimé Césaire, *Discourse on Colonialism* (New York: Monthly Review Press, 2000), 45.

148. Césaire, *Discourse on Colonialism*, 45.

149. Césaire, *Discourse on Colonialism*, 73.

150. Robyn Kelly, Introduction to *Discourse on Colonialism* (New York: Monthly Review Press, 2000), 25.

151. Said, "Culture and Imperialism," 78.

152. Said, *Culture and Imperialism*, 321.

153. Said, *Culture and Imperialism*, 216.

154. Said, *Culture and Imperialism*, 282.

155. Said, *Culture and Imperialism*, 283.

156. Said, *Culture and Imperialism*, 285.

157. Said, "Opponents, Audiences," 119.

158. See, for instance, Habermas's idea of the "progressive development of international law." Jurgen Habermas, *The Divided West* (Cambridge, UK: Polity Press, 2006), 35.

159. Edward Said, "Always on Top," *London Review of Books*, 25.6 (March 2003), https://www.lrb.co.uk/the-paper/v25/n06/edward-said/always-on-top. Last accessed March 24, 2022.

160. Said, "Always on Top."

161. Ferguson makes this argument frequently, most extensively in *Colossus: The Rise and Fall of American Empire* (New York: Penguin, 2009).

162. Said, "Always on Top."

163. Said, "Always on Top."

164. Said, "Always on Top."

## BRIDGE

1. Said and Mohr, *After the Last Sky*, 130.

2. Said, "Reflections on Exile," 181.

3. Edward Said, *Representations of the Intellectual: The 1993 Reith Lectures* (New York: Vintage Books, 1996), 53.

4. Said, "Reflections on Exile," 184.

## 4

1. Edward Said, "The Public Role of Writers and Intellectuals," in *Humanism and Democratic Criticism* (New York; Columbia University Press, 2004), 141 [Originally published in *The Nation*, (September 17, 2001)].

2. Said, "Public Role of Writers," 142.

3. Edward Said, "The Public Role of Writers and Intellectuals," *Humanism and Democratic Criticism* (New York: Columbia University Press, 2004), 141.

4. Edward Said, "Introduction to Erich Auerbach's Mimesis," in *Humanism and Democratic Criticism* (New York: Columbia University Press, 2004), 91.

5. Said, "Public Role of Writers," 142–43.

6. Said, *Culture and Imperialism*, 336.

7. "The World, the Text, and the Critic" first appeared in Josue V. Harari (ed.), *Textual Strategies: Perspectives in Post-Structuralist Criticism* (Ithaca, NY: Cornell University Press, 1979), 161–88. Throughout this chapter, as in earlier chapters, I refer to the version in Said's collection of essays *The World, the Text, and the Critic*.

8. Edward Said, "Interview With Edward Said," *Diacritics*, 6.3 (1976), 37.

9. Edward Said, "Orientalism 25 Years Later: Worldly Humanism v. the Empire-Builders," *Counterpunch*, August 5, 2015 (2003), http://www.counterpunch.org/2003/08/05/orientalism/. Last accessed March 24, 2022.

10. Roland Barthes, "The Death of the Author," in *Image Music Text*, new ed. (London: Fontana Press, 1987), 146.

11. Barthes, "Death of the Author," 146.

12. Julia Kristeva, "Word, Dialogue, and Novel," in Leon S. Roudiez (ed.), *Desire in Language: A Semiotic Approach to Literature and Art* (New York: Columbia University Press, 1980/1977), 65.

13. Kristeva first used the term *inter-textuality* in "Word, Dialogue and Novel" (1966) and in "The Bounded Text" (1966–67), both in *Desire in Language.* Derrida argues in *Of Grammatology* that the "concept of history itself" is located "within a logocentric epoch." [Jacques Derrida, *Of Grammatology*, trans. Gayatri Chakravorty Spivak (Baltimore: Johns Hopkins University Press, 1976), 5]. For more on Derrida and the death of the author, see Seán Burke, *The Death and Return of the Author* (Edinburgh, UK: Edinburgh University Press, 2008).

14. Said, "On Originality," in *The World, the Text, and the Critic*, 130 [originally, "On Originality," in Monroe Engle (ed.), *Uses of Literature* (Cambridge, MA: Harvard University Press, 1973), 49–65].

15. Said, "World, the Text," 35.

16. Said, *Culture and Imperialism*, 259.

17. See, for instance, J. G. A. Pocock, "The History of Political Thought: A Methodological Inquiry," *Political Thought and History: Essays on Theory and Method* (Cambridge, UK: Cambridge University Press, 2009), and Quentin Skinner, *Liberty Before Liberalism* (Cambridge, UK: Cambridge University Press, 1998).

18. For an overview of the "linguistic turn," see John E. Toews, "Intellectual History after the Linguistic Turn: The Autonomy of Meaning and the Irreducibility of Experience," *American Historical Review*, 92.4 (1987), 879–907.

19. Dabashi argues that an intellectual genealogy of *Orientalism* "can in fact completely bypass Michel Foucault and trace its origin to Quentin Skinner's philosophical hermeneutics on political theory and the link he proposes between social meaning and social action." Hamid Dabashi, "On Exilic Intellectuals (1994)," in *On Edward Said: Remembrances of Things Past* (New York: Haymarket, 2020), 97. See Tully's reflections on the overlap of thinkers who have most influenced his thought (Skinner, Foucault, Said) in James Tully, "Political Philosophy as a Critical Activity," *Political Theory*, 30.4 (2002), 535. See also the linkages to the Cambridge School that Abass Manoochehri makes in "Edward Said: An Emancipatory Narrative," *International Journal of Humanities and Social Science*, 6.10 (2016), 146.

20. Pocock, "History of Political Thought," 3. Pocock argues that the reason we congregate our intellectual interests around particular thinkers has less to do with the timeless truths their works reveal or the clearly superior quality of their insights and more to do with the "social and intellectual traditions in which we conduct our thinking." Pocock, "History of Political Thought," 4.

21. Ian Hall, "The History of International Thought and International Relations Theory: From Context to Interpretation," *International Relations*, 31.3 (2017), 254.

22. For examples of thoughtful, contextualist-oriented scholarship on non-European political thought, see Juan Pablo Scarfi, *The Hidden History of International Law in the Americas* (Oxford, UK: Oxford University Press, 2017), and Banu Turnaoğlu, *The Formation of Turkish Republicanism* (Princeton, NJ: Princeton University Press, 2017).

23. For instance, David Armitage, *The Ideological Origins of the British Empire* (Cambridge, UK: Cambridge University Press, 2000); Sankar Muthu, *Enlightenment Against Empire* (Princeton, NJ: Princeton University Press, 2003); Jennifer Pitts, *A Turn to Empire* (Princeton, NJ: Princeton University Press, 2005).

24. Duncan Bell, *Reordering the World: Essays on Liberalism and Empire* (Princeton, NJ: Princeton University Press, 2016); Karuna Mantena, *Alibis of Empire* (Princeton, NJ: Princeton University Press, 2010).

25. See, for instance, Karuna Mantena, "Gandhi's Critique of the State: Sources, Contexts, Conjunctures," *Modern Intellectual History*, 9.3 (2012), 535–63. See also Duncan Bell (ed.), *Empire, Race, and Global Justice* (Cambridge, UK: Cambridge University Press, 2019), and Adom Getachew and Jennifer Pitts, "Democracy and Empire," in Jennifer Pitts and Getachew (eds.), *W. E. B. Du Bois's International Writings* (Cambridge, UK: Cambridge University Press, 2021).

26. Said, *Culture and Imperialism*, xxi; Edward Said, "Opponents, Audience, Constituencies, and Communities," *Critical Inquiry*, 9.1 (1982), 119.

27. See Fred Dallmayr, "Beyond Monologue: For a Comparative Political Theory," *Perspectives on Politics*, 2.2 (2004), 249–57, and Leigh Jenco, "Recentering Political Theory: The Promise of Mobile Locality," *Cultural Critique*, 79.1 (2011), 27–59.

28. Bruce Robbins, "American Intellectuals and Middle East Politics: An Interview with Edward W. Said," (1988), Viswanathan, ed., *Power, Politics, and Culture*, 340..

29. Interview with Gauri Viswanathan, 1996, in Edward Said, "Language, History, and the Production of Knowledge," in *Power, Politics, and Culture*, 263.

30. Edward Said, "Secular Criticism," in *The World, the Text, and the Critic*, 25 [originally, Edward Said, "Secular Criticism," *Raritan: A Quarterly Review*, 2.3 (1983), 1–26].

31. Said, "Interview," *Diacritics* 39.

32. Ashcroft and Ahluwalia, *Edward Said: The Paradox of Identity*, 42.

33. Said, *Culture and Imperialism*, 259.

34. Said, "American Intellectuals," 335.

35. Edward Said, "Representing the Colonized: Anthropology's Interlocutors," *Critical Inquiry*, 15.2 (1989), 212.

36. Rajagopalan Radhakrishnan, "Edward Said's *Culture and Imperialism:* A Symposium," *Social Text*, 40 (1994), 18.

37. Edward Said, "Identity, Authority, and Freedom: The Potentate and the Traveler," *boundary 2*, 21.3 (1994), 11.

38. Edward Said, "Humanism's Sphere," in *Humanism and Democratic Criticism*, 11.

39. Edward Said, "Vico: Autodidact and Humanist," *Centennial Review*, 11.3 (1967), 352.

40. Edward Said, *Beginnings* (New York: Basic Books, 1975), 349.

41. Said, "Humanism's Sphere," 6; Edward Said, "Criticism, Culture, and Performance," in *Power, Politics, and Culture*, 127; Edward Said, "The Return to Philology," in *Humanism and Democratic Criticism* (New York: Columbia University Press, 2004), 80.

42. Said, "Opponents, Audiences," 9.

43. *Humanism and Democratic Criticism* also includes a version of "The Public Role of Writers and Intellectuals," updated to reflect the events of September 11 and the imminent war with Iraq.

44. Stathis Gourgouris, "The Late Style of Edward Said / ستاثيس جورجوريس," *Alif: Journal of Comparative Poetics*, 25 (2004), 40.

45. James Pannero, "Palestinian Authority: Culture Wars and the Legacy of Edward Said," *Claremont Review of Books*, 5.1 (2004/2005), https://claremontreviewofbooks.com/palestinian-authority/

46. Edward Said, *Orientalism* (New York: Penguin, 1995), 339.

47. Said, "Humanism's Sphere," 8.

48. Said, "Humanism's Sphere," 10.

49. Said, "Humanism's Sphere," 11.

50. Said, "Humanism's Sphere," 11.

51. Said, "Humanism's Sphere," 11.

52. See, for instance, and Allan Bloom, *The Closing of the American Mind* (New York: Simon & Schuster, 1987), or one of the eleven editions of the *Western Heritage* textbooks coedited by Donald Kagan, Steven Ozment, Frank M. Turner, and Alison Frank (New York: Macmillan, 1979–2013).

53. Edward Said, "Intellectuals in the Postcolonial World," *Salmagundi*, 70.71 (1986), 54.

54. Said, "Return to Philology," 68.

55. Said, "The Art of Displacement: Mona Hatoum's Logic of Irreconcilables," 109.

56. Said, "The Politics of Knowledge," in *Reflections on Exile*, 377 [originally in *Raritan*, 11.1 (1991)].

57. Said, "Politics of Knowledge," 377.

58. Said, "Identity, Authority, and Freedom," 16.

59. Said, "Always on Top," 17.

60. Aimé Césaire, *Discourse on Colonialism* (New York; Monthly Review Press, 2000), 75.

61. Ella Myers, *Worldly Ethics: Democratic Politics and Care for the World* (Durham, NC: Duke University Press, 2013), 1.

62. Judith Butler, *Precarious Life: The Powers of Mourning and Violence* (New York: Verso Books, 2004).

63. Richard Cohen, Introduction, in Emanuel Levinas, *Humanism of the Other* (Urbana: University of Illinois Press, 2006), ix; Emmanuel Levinas, "Useless Suffering," trans. Richard Cohen, in Robert Bernasconi and David Wood (eds.), *The Provocation of Levinas: Rethinking the Other*, (New York: Routledge, 1988), 159.

64. Bonnie Honig, "Antigone's Two Laws: Greek Tragedy and the Politics of Humanism," *New Literary History*, 41.1 (2010), 1.

65. Michael Goodhart, "Constructing Dignity: Human Rights as a Praxis of Egalitarian Freedom," *Journal of Human Rights*, 17.4 (2018), 404. See also Or Rosenboim's important exploration of the spiritual (explicitly Catholic) origins of the human-rights-as-dignity argument made by scholars and theologians in the 1940s, particularly chapter 6, "Writing a World Constitution," in *The Emergence of Globalism: Visions of World Order in Britain and the United States, 1939–1950* (Princeton, NJ: Princeton University Press, 2017).

66. Michael Ignatieff, *Human Rights as Politics and Idolatry* (Princeton, NJ: Princeton University Press, 2001), 88.

67. For more on Ignatieff's foreign policy as liberal imperialism, see Jeanne Morefield, *Empires without Imperialism: Anglo-American Decline and the Politics of Deflection* (Oxford, UK: Oxford University Press, 2014), chap. 6. Ignatieff was one of the architects of the Responsibility to Protect (R2P) Doctrine. See International Commission on Intervention and State Sovereignty, *The Responsibility to Protect: Report of the International Commission on Intervention and State Sovereignty* (Ottawa, ON: International Development Research Centre, 2001). For a razor-sharp, Saidian-influenced critique of Ignatieff and R2P, see Jessica Whyte, "Always on Top: The Responsibility to Protect and the Persistence of Colonialism," in Jyotsna Singh and David Kim (eds.), *The Postcolonial World* (New York: Routledge, 2016).

68. Said, *Humanism and Democratic Criticism*, 142–43.

69. Said, "Humanism's Sphere," 12.

70. Thus failing, in Valdez's words, to "consider intellectual resources and political practices from outside the West." Valdez, *Toward Transnational Cosmopolitanism*, 4.

71. Edward Said, "The Changing Basis of Humanistic Study and Practice," 47.

72. Michael Ignatieff, "Democracy Versus Democracy: The Populist Challenge to Liberal Democracy," *LSE Public Policy Review* (July 20, 2020), https://ppr.lse.ac.uk/articles/10.31389/lseppr.2/. Last accessed March 25, 2022.

73. Benjamin Novak, "Michael Ignatieff on the Crisis of Universalism and the Return of the Leviathan," *Budapest Beacon*, January 16, 2016, https://budapestbeacon.com/michael-ignatieff-on-the-crisis-of-universalism/. Last accessed March 25, 2022.

74. Michael Ignatieff, "The New World Disorder," *New York Review of Books*, September 25, 2014, https://www.nybooks.com/articles/2014/09/25/new-world-disorder/. Last accessed March 25, 2022.

75. Michael Ignatieff, "American Empire: The Burden," *New York Times Magazine*, January 5, 2003, https://www.nytimes.com/2003/01/05/magazine/the-american-empire-the-burden.html. Last accessed March 25, 2022.

76. Michael Ignatieff, "Barbarians at the Gate?" *New York Review of Books*, February 28, 2002, http://www.nybooks.com/articles/archives/2002/feb/28/barbarians-at-the-gate/. Last accessed March 25, 2022.

77. Michael Ignatieff, *Human Rights as Politics and Idolatry* (Princeton, NJ: Princeton University Press, 2003); Michael Ignatieff, "The Seductiveness of Moral Disgust," *Index on Censorship*, 24.5 (1995), 22–38.

78. In 2004, Michael Ward posted a "Create Your Own Thomas Friedman Op-Ed Column" spoof on the website McSweeney's in the form of a Mad Lib that became an instant classic. It begins, not surprisingly, with "Last week's events in [*country in the news*] were truly historic, although we may not know for years or even decades what their final meaning is." Michael Ward, "Create Your Own Thomas Friedman Op-Ed Column," *McSweeney's*, April 28, 2004, https://www.mcsweeneys.net/articles/create-your-own-thomas-friedman-op-ed-column. Last accessed March 26, 2022.

79. Michael Ignateiff, "The Challenge of the Challenges of American Imperial Power," *Naval War College Review*, 56.2 (2003), 53.

80. Michael Ignatieff, "The Duty to Protect Is Still Urgent," *New York Times*, September 13, 2013, https://www.nytimes.com/2013/09/14/opinion/the-duty-to-protect-still-urgent.html. Last accessed March 16, 2022.

81. Ignatieff, "Barbarians at the Gate?"

82. Just before the war with Iraq in 2003, Ignatieff insisted that our "contemporary situation in global politics has no precedent since the age of the later Roman emperors." Ignatieff, "Barbarians at the Gate?"

83. Ignatieff, "New World Disorder."

84. Daniel Neep, *Occupying Syria Under the French Mandate Insurgency, Space and State Formation* (Cambridge, UK: Cambridge University Press, 2012). See also Priya Satia, "The Defense of Inhumanity: Air Control and the British Idea of Arabia," *American Historical Review*, 111.1 (2006), 16–51.

85. See, for instance, Ayse Tekdal Fildis's work on the destabilizing French imperial practices in Syria in "The Troubles in Syria: Spawned by French Divide and Rule," *Middle East Policy Council*, 28.4 (2011). See also Rashid Khalidi, "The Persistence of the Sykes-Picot Frontiers in the Middle East," *London Review of International Law*, 4. 2 (2016).

86. Edward Said, "The Intellectuals and the War," in *Power, Politics, and Culture*, 363 [originally in *Middle East Report*, 171 (1991), 15–20].

87. Edward Said, "Orientalism 25 Years Later."

88. See Fouad Ajami, "Two Faces, One Terror," *Wall Street Journal*, November 11, 2002, https://www.wsj.com/articles/SB1036979367456776108. Last accesed March 26, 2022. See also, Ignatieff, "American Empire."

89. Homi Bhabha, "Adagio," in Homi Bhabha and W. J. T. Mitchell (eds.), *Edward Said: Continuing the Conversation* (Chicago: University of Chicago Press, 2005), 12.

90. Edward Said, "Orientalism 25 Years Later."

91. Said, "Public Role of Writers," 142–43.

92. Said, "Return to Philology," 61.

93. Said, *Representations of the Intellectual*, 102.

94. Said, "Permission to Narrate (1984)," in *The Politics of Dispossession*, 250. "Israel's invasion in 1982 caused 19,085 deaths and left 31,915 wounded, overwhelmingly civilians." See *Targeting Homes, Shelters and Shelter Seekers During Operation Cast Lead in the Context of Israeli Military Practice* (Cairo, Egypt: Housing and Land Rights Network, Habitat International Coalition to the UN Fact-Finding Mission on the Gaza Conflict, July 29, 2009), 21, http://www.hlrn.org/img/violation/Submission.pdf. Last accessed March 26, 2022. See also Rashid Khalidi, *Under Siege: PLO Decisionmaking During the 1982 War* (New York: Columbia University Press, 2014).

95. Said, "Permission to Narrate," 247.

96. Said, "Permission to Narrate," 248. The ease with which the state of Israel (led by the reactionary Trump-clone, Benjamin Netanyahu) has continued to employ this logic of "self-defense" since Said wrote these words is truly arresting. See Bashir Abu-Manneh, "As an Occupier, Israel Has No Right to 'Self-Defense,'" *Jacobin*, May 16, 2021, https://jacobinmag.com/2021/05/israel-palestine-right-to-self-defense-justification-for-war-article-51-un-charter. Last accessed March 26, 2022.

97. Said, "Permission to Narrate," 250.

98. Said, "Permission to Narrate," 254.

99. For a theoretically rich and political powerful analysis of the way Palestinian life is "ordered" through checkpoints, see Hagar Kotef, *Movement and the Ordering of Freedom: On Liberal Governances of Mobility* (Durham, NC: Duke University Press, 2015).

100. Dennis Ross, "Stop Giving Palestinians a Pass," *New York Times*, January 4, 2015, https://www.nytimes.com/2015/01/05/opinion/stop-giving-palestinians-a-pass.html. Last accessed March 25, 2022.

101. Joe Biden's equally chilling, "unwavering support" for Israel's "right to defend itself"—despite the right-wing Israeli incursions and Palestinian evictions that created the conditions for this current conflict in the first place, despite the massive

military imbalance, despite the disproportionate death of Palestinian civilians—suggests that this shocking level of deflective unseeing remains intact among a large section of the US military-industrial establishment. See White House Briefing, "Readout of President Joseph R. Biden, Jr. Call With Prime Minister Benjamin Netanyahu of Israel," May 12, 2021, https://www.whitehouse.gov/briefing-room/statements-releases/2021/05/19/readout-of-president-joseph-r-biden-jr-call-with-prime-minister-benjamin-netanyahu-of-israel-5/. Last accessed March 26, 2022.

102. Said, "Return to Philology," 83.

103. Edward Said, "Sanctum of the Strong," in *The Politics of Dispossession*, 275.

104. Said, *Orientalism*, 57.

105. Said, *Orientalism*, 283.

106. Said, *Humanism and Democratic Criticism*, 142.

107. Indeed, as Rashid Khalidi argues, Zionism itself—which was "for two decades the coddled stepchild of British colonialism"—later successfully and ironically rebranded itself as an "anticolonial movement." Rashid Khalidi, *The One Hundred Years War Against Palestine: A History of Settler Colonialism and Resistance, 1917–2017* (New York: Metropolitan Books, 2020), 13.

108. Edward Said, *The Question of Palestine* (New York: Vintage Books, 1979), 13–15.

109. As he puts it, the Balfour Declaration is an imperialist document because it was "made a) by a European power, b) about a non-European territory, c) in flat disregard of both the presence and wishes of the native majority residents in the territory, and d) it took the form of a promise about this same territory to another foreign group, so that this foreign group might, quite literally, *make* this territory a national home for the Jewish people." Said, *Question of Palestine*, 15.

110. Edward Said, "Traveling Theory Reconsidered," in *Reflections on Exile*, 451 [originally "Traveling Theory Reconsidered," in Robert M. Polhemus and Roger B. Henkle (eds.), *Critical Reconstructions: The Relationship of Fiction and Life* (Stanford, CA: Stanford University Press, 1994)].

111. Said, *Culture and Imperialism*, xiii.

112. Charles Mills, "White Ignorance," in *Black Rights, White Wrongs: The Critique of Racial Liberalism* (Oxford, UK: Oxford University Press, 2017).

113. See Michael Walzer, *On Toleration* (London: Yale University Press, 1997), and Michael Walzer, *Thick and Thin: Moral Argument at Home and Abroad* (Notre Dame, IN: Notre Dame Press, 1994).

114. Michael Walzer, *Just and Unjust Wars: A Moral Argument With Historical Illustrations* (New York: Basic Books, 2006); Walzer, *On Toleration*; Michael Walzer, *The Paradox of Liberation* (New Haven, CT: Yale University Press, 2015); Michael Walzer, "Political Action: The Problem of Dirty Hands," *Philosophy and Public Affairs*, 2 (1973).

115. Walzer has, for instance, penned more than three hundred articles for *Dissent*.

116. The Edward Said Papers in the Archival Collections of Columbia University, Box 119, Folder 14, Series II.2: "Response – Michael Walzer – Exodus and Revolution, 1986."

117. Michael Walzer and Edward W. Said, "An Exchange: 'Exodus and Revolution,'" *Grand Street*, 5.4 (1986), 246.

118. Walzer and Said, "Exchange," 246.

119. Edward Said, "Michael Walzer's 'Exodus and Revolution': A Canaanite Reading," *Grand Street*, 5.2 (1986), 90.

120. Michael Walzer, *Exodus and Revolution* (New York: Basic Books, 1985), 25.

121. Said, "Michael Walzer's 'Exodus and Revolution,'" 89.

122. Said, "Michael Walzer's 'Exodus and Revolution,'" 89.

123. Said, "Michael Walzer's 'Exodus and Revolution,'" 89.

124. Said, "Michael Walzer's 'Exodus and Revolution,'" 87, 89.

125. Said, "Michael Walzer's 'Exodus and Revolution,'" 93.

126. Said, "Michael Walzer's 'Exodus and Revolution,'" 89.

127. Said, "Michael Walzer's 'Exodus and Revolution,'" 106.

128. Said, "Michael Walzer's 'Exodus and Revolution,'" 101.

129. Said, "Michael Walzer's 'Exodus and Revolution,'" 98.

130. Walzer and Said, "Exchange," 253.

131. Walzer and Said, "Exchange," 253.

132. See Walzer's response to Andrew March's mild criticism in "Islamism and the Left: An Exchange," *Dissent*, Winter 2015, https://www.dissentmagazine.org/article/islamism-and-left-exchange. Last accessed March 25, 2022.

133. Michael Walzer, "What the Protesters Need to Win," *Tablet*, June 3, 2020, https://www.tabletmag.com/sections/news/articles/michael-walzer-race-protests. Last accessed March 25, 2022.

134. Michael Walzer, "A Note on Racial Capitalism," *Dissent*, July 29, 2020, https://www.dissentmagazine.org/online_articles/a-note-on-racial-capitalism. Last accessed March 26, 2022.

135. Olúfẹ́mi O. Táíwò and Liam Kofi Bright, "A Response to Michael Walzer," *Dissent*, August 7, 2020, https://www.dissentmagazine.org/online_articles/a-reply-to-olufemi-o-taiwo-and-liam-kofi-bright. Last accessed March 26, 2022.

136. Medea Benjamin and Nicolas J. S. Davies, "The Staggering Death Toll in Iraq," *Salon*, March 10, 2018, https://www.salon.com/2018/03/19/the-staggering-death-toll-in-iraq_partner/. Last accessed March 26, 2022.

137. See Ignatieff's comments on this panel in Christina Pazzanese, "Cruel Summer: Violence in the Middle East and What It Means for the Future," *Harvard Gazette*, September 11, 2014, http://news.harvard.edu/gazette/story/2014/09/cruel-summer/. Last accessed March 25, 2022.

138. See Rogers Smith, "The Stories We Tell Ourselves," *PS: Political Science and Politics*, 51.4 (2018), 895–99, and Rogers Smith, *That Is Not Who We Are! Populism and Peoplehood* (New Haven, CT: Yale University Press, 2020).

139. Liberalism, Walzer commented in the spring of 2020, "determines not who we are but how we are who we are—how we enact our ideological commitments." Michael Walzer, "What It Means to Be a Liberal," *Dissent*, Spring 2020, https://www.dissentmagazine.org/article/what-it-means-to-be-liberal. Last accessed March 26, 2022.

140. Jeffrey Isaac, "It's Happening Here and Now: Thoughts on the Recent Immigration Detentions and William E. Connolly's 'Aspirational Fascism,'" *Public Seminar*, June 25, 2018, https://publicseminar.org/2018/06/its-happening-here-and-now/. Last accessed March 26, 2022.

141. John Ikenberry, "The Plot Against American Foreign Policy: Can the Liberal Order Survive?" *Foreign Affairs,* 96.3 (May/June, 2017), 2.

142. William Connolly, *Aspirational Fascism: The Study for Multifaceted Democracy Under Trumpism* (Minneapolis: University of Minnesota Press, 2017).

143. From as early as 2015, numerous media outlets have taken up the *Mein Kampf* story, including the *Independent* (https://www.independent.co.uk/news/world/americas/us-politics/donald-trump-adolf-hitler-books-bedside-cabinet-ex-wife-ivana-trump-vanity-fair-1990-a7639041.html, last accessed March 26, 2022), Snopes (https://www.snopes.com/fact-check/trump-hitler-mein-kampf/, last accessed March 26, 2022), and the *Guardian* (https://www.theguardian.com/commentisfree/2018/oct/30/trump-borrows-tricks-of-fascism-pittsburgh, last accessed March 26, 2022). For Trump and the Frankfurt School, see Henry Giroux, "Donald Trump and Neo-Fascism in America," *Arena Magazine*, 104 (2016); Douglas Kellner, *American Nightmare: Donald Trump, Media Spectacle, and Authoritarian Populism* (Boston: Sense, 2016); and Alex Ross, "The Frankfurt School Knew Trump Was Coming," *New Yorker*, December 5, 2016.

144. See Alison Griswold, "'The Origins of Totalitarianism,' Hannah Arendt's Definitive Guide to How Tyranny Begins, Has Sold Out on Amazon," *Quartz*, January 29, 2017, https://qz.com/897517/the-origins-of-totalitarianism-hannah-arendts-defining-work-on-tyranny-is-out-of-stock-on-amazon/. Last accessed March 26, 2022.

145. Hannah Arendt, *Eichmann in Jerusalem* (New York: Penguin Books, 2006), 252.

146. Hannah Arendt, *The Origins of Totalitarianism* (New York: Meridian Books, 1958), 155.

147. Hannah Arendt, *The Human Condition* (Chicago: University of Chicago Press, 1958), 28.

148. Arendt, *Human Condition*, 115.

149. Arendt, *Human Condition*, 53.

150. See Michiel Bot's translation of this entry, entitled "The National Principle" (1952), *The Hannah Arendt Center for Politics and Humanities*, November 24, 2014, https://hac.bard.edu/amor-mundi/the-nation-principle-2014-11-24.

151. Arendt, *Origins of Totalitarianism*, 94.

152. Hannah Arendt, *Thinking Without a Banister: Essays in Understanding, 1953–1975* (New York: Shocken Press, 2018), v.

153. Arendt contrasted her own banister-less method with the idea of "groundless thinking" in *Thinking Without a Banister*, 473.

154. See Arendt on "Occidental antiquity," see *Human Condition*, 27.

155. Hannah Arendt, *Between Past and Future* (New York: Viking Press, 1968), 28–29.

156. Myers describes "care for the world" as a "world-centered democratic ethos" that "aims to incite and sustain collective care for conditions, care that is expressed in associative efforts to affect particular 'worldly things.'" Myers, *Worldly Ethics*, 2.

157. Arendt, *Human Condition*, 71.

158. "Westerners have assumed the integrity and the inviolability of their cultural masterpieces, their scholarship, their worlds of discourse; the rest of the world stands petitioning for attention at our windowsill." Said, *Culture and Imperialism*, 259. "In this context the interlocutor is someone who has perhaps been found clamoring on the doorstep." Said, "Representing the Colonized," 210.

159. Said, *Culture and Imperialism,* 332.

160. Said, *Culture and Imperialism*, 332.

161. Said, "Intellectuals in the Postcolonial World," 54.

162. Said, "Politics of Knowledge," 382.

163. Said, *Culture and Imperialism*, xx.

164. Edward Said, "An Unresolved Paradox," *MLA Newsletter*, 31.2 (1999), 3.

165. Said, "The One-State Solution"; Said, *Culture and Imperialism*, 334; Edward Said, "Orientalism Once More," *Development and Change*, 35.5 (2004), 877 (reprint of a speech given by Said "on the occasion of the awarding of the degree of Doctor Honoris Causa at the Academic Ceremony on the 50th Anniversary of the Institute of Social Studies," the Hague, May 21, 2003).

166. Edward Said, "Orientalism Reconsidered," *Cultural Critique*, 1 (1985), 94. See, for instance, Lisa Lowe on the colonial "intimacy" of African and Asian labor in the British West Indies, communities of "slaves, indentured and mixed free peoples living together." Lisa Lowe, "The Worldliness of Intimacy," in Ned Curthoys and Debjani Ganguly (eds.), *Edward Said: Legacy of a Public Intellectual* (Melbourne: Melbourne University Press, 2007), 135.

167. Said, "The Changing Bases of Humanistic Study and Practice," in *Humanism and Democratic Criticism*, 50.

168. Paul A. Bové, "Hope and Reconciliation: A Review of Edward W. Said," *boundary 2*, 20.2 (1993), 268.

169. Said, *Culture and Imperialism*, 274.

170. Said, "Unresolved Paradox," 3.

171. Gurminder Bambra and John Holmwood, "Colonialism, Postcolonialism and the Liberal Welfare State," *New Political Economy*, 23.5 (2018), 581.

172. Stuart Schrader, *Badges Without Borders: How Global Counterinsurgency Transformed American Policing* (Berkeley: University of California Press, 2019), 195.

173. Said, *Culture and Imperialism*, 54, 216.

174. Bruce Robbins, "American Intellectuals and Middle East Politics: An Interview with Edward W. Said," (1988), Viswanathan, ed., *Power, Politics, and Culture*, 340.

175. Interview with Jacqueline Rose, 1997–98, in Edward Said, "Returning to Ourselves," in *Power, Politics, and Culture*, 425–26.

176. Said, *Orientalism*, 240.

177. Edward Said, "Truth and Reconciliation," *Al-Ahram Weekly*, 412 (January 20, 1999).

178. Edward W. Said, "Invention, Memory, and Place," *Critical Inquiry* 26.2 (2000), 191.

179. Said, "Invention, Memory, and Place," 192.

180. Said, "Invention, Memory, and Place," 192.

181. Said, "One-State Solution."

182. Judith Butler, "Versions of Bi-nationalism in Said and Buber," in Rosi Braidotti and Paul Gilroy (eds.), *Conflicting Humanities* (London: Bloomsbury 2016), 189.

183. Said, "Public Role of Writers," 143. The world itself remains saturated with examples of such irreconcilable histories and experiences, often generated through precisely the colonial and imperial practices that bring societies, communities, and cultures together in the first place. In the pervasive settler states of Canada, Australia, New Zealand, and the United States, for instance, a history of systematic violence against Indigenous people not only dramatically reduced their numbers and weakened their cultures, but it also created a political present in which calls for indigeneity and autonomy often work directly at odds with a politics of recognition and liberal multiculturalism. See, for instance, Dirk Moses, "Official Apologies, Reconciliation, and Settler Colonialism: Australian Indigenous Alterity and Political Agency," *Citizenship Studies*, 15. 2 (2011), 145–59; Audra Simpson, "Whither Settler Colonialism?" *Settler Colonial Studies*, 6.4 (2016), 438–45; and Lorenzo Veracini, *Settler Colonialism a Theoretical Overview* (New York: Palgrave, 2010).

184. Said, "Public Role of Writers," 143.

185. Edward Said, "Humanism and Heroism," *PMLA*, 115.3 (2000), 290.

186. Chantal Mouffe, *For a Left Populism* (London: Verso, 2018).

187. Chantal Mouffe, "Carl Schmitt and the Paradox of Liberal Democracy," *Canadian Journal of Law and Jurisprudence*, 10.1 (1997), 25.

188. One sees something similar in Connolly's reading of pluralism. At the end of the day, he argues, no matter how much theorists like Agamben, Hardt, and Negri may teach us about the "ambiguities circulating through state sovereignty," democratic politics still entails a foundational "positional respect" for the state and its institutions. William Connolly, *Pluralism* (Durham, NC: Duke University Press, 2005), 146.

189. Said, "Return to Philology," 68; Edward Said, "The Satanic Verses and Democratic Freedoms," *Black Scholar*, 20.2 (1989), 18.

190. See James Tully, "Deparochializing Political Theory and Beyond: A Dialogue Approach to Comparative Political Thought," *Journal of World Philosophies* 1 (2016): 51–74, and James Tully, "On Global Citizenship," in *On Global Citizenship: James Tully in Dialogue* (London: Bloomsbury, 2014).

191. Said, *Culture and Imperialism*, 48. For more on Antonio Gramsci's reading of "collective will," see "The Modern Prince," in Quintin Hoare and Geoffrey Nowell Smith (eds.), *Selections from the Prison Notebooks of Antonio Gramsci* (London: Lawrence and Wishart, 1971), especially 123.

192. Said, "Orientalism Once More," 877.

193. Said, "Return to Philology," 83.

**5**

1. Edward Said, "Representing the Colonized: Anthropology's Interlocutors," *Critical Inquiry*, 15.2 (1989), 211, 210.

2. Said, "Representing the Colonized," 217. The allusion comes from William Butler Yeats's 1929 poem "Blood and Moon." In this late poem, Yeats ruminates on the way poets, artists, and philosophers build "towers" to concepts that preoccupy them, that lift them out (and eventually bring them back) "to mankind." Oliver Goldsmith was a late-eighteenth-century Anglo-Irish playwright and novelist with a particular penchant for beautiful, carefully crafted prose. Thus did Yeats describe him as "deliberately sipping at the honey-pot of his mind." See W. B. Yeats, "Blood and the Moon," in *The Winding Stair* (New York: Scribner Books, 2011).

3. Said, "Representing the Colonized," 215.

4. Edward Said, "The Public Role of Writers and Intellectuals," *Nation, Language, and the Ethics of Translation*, eds Sandra Bermann, Michael Wood, 24.

5. Said, *Representations of the Intellectual*, xvii.

6. Said, "Representing the Colonized," 225.

7. Joesph Masad, "The Intellectual Life of Edward Said," *Journal of Palestine Studies*, 33.3 (2004), 7.

8. See BBC Radio 4, webpage "About the Reith Lectures,": https://www.bbc.co.uk/programmes/articles/4ZTNLKgrG2mSzfgC1ZYlNmV/about-the-reith-lectures (last accessed March 23, 2022).

9. Said, *Representations of the Intellectual*, x.

10. Curthoys and Ganguly, Introduction, *Edward Said: The Legacy of a Public Intellectual*, 1.

11. Timothy Brennan, "Place of Mind, Occupied Lands: Edward Said and Philology," *Arab World Geographer/Le Géographe du monde arabe*, 7.1–2 (2004), 49.

12. Said, *Representations of the Intellectual*, 11.

13. Edward Said, "The Public Role of Writers and Intellectuals," in Sandra Bermann and Michael Wood (eds.), *Nation, Language, and the Ethics of Translation* (Princeton, NJ: Princeton University Press, 2005), 16.

14. Said, "Public Role of Writers and Intellectuals," in Bermann and Woods, *Nation, Language*, 16.

15. See, for instance, Jurgen Habermas, *The Structural Transformation of the Public Sphere* (New York: Polity Press, 1992), and Jurgen Habermas, *Theory of Communicative Action*, Vol. 1: *Reason and the Rationalization of Society* (New York: Polity Press, 1986).

16. Jurgen Habermas, *Knowledge and Human Interests* (London: Heinemann, 1972), 9. See also Rainer Forst, *The Right to Justification* (New York: Columbia University Press, 2007).

17. Michael Freeden, *Ideologies and Political Theory: A Conceptual Approach* (Oxford, UK: Clarendon Press, 1996), 1.

18. See Alan Finlayson and James Martin, "'It Ain't What You Say . . . ': British Political Studies and the Analysis of Speech and Rhetoric," *British Politics*, 3.4 (2008), 445–64; Freeden, *Ideologies and Political Theory*; Ernesto Laclau, "Ideology

and Post-Marxism," *Journal of Political Ideologies*, 11.2 (2006), 103–14; and Richard Shorten, "Why Bad Books Matter: Past and Future Directions for Understanding Reactionary Ideology," *Politics, Religion, and Ideology*, 20.4 (2019), 401–22.

19. Michael Freeden, "Practising Ideology and Ideological Practices," *Political Studies*, 48.2 (2000), 302, 320.

20. Edward Said, *Orientalism* (New York: Penguin, 1995), 240, 22.

21. Said, *Orientalism*, 23.

22. Neeladri Bhattacharya, Suvir Kaul, and Ania Loomba, "Edward Said: In Conversation with Neeladri Bhattacharya, Suvir Kaul, and Ania Loomba, New Delhi, 16 December 1997," *Interventions: International Journal of Postcolonial Studies*, 1.1 (1998), 92.

23. Edward Said, "Interview With Edward Said," *Diacritics*, 6.3 (1976), 47.

24. Said, "Interview," *Diacritics*, 47.

25. Said, "Interview," *Diacritics*, 47.

26. Edward Said, "Orientalism Once More," *Development and Change*.

27. Edward Said, *Covering Islam: How the Media and the Experts Determine How We See the Rest of the World* (New York: Vintage Books, 1997), xi–xii.

28. Edward Said, "Orientalism 25 Years Later: Worldly Humanism v. the Empire-Builders," *Counterpunch*, August 4, 2003, http://www.counterpunch.org/2003/08/05/orientalism/

29. Said, *Orientalism*, 322.

30. Edward Said, Introduction, Edward Said and Christopher Hitchens (eds.), *Blaming the Victims: Spurious Scholarship and the Palestinian Questions* (London: Verso, 1988), 8.

31. Robert Vitalis, *White World Order, Black Power Politics: The Birth of American International Relations* (Ithaca, NY: Cornell University Press, 2017), 4.

32. Rashid Khalidi, "Edward Said and the American Public Sphere: Speaking Truth to Power," in Paul A. Bové (ed.), *Edward Said and the Work of the Critic* (Durham, NC: Duke University Press, 2000), 155, 153.

33. Said, "Orientalism Once More," 877.

34. Said, "Representing the Colonized," 215.

35. Ignatieff is listed as one of the core contributors to the commission's original report. See International Commission on Intervention and State Sovereignty, *The Responsibility to Protect: Report of the International Commission on Intervention and State Sovereignty* (Ottawa, ON: International Development Research Centre, 2001).

36. According to the Global Centre for the Responsibility to Protect, "The Responsibility to Protect has also been invoked in more than 50 Human Rights Council resolutions and 13 General Assembly resolutions. These resolutions and their related preventive and—as a last resort—coercive measures, have demonstrated that collective action to protect populations at risk is possible." Global Centre for the Responsibility to Protect, "What Is R2P?" May 12, 2014, https://www.globalr2p.org/what-is-r2p/#:~:text=R2P%20has%20been%20invoked%20in,of%20genocide%2C%20prevention%20of%20armed. Last accessed March 27, 2022.

37. Jessica Whyte, "Always on Top? The Responsibility to Protect and the Persistence of Colonialism," in Jyotsna G. Singh and David D. Kim (eds.), *The

*Postcolonial World* (London: Routledge, 2016), 319. See also Ray Bush, Giuliano Martiniello, and Claire Mercer, "Humanitarian Imperialism," *Review of African Political Economy*, 38.129 (2011).

38. Said, "Representing the Colonized," 214.

39. Jennifer J. Li, Richard S. Girven, and Norah Griffin, *Meeting the Language and Culture Training Needs of the U.S. Department of Defense Personnel: An Evaluation of the Language Training Center Program* (Santa Monica, CA: RAND, 2019), xi.

40. See the article on Rhodes by David Samuels, "The Aspiring Novelist Who Became Obama's Foreign Policy Guru," *New York Times Magazine*, May 5, 2016, https://www.nytimes.com/2016/05/08/magazine/the-aspiring-novelist-who-became-obamas-foreign-policy-guru.html. See also Mathew Yglesia's interesting exposé of the controversy caused by the interview in which Rhodes uttered this phrase, "The Raging Controversy Over a Profile of Ben Rhodes, Explained," *Vox*, May 12, 2016, https://www.vox.com/2016/5/12/11655668/ben-rhodes. Since the publication of that article, "the Blob" has become the moniker du jure for critics of the foreign policy establishment, particularly for realists like Patrick Porter, who want to see both war and the reach of the American military significantly curtailed.

41. See Edward Said, "Orientalism: An Exchange—Edward W. Said and Oleg Grabar, reply by Bernard Lewis," *New York Review*, August 12, 1982.

42. See Kurt M. Campbell (ed.), *In Search of an American Grand Strategy for the Middle East: A Report of the Aspen Strategy Group* (Washington, DC: Aspen Institute, 2004), 9.

43. Michael Hirsch, "The Lewis Doctrine," *Prospect*, February 20, 2005, https://www.prospectmagazine.co.uk/magazine/thelewisdoctrine

44. Said, *Orientalism*, 343.

45. Said, "Representing the Colonized," 214.

46. Said, "Orientalism 25 Years Later."

47. Said, "Representing the Colonized," 215.

48. Michael Ignatieff, "Living Fearlessly in a Fearful World," Whitman College commencement address, May 26, 2004, quoted in Jeanne Morefield, *Empires without Imperialism: Anglo-American Decline and the Politics of Deflection* (Oxford, UK: Oxford University Press, 2014), 3.

49. Said, *Representations of the Intellectual*, 11.

50. Bhattacharya, Kaul, and Loomba, "Edward Said," 92.

51. Said, *Representations of the Intellectual*, 11.

52. Said, *Representations of the Intellectual*, 11.

53. Said, *Representations of the Intellectual*, xii.

54. Said, *Representations of the Intellectual*, 5.

55. Edward Said, "The Future of Criticism," in *Reflections on Exile*, 171.

56. Said, *Representations of the Intellectual*, 74.

57. Edward Said, "Opponents, Audiences, Constituencies, and Community," *Critical Inquiry*, 9.1 (1982), 19.

58. Edward Said, "On Defiance and Taking Positions," in *Reflections on Exile*, 502.

59. Said, *Representations of the Intellectual*, 53.

60. Said, *Representations of the Intellectual*, 13.

61. Said, *Representations of the Intellectual*, 11.

62. Said, *Representations of the Intellectual*, 11.

63. Said, *Representations of the Intellectual*, 23

64. Said, "On Defiance," 503.

65. Said, *Representations of the Intellectual*, 62.

66. Said, *Representations of the Intellectual*, 63.

67. Said, "Michael Walzer's 'Exodus and Revolution': A Canaanite Reading," 105.

68. Said, *Representations of the Intellectual*, 64.

69. Said, "Intellectual Exile: Expatriates and Marginals," *Representations of the Intellectual*, 52.

70. Said, *Representations of the Intellectual*, 53.

71. Said, "Intellectual Exile: Expatriates and Marginals," *Representations of the Intellectual*, 53.

72. Theodore Adorno, *Minima Moralia: Reflections From a Damaged Life* (London: Verso, 1951), 39; Edward Said, *Representations of the Intellectual*, 56.

73. Said, *Representations of the Intellectual*, 59.

74. Said, *Representations of the Intellectual*, 98.

75. Said, "Representing the Colonized," 55–56.

76. Said, "On Defiance," 504.

77. Antonio Gramsci, "The Study of Philosophy," in *The Prison Notebooks* (New York: International, 1992), 324.

78. Bhattacharya, Kaul, and Loomba, "Edward Said," 91 (italics mine). Said was both an extraordinarily careful reader of Gramsci and one of the first academics in America to begin teaching *The Prison Notebooks* in the 1970s.

79. Said, *Culture and Imperialism* (New York: Vintage Books, 1994), xvii, xxiii.

80. Said, *Representations of the Intellectual*, 33 (italics mine).

81. Said, *Representations of the Intellectual*, 33.

82. Edward Said, "A Tragic Convergence," in *The Politics of Dispossession*, 285 (originally published in the *New York Times*, January 11, 1991).

83. Edward Said, "Ignorant Armies Clash by Night," in *The Politics of Dispossession*, 293.

84. Edward Said, "Nationalism, Human Rights, and Interpretation," in *Reflections on Exile*, 423.

85. Said, *Culture and Imperialism*, 336.

86. Said, *Representations of the Intellectual*, xvii.

87. Said, *Representations of the Intellectual*, xvii.

88. Aimé Césaire, *Discourse on Colonialism* (New York: Monthly Review Press, 2000), 38.

89. Said, *Representations of the Intellectual*, xvii.

90. Said, *Representations of the Intellectual*, xvii.

91. "From all these continents, under whose eyes Europe today raises up her tower of opulence, there has flowed out for centuries toward that same Europe diamonds and oil, silk and cotton, wood and exotic products. Europe is *literally* the creation of the Third World. The wealth which smothers her is that which was stolen from the

under developed peoples." Frantz Fanon, *Wretched of the Earth*, trans. Constance Farrington (New York: Grove Press, 1963), 102.

92. Said, "On Defiance," 504.

93. Edward Alexander, "Professor of Terror," *Commentary*, August 1989, https://www.commentarymagazine.com/articles/professor-of-terror/

94. Joshua Muravchik, "Enough Said: The False Scholarship of Edward Said," *World Affairs*, 175.6 (2013), 16.

95. Muravchik, "Enough Said," 21, 18.

96. Michael Walzer and Edward W. Said, "An Exchange: 'Exodus and Revolution,'" *Grand Street*, 5.4 (1986), 246.

97. Walzer and Said, "Exchange," 249. For an interesting take on the language of "rage" and Palestine, see Mark Krupnick, "Discourse and Palestinian Rage," *Tikkun*, 4.6 (1986).

98. Walzer and Said, "Exchange," 249.

99. Karen Arenson, "Columbia Debates a Professor's 'Gesture,'" *New York Times*, October 19, 2000, www.nytimes.com/2000/10/19/nyregion/columbia-debates-a-professor-s-gesture.html. Last accessed March 27, 2022.

100. Bill Mullen, "Throwing Stones in Glass Houses: The ASA and the Road to Academic Boycott," *American Quarterly*, 67.4 (2015), 1076.

101. Brennan, "Place of Mind," 56. See also Jeffrey St. Claire's reflections on the stone-throwing controversy in "The Parable of the Stone and the Slap," *Counterpunch*, March 30, 2018, https://www.counterpunch.org/2018/03/30/the-parable-of-the-stone-and-the-slap/. Last accessed March 27, 2022.

102. See, for instance, the Grand Strategy programs set up at Yale (funded largely through the donations of right-wing philanthropists like Roger Hertog) to educate future leaders in the history of imperial strategy. Yale University, "Brady-Johnson Program in Grand Strategy," 2022, https://grandstrategy.yale.edu/#:~:text=The%20Brady%2DJohnson%20Program%20in%20Grand%20Strategy%20offers%20a%20year,%2C%20politics%2C%20and%20social%20change. Last accessed March 27, 2022. Similar programs have been set up at Duke, Texas, Columbia, and Temple.

103. Ashcroft and Ahluwalia, *Edward Said: The Paradox of Identity*, 46.

104. Yes, Said argues, exile means "that you are always to be marginal," but "if you can experience that fate not as a deprivation and as something to be bewailed but as a sort of freedom . . . that is a unique pleasure." Said, *Representations of the Intellectual*, 62.

105. Ian Buruma, 'Real Wounds, Unreal Wounds: The Romance of Exile," *The New Republic*, February 12, 2001, 34.

106. Sean Scalmer, "Edward Said and the Sociology of Intellectuals," in Curthoys and Ganguly (eds.), *Edward Said: The Legacy of a Public Intellectual*, 44.

107. Hamid Dabashi, *On Edward Said: Remembrances of Things Past* (New York: Haymarket, 2020), 100.

108. Edward Said and Henry Giroux, "Writing the Public Good Back Into Education: Reclaiming the Role of the Public Intellectual," in Jeffrey Di Leo and Peter Hitchcock (eds.), *The New Public Intellectual: Politics, Theory, and the Public Sphere* (New York: Palgrave, 2016).

109. See "An interview with Edward Said (1999)," in *The Edward Said Reader*, eds. Moustafa Bayoumi and Andrew Rubin, 419–44 (New York: Vintage Books, 2000); David Price, "How the FBI Spied on Edward Said," *Counterpunch*, January 13, 2006, https://www.counterpunch.org/2006/01/13/how-the-fbi-spied-on-edward-said/. Last accessed March 27, 2022.

110. See University Provost Jonathan Cole responding to questions about Said in 2000, in Jonathan Cole, "The University Responds to Said," *Columbia Spectator*, 124.109 (2000), http://spectatorarchive.library.columbia.edu/cgi-bin/columbia?a=d&d=cs20001020-01.2.35. Employees at Princeton and Columbia (as well as his alma mater, Harvard) also gave FBI agents important biographical and education information on Said. See Price, "How the FBI Spied."

111. Walter Armbrust, *Mass Culture and Modernism in Egypt* (Cambridge, UK: Cambridge University Press, 1992), 221.

112. Wouter Capitain, "Edward Said on Popular Music," *Popular Music and Society*, 40.1 (2017), 50.

113. Neil Lazarus, "Representations of the Intellectual," *Research in African Literatures: Edward Said, Africa, and Cultural Criticism*, 36.3 (2005), 141.

114. Aijaz Ahmad, *In Theory: Classes, Nations, and Literatures* (London: Verso, 1994), 98. Paul Tiyambe Zeleza also believed that Said's understanding of the relationship between writers and exile "clearly shows strong class biases." Paul Tiyambe Zeleza, "The Politics and Poetics of Exile: Edward Said in Africa," *Research in African Literatures*, 36.3 (2005), 14.

115. Jules Boykoff, "Riding the Lines: Academia, Public Intellectual Work, and Scholar-Activism," *Sociology of Sport Journal*, 35 (2018), 81–88. Likewise, Indigenous activist-scholars have also taken inspiration from Said's words, deploying them specifically to explore and support denaturalizing forms of Indigenous media interventions. See Miranda Brady and John Kelly, *We Interrupt This Program: Indigenous Media Tactics in Canadian Culture* (Vancouver: University of British Columbia Press, 2017), 11.

116. The Edward Said Papers in the Archival Collections of Columbia University, Box 119.

117. Said, "On Defiance," 504.

118. The Edward Said Papers in the Archival Collections of Columbia University, Box 119.

119. Edward Said, *The Pen and the Sword: Conversations with David Barsamian* (New York: Hawymarket press, 1994), 138.50.

120. Said, *Representations of the Intellectual*, 32.

121. See Said's moving tribute to the young activist Rachel Corrie, who was run down by an Israeli bulldozer as she fought to stop the destruction of Palestinian homes in Rafah in 2002. Edward Said, "Dignity and Solidarity" *Al-Hayat*, July 2, 2003 [reprinted in Moustafa Bayoumi and Andrew Rubin (eds.), *The Selected Works of Edward Said, 1966–2006* (New York: Vintage Books, 2019)].

122. Said, "Secular Criticism," in *The World, the Text, and the Critic*, 28 [originally, Edward Said, "Secular Criticism," *Raritan: A Quarterly Review*, 2.3 (1983), 1–26].

123. Cindi Katz and Neil Smith, "An Interview With Edward Said," *Environment and Planning D: Society and Space*, 21.6 (2003), 642.

124. "I write at a distance. I haven't experienced the ravages." Said and Mohr, *After the Last Sky*, 130.

125. Edward Said, "Edward Said Talks to Jacqueline Rose," *Edward Said and the Work of the Critic: Speaking Truth to Power* (Durham, NC: Duke University Press, 2000), 23.

126. Affirmation of the Palestinian Right of Return, 462 AL-AHRAM, March 9–15, 2000, https://archive.globalpolicy.org/security-council/index-of-countries-on-the-security-council-agenda/israel-palestine-and-the-occupied-territories/38363.html. Last accessed March 27, 2022. Declaration signed by one hundred prominent Palestinians from Palestine, Israel, Jordan, Lebanon, Syria, the Arabian Gulf, Europe, the United Kingdom, and the United States, including Said and numerous scholars, such as Ibrahim Abu Lughod, and diplomats like Haider Abdel-Shafi (Palestinian chief negotiator at the Madrid Peace Conference, 1991), and many others.

127. Bruce Robbins, "Elitism, Progress, and Other Transgressions: On Edward Said's 'Voyage In,'" *Social Text*, 40 (1994), 34.

128. Scalmer, "Edward Said," 48.

129. James Clifford, "Review: *Orientalism*, by Edward Said," *History and Theory*, 19.2 (1980), 263–64, 274.

130. Said, *Representations of the Intellectual*, 59.

131. Edward Said, "Reflections on Exile,", 184.

132. Said, "The Art of Displacement: Mona Hatoum's Logic of Irreconcilables,", 17.

133. Said, *Representations of the Intellectual*, 63–64.

134. Jillian Steinhauer, "An Escape Room Where You Can't Escape Your Privilege," *New York Times*, June 23, 2019, https://www.nytimes.com/2019/07/23/arts/design/escape-room-creative-time.html. Last accessed March 27, 2022.

135. Said, "Secular Criticism," 29. One sees this, for instance, in the outsized influence of Gramsci and Adorno on his thought.

136. Said, "Opponents, Audiences," 135; Said, "Secular Criticism," 29.

137. See Brennan's analysis of Said's critique of Marx and elitism. "Said accused Marx of elitist scorn, referring to *The Eighteenth Brumaire of Louis Napolean*, where Marx says of the French peasantry in 1848, 'They could not represent themselves, they must be represented.'" Brennan, "Places of Mind," 59.

138. Said, "Opponents, Audiences," 135.

139. Said, "Secular Criticism," 28.

140. Said, "Secular Criticism," 29.

141. Wael Hallaq, *Restating Orientalism: A Critique of Modern Knowledge* (New York: Columbia University Press, 2018), 239.

142. Robert Tally, "Said, Marxism, and Spatiality: Wars of Position in Oppositional Criticism," *ariel: A Rieview of International English Literature*, 51.1 (2020), 88.

143. Hallaq, *Restating Orientalism*, 240, 103.

144. Khaled Furani, "Said and the Religious Other," *Comparative Studies in Society and History*, 52.3 (2010), 618, 624.

145. Tally, "Said, Marxism, and Spatiality," 97.

146. Rajagopalan Radhakrishnan, "Edward Said's *Culture and Imperialism*: A Symposium," *Social Text*, 40 (1994), 19.

147. See Said's response in Radhakrishnan, "Edward Said's *Culture and Imperialism*," 24.

148. Ahmad, *In Theory*, 164; E. San Juan Jr., "Edward Said's Affiliations," *Atlantic Studies*, 3.1 (2006), 52.

149. Said, "Representing the Colonized," 217.

## 6

1. Julien Benda, *The Treason of the Intellectuals* (New York: Transaction, 2006), 27.

2. Edward Said, "The Treason of the Intellectuals," *Al-Ahram Weekly*, June 24–30, 1999.

3. Pitts notes approvingly that such an approach can be found in the work of David Scott and other postcolonial scholars. Jennifer Pitts, "Political Theory of Empire and Imperialism," *Annual Review of Political Science*, 13 (2010), 227.

4. Pitts, "Political Theory of Empire," 227.

5. Edward Said, "Orientalism Once More," *Development and Change*, 35.5 (2004), 877.

6. Edward Said, "Orientalism Once More," lecture delivered on the occasion of the awarding of the degree of doctor honoris causa at the academic ceremony on the fiftieth anniversary of the Institute of Social Studies, the Hague, the Netherlands, May 21, 2003, 4.

7. Barry Hindress, "Political Theory and Actually Existing Liberalism," *Critical Review of International Social and Political Philosophy*, 11.3 (2008), 347–52.

8. John Rawls, *Justice as Fairness: A Restatement* (Cambridge, MA: Harvard University Press, 2000), 1.

9. See Donald Moon's 2003 review article "Liberalism, Autonomy, and Moral Philosophy," *Political Theory*, 31.1 (2003), 125–35, for a sense of the Rawlsian intellectual landscape with regard to pluralism.

10. See, for instance, Simone Chambers, "The Politics of Equality: Rawls on the Barricades," *Perspectives on Politics*, 4.1 (2006).

11. John Rawls, *A Theory of Justice* (Cambridge, MA: Harvard University Press, 1971), viii.

12. John Rawls, "Justice as Fairness: Political Not Metaphysical," *Philosophy and Public Affairs*, 14.3 (1985), 225.

13. John Rawls, *The Law of Peoples* (Cambridge, MA: Harvard University Press, 1999), 3, 57.

14. For important work on these entanglements, see Antony Anghie, *Imperialism, Sovereignty, and the Making of International Law* (Cambridge, UK: Cambridge University Press, 2005), and Andrew Fitzmaurice, "Liberalism and Empire in Nineteenth-Century International Law," *American Historical Review*, 117.1 (2012), 122–40.

15. Rawls, *Law of Peoples*, 5, 75–78. See also Murad Idris, "The Kazanistan Papers: Reading the Muslim Question in the John Rawls Archives," *Perspectives on Politics,* 19.1 (2021).

16. Michael Blake, *Justice and Foreign Policy* (Oxford, UK: Oxford University Press, 2013), 46, 3, 5.

17. Hindress, "Political Theory," 347.

18. Michael Freeden, *Liberal Languages* (Princeton, NJ: Princeton University Press, 2005), 20.

19. Harold Laski, *The Rise of European Liberalism* (London: George Allen and Unwin, 1936), 12.

20. Laski, *Rise of European Liberalism*, 12.

21. Duncan Bell, "What Is Liberalism?" *Political Theory*, 42.6 (2014), 693.

22. Bell, "What Is Liberalism?" 685.

23. Bell, "What Is Liberalism?" 689–90.

24. See Katrina Forrester, *In the Shadow of Justice: Postwar Liberalism and the Remaking of Modern Philosophy* (Princeton, NJ: Princeton University Press, 2019), and Samuel Moyn, "The Doctor's Plot: The Origins of the Philosophy of Human Rights," in Duncan Bell (ed.), *Empire, Race, and Global Justice* (Cambridge, UK: Cambridge University Press, 2019).

25. Katrina Forrester, "The Future of Political Philosophy," *Boston Review*, September 2019, https://bostonreview.net/articles/katrina-forrester-future-political-philosophy/. Last accessed March 27, 2022.

26. Forrester, "Future of Political Philosophy."

27. Francis Fukuyama, "The End of History?" *National Interest*, 16 (1989), 4.

28. Pitts, "Political Theory of Empire," 220.

29. Uday Singh Mehta, *Liberalism and Empire: A Study in Nineteenth-Century British Liberal Thought* (Chicago: University of Chicago Press, 1999), 1–2.

30. Helena Rosenblatt, *The Lost History of Liberalism: From Ancient Rome to the Twenty-first Century* (Princeton, NJ: Princeton University Press, 2018), 5.

31. Duncan Bell, *Reordering the World: Essays on Liberalism and Empire* (Princeton, NJ: Princeton University Press, 2015), 5.

32. Bell, *Reordering the World*, 364. Andrew Fitzmaurice similarly concentrates on self-described liberal jurists and political figures well known in their time but hardly household names for political theorists today. See Andrew Fitzmaurice, "Liberalism and Empire in International Nineteenth-Century International Law," 122–40.

33. Fitzmaurice, "Liberalism and Empire in International Nineteenth-Century International Law," 122.

34. Pitts, "Political Theory of Empire," 212.

35. Edward Said, "Nationalism, Human Rights, and Interpretation," in *Reflections on Exile and Other Essays*, 423 [originally in *The Oxford Amnesty Lectures* (New York: Basic Books, 1992), 175–205]. Hindress quotes Said here in "Political Theory," 350.

36. Pitts, "Political Theory of Empire," 227. Pitts finds this kind of connection in the work of David Scott and other postcolonial scholars.

37. Jennifer Pitts, *Boundaries of the International: Law and Empire* (Cambridge, MA: Harvard University Press, 2018), 27.

38. Jeanne Morefield, *Empires without Imperialism: Anglo-American Decline and the Politics of Deflection* (Oxford, UK: Oxford University Press, 2014).

39. For the clearest articulation of the post-Bush-era revival of liberal international principle, see the final paper of the Princeton Project on National Security, G. John Ikenberry and Anne-Marie Slaughter (eds.), *Forging a World of Liberty Under Law: U.S. National Security in the Twenty-first Century* (Princeton, NJ: Woodrow Wilson School of Public and International Affairs, Princeton University, 2006).

40. Ignatieff, for instance, was one of the original contributors to International Commission on Intervention and State Sovereignty, *The Responsibility to Protect: Report of the International Commission on Intervention and State Sovereignty* (Ottawa, ON: International Development Research Centre, 2001).

41. Samuels, "The Aspiring Novelist Who Became Obama's Foreign Policy Guru."

42. G. John Ikenberry, "The Plot Against American Foreign Policy," *Foreign Affairs*, 96.3 (2017), 2.

43. G. John Ikenberry, "The End of the Liberal International Order?" *International Affairs*, 94.1 (2018), 7.

44. Ikenberry, "End of the Liberal International Order?" 7.

45. Blake, *Justice and Foreign Policy*, 84.

46. See the various essays on precisely this denial in G. John Ikenberry, Thomas Knock, Anne-Marie Slaughter, and Tony Smith (eds.), *The Crisis in American Foreign Policy: Wilsonianism in the Twenty-first Century*, (Princeton, NJ: Princeton University Press, 2009).

47. Michael Desch, "Roundtable Review," *H-Diplo Roundtable Review*, 10.27 (2009), 13.

48. Inderjeet Parmar, "Foreign Policy Fusion: Liberal Interventionists, Conservative Nationalists and Neoconservative: The New Alliance Dominating the US Foreign Policy Establishment," *International Politics*, 46.2/3 (2009), 178.

49. Parmar, "Foreign Policy Fusion," 178.

50. See Michael Hirsch, "Why Liberal Internationalism Is Still Indispensable—and Fixable," *Foreign Policy*, December 5, 2020, https://foreignpolicy.com/category/review/. For more on Biden's foreign policy team, see Michael Crowley, "An Obama Restoration of Foreign Policy? Familiar Faces Could Fill Biden's Team," *New York Times*, January 20, 2021, https://www.nytimes.com/2020/11/09/us/politics/biden-cabinet.html. Last accessed March 27, 2022.

51. According to Du Bois, the "problem of the twentieth century is the problem of the color-line—the relation of the darker to the lighter races of men in Asia and Africa, in America and the islands of the sea." W. E. B. Du Bois, *Souls of Black Folk*, ed. David W. Blight and Robert Gooding-Williams (Boston: Bedford Books, 1997), 45. For new work on the idea of global Jim Crow, see Justin Leroy, "Black History in Occupied Territory: On the Entanglements of Slavery and Settler Colonialism," *Theory and Event*, 19.4 (2016), and Zine Magubane, "American Sociology's Racial Ontology: Remembering Slavery, Deconstructing Modernity, and Charting the Future of Global Historical Sociology," *Cultural Sociology*, 10.3 (2016). For more on the

relationship between Wilson and the South African general Jan Smuts, see Adom Getachew, *Worldmaking After Empire*. For more on the role Wilson played in formulating a liberal theory of international relations that Tony Smith calls "progressive imperialism," see Tony Smith, *Why Wilson Matters: The Origin of American Liberal Internationalism and Its Crisis Today* (Princeton, NJ: Princeton University Press, 2019), 66.

52. See Morefield, *Empires without Imperialism*, for a more detailed discussion of early-twentieth-century liberal imperialism/internationalism and the ties of its founders to imperial and race politics. See also Daniel Deudney and G. John Ikenberry's recent (and highly convenient) pivot from Wilson (in the wake of Black Lives Matter protests) to a "Rooseveltian" foreign policy tradition, "The Intellectual Foundations of the Biden Revolution," *Foreign Policy*, July 2, 2021, https://foreignpolicy.com/2021/07/02/biden-revolution-roosevelt-tradition-us-foreign-policy-school-international-relations-interdependence/. Last accessed March 27, 2022.

53. See James Tully on the complexities of "informal imperialism" in "Lineages of Contemporary Imperialism," in Duncan Kelly (ed.), *Lineages of Empire: The Historical Roots of British Imperial Thought* (Oxford, UK: British Academy, Oxford University Press, 2009), 3–29.

54. Patrick Porter, "A World Imagined: Nostalgia and the Liberal Order," CATO Policy Analysis, no. 843, June 5, 2018, https://www.cato.org/publications/policy-analysis/world-imagined-nostalgia-liberal-order. Last accessed March 27, 2022.

55. Porter, "World Imagined" (italics mine).

56. Hedley Bull, *The Anarchical Society: A Study of Order in World Politics* (London: Macmillan, 1977), 209.

57. G. John Ikenberry, *Liberal Hegemony: The Origins, Crisis, and Transformation of the American World Order* (Princeton, NJ: Princeton University Press, 2012).

58. The IR literature on hegemony is enormous. See, for instance, Robert Keohane, *After Hegemony: Cooperation and Discord in the World Political Economy* (Princeton, NJ: Princeton University Press, 1984); Richard Ned Lebow and Simon Reich, *Goodbye Hegemony! Power and Influence in the Global System* (Princeton, NJ: Princeton University Press, 2014); Carla Norrlof, *America's Global Advantage: US Hegemony and International Cooperation* (Cambridge, UK: Cambridge University Press, 2010); and Joseph Nye, *Bound to Lead: The Changing Nature of American Power* (New York: Basic Books, 1990).

59. See David Armitage, *The Ideological Origins of the British Empire* (Cambridge, UK: Cambridge University Press, 2000); Mehta, *Liberalism and Empire*; and Edward Said, *Culture and Imperialism* (New York: Vintage Books, 1994).

60. See Duncan Bell (ed.), *Empire, Race, and Global Justice* (Cambridge, UK: Cambridge University Press, 2019); Charles Mills, *Black Rights, White Wrongs: The Critique of Racial Liberalism* (Oxford, UK: Oxford University Press, 2017); and Charles Mills, *The Racial Contract* (Ithaca, NY: Cornell University Press, 1997). For more on liberalism's internal colonies, see Barbara Arneil's important book *Domestic Colonies: The Turn Inward to Colony* (Oxford, UK: Oxford University Press, 2018).

61. See John Locke, chap. 5, "On Property," in *Second Treatise of Government* (New York; Hackett, 1980), 18. See in particular Alexis de Tocqueville's thoughts

on colonization and domination in *Writing on Empire and Slavery* (Baltimore, MD; Johns Hopkins University Press, 2003), 61, and John Stuart Mill, *On Liberty and the Subjection of Women* (New York: Penguin, 2006), 16.

62. Morefield, *Empires without Imperialism*. For a liberal internationalist view on the "universal values" of liberalism in our era, see Anne-Marie Slaughter, "How to Succeed in the Networked World: A Grand Strategy for the Digital Age," *Foreign Affairs*, 96.6 (2016), 87.

63. Michael Ignatieff, "Reimagining a Global Ethic," *Ethics and International Affairs*, 26.1 (2012), 12.

64. Ignatieff, "Reimagining a Global Ethic," 18. Not unsurprisingly for the man who helped invent the interventionist R2P doctrine, in this article, Ignatieff uses the sometimes contradiction between respecting the sovereign autonomy of states and ethical imperative to protect human rights as an example of two such "competing ethical goals."

65. G. John Ikenberry, "Liberal Internationalism 3.0: America and the Dilemmas of Liberal World Order," *Perspectives on Politics*, 7.1 (2009), 71.

66. G. John Ikenberry, "America Self-Contained? Obama's Pragmatic Internationalism," *American Interest*, 2014, https://www.the-american-interest.com/2014/04/08/obamas-pragmatic-internationalism/. Last accessed March 27, 2022.

67. Ikenberry, "Plot Against American Foreign Policy," 2.

68. G. John Ikenberry, "Why the Liberal World Order Will Survive," *Ethics and International Affairs*, 32.1 (2018), 24.

69. Michael Ignatieff, "Reimagining a Global Ethic," *Ethics and International Affairs*, 1 (2012), http://www.ethicsandinternationalaffairs.org/2012/reimagining-a-global-ethic-full-text/. Last accessed March 27, 2022. For another example, see Daniel Deudney and G. John Ikenberry's argument that a liberal democratic "grand strategy for the present and future" can be built "on deep historical foundations and more recent U.S. foreign policy initiatives." Daniel Deudney and G. John Ikenberry, "Democratic Internationalism an American Grand Strategy for a Post-exceptionalist Era," working paper, Council on International Relations: International Institutions and Global Governance Program (New York, 2012), 8.

70. G. John Ikenbery, *After Victory: Institutions, Strategic Restraint, and the Rebuilding of Order After Major Wars* (Princeton, NJ: Princeton University Press, 2009), 27.

71. Ikenberry, "Liberal World Order Will Survive," 24.

72. Slaughter and Ikenberry, *Forging a World*, 6.

73. Anne-Marie Slaughter, *The Idea That Is America* (New York: Basic Books, 2008), xvi, 233.

74. Slaughter, *Idea That Is America*, 215.

75. Frank Lechner, *The American Exception* (New York: Palgrave, 2017), 190–91; David Vine, "The United States Probably Has More Military Bases Than Any Other People, Nation, or Empire in History," *Nation*, September 14, 2015, https://www.thenation.com/article/world/the-united-states-probably-has-more-foreign-military-bases-than-any-other-people-nation-or-empire-in-history/. Last accessed March 27, 2022.

76. Schmitt argues in *Political Theology* that all meaningful, modern conceptions of the state are "secularized theological concepts." In essence, for Schmitt, political philosophers theorize sovereignty much as theologians theorize the existence of God. See, Carl Schmitt, *Political Theology* (University of Chicago: University of Chicago Press, 2006).

77. See Patrick Porter, "Why America's Grand Strategy Has Not Changed: Power, Habit, and the U.S. Foreign Policy Establishment," *International Security*, 42.4 (2018), 12.

78. See Inderjeet Parmar's important historical study of think tanks in the United Kingdom and the United States and the relation of both to imperialism in *Think Tanks and Power in Foreign Policy: A Comparative Study of the Role and Influence of the Council on Foreign Relations and the Royal Institute of International Affairs, 1939–1945* (London: Palgrave, 2004).

79. G. John Ikenberry, "The Future of the Liberal World Order: Internationalism After America," *Foreign Affairs*, 90.3 (2011), 61; Daniel Deudney and G. John Ikenberry, "Liberal World: The Resilient Order," *Foreign Affairs*, 97.4 (2018), 18.

80. Ikenberry, "Future of the Liberal World Order," 61.

81. G. John Ikenberry, *Liberal Leviathan, The Origins, Crisis, and Transformation of the American World Order* (Princeton, NJ: Princeton University Press, 2012), 10.

82. Ikenberry, *Liberal Leviathan*, 6.

83. For more on "zones of conflict" and "zones of peace," see Robert Keohane, "Hobbes' Dilemma and Institutional Change in World Politics: Sovereignty in International Society," in *Power and Governance in a Partially Globalized World* (London: Routledge, 2002). For more on realism and Hobbes see, for instance, Hans Morgenthau, who associated Hobbes with the "ubiquity of power." Hans Morgenthau, *Politics Among Nations* (New York: McGraw-Hill, 2005), 220. He refers to his understanding of the state of nature as the "stock in trade" of disciplinary IR. Hans Morgenthau, *Scientific Man Versus Power Politics* (Chicago: University of Chicago Press, 1946), 113. The more diagnostic Martin Wight also identifies Hobbes with a "realist" tradition strain in the history of international thought (along with a "ratio-nalist" and a "revolutionist" tradition). See Martin Wight, *International Theory: The Three Traditions* (London: Holmes and Meier, 1992), 17. Contemporary realists like Keohane continue to think about "Hobbes's dilemma" as a security dilemma, a description of the world in which a "war of all against all" reigns supreme unless tempered by sovereignty and/or institutions. Keohane's version of Hobbes and IR has been challenged by some scholars of the history of political thought who seek to contextualize it. See, for instance, Haig Patapan, "Thomas Hobbes on Leadership and International Relations," in Ian Hall and Lisa Hill (eds.), *British International Thinkers from Hobbes to Namier* (London: Palgrave, 2009).

84. Hedley Bull, "Hobbes and the International Anarchy," *Social Research*, 41 (1977), 327–52.

85. Bull, "Hobbes and International Anarchy," 729.

86. Thomas Hobbes, *Leviathan* (Oxford, UK: Clarendon Press, 1909), 132.

87. Hobbes, *Leviathan*, 153.

88. Philip Pettit, "Liberty and the Leviathan," *Politics, Philosophy, and Economics,* 4.1 (2005), 142.

89. See, for instance, Steven Masekura and Erez Manela (eds.), *The Development Century: A Global History* (Cambridge, UK: Cambridge University Press, 2018), and Nikhil Singh, *Race and America's Long War* (Los Angeles: University of California Press, 2019).

90. See Andrew Bacevich, *The Age of Illusions: How America Squandered Its Cold War* (New York: Metropolitan Books, 2020), and Stephen Kinser, *Overthrow: America's Century of Regime Change, From Hawaii to Iraq* (New York: Times Books, 2006).

91. Michael Ignatieff, "Isaiah Berlin Lecture: Liberal Values in Tough Times," the Isaiah Berlin lecture, Liberal International, the Canadian Club, National Liberal Club, Whitehall Palace, London, July 8, 2009, 5. https://www.macleans.ca/uncategorized/liberalism-is-not-a-bloodless-breviary-for-rootless-cosmopolitans/. Last accessed March 27, 2022.

92. Francis Fukuyama, G. John Ikenberry, and Thomas Wright, "Report of the Grand Strategic Choices Working Group," *Princeton Project on National Security*, 2008, https://web.archive.org/web/20170702133156/http://www.princeton.edu/~ppns/conferences/reports/fall/GSC.pdf.

93. Michael Ignatieff, *Empire Lite* (London: Vintage Books, 2003), 112.

94. Porter, "America's Grand Strategy," 11.

95. See Nobel Prize, "The Nobel Peace Prize for 2009," October 9, 2009, https://www.nobelprize.org/prizes/peace/2009/press-release/. See Twitter, @realDonaldTrump, January 24, 2016, 7:08 a.m. This can be found on the Trump Twitter archive, https://www.thetrumparchive.com/?results=1&dates=%5B%222016-01-22%22%2C%222016-01-25%22%5D. Last accessed March 27, 2022.

96. Lindsay Koshgarian, "Biden's Unconscionable Military Budget," *Foreign Policy in Focus*, June 3, 2021, https://fpif.org/bidens-unconscionable-military-budget/. Last accessed March 27, 2022. This continues a long-standing trend. The percentage of resources devoted to the military in Obama's proposed 2015 national budget was only slightly smaller than Trump's in 2018. For information on military spending and Barack Obama's 2015 budget proposal, see Jasmine Tucker, "President's 2015 Budget in Pictures," *National Priorities Project*, March 19, 2014, https://www.nationalpriorities.org/analysis/2014/presidents-2015-budget-in-pictures/. Last accessed March 27, 2022.For information on military spending and Donald Trump's 2019 budget proposal, see Peace Action, "2019_TrumpDiscretionaryBudget," 2019, https://www.peaceaction.org/what-we-do/campaigns/pentagon-spending/2019_trumpdiscretionarybudget/. Last accessed March 27, 2022.

97. Said, *Culture and Imperialism*, xvii.

98. Freeden, *Liberal Languages*, 20; James Tully, *Public Philosophy in a New Key*, Vol 2 (Cambridge, UK: Cambridge University Press, 2008), 244.

99. Said, "Interview With Edward Said," *Diacritics*, 47.

100. Mehta, *Liberalism and Empire*, 1.

101. Jeanne Morefield, *Covenants Without Swords: Idealist Liberalism and the Spirit of Empire* (Princeton, NJ: Princeton University Press, 2005), 2.

102. Mehta, *Liberalism and Empire*, 8.

103. Mehta, *Liberalism and Empire*, 20.

104. Fitzmaurice, "Liberalism and Empire in the Nineteenth-Century International Law," 122.

105. G. John Ikenberry, "Liberalism and Empire: Logics of Order in the American Unipolar Age," *Review of International Studies*, 30.4 (2004), 630.

106. Jeffrey Isaac, "Last Call: Why Leftists Should Vote for Clinton," *Dissent*, November 3, 2016, https://www.dissentmagazine.org/blog/last-call-leftists-vote-hillary-clinton. Last accessed March 27, 2022.

107. Jeffrey Anderson, G. John Ikenberry, and Thomas Risse (eds.), *The End of the West? Crisis and Change in the Atlantic Order* (Ithaca, NY: Cornell University Press, 2008); Yoichi Funabashi and G. John Ikenberry (eds.), *The Crisis of Liberal Internationalism: Japan and the World Order* (Washington, DC: Brookings Institute Press, 2019); G. John Ikenberry, Thomas J. Knock, Anne-Marie Slaughter, and Tony Smith, *The Crisis of American Foreign Policy: Wilsonianism in the Twenty-first Century* (Princeton, NJ: Princeton University Press, 2008); Ikenberry, *Liberal Leviathan*. This obviously does not include the many articles written by Ikenberry in which the word *crisis* appears in the title, nor can it fully convey the near-ubiquity of the word in the corpus of Ikenberry's work.

108. Ikenberry, *Liberal Leviathan*, 334.

109. Ikenberry, *Liberal Leviathan*, 31.

110. Ikenberry, "The End of Liberal International Order," *International Affairs*, 94.1 (2018), 7.

111. Ikenberry, "Future of the Liberal World Order," 57; Ikenberry, "Plot Against American Foreign Policy," 7.

112. G. John Ikenberry, *A World Safe for Democracy: Liberal Internationalism and the Crises of Global Order* (New Haven, CT: Yale University Press, 2020), 2.

113. Ikenberry, *World Safe for Democracy*, 216, 21, 247.

114. Ikenberry, *World Safe for Democracy*, 215.

115. Ikenberry, *World Safe for Democracy*, 253.

116. Ikenberry, *World Safe for Democracy*, 254.

117. Duncan Bell, "International Relations and Intellectual History," in *Oxford Handbook of Historical International Relations,* eds. Mlada Bukovansky, Edward Keene, Maja Spanu, and Christian Reus-Smit (Oxford, UK: Oxford University Press, forthcoming 2022).

118. Jennifer Pitts, "Political Theory of Empire and Imperialism," 227.

119. Said, *Culture and Imperialism*, 80.

120. Said, *Culture and Imperialism*, xxiii.

121. Said, *Orientalism* (New York: Penguin, 1995), 42, 4.

122. Said, "Interview," *Diacritics*, 47.

123. Said, "Interview," *Diacritics*, 47; Edward Said, "Orientalism 25 Years Later."

124. Morefield, *Empires without Imperialism*, 7.

125. Daniel Deudney and G. John Ikenberry, "Liberal World: The Resilient Order," *Foreign Affairs*, 97 (2018), 18.

126. Lionel Curtis, *The Commonwealth of Nations: An inquiry into the Nature of Citizenship in the British Empire and the Mutual Relations of the Several Communities Thereof* (London: Macmillan, 1916), 166, quoted in Morefield, *Empires without Imperialism*, 124.

127. See David Patrick Geggus (ed.), *The Impact of the Haitian Revolution in the Atlantic World* (Charleston: University of South Carolina Press, 2020).

128. See Helen Quane, "The United Nations and the Evolving Right to Self-Determination," *International and Comparative Law Quarterly*, 47.3 (1998). In a gesture of protest, the one Black member of the US delegation, Zelma Watson George, stood up and applauded as the resolution was adopted anyway. See "Telegram From the Mission at the United Nations to the Department of State," December 15, 1960, US Department of State, Office of the Historian, https://history.state.gov/historical-documents/frus1958-60v02/d260. Last accessed March 27, 2022.

129. Said, "Travelling Theory Reconsidered," in *Reflections on Exile,* 452.

130. Mohandas K. Gandhi, *Hind Swaraj and Other Writings* (Cambridge, UK: Cambridge University Press, 2009), 27.

131. Said, "Nationalism, Human Rights," 423.

132. Said, *Culture and Imperialism*, xxiii, 37.

133. Edward Said, "Intellectuals in the Post-Colonial World," *Salmagundi*, 70.71 (1986), 59.

134. Niall Ferguson, *Colossus: The Rise and Fall of American Empire* (New York: Penguin, 2009), 174.

135. Said, "Always on Top."

136. Said, "Intellectuals in the Post-Colonial World," 59.

137. Said, *Culture and Imperialism*, 22.

138. Barack Obama, speech at West Point, May 28, 2014. For transcript see, Catherine A. Traywick, "Read the Transcript," May 28, 2014, https://obamawhitehouse.archives.gov/the-press-office/2014/05/28/remarks-president-united-states-military-academy-commencement-ceremony. Last accessed March 27, 2022.

139. *National Security Strategy of the United States of America: December 2017*, https://trumpwhitehouse.archives.gov/wp-content/uploads/2017/12/NSS-Final-12-18-2017-0905.pdf. See also "Remarks by the President to the 72nd Session of the United Nations General Assembly," https://trumpwhitehouse.archives.gov/briefings-statements/remarks-president-trump-72nd-session-united-nations-general-assembly/.

140. In a meeting with lawmakers about immigration, Trump was quoted as saying; "Why are we having all these people from shithole countries come here?" See Lauren Gambino, "Trump Pans Immigration Proposal as Bringing People From 'Shithole Countries,' January 12, 2018. https://www.theguardian.com/us-news/2018/jan/11/trump-pans-immigration-proposal-as-bringing-people-from-shithole-countries.

141. For Trump on Iran and "obliteration," see Julian Borger and Patrick Wintour, "Trump Threatens 'Obliteration' After Iran Suggests He Has a 'Mental Disorder,'" *Guardian*, June 25, 2019, https://www.theguardian.com/world/2019/jun/25/trump-iran-rouhani-insults-sanctions-threats. Last accessed March 17, 2022. Trump threatened North Korea's leader with his "nuclear button" in a tweet from January 2, 2018,

https://www.thetrumparchive.com/?dates=%5B%222018-01-01%22%2C%222018-01-03%22%5D. Last accessed March 22, 2022.

142. Ikenberry, "Liberal World Order Will Survive," 28.

143. Sophie Tatum, "Trump Defends Putin: 'You Think Our Country's So Innocent?'" *CNN*, February 6, 2017, https://www.thetrumparchive.com/?dates=%5B%222018-01-01%22%2C%222018-01-03%22%5D. Last accessed March 27, 2022.

144. Ikenberry, "Plot Against American Foreign Policy," 1.

145. Edward Said, "Representing the Colonized: Anthropology's Interlocutors," *Critical Inquiry*, 15.2 (1989), 215.

146. "The Treason of the Intellectuals," *Al-Ahram Weekly*, 435, June 24-30, 1999.

147. Said, "The Public Role of Writers and Intellectuals," in *Humanism and Democratic*, 142.

148. Said, "The Public Role of Writers and Intellectuals," *Humanism and Democratic Criticism,* 142-43.

149. Weiyi Cai, Josh Holder, Lauren Leatherby, Eleanor Lutz, Scott Reinhard, and Karen Yourish, "The Toll of Eight Days of Conflict in Gaza and Israel," *New York Times*, May 17, 2021, https://www.nytimes.com/interactive/2021/05/17/world/middleeast/israel-palestine-gaza-conflict-death-toll.html. Last accessed March 27, 2022. Despite the starkly disproportionate nature of the violence, despite the right-wing settler movement that prompted the protests and despite Netanyahu's crass commitment to levying a "heavy price" on Gaza, Joe Biden responded to the situation with a dismissive—and deeply deflective—quip: "Israel has the right to defend itself." Rebecca Falconer, "Biden: 'Israel has a right to defend itself,'" *Axios*, May 13, 2021, https://www.axios.com/biden-israel-right-defend-itself-gaza-41510149-a7a3-4051-b926-c4a78bb639f4.html

150. This video went viral on a number of different platforms, including Twitter and Facebook. It can be seen at Middle East Monitor, "Israel Releases Jerusalem Woman Who Questioned Soldier's Morals," May 10, 2021, https://www.middleeastmonitor.com/20210510-israel-releases-jerusalem-woman-who-questioned-soldiers-morals/. Last accessed March 27, 2022.

151. See history of the conservatory at the Edward Said National Conservatory of Music, Birzeit University, "History," 2022, http://ncm.birzeit.edu/en/history

152. The Edward Said National Conservatory of Music, Birzeit University, "The Palestine Youth Orchestra," 2022, http://ncm.birzeit.edu/en/pyo/60. Last accessed March 28, 2022.

153. Said and Mohr, *After the Last Sky*, 166.

154. Said, *Culture and Imperialism*, 336.

# CODA

1. Said, "Reflections on Exile," in *Reflections on Exile*, 171.

# Index

academy:
  challenges to authority,
    xxviii, 149–51
  disciplinary borders, xxviii–
    xxxviii, xl, 166
  identity as detached observer, 134,
    146–47, 150–51
  intellectual middlemen (the "Blob"),
    139–42, 166, 175–76, 193,
    212n64, 246n40
  interdisciplinary thought, xxxiv,
    xxxvi–xlii
  lack of interest in Said, xv–xvi, xix–
    xxi, xxiv, xxviii–xxix, xlvii
  neoconservatives, xxviii–xxix
  neoliberalism, 154–55
  Orientalism, 140–42
  public intellectuals, 137, 139–42,
    146–48, 150–51
  Said's perspectives, xl, 154–55
  scholar-activists, 29–30, 155–59.
    *See also* international relations (IR);
      political science; political theory;
      Said, Edward, career as professor
Adorno, Theodore:
  Dallmayr's critique, 27–30
  exilic perspective, 146–48, 158–59
  *Minima Moralia,* 4, 146–47, 158
  *Negative Dialectics,* 27–28

Said's interest in, 4, 146–
  48, 250n132
affiliation and filiation:
  about, l, 9–13, 205
  affiliation (culture), 9–13
  *After the Last Sky,* 2, 18–21
  attachment/detachment, 2,
    12–13, 17–21, 38
  constructedness, 10–13, 18–21, 205
  denaturalization of culture, 9–11, 13
  exilic perspective, 9–13, 21–22,
    38–39, 205
  family, 10–11, 13
  filiation (nature), 9–13
  identification, 37–41, 43
  imperialism, 12–13, 56, 84, 98, 167,
    191, 200–201
  national identities, 8–9,
    12–13, 18–19
  pronouns ("we," "us," and
    "them"), 38–41
  resistance to reconciliation,
    13, 21, 28
Afghanistan, 166, 172–73
Al-Afifi, Maryam, 202–3, 260n146
Africa:
  Arendt's boomerang effect, xlii–
    xlv, 121–23

261

# About the Author

**Jeanne Morefield** is associate professor of political theory at Oxford University; Tutorial Fellow at New College (Oxford); and Non–Residential Fellow at the Quincy Institute for Responsible Statecraft (Washington, DC). She is author of *Empires without Imperialism: Anglo American Decline and the Politics of Deflection* (Oxford University Press, 2014) and *Covenants without Swords: Idealist Liberalism and the Spirit of Empire* (Princeton University Press, 2005).